THE ONE minute bible

:00 :10 :20 :30 :40 :50 1:00

4 students

with
daily
applications
for living

editor **John R. Kohlenberger III**
applications by **Doug Fields**
design and illustration **Kyle Webb**

from The Living Bible

GARBORG'S Inc.
Bloomington, MN 55431

The One-Minute Bible™ for Students

Copyright © 1993 by Garborg's Heart 'n Home, Inc.
Bloomington, Minnesota 55431

Commentary © 1993 by Doug Fields
Design by Kyle Webb

All Scripture in **The One-Minute Bible™ for Students** is taken
from The Living Bible © 1971. Used by permission of Tyndale House
Publishers, Inc., Wheaton, IL 60189.
All rights reserved.

Published in association with the literary agency
of Alive Communications, P.O. Box 49068,
Colorado Springs, Colorado 80949.

PRINTED IN THE UNITED STATES OF AMERICA

table of CONTENTS

table of

CONTENTS

The Bible is the greatest of all books. More than a book, it is in fact a collection of sixty-six books written over the span of sixteen centuries by kings and peasants, poets and prophets.

The books of the Law, Genesis through Deuteronomy, recount the early history of humanity and the great covenant at Sinai by which the living God of the universe bound Himself to the nation of Israel. The historical books of Joshua through Esther highlight the covenant history of Israel, noting both Israel's successes and failures in keeping the covenant and God's patience and grace in enforcing its terms.

The books of poetry and wisdom, Job through Song of Songs, celebrate the God of Israel for His goodness, His holiness, and His accessibility to all who approach Him on His terms. Wisdom offers timeless principles for a successful life in relation to God and His creation.

The prophets, Isaiah through Malachi, were the preachers of old. They proclaimed to the Israelites their failure to honor covenant obligations to their God, warned them of His impending righteous judgment, and offered hope to all nations of His coming salvation.

The Gospels, Matthew through John, tell of the life and teaching of Jesus the Messiah, the promised Savior of Israel and the nations. The book of Acts recounts the early history of the Christian church as the followers of Jesus take his message to the farthest corners of the globe.

The letters or epistles, Romans through Jude, were written by the first leaders of the church to Christian congregations and their leadership, offering encouragement, discipline, teaching, and hope. The book of Revelation tells of the end of this present world and of the establishment of the new heavens and new earth in which God will live with His people forever.

We hope *The One-Minute Bible™ for Students* offers you a taste of God's Word that will not be fully satisfied by our bite-sized sampling. We encourage you to read daily from a full-text Bible, perhaps even following an annual read-through-the-Bible plan.

- The Editor

a note to

STUDENTS

Every day I hear students' thoughts, concerns, doubts, and **questions** about life, Christianity, God, and the Bible. In *The One-Minute Bible™ for Students*, I try to provide clear understandable answers—**God's answers.** The 366 daily applications in *The One-Minute Bible™ for Students* are intended to help you **immediately** apply God's Word to **your** life.

Here's one principle to remember while reading *The One-Minute Bible™ for Students:* **Don't give up** if you don't understand. Some parts of the Bible are **tough** to understand. **Keep reading!** Ask questions! Pray that God would make His Word **clear** to you. **Keep going...**

you can do it!

I applaud you for digging in and learning about God. **My prayer** is that your faith will grow as you take regular doses of His Word.

a note to

This product was designed to meet the **needs** of your son or daughter. If your child has no Bible background, this book will serve as a **perfect** introductory tool! I've found that almost anyone will give a minute a day to the **greatest** book ever written. Or, if your child has grown up in the church or is a mature Christian, *The One-Minute Bible™ for Students* will be a **powerful** devotional resource. The content is intended to foster and encourage **spiritual** maturity.

Put this book in your child's hands, comment on the **ease** of the readings, and leave him or her alone to **discover** God's Word.

My **prayer** is that this book will **ignite** a desire to consume more of God's love letter.

a note to

YOUTH WORKERS

As a **youth pastor** and author of over a dozen books, I can't think of any book, aside from the Bible itself, that I'm more **excited** for my students to read than *The One-Minute Bible™ for Students*. This book will not only help students understand the Bible, but it emphasizes God's **passionate** and **unconditional** love for them and will challenge them to **respond.**

Youth ministry is tough in today's world! As you know, most students are not reading the Bible. We are ministering to a **biblically illiterate** generation. They need tools to guide them through the scriptures and **help** them understand God's Word.

My prayer is that *The One-Minute Bible™ for Students* will assist you in your ministry to students. I've written a 52-week teaching and discussion curriculum to accompany this book. It may be used for Sunday School or a mid-week meeting. **Contact me** if you're interested.

Doug Fields

Students, parents, and youth workers can write to me at:
**21612 Plano Trabuco Q-30
Trabuco Canyon, CA 92679**

answers to some common

Where do I begin?
The One-Minute Bible™ for Students offers 366 daily one-minute readings from the world's greatest literary treasure...the Bible. Each day of the year, the date is indicated at the top of the page. Although this provides a one-year reading plan, you can start whenever you'd like—you don't have to limit yourself to starting in January or to reading one page a day!

Is this the entire Bible?
Although every day contains selections from the Bible, *The One-Minute Bible™ for Students* isn't a complete Bible. Reading one minute a day will allow you to survey the heart of the Bible in one year. If you want more, we've provided related texts at the end of the book to direct you to nearly 1,800 passages of scripture that will further your understanding of the topics covered in that day's reading.

How much of the Bible is covered?
The One-Minute Bible™ for Students begins with the first verse of Genesis and ends with the last verse of Revelation. Readings follow the general flow of biblical history, interspersed with several topical series for occasions such as Easter and Mother's Day. The 700 selected scriptures and 1,800 related texts present the key themes of the Bible and draw from all 66 books. Great care was taken to ensure that each text has the same meaning in *The One-Minute Bible™ for Students* as it does in its larger context in the Bible.

What happens if I don't read every day?
If you fall behind in the suggested daily reading program, don't worry! You can make up one week in seven minutes, half a month in 15. But again, don't be discouraged by failing to follow our schedule. If you get behind, simply jump back in where you left off and

"Just Read It"

a note about the different daily

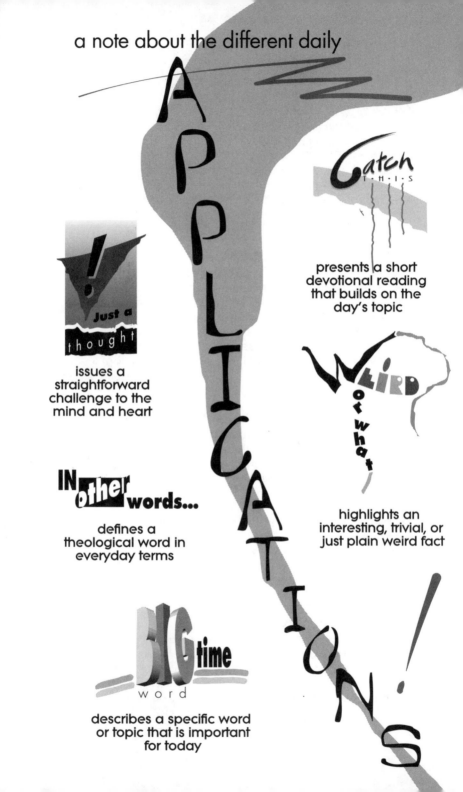

APPLICATIONS!

Just a thought
issues a
straightforward
challenge to the
mind and heart

IN other words...
defines a
theological word in
everyday terms

BIG time word
describes a specific word
or topic that is important
for today

Catch T·H·I·S
presents a short
devotional reading
that builds on the
day's topic

Weird or what
highlights an
interesting, trivial, or
just plain weird fact

a note about the different daily

APPLICATIONS!

personality plus

features a short biographical sketch of a biblical character

ONE MINUTE MEMORY

extracts from the scripture reading a truly memorable verse

Give it a try

offers involvment with the text through written expression

WHAT'S it mean

clarifies the message of the text with background information and application

CHECK IT OUT

directs students to other scriptures that shed more light on the subject

books of the **Bible**

OLD Testament

Genesis
Exodus
Leviticus
Numbers
Deuteronomy
Joshua
Judges
Ruth
1 Samuel
2 Samuel
1 Kings
2 Kings
1 Chronicles
2 Chronicles
Ezra
Nehemiah
Esther
Job
Psalms
Proverbs
Ecclesiastes
Song of Songs
Isaiah
Jeremiah
Lamentations
Ezekiel
Daniel
Hosea
Joel
Amos
Obadiah
Jonah
Micah
Nahum
Habakkuk
Zephaniah
Haggai
Zechariah
Malachi

NEW Testament

Matthew
Mark
Luke
John
Acts
Romans
1 Corinthians
2 Corinthians
Galatians
Ephesians
Philippians
Colossians
1 Thessalonians
2 Thessalonians
1 Timothy
2 Timothy
Titus
Philemon
Hebrews
James
1 Peter
2 Peter
1 John
2 John
3 John
Jude
Revelation

JAN

Sin will keep you
from this Book.

This Book will
keep you from sin.

**Dwight L. Moody
(1837-1899)**
American Evangelist

IN THE BEGINNING

CREATION science C²

Catch T·H·I·S

When God began creating the heavens and the earth, the earth was a shapeless, chaotic mass, with the Spirit of God brooding over the dark vapors.

♦ Before anything else existed, there was Christ, with God. He has always been alive and is himself God. He created everything there is—nothing exists that he didn't make. Eternal life is in him, and this life gives light to all mankind. His life is the light that shines through the darkness—and the darkness can never extinguish it.

♦ Praise the Lord, O heavens! Praise him from the skies! Praise him, all his angels, all the armies of heaven. Praise him, sun and moon and all you twinkling stars. Praise him, skies above. Praise him, vapors high above the clouds.

Let everything he has made give praise to him. For he issued his command, and they came into being; he established them forever and forever. His orders will never be revoked.

Genesis 1:1-2; John 1:1-5; Psalm 148:1-6

:00
:10
:20
:30
:40
:50
:60
done

These few verses sure cause big debates in science class. Unfortunately, there are no quick or easy answers in the creation and evolution controversy. Believers in evolution claim our world **suddenly** exploded into existence billions of years ago...pits of slime somehow **sprouted legs** and started **growing chest hair.** It's a good story for those who don't believe in God or the Bible. The Bible informs us that **God created** the earth, and through Him all things were made...including us.

Actually, it takes less faith to **believe God** created this world and us than it does to believe our complex minds and bodies evolved from a "big bang" and a drop of ooze.

God created each of us in His image. Try thinking about that the next **twenty-one times** you look in the mirror. Your uniqueness is no accident!

CHECK IT OUT

LET THERE BE LIGHT

The Bible uses the term **"light"** on many different occasions. In Matthew 5:14-16 Jesus uses the illustration of "light" to challenge and remind Christians that their life is a daily example. Jesus says, "You are the world's light...don't hide your light! Let it shine for all; **let your good deeds glow** for all to see, so that they will praise your heavenly Father."

Being a light to the world is a high calling! It's a pretty wild thought to realize you may be the only example of Christianity your friends ever see. **Are you shining bright?** If not, what are a few things you could do to be a stronger **light for God?**

:00

:10

:20

:30

:40

:50

:60

T hen God said, "Let there be light." And light appeared. And God was pleased with it and divided the light from the darkness. He called the light "daytime," and the darkness "nighttime." Together they formed the first day.

♦ O Lord, you are my light! You make my darkness bright.

♦ The Lord is my light and my salvation; he protects me from danger—whom shall I fear?

♦ Later, in one of his talks, Jesus said to the people, "I am the Light of the world. So if you follow me, you won't be stumbling through the darkness, for living light will flood your path."

♦ There shall be nothing in the city that is evil; for the throne of God and of the Lamb will be there, and his servants will worship him. And they shall see his face; and his name shall be written on their foreheads. And there will be no night there—no need for lamps or sun—for the Lord God will be their light; and they shall reign forever and ever.

Genesis 1:3-5; 2 Samuel 22:29; Psalm 27:1; John 8:12; Revelation 22:3-5

d o n e

CREATION

And God said, "Let the vapors separate to form the sky above and the oceans below." So God made the sky, dividing the vapor above from the water below. This all happened on the second day.

♦ The heavens are telling the glory of God; they are a marvelous display of his craftsmanship. Day and night they keep on telling about God. Without a sound or word, silent in the skies, their message reaches out to all the world.

♦ I will thank you publicly throughout the land. I will sing your praises among the nations. Your kindness and love are as vast as the heavens. Your faithfulness is higher than the skies.
Yes, be exalted, O God, above the heavens. May your glory shine throughout the earth.

♦ But our God formed the earth by his power and wisdom, and by his intelligence he hung the stars in space and stretched out the heavens. It is his voice that echoes in the thunder of the storm clouds. He causes mist to rise upon the earth; he sends the lightning and brings the rain, and from his treasuries he brings the wind.

Genesis 1:6-8; Psalms 19:1-3; 57:9-11; Jeremiah 10:12-13

Just a thought

If God is powerful enough to create this huge playground we call "earth," don't you think He's mighty enough to have created you EXACTLY as He intended?

3

JAN

:00
:10
:20
:30
:40
:50
1:00
FINISH

IN other words...

FEAR

To fear God doesn't mean to be afraid of Him or fear some type of unknown punishment or terror.

To fear God means to **respect** Him, to honor Him, to be **amazed** by His greatness, and admire all He has done for you and this world. When you have nothing to say but "WOW" when describing God, you're on your way to fearing Him. An attitude of fear and **AWE** is pleasing to God and is the first step toward gaining wisdom.

When you close this book, take a minute to say **"WOW"** to all God has done for you.

:00
:10
:20
:30
:40
:50
:60   done

Then God said, "Let the water beneath the sky be gathered into oceans so that the dry land will emerge." And so it was. Then God named the dry land "earth," and the water "seas." And God was pleased. And he said, "Let the earth burst forth with every sort of grass and seed-bearing plant, and fruit trees with seeds inside the fruit, so that these seeds will produce the kinds of plants and fruits they came from." And so it was, and God was pleased. This all occurred on the third day.

♦ "Have you no respect at all for me?" the Lord God asks. "How can it be that you don't even tremble in my presence? I set the shorelines of the world by perpetual decrees, so that the oceans, though they toss and roar, can never pass those bounds. Isn't such a God to be feared and worshiped?"

♦ The tender grass grows up at his command to feed the cattle, and there are fruit trees, vegetables, and grain for man to cultivate, and wine to make him glad, and olive oil as lotion for his skin, and bread to give him strength.

Genesis 1:9-13; Jeremiah 5:22; Psalm 104:14-15

4

CREATION

Sun ★ Moon & Stars

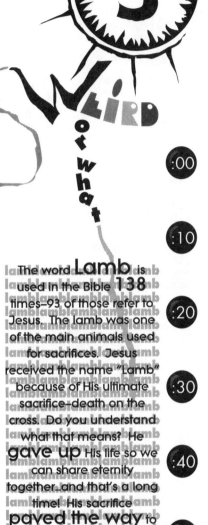

Then God said, "Let bright lights appear in the sky to give light to the earth and to identify the day and the night; they shall bring about the seasons on the earth, and mark the days and years." And so it was. For God had made two huge lights, the sun and moon, to shine down upon the earth—the larger one, the sun, to preside over the day and the smaller one, the moon, to preside through the night; he had also made the stars. And God set them in the sky to light the earth, and to preside over the day and night, and to divide the light from the darkness. And God was pleased. This all happened on the fourth day.

♦ No temple could be seen in the city, for the Lord God Almighty and the Lamb are worshiped in it everywhere. And the city has no need of sun or moon to light it, for the glory of God and of the Lamb illuminate it. Its light will light the nations of the earth, and the rulers of the world will come and bring their glory to it. Its gates never close; they stay open all day long—and there is no night! And the glory and honor of all the nations shall be brought into it. Nothing evil will be permitted in it—no one immoral or dishonest—but only those whose names are written in the Lamb's Book of Life.

Genesis 1:14-19; Revelation 21:22-27

WEIRD or what

The word **Lamb** is used in the Bible **138** times—93 of those refer to Jesus. The lamb was one of the main animals used for sacrifices. Jesus received the name "Lamb" because of His ultimate sacrifice-death on the cross. Do you understand what that means? He **gave up** His life so we can share eternity together..and that's a long time! His sacrifice **paved the way** to heaven. To get there, all we have to do is follow **in His steps.**

:00
:10
:20
:30
:40
:50
:60
end

5

CHECK IT OUT

ALL CREATURES

It's great to know that God not only created animals, but **He cares** about them as well. What's even more incredible is the truth that God cares **more about us** than animals. Jesus said, "Not one sparrow can fall to the ground without your Father knowing it. And the very **hairs** of your head are all numbered. So don't worry! You are more valuable to Him than many sparrows." (Matthew 10:29-31)

Next time you see an animal, let it be a reminder of how much **God loves you.** You are His special creation! **So special** that the number of hairs on your head is no secret to God. You might even say, "Not one hair can fall into the **bathroom sink** without God knowing about it."

Now, **that's concern!**

:00
:10
:20
:30
:40
:50
:60

d o n e

   Then God said, "Let the waters teem with fish and other life, and let the skies be filled with birds of every kind." So God created great sea animals, and every sort of fish and every kind of bird. And God looked at them with pleasure, and blessed them all. "Multiply and stock the oceans," he told them, and to the birds he said, "Let your numbers increase. Fill the earth!" That ended the fifth day.

♦ O Lord, what a variety you have made! And in wisdom you have made them all! The earth is full of your riches.

There before me lies the mighty ocean, teeming with life of every kind, both great and small. And look! See the ships! And over there, the whale you made to play in the sea. Every one of these depends on you to give them daily food. You supply it, and they gather it. You open wide your hand to feed them, and they are satisfied with all your bountiful provision.

Genesis 1:20-23; Psalm 104:24-28

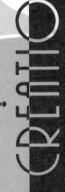

And God said, "Let the earth bring forth every kind of animal—cattle and reptiles and wildlife of every kind." And so it was. God made all sorts of wild animals and cattle and reptiles. And God was pleased with what he had done.

♦ I have no complaint about the sacrifices you bring to my altar, for you bring them regularly. But it isn't sacrificial bullocks and goats that I really want from you. For all the animals of field and forest are mine! The cattle on a thousand hills! And all the birds upon the mountains! If I were hungry, I would not mention it to you—for all the world is mine and everything in it. No, I don't need your sacrifices of flesh and blood. What I want from you is your true thanks; I want your promises fulfilled. I want you to trust me in your times of trouble, so I can rescue you and you can give me glory.

Genesis 1:24-25; Psalm 50:8-15

IN other words...

SACRIFICE

There are several types of **sacrifices** mentioned throughout the Bible. People made sacrifices when they wanted to get right with God. At that time, tradition instructed a person to sacrifice [kill] an animal as a type of payment to God for sin, resulting in forgiveness. Jesus changed all that when He died on the cross. Once and for all He paid the debt for our sin.... The world hasn't gotten over it yet.

:00

:10

:20

:30

:40

:50

done :60

MANKIND: THE IMAGE OF GOD

Catch THIS

These verses **are awesome!** God created us in His image and views His creation as very good. Not average. **Not weird.** Not ugly. But **very good!** If that truth doesn't get you excited, you'd better **check your pulse**...you might already be dead.

Take a minute and **thank God** for that image of yours. Rest in the truth that no matter what you think of yourself and your body, God sees it as good... **VERY Good.**

:00
:10
:20
:30
:40
:50
:60 done

Then God said, "Let us make a man—someone like ourselves, to be the master of all life upon the earth and in the skies and in the seas." So God made man like his Maker. Like God did God make man; Man and maid did he make them. And God blessed them and told them, "Multiply and fill the earth and subdue it; you are masters of the fish and birds and all the animals. And look! I have given you the seed-bearing plants throughout the earth and all the fruit trees for your food. And I've given all the grass and plants to the animals and birds for their food." Then God looked over all that he had made, and it was excellent in every way. This ended the sixth day.

Genesis 1:26-31

8

GOD RESTS

Now at last the heavens and earth were successfully completed, with all that they contained. So on the seventh day, having finished his task, God ceased from this work he had been doing, and God blessed the seventh day and declared it holy, because it was the day when he ceased this work of creation.

♦ Remember to observe the Sabbath as a holy day. For in six days the Lord made the heaven, earth, and sea, and everything in them, and rested the seventh day; so he blessed the Sabbath day and set it aside for rest.

♦ Another time, on a Sabbath day as Jesus and his disciples were walking through the fields, the disciples were breaking off heads of wheat and eating the grain.

Some of the Jewish religious leaders said to Jesus, "They shouldn't be doing that! It's against our laws to work by harvesting grain on the Sabbath."

But Jesus replied, "Didn't you ever hear about the time King David and his companions were hungry, and he went into the house of God—Abiathar was High Priest then—and they ate the special bread only priests were allowed to eat? That was against the law too. But the Sabbath was made to benefit man, and not man to benefit the Sabbath. And I, the Messiah, have authority even to decide what men can do on Sabbath days!"

Genesis 2:1-3; Exodus 20:8, 11;
Mark 2:23-28

Just a thought

Don't you think that if God found the time to rest after all He did, you can spend some time enjoying His good work?

:00
:10
:20
:30
:40
:50
1:00

FINISH

9

The First **Man** and **Woman**

ADAM EVE

BIG time
word

"Joined" is an important word to understand, because it's a very graphic description of sex. That's right...**SEX!** Sex wasn't invented by a group of explorers. Sex was God's idea. He created it. But from the very beginning God sets a standard for sex by informing us that sex joins **husband and wife** into "one flesh." It's sort of reverse arithmetic: two become **ONE.** God wants us to become one flesh with only one other person. Just like Adam and Eve, that one other person is to be our spouse. **What a beautiful gift from God!** It's worth the wait!

The time came when the Lord God formed a man's body from the dust of the ground and breathed into it the breath of life. And man became a living person.

The Lord God placed the man in the Garden of Eden as its gardener, to tend and care for it. But the Lord God gave the man this warning: "You may eat any fruit in the garden except fruit from the Tree of Conscience—for its fruit will open your eyes to make you aware of right and wrong, good and bad. If you eat its fruit, you will be doomed to die."

And the Lord God said, "It isn't good for man to be alone; I will make a companion for him, a helper suited to his needs."

Then the Lord God caused the man to fall into a deep sleep, and took one of his ribs and closed up the place from which he had removed it, and made the rib into a woman, and brought her to the man.

"This is it!" Adam exclaimed. "She is part of my own bone and flesh! Her name is 'woman' because she was taken out of a man." This explains why a man leaves his father and mother and is joined to his wife in such a way that the two become one person. Now although the man and his wife were both naked, neither of them was embarrassed or ashamed.

Genesis 2:7, 15-18, 21-25

11

O Lord our God, the majesty and glory of your name fills all the earth and overflows the heavens. You have taught the little children to praise you perfectly. May their example shame and silence your enemies! When I look up into the night skies and see the work of your fingers—the moon and the stars you have made—I cannot understand how you can bother with mere puny man, to pay any attention to him!

And yet you have made him only a little lower than the angels and placed a crown of glory and honor upon his head.

You have put him in charge of everything you made; everything is put under his authority: all sheep and oxen, and wild animals too, the birds and fish, and all the life in the sea. Jehovah, our Lord, the majesty and glory of your name fills the earth.

Psalm 8

done!

Give it a try

This Psalm was written to express thankfulness for all God has done.

What are **three** things you are thankful for today?

1 _____

2 _____

3 _____

11

JAN 12

WHAT'S **it** mean

THE FIRST SIN

Satan is not a make-believe character created to scare us. **Satan is real.** The Bible refers to Satan many times and gives him several names: Evil One, Serpent or **Snake,** Murderer, Roaring Lion, Liar, **Tempter,** Dragon, and the Devil. These aren't great names to have.

Satan's role started when he **tempted** Adam and Eve to disobey God. Their act of **rebellion** is known as the first or "original" **sin.** This sin led our entire world into more sin and **disobedience.**

Since then, this world has gotten pretty bad. Death, violence, pain, and wickedness are everywhere. But there's **hope in the midst** of this mess! If you read to the end of this book, you'll see how **God has His way** with Satan.

The serpent was the craftiest of all the creatures the Lord God had made. So the serpent came to the woman. "Really?" he asked. "**None** of the fruit in the garden? God says you mustn't eat **any** of it?"

"Of course we may eat it," the woman told him. "It's only the fruit from the tree at the **center** of the garden that we are not to eat. God says we mustn't eat it or even touch it, or we will die."

"That's a lie!" the serpent hissed. "You'll not die! God knows very well that the instant you eat it you will become like him, for your eyes will be opened—you will be able to distinguish good from evil!"

The woman was convinced. How lovely and fresh looking it was! And it would make her so wise! So she ate some of the fruit and gave some to her husband, and he ate it too. And as they ate it, suddenly they became aware of their nakedness, and were embarrassed. So they strung fig leaves together to cover themselves around the hips. That evening they heard the sound of the Lord God walking in the garden; and they hid themselves among the trees.

Genesis 3:1-8

DONE

12

God Judges the First Sin

ONE MINUTE MEMORY

The Lord God called to Adam, "Why are you hiding?" And Adam replied, "I heard you coming and didn't want you to see me naked. So I hid."

"Who told you you were naked?" the Lord God asked. "Have you eaten fruit from the tree I warned you about?"

"Yes," Adam admitted, "but it was the woman you gave me who brought me some, and I ate it."

Then the Lord God asked the woman, "How could you do such a thing?"

"The serpent tricked me," she replied.

So the Lord God said to the serpent, "This is your punishment: You are singled out from among all the domestic and wild animals of the whole earth—to be cursed. You shall grovel in the dust as long as you live, crawling along on your belly. From now on you and the woman will be enemies, as will your offspring and hers. You will strike his heel, but he will crush your head."

Then God said to the woman, "You shall bear children in intense pain and suffering; yet even so, you shall welcome your husband's affections, and he shall be your master."

♦ So there is now no condemnation awaiting those who belong to Christ Jesus.

Genesis 3:9-16; Romans 8:1

So there is now no condemnation awaiting those who belong to Christ Jesus.

Romans 8:1

:00

:15

:30

:45

:60

done

CHECK IT OUT

GOD EXILES ADAM AND EVE FROM THE GARDEN

And to Adam, God said, "Because you listened to your wife and ate the fruit when I told you not to, I have placed a curse upon the soil. All your life you will struggle to extract a living from it. It will grow thorns and thistles for you, and you shall eat its grasses. All your life you will sweat to master it, until your dying day. Then you will return to the ground from which you came. For you were made from the ground, and to the ground you will return."

The man named his wife Eve (meaning "The life-giving one"), for he said, "She shall become the mother of all mankind"; and the Lord God clothed Adam and his wife with garments made from skins of animals.

Then the Lord said, "Now that the man has become as we are, knowing good from bad, what if he eats the fruit of the Tree of Life and lives forever?" So the Lord God banished him forever from the Garden of Eden, and sent him out to farm the ground from which he had been taken. Thus God expelled him, and placed mighty angels at the east of the Garden of Eden, with a flaming sword to guard the entrance to the Tree of Life.

♦ Everyone dies because all of us are related to Adam, being members of his sinful race, and wherever there is sin, death results. But all who are related to Christ will rise again.

Genesis 3:17-24; 1 Corinthians 15:22

It sounds **depressing** to read that we will **die** because of our disobedience. You may even be thinking, **"What** did I do wrong?" The answer is, "Just like the rest of us, **you were born** into a sinful world where death goes along with living."

It's **good news** to know that our future is in God's hands and that it's one filled with **hope.** One day God will get rid of sin and death. The Bible **informs us** in Romans 8:20-21, "Sin and death will disappear, and the world around us will share in the **glorious freedom** from sin which God's children enjoy."

If you are **one** of God's children, get ready to **party!**

If not...**yikes.**

:00

:10

:20

:30

:40

:50

:60

done

ONE MINUTE MEMORY

Death in Adam, Life in Christ

When Adam sinned, sin entered the entire human race. His sin spread death throughout all the world, so everything began to grow old and die, for all sinned. (We know that it was Adam's sin that caused this) because although, of course, people were sinning from the time of Adam until Moses, God did not in those days judge them guilty of death for breaking his laws—because he had not yet given his laws to them nor told them what he wanted them to do. So when their bodies died it was not for their own sins since they themselves had never disobeyed God's special law against eating the forbidden fruit, as Adam had.

What a contrast between Adam and Christ who was yet to come! And what a difference between man's sin and God's forgiveness!

For this one man, Adam, brought death to many through his sin. But this one man, Jesus Christ, brought forgiveness to many through God's mercy. Adam's one sin brought the penalty of death to many, while Christ freely takes away many sins and gives glorious life instead. The sin of this one man, Adam, caused death to be king over all, but all who will take God's gift of forgiveness and acquittal are kings of life because of this one man, Jesus Christ.

♦ For the wages of sin is death, but the free gift of God is eternal life through Jesus Christ our Lord.

Romans 5:12-17; 6:23

For the wages of sin is death, but the free gift of God is eternal life through Jesus Christ our Lord.

Romans 6:23

:00

:15

:30

:45

:60

done

15

CAIN THE FIRST ABEL MURDER

Then Adam had sexual intercourse with Eve his wife, and she conceived and gave birth to a son, Cain (meaning "I have created"). For, as she said, "With God's help, I have created a man!" Her next child was his brother, Abel.

Abel became a shepherd, while Cain was a farmer. At harvest time Cain brought the Lord a gift of his farm produce, and Abel brought the fatty cuts of meat from his best lambs, and presented them to the Lord. And the Lord accepted Abel's offering, but not Cain's. This made Cain both dejected and very angry, and his face grew dark with fury.

"Why are you angry?" the Lord asked him. "Why is your face so dark with rage? It can be bright with joy if you will do what you should! But if you refuse to obey, watch out. Sin is waiting to attack you, longing to destroy you. But you can conquer it!"

One day Cain suggested to his brother, "Let's go out into the fields." And while they were together there, Cain attacked and killed his brother.

But afterwards the Lord asked Cain, "Where is your brother? Where is Abel?"

"How should I know?" Cain retorted. "Am I supposed to keep track of him wherever he goes?"

But the Lord said, "Your brother's blood calls to me from the ground. What have you done? You are hereby banished from this ground which you have defiled with your brother's blood."

Genesis 4:1-11

Catch T·H·I·S

It doesn't take the IQ of a **brain surgeon** to recognize Cain's jealousy. He compared his gift with Abel's and he lost. Instead of attacking his **own** problem of jealousy, he attacked his brother and killed him. Not exactly a **fairy-tale** ending, right?

Jealous people are typically not **happy** with who they are. They spend too much time **comparing** themselves to others and trying to conform to another's style, personality, or look. This comparison game leaves them feeling like losers because they'll always find someone stronger, smarter, more athletic, or **better-looking** than they are.

Fortunately, God doesn't play the comparison game with us. **He doesn't care** if we are tan, fat, thin, athletic, or smart. God is interested in our hearts. If you can understand this truth, you'll find no reason for jealousy. **He loves you** just the way you are...so thank Him and **celebrate** your creation.

:00
:10
:20
:30
:40
:50
:60
done

Noah personality plus

Noah was the only truly righteous man living on the earth at that time. He tried always to conduct his affairs according to God's will. And he had three sons—Shem, Ham, and Japheth.

Meanwhile, the crime rate was rising rapidly across the earth, and, as seen by God, the world was rotten to the core.

As God observed how bad it was, and saw that all mankind was vicious and depraved, he said to Noah, "I have decided to destroy all mankind; for the earth is filled with crime because of man. Yes, I will destroy mankind from the earth. Make a boat from resinous wood, sealing it with tar; and construct decks and stalls throughout the ship.

"Look! I am going to cover the earth with a flood and destroy every living being—everything in which there is the breath of life. All will die. But I promise to keep you safe in the ship, with your wife and your sons and their wives. Bring a pair of every animal—a male and a female—into the boat with you, to keep them alive through the flood.

"Store away in the boat all the food that they and you will need." And Noah did everything as God commanded him.

Genesis 6:9-14, 17-19, 21-22

Rarely related with the story of **Noah and the Ark** is the fact that Noah was a man who **walked with God.** Noah lived during a time period when sin was everywhere, people were wicked, and the world was full of evil. Noah is a **hero** because he remained faithful to God, and **God was faithful** to him and honored him by choosing him and his wife to repopulate the **world.**

Are you **open to God** using you to do great things? Prepare yourself by remaining faithful during difficult times. **You never know** how or when God may choose **to use you.**

:00

:10

:20

:30

:40

:50

:60

the End

THE GREAT FLOOD

[Noah] was 600 years old when the flood came. He boarded the boat with his wife and sons and their wives, to escape the flood. With him were all the various kinds of animals—those for eating and sacrifice, and those that were not, and the birds and reptiles. They came into the boat in pairs, male and female, just as God commanded Noah.

One week later, when Noah was 600 years, two months, and seventeen days old, the rain came down in mighty torrents from the sky, and the subterranean waters burst forth upon the earth.

For forty days the roaring floods prevailed, covering the ground and lifting the boat high above the earth. As the water rose higher and higher above the ground, the boat floated safely upon it; until finally the water covered all the high mountains under the whole heaven.

All existence on the earth was blotted out—man and animals alike, and reptiles and birds. God destroyed them all, leaving only Noah alive, and those with him in the boat.

♦ Noah was another who trusted God. When he heard God's warning about the future, Noah believed him even though there was then no sign of a flood, and wasting no time, he built the ark and saved his family. Noah's belief in God was in direct contrast to the sin and disbelief of the rest of the world—which refused to obey—and because of his faith he became one of those whom God has accepted.

Genesis 7:6-12, 17-19, 23; Hebrews 11:7

:00

:10 It's not clear what the ark **looked** like. All we can do is guess. But we do know its

:20 dimensions. It was **300 cubits** in length, **50 cubits** in width, and

:30 **30 cubits** in height. If that doesn't help you any, you can figure out the size of the

:40 boat by multiplying **21** inches per cubit. If you don't want the math challenge but want to use the answers to

:50 stump a friend, turn this book upside down for the dimensions.

:60 ANSWER: It's 525 feet long, 87 feet 6 inches wide, and 52 feet 6 inches high.

 end

AFTER THE FLOOD

WHAT'S it mean

God didn't forget about Noah and all the animals in the boat! He sent a wind to blow across the waters, and the floods began to disappear.

After another forty days, Noah opened a porthole and released a raven that flew back and forth until the earth was dry. Meanwhile he sent out a dove to see if it could find dry ground, but the dove found no place to light, and returned to Noah, for the water was still too high. So Noah held out his hand and drew the dove back into the boat.

Seven days later Noah released the dove again, and this time, toward evening, the bird returned to him with an olive leaf in her beak. So Noah knew that the water was almost gone.

Noah, his wife, and his sons and their wives all disembarked, along with all the animals, reptiles, and birds—all left the ark in pairs and groups.

Then Noah built an altar and sacrificed on it some of the animals and birds God had designated for that purpose. And Jehovah was pleased with the sacrifice and said to himself, "I will never do it again—I will never again curse the earth, destroying all living things, even though man's bent is always toward evil from his earliest youth, and even though he does such wicked things."

Genesis 8:1, 6-9a, 10-11, 18, 21

These last two verses are referred to as the **Noahic Covenant.** A covenant is an oath or a **promise** made by God. The Noahic Covenant is the promise God made to Noah—and to all of us who would be alive in the future—that He will **never** again destroy the earth by flooding. **That's good news!**

As you read the Bible, you can always look to God's covenants with **confidence** that He will keep His promises.

Take a minute to thank God for His promises.

DONE

20 jan

personality plus Abraham

:00
:10
:20
:30
:40
:50
:60

Abram, later called Abraham, is one of the **most popular** people in the Bible. He is known as the **"Father** of the **faithful."** Like Noah, Abraham was a faithful person who put **God first.** His first test of faith was to leave his country and family and travel to an unknown land. He left this security because he was **confident** in God's vision. He trusted God so much that he was willing to offer his only child, Isaac, as a sacrifice to prove this faithfulness.

God **rewarded** Abraham's faithfulness. As you read about Abraham, think about how you can show God your faithfulness. He has a **vision** for your life.

Are you **ready?**
Available?
Faithful?
Willing?

How about **today?**

Let Him know.

God had told Abram, "Leave your own country behind you, and your own people, and go to the land I will guide you to. If you do, I will cause you to become the father of a great nation; I will bless you and make your name famous, and you will be a blessing to many others. I will bless those who bless you and curse those who curse you; and the entire world will be blessed because of you."

So Abram departed as the Lord had instructed him, and Lot went too; Abram was seventy-five years old at that time. He took his wife Sarai, his nephew Lot, and all his wealth—the cattle and slaves he had gotten in Haran—and finally arrived in Canaan. Traveling through Canaan, they came to a place near Shechem, and set up camp beside the oak at Moreh. (This area was inhabited by Canaanites at that time.)

Then Jehovah appeared to Abram and said, "I am going to give this land to your descendants." And Abram built an altar there to commemorate Jehovah's visit.

Genesis 12:1-7

the End

Afterwards Jehovah spoke to Abram in a vision, and this is what he told him: "Don't be fearful, Abram, for I will defend you. And I will give you great blessings."

But Abram replied, "O Lord Jehovah, what good are all your blessings when I have no son? For without a son, some other member of my household will inherit all my wealth."

Then Jehovah told him, "No, no one else will be your heir, for you will have a son to inherit everything you own."

Then God brought Abram outside beneath the nighttime sky and told him, "Look up into the heavens and count the stars if you can. Your descendants will be like that—too many to count!" And Abram believed God; then God considered him righteous on account of his faith.

♦ Now this wonderful statement—that he was accepted and approved through his faith—wasn't just for Abraham's benefit. It was for us, too, assuring us that God will accept us in the same way he accepted Abraham—when we believe the promises of God who brought back Jesus our Lord from the dead. He died for our sins and rose again to make us right with God, filling us with God's goodness.

Genesis 15:1-6; Romans 4:23-25

IN other words...
RIGHTEOUS

The words "righteous" and "righteousness" are used many times in the Bible. A righteous person is someone who has an intimate relationship with God and constantly lives to please Him and do what's right.

In the Old Testament a righteous person is someone who fears God and lives his life by keeping God's commandments.

In the New Testament, Jesus goes beyond the definition of doing and focuses more on being. He places higher priority on a person's heart (being) than his behavior (doing). A person with a righteous heart automatically wants to do what's right.

:00
:10
:20
:30
:40
:50
:60

How's your heart today?   done

21

22

JAN

:00

:10

:20

:30

:40

:50

1:00

◻ FINISH

Just a thought

God's **ability** to perform **miracles** in **your** life and answer your prayers doesn't **depend** on how young or **old** you are.

Fortunately, God isn't confined to **OUR** limited way of thinking...

remember,

He's **God!**

ISHMAEL & (ABRAHAM'S SONS) ISAAC

But Sarai and Abram had no children. So Sarai took her maid, an Egyptian girl named Hagar, and gave her to Abram to be his second wife.

"Since the Lord has given me no children," Sarai said, "you may sleep with my servant girl, and her children shall be mine." And Abram agreed. (This took place ten years after Abram had first arrived in the land of Canaan.) So he slept with Hagar, and she conceived; and when she realized she was pregnant, she became very proud and arrogant toward her mistress Sarai.

So Hagar gave Abram a son, and Abram named him Ishmael. (Abram was eighty-six years old at this time.)

♦ Then God did as he had promised, and Sarah became pregnant and gave Abraham a baby son in his old age, at the time God had said; and Abraham named him Isaac (meaning "Laughter!"). Eight days after he was born, Abraham circumcised him, as God required. (Abraham was 100 years old at that time.)

♦ Abraham trusted God. . . . Sarah, too, had faith, and because of this she was able to become a mother in spite of her old age, for she realized that God, who gave her his promise, would certainly do what he said.

Genesis 16:1-4a, 15-16; 21:1-5; Hebrews 11:8a,11

Abraham offers Isaac as a sacrifice

Later on, God tested Abraham's (faith and obedience). "Abraham!" God called.

"Yes, Lord?" he replied.

"Take with you your only son—yes, Isaac whom you love so much—and go to the land of Moriah and sacrifice him there as a burnt offering upon one of the mountains which I'll point out to you!"

When they arrived at the place where God had told Abraham to go, he built an altar and placed the wood in order, ready for the fire, and then tied Isaac and laid him on the altar over the wood. And Abraham took the knife and lifted it up to plunge it into his son, to slay him.

At that moment the Angel of God shouted to him from heaven, "Abraham! Abraham!"

"Yes, Lord!" he answered.

"Lay down the knife; don't hurt the lad in any way," the Angel said, "for I know that God is first in your life—you have not withheld even your beloved son from me." Then Abraham noticed a ram caught by its horns in a bush. So he took the ram and sacrificed it, instead of his son, as a burnt offering on the altar.

♦ In this act we see what real love is: it is not our love for God but his love for us when he sent his Son to satisfy God's anger against our sins.

Genesis 22:1-2, 9-13; 1 John 4:10

d o n e !

Give it a try

God tested Abraham's faith by seeing if he loved his son **more than Him.**
What is it that you love **more than anything else?**
Write your answer in the blank space below.

"For I know that God is first in your life—you have not withheld even your _____ from me."

Is this true? ☐YES ☐NO

If your answer is no, what do you need to do to make God the greatest love in your life?

:00

:10

:20

:30

:40

:50

1:00

Just a thought

Everyone is a favorite creation to God!

God's love for you has **nothing** to do with your

background, skin color, financial situation, IQ, or **even** your **neighborhood.**

Take a look at yourself...you're one of God's **favorite** creations.

ESAU & (ISAAC'S SONS) JACOB

This is the story of Isaac's children: Isaac was forty years old when he married Rebekah, the daughter of Bethuel the Aramean from Paddam-aram. Rebekah was the sister of Laban. Isaac pleaded with Jehovah to give Rebekah a child, for even after many years of marriage she had no children. Then at last she became pregnant. And it seemed as though children were fighting each other inside her!

"I can't endure this," she exclaimed. So she asked the Lord about it.

And he told her, "The sons in your womb shall become two rival nations. One will be stronger than the other; and the older shall be a servant of the younger!"

And sure enough, she had twins. The first was born so covered with reddish hair that one would think he was wearing a fur coat! So they called him "Esau." Then the other twin was born with his hand on Esau's heel! So they called him Jacob (meaning "Grabber"). Isaac was sixty years old when the twins were born.

As the boys grew, Esau became a skillful hunter, while Jacob was a quiet sort who liked to stay at home. Isaac's favorite was Esau, because of the venison he brought home, and Rebekah's favorite was Jacob.

Genesis 25:19-28

ESAU SELLS OUT

WHAT'S it mean?

One day Jacob was cooking stew when Esau arrived home exhausted from the hunt.

Esau: *"Boy, am I starved! Give me a bite of that red stuff there!" (From this came his nickname "Edom," which means "Red Stuff.")*
Jacob: *"All right, trade me your birthright for it!"*
Esau: *"When a man is dying of starvation, what good is his birthright?"*
Jacob: *"Well then, vow to God that it is mine!"*

And Esau vowed, thereby selling all his eldest-son rights to his younger brother. Then Jacob gave Esau bread, peas, and stew; so he ate and drank and went on about his business, indifferent to the loss of the rights he had thrown away.

♦ "I have loved you very deeply," says the Lord.

But you retort, "Really? When was this?" And the Lord replies, "I showed my love for you by loving your father, Jacob. I didn't need to. I even rejected his very own brother, Esau, and destroyed Esau's mountains and inheritance, to give it to the jackals of the desert.

♦ Watch out that no one becomes involved in sexual sin or becomes careless about God as Esau did: he traded his rights as the oldest son for a single meal. And afterwards, when he wanted those rights back again, it was too late, even though he wept bitter tears of repentance. So remember, and be careful.

Genesis 25:29-34; Malachi 1:2-3; Hebrews 12:16-17

A **birthright** was a special privilege given to the oldest son. The one with the birthright received the **blessing** of the father and all the father had built and accomplished. In the case of Esau and Jacob, it was about more than gaining their dad's money: It was about receiving special blessings from God.

Today, we have the opportunity to receive the birthright that God intended for Jesus. Jesus is both the only Son of God and the firstborn of God. By having a relationship with Jesus, **we can share** in the blessings intended for Him. The Bible says, "We should behave like God's very own children.... And since we are his children, we will share his **treasures**–for all God gives to his Son Jesus is now ours too."

(Romans 8:13,17)

Congratulations!

personality Plus Joseph

Joseph is another example of **good** things happening to a **faithful** man.

Joseph was abducted by his brothers and sold into slavery. But God was with him and took **care** of him. Joseph's life illustrates this truth:

"When you are **obedient** to God you can **conquer** any obstacle put in your way." Joseph's statement supports this. "As for you, you meant evil against me; but God meant it for good."

Joseph believed that no matter **what** harm his enemies might inflict upon him, **God** would remain **faithful** and come through.

Be faithful **today** and see if any good happens to **you.**

:00

:10

:20

:30

:40

:50

:60

J acob's son Joseph was now seventeen years old. His job, along with his half-brothers, the sons of his father's wives Bilhah and Zilpah, was to shepherd his father's flocks. But Joseph reported to his father some of the bad things they were doing. Now as it happened, Israel loved Joseph more than any of his other children, because Joseph was born to him in his old age. So one day Jacob gave him a special gift—a brightly colored coat. His brothers of course noticed their father's partiality, and consequently hated Joseph; they couldn't say a kind word to him. One night Joseph had a dream and promptly reported the details to his brothers, causing even deeper hatred.

"Listen to this," he proudly announced. "We were out in the field binding sheaves, and my sheaf stood up, and your sheaves all gathered around it and bowed low before it!"

Then he had another dream and told it to his brothers. "Listen to my latest dream," he boasted. "The sun, moon, and eleven stars bowed low before me!" This time he told his father as well as his brothers; but his father rebuked him. "What is this?" he asked. "Shall I indeed, and your mother and brothers come and bow before you?" His brothers were fit to be tied concerning this affair, but his father gave it quite a bit of thought and wondered what it all meant.

Genesis 37:2b-7, 9-11

the End

God also gave Abraham the ceremony of circumcision at that time, as evidence of the covenant between God and the people of Abraham. And so Isaac, Abraham's son, was circumcised when he was eight days old. Isaac became the father of Jacob, and Jacob was the father of the twelve patriarchs of the Jewish nation. These men were very jealous of Joseph and sold him to be a slave in Egypt. But God was with him, and delivered him out of all of his anguish, and gave him favor before Pharaoh, king of Egypt. God also gave Joseph unusual wisdom so that Pharaoh appointed him governor over all Egypt, as well as putting him in charge of all the affairs of the palace.

But a famine developed in Egypt and Canaan, and there was great misery for our ancestors. When their food was gone, Jacob heard that there was still grain in Egypt, so he sent his sons to buy some. The second time they went, Joseph revealed his identity to his brothers, and they were introduced to Pharaoh. Then Joseph sent for his father Jacob and all his brothers' families to come to Egypt, seventy-five persons in all. So Jacob came to Egypt, where he died, and all his sons.

♦ Jacob lived seventeen years after his arrival, so that he was 147 years old at the time of his death.

Acts 7:8-15; Genesis 47:28

IN other words...

DELIVERED

Joseph is one of many examples of God delivering someone from evil, pain, or a specific situation. Other words that could be used to help define "delivered" are **rescued, saved,** or **escaped.** God's deliverance can give you **hope** for daily living.

Jesus taught His followers to pray using words like these: "Don't bring us into temptation, but deliver us from the evil one."

What's an area in **your life** that you need to be **rescued** from? **Ask** God to deliver you. He's done it **millions** of times. He **can** do it for you.

:00 :10 :20 :30 :40 :50 done :60

27

28 JAN

ONE MINUTE MEMORY

And we know
that all that
happens to us
is working
for our good
if we love God
and are
fitting into
his plans.

Romans 8:28

:00
:15
:30
:45
:60

done

Now that their father was dead, Joseph's brothers were frightened.

"Now Joseph will pay us back for all the evil we did to him," they said.

So they sent him this message: "Before he died, your father instructed us to tell you to forgive us for the great evil we did to you. We servants of the God of your father beg you to forgive us." When Joseph read the message, he broke down and cried.

Then his brothers came and fell down before him and said, "We are your slaves."

But Joseph told them, "Don't be afraid of me. Am I God, to judge and punish you? As far as I am concerned, God turned into good what you meant for evil, for he brought me to this high position I have today so that I could save the lives of many people. No, don't be afraid. Indeed, I myself will take care of you and your families." And he spoke very kindly to them, reassuring them.

"Soon I will die," Joseph told his brothers, "but God will surely come and get you, and bring you out of this land of Egypt and take you back to the land he promised to the descendants of Abraham, Isaac and Jacob."

♦ And we know that all that happens to us is working for our good if we love God and are fitting into his plans.

Genesis 50:15-21, 24; Romans 8:28

28

blameless blessed Job personality Plus

29 jan

There lived in the land of Uz a man named Job—a good man who feared God and stayed away from evil. He had a large family of seven sons and three daughters, and was immensely wealthy, for he owned 7,000 sheep, 3,000 camels, 500 teams of oxen, 500 female donkeys, and employed many servants. He was, in fact, the richest cattleman in that entire area.

One day as the angels came to present themselves before the Lord, Satan, the Accuser, came with them.

Then the Lord asked Satan, "Have you noticed my servant Job? He is the finest man in all the earth—a good man who fears God and will have nothing to do with evil."

"Why shouldn't he when you pay him so well?" Satan scoffed. "You have always protected him and his home and his property from all harm. You have prospered everything he does—look how rich he is! No wonder he 'worships' you! But just take away his wealth, and you'll see him curse you to your face!"

And the Lord replied to Satan, "You may do anything you like with his wealth, but don't harm him physically."

So Satan went away.

Job 1:1-3, 6, 8-12

Job was one of the most **righteous,** richest, well-known, respected people in his world. There was **no wrong** found in him. But unlike the other characters we've already looked at, Job **suffered** tragically. It's an unbelievable story!

No matter **how** incredible the pain, Job was able to keep his **faith**. He never blamed God. Job is **proof** that one can endure incredible pain and still remain confident in God. Job's life reminds us that **God remains God,** no matter how happy and wealthy or sad and poor we might be. His statement sums this up:

> "The Lord gave me everything I had, and they were his to take away. Blessed be the name of the Lord."
>
> (Job 1:21)

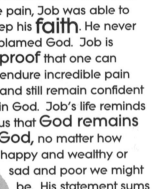

:00
:10
:20
:30
:40
:50
:60

the End

29

JOB
LOSES BIG

No one **wakes up** in the morning and hopes for a **lousy** day. Crummy days just seem to happen without any warning. It would be great if someone called ahead to **warn us** about potentially dreadful days. We wouldn't even have to get out of bed. **Dream on**, right? The truth is, bad days happen!

Next time you have a terrible day, realize you're **not alone.** People have been having them for thousands of years, and you're going to record several more on your life scroll before it's over.

Consider yourself lucky you weren't created to be Job. **Talk about a lousy day**...it doesn't get any worse. What's interesting about Job is that he didn't **blame** God for his pain. This is **amazing!** It's so easy to blame God. But Job chose a different response. If today or tomorrow screams "lousy," remember **Job's example.**

Not long afterwards when Job's sons and daughters were dining at the oldest brother's house, tragedy struck.

A messenger rushed to Job's home with this news: "Your oxen were plowing, with the donkeys feeding beside them, when the Sabeans raided us, drove away the animals, and killed all the farmhands except me. I am the only one left."

While this messenger was still speaking, another arrived with more bad news: "The fire of God has fallen from heaven and burned up your sheep and all the herdsmen, and I alone have escaped to tell you."

Before this man finished, still another messenger rushed in: "Three bands of Chaldeans have driven off your camels and killed your servants, and I alone have escaped to tell you."

As he was still speaking, another arrived to say, "Your sons and daughters were feasting in their oldest brother's home, when suddenly a mighty wind swept in from the desert and engulfed the house so that the roof fell in on them and all are dead; and I alone escaped to tell you."

Then Job stood up and tore his robe in grief and fell down upon the ground before God. "I came naked from my mother's womb," he said, "and I shall have nothing when I die. The Lord gave me everything I had, and they were his to take away. Blessed be the name of the Lord." In all of this Job did not sin or revile God.

Job 1:13-22

:00
:10
:20
:30
:40
:50
:60
done

31 JAN

Now the angels came again to present themselves before the Lord, and Satan with them.

"Well, have you noticed my servant Job?" the Lord asked [Satan]. "He is the finest man in all the earth—a good man who fears God and turns away from all evil. And he has kept his faith in me despite the fact that you persuaded me to let you harm him without any cause."

"Skin for skin," Satan replied. "A man will give anything to save his life. Touch his body with sickness, and he will curse you to your face!"

"Do with him as you please," the Lord replied; "only spare his life."

So Satan went out from the presence of the Lord and struck Job with a terrible case of boils from head to foot. Then Job took a broken piece of pottery to scrape himself and sat among the ashes.

His wife said to him, "Are you still trying to be godly when God has done all this to you? Curse him and die."

But he replied, "You talk like some heathen woman. What? Shall we receive only pleasant things from the hand of God and never anything unpleasant?" So in all this Job said nothing wrong.

Job 2:1, 3-10

done!

Give it a try

Even when life is going well, it's easier to focus on the negative than the positive. In the midst of pain it's even more difficult to recognize anything good about life.

Write down **three** good things you want to do **next month:**

1 _____

2 _____

3 _____

Write down **two** good things that happened to you this month:

1 _____

2 _____

31

FEB

It ain't those
parts of the
Bible that I
can't understand
that bother me,
it is the parts
that I do understand.

**Mark Twain
(1835-1910)**
American Author

IS SUFFERING
always punishment?

When hen three of Job's friends heard of all the tragedy that had befallen him, they got in touch with each other and traveled from their homes to comfort and console him. Their names were Eliphaz the Temanite, Bildad the Shuhite, and Zophar the Naamathite. Job was so changed that they could scarcely recognize him. Wailing loudly in despair, they tore their robes and threw dust into the air and put earth on their heads to demonstrate their sorrow. Then they sat upon the ground with him silently for seven days and nights, no one speaking a word; for they saw that his suffering was too great for words.

♦ At last Job spoke, and cursed the day of his birth.

♦ A reply to Job from Eliphaz the Temanite: "Stop and think! Have you ever known a truly good and innocent person who was punished? Experience teaches that it is those who sow sin and trouble who harvest the same. They die beneath the hand of God.

♦ "My advice to you is this: Go to God and confess your sins to him.

"How enviable the man whom God corrects! Oh, do not despise the chastening of the Lord when you sin. For though he wounds, he binds and heals again.

"I have found from experience that all of this is true. For your own good, listen to my counsel."

Job 2:11-13; 3:1; 4:1, 7-9; 5:8, 17-18, 27

word

COMFORT
+EMPATHY
CONSOLE

Empathy is **possessing** and showing genuine **interest** and **concern** in what is happening. With empathy you can actually **feel** the pain of others. If you express empathy you don't need to know what to say, how to act, or what Bible verse to quote.

People around you are experiencing tragedies on a daily basis. Your empathy for their situation will **reveal God's love.** Where there is empathy, there is support; where there is support, there is encouragement; and where there is **encouragement,** there is love.

Next time a friend is in pain and you don't know what to say, don't worry. Your empathy will communicate the right words: **"I care!"**

35

2 FEB

CHECK IT OUT

JOB PROTESTS

God **heard** the prayers of Job thousands of years ago and He hears our prayers today! God doesn't always choose to answer them when WE want them answered, but He **ALWAYS** hears them. We can be **confident** that God is not hard of hearing!

In Luke 18:1-11, Jesus explains our need to **pray consistently** and to keep praying until an answer comes. Jesus said, "God will surely give justice to his people who plead with him day and night. Yes! He will answer them quickly!"

Next time you get the **urge to worry,** try replacing your worry with a **prayer.** Worrying won't help you at all, but your prayers **will be heard** by the One who can make things happen.

Keep **praying!**

:00

:10

:20

:30

:40

:50

:60

d o n e

The reply of Job:
"How long are you going to trouble me, and try to break me with your words? Ten times now you have declared I am a sinner. Why aren't you ashamed to deal with me so harshly? And if indeed I was wrong, you have yet to prove it. You think yourselves so great? Then prove my guilt!

"The fact of the matter is that God has overthrown me and caught me in his net. I scream for help and no one hears me. I shriek, but get no justice."

• Job's final defense:
"I vow by the living God, who has taken away my rights, even the Almighty God who has embittered my soul, that as long as I live, while I have breath from God, my lips shall speak no evil, my tongue shall speak no lies. I will never, never agree that you are right; until I die I will vow my innocence. I am not a sinner—I repeat it again and again. My conscience is clear for as long as I live."

Job 19:1-7; 27:1-6

36

GOD ANSWERS JOB

Then the Lord answered Job from the whirlwind:

"Why are you using your ignorance to deny my providence? Now get ready to fight, for I am going to demand some answers from you, and you must reply."

"Where were you when I laid the foundations of the earth? Tell me, if you know so much. Do you know how its dimensions were determined, and who did the surveying? What supports its foundations, and who laid its cornerstone as the morning stars sang together and all the angels shouted for joy?"

♦ *The Lord went on:*

"Do you still want to argue with the Almighty? Or will you yield? Do you—God's critic—have the answers?"

Then Job replied to God:

"I am nothing—how could I ever find the answers? I lay my hand upon my mouth in silence. I have said too much already."

Then the Lord spoke to Job again from the whirlwind:

"Stand up like a man and brace yourself for battle. Let me ask you a question, and give me the answer. Are you going to discredit my justice and condemn me so that you can say you are right?"

Job 38:1-7; 40:1-8

Job **screamed** out because of his pain, anguish, and torment. **Do you blame him?** What's totally unexpected is God's response to Job. Instead of answering Job's cry and explaining why a good person can suffer, God instead reminds Job **of His greatness.** God points to the fact that He is **awesome.** Job listens and does the only thing he can in God's presence–he shuts his mouth.

Be reminded today that God is **bigger** than your ability to understand Him. Just take a survey of His incredible creations and you may end up **speechless, too!**

:00

:10

:20

:30

:40

:50

:60

end

GOD restores JOB

4

FEB

Just a thought

God doesn't promise to give the faithful twice as much as they had before, but He has a way of rewarding faithfulness in terms that can't be measured.

:OO

:1O

:2O

:3O

:4O

:5O

1:OO

FINISH

Then Job replied to God:
"I know that you can do anything and that no one can stop you. You ask who it is who has so foolishly denied your providence. It is I. I was talking about things I knew nothing about and did not understand, things far too wonderful for me."
"(You said,) 'Listen and I will speak! Let me put the questions to you! See if you can answer them!'"
"(But now I say,) 'I had heard about you before, but now I have seen you, and I loathe myself and repent in dust and ashes.'"

After the Lord had finished speaking with Job, he said to Eliphaz the Temanite:
"I am angry with you and with your two friends, for you have not been right in what you have said about me, as my servant Job was. Now take seven young bulls and seven rams and go to my servant Job and offer a burnt offering for yourselves; and my servant Job will pray for you, and I will accept his prayer on your behalf, and won't destroy you as I should because of your sin, your failure to speak rightly concerning my servant Job."

So Eliphaz the Temanite, and Bildad the Shuhite, and Zophar the Naamathite did as the Lord commanded them, and the Lord accepted Job's prayer on their behalf.

Then, when Job prayed for his friends, the Lord restored his wealth and happiness! In fact, the Lord gave him twice as much as before!

Job 42:1-10

38

BEATITUDES: POOR IN SPIRIT

WHAT'S **it** mean

O ne day as the crowds were gathering, [Jesus] went up the hillside with his disciples and sat down and taught them there.

"Humble men are very fortunate!" he told them, "for the Kingdom of Heaven is given to them."

♦ It is a broken spirit you want—remorse and penitence. A broken and a contrite heart, O God, you will not ignore.

♦ The high and lofty One who inhabits eternity, the Holy One, says this: I live in that high and holy place where those with contrite, humble spirits dwell; and I refresh the humble and give new courage to those with repentant hearts.

♦ Dear brothers, how can you claim that you belong to the Lord Jesus Christ, the Lord of glory, if you show favoritism to rich people and look down on poor people? Judging a man by his wealth shows that you are guided by wrong motives.

Listen to me, dear brothers: God has chosen poor people to be rich in faith, and the Kingdom of Heaven is theirs, for that is the gift God has promised to all those who love him.

Matthew 5:1-3; Psalm 51:17; Isaiah 57:15; James 2:1, 4-5

"Beatitudes" is a name given to a special sermon from Jesus. Jesus introduced a new way of thinking that was radically different from the way the world thought.
Here's what He said:

- mourn and you'll be **COMFORTED.**

- be meek and you'll be **HAPPY.**

- do what is right and you'll be **SATISFIED.**

- show mercy and **MERCY** will be shown to you.

- have a pure heart and you'll **SEE God.**

- bring peace to others and you'll be **God's CHILD.**

- be treated badly for doing good and you'll be **REWARDED.**

If you can follow these teachings, you will **definitely** stand out... there's no question about it. But look at the promised outcomes....

Seem too good to be true?

Give it a **try** and find out!

DONE

39

:00

:10

:20

:30

:40

:50

1:00

Just a

thought

Next time you **worry** about your **future** be reminded that God has **already** taken care of the **ultimate** future

and wants you to **know** it.

When you know it, you'll **experience** a new peace and **hope** for living **today.**

T H E BEATITUDES: THOSE WHO

Those who mourn are fortunate! for they shall be comforted.

♦ The Spirit of the Lord God is upon me, because the Lord has anointed me to bring good news to the suffering and afflicted. He has sent me to comfort the brokenhearted, to announce liberty to captives, and to open the eyes of the blind. He has sent me to tell those who mourn that the time of God's favor to them has come, and the day of his wrath to their enemies. To all who mourn in Israel he will give:

> *beauty for ashes;*
> *joy instead of mourning;*
> *praise instead of heaviness.*

For God has planted them like strong and graceful oaks for his own glory.

♦ I heard a loud shout from the throne saying, "Look, the home of God is now among men, and he will live with them and they will be his people; yes, God himself will be among them. He will wipe away all tears from their eyes, and there shall be no more death, nor sorrow, nor crying, nor pain. All of that has gone forever."

Matthew 5:4; Isaiah 61:1-3;
Revelation 21:3-4

40

F E B

The Beatitudes: The Meek

The meek and lowly are fortunate! for the whole wide world belongs to them.

♦ Never envy the wicked! Soon they fade away like grass and disappear. Trust in the Lord instead. Be kind and good to others; then you will live safely here in the land and prosper, feeding in safety.

Be delighted with the Lord. Then he will give you all your heart's desires. Commit everything you do to the Lord. Trust him to help you do it, and he will. Your innocence will be clear to everyone. He will vindicate you with the blazing light of justice shining down as from the noonday sun.

Rest in the Lord; wait patiently for him to act. Don't be envious of evil men who prosper.

Stop your anger! Turn off your wrath. Don't fret and worry—it only leads to harm. For the wicked shall be destroyed, but those who trust the Lord shall be given every blessing. Only a little while and the wicked shall disappear. You will look for them in vain. But all who humble themselves before the Lord shall be given every blessing and shall have wonderful peace.

Matthew 5:5; Psalm 37:1-11

But all who humble themselves before the Lord shall be given every blessing, and shall have wonderful peace.

Psalm 37:11

THE BEATITUDES: HUNGRY FOR RIGHTEOUSNESS

Happy are those who long to be just and good, for they shall be completely satisfied.

♦ As the deer pants for water, so I long for you, O God. I thirst for God, the living God. Where can I find him to come and stand before him?

♦ Jesus replied that people soon became thirsty again after drinking this water. "But the water I give them," he said, "becomes a perpetual spring within them, watering them forever with eternal life."

♦ Jesus replied, "I am the Bread of Life. No one coming to me will ever be hungry again. Those believing in me will never thirst."

♦ On the last day, the climax of the holidays, Jesus shouted to the crowds, "If anyone is thirsty, let him come to me and drink. For the Scriptures declare that rivers of living water shall flow from the inmost being of anyone who believes in me." (He was speaking of the Holy Spirit, who would be given to everyone believing in him.)

♦ The Spirit and the bride say, "Come." Let each one who hears them say the same, "Come." Let the thirsty one come—anyone who wants to; let him come and drink the Water of Life without charge.

Matthew 5:6; Psalm 42:1-2;
John 4:13-14; 6:35; 7:37-39a;
Revelation 22:17

Catch T·H·I·S

These are good scriptures to recall next time you swing open the refrigerator and exclaim, **"I'm starving!"** If you're like most people, you'll spend a few minutes checking out all the food and then say, **"There's nothing to eat."** So you slam the door, frustrated, hungry, and in search of some **munchies.**

Though Jesus doesn't promise we'll have a life-time supply of pizza, **Ding-Dongs™,** and potato chips, He does guarantee that we'll never go hungry or thirsty if we **believe** in Him. Jesus isn't talking about how to make sure our stomachs never growl. He's referring to our spiritual needs and how He can completely satisfy them. Picture Jesus' promise as being like living next door to a grocery store that's open 24 hours every day, filled with **free** all-you-can-eat food. Jesus' assurance is even better than that, because you never have to leave your home and His "food" is **completely healthy.**

How can you eat from the **"Bread of Life"** today?

:00
:10
:20
:30
:40
:50
:60
done

for they shall be shown mercy.

♦ For the Lord your God is
merciful—he will not abandon you
nor destroy you nor forget the
promises he has made to
your ancestors.

♦ O God enthroned in heaven, I lift
my eyes to you.

We look to Jehovah our God for his
mercy and kindness just as a servant
keeps his eyes upon his master or a
slave girl watches her mistress for the
slightest signal. Have mercy on us,
Lord, have mercy. For we have had
our fill of contempt and of the
scoffing of the rich and proud.

♦ I don't want your sacrifices—I want
your love; I don't want your
offerings—I want you to know me.

♦ No, he has told you what he wants,
and this is all it is: to be fair, just,
merciful, and to walk humbly with
your God.

♦ You will be judged on whether or
not you are doing what Christ wants
you to. So watch what you do and
what you think; for there will be no
mercy to those who have shown no
mercy. But if you have been merciful,
then God's mercy toward you will
win out over his judgment
against you.

*Matthew 5:7; Deuteronomy 4:31;
Psalm 123:1-4; Hosea 6:6; Micah 6:8;
James 2:12-13*

FEB
9

the merciful

BEATITUDES

IN **other** words...
MERCY

Mercy is showing **compassion** or **empathy.** It's
given by God to meet
the needs of His
people and to care
for them.

:00

Mercy starts with God.
God shows mercy
to us as His followers
because He has
compassion and
cares for us. But
mercy doesn't stop
with God! We can
also express **mercy
to others** in need.

:10

:20

:30

Can you think of **one**
person who is in need
of your mercy? How
can you **show** this
person mercy
TODAY?

:40

:50

done :60

43

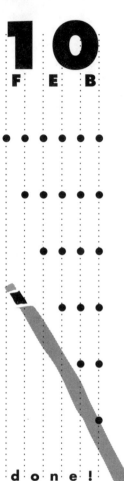

10
F E B

d o n e !

Happy are those whose hearts are pure, for they shall see God.

✦ Who may climb the mountain of the Lord and enter where he lives? Who may stand before the Lord? Only those with pure hands and hearts, who do not practice dishonesty and lying. They will receive God's own goodness as their blessing from him, planted in their lives by God himself, their Savior.

✦ Create in me a new, clean heart, O God, filled with clean thoughts and right desires.

✦ Run from anything that gives you the evil thoughts that young men often have, but stay close to anything that makes you want to do right. Have faith and love, and enjoy the companionship of those who love the Lord and have pure hearts.

✦ And so, dear brothers, now we may walk right into the very Holy of Holies, where God is, because of the blood of Jesus.

And since this great High Priest of ours rules over God's household, let us go right in to God himself, with true hearts fully trusting him to receive us because we have been sprinkled with Christ's blood to make us clean and because our bodies have been washed with pure water.

Matthew 5:8; Psalms 24:3-5; 51:10; 2 Timothy 2:22; Hebrews 10:19,21-22

The scripture in 2 Timothy 2:22 gives you an **action plan** on how to remain pure in heart. **Here it is:**

Give it a try

1. Run from the things that give you **evil thoughts**.
2. Stay **close** to anything that makes you **do right**.
3. Have **faith** and **love**.
4. **Enjoy** the company of others who **love God** and live by this plan.

Do you have at least one friend who could help you meet number four?

Write three qualities you admire about this friend.

1 _____ 2 _____ 3 _____

Sometime real soon, let this friend know how important he or she is to you and your faith.

44

THE BEATITUDES:
THE PEACEMAKERS

Happy are those who strive for peace—they shall be called the sons of God.

♦ Sons and daughters, come and listen and let me teach you the importance of trusting and fearing the Lord. Do you want a long, good life? Then watch your tongue! Keep your lips from lying. Turn from all known sin and spend your time in doing good. Try to live in peace with everyone; work hard at it.

♦ But the good man—what a different story! For the good man—the blameless, the upright, the man of peace—he has a wonderful future ahead of him. For him there is a happy ending. But evil men shall be destroyed, and their posterity shall be cut off.

♦ "There is no peace," says the Lord, "for the wicked."

♦ Don't quarrel with anyone. Be at peace with everyone, just as much as possible.

♦ The wisdom that comes from heaven is first of all pure and full of quiet gentleness. Then it is peace-loving and courteous. It allows discussion and is willing to yield to others; it is full of mercy and good deeds. It is wholehearted and straightforward and sincere.

Matthew 5:9; Psalms 34:11-14; 37:37-38; Isaiah 48:22; Romans 12:18; James 3:17

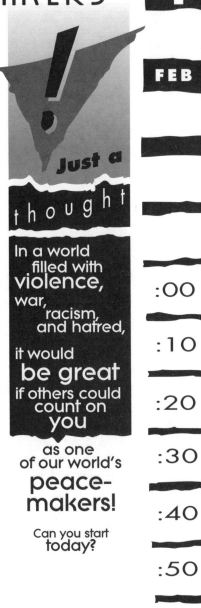

Just a thought

In a world filled with **violence,** war, racism, and hatred, it would **be great** if others could count on **you** as one of our world's **peace-makers!** Can you start **today?**

:00
:10
:20
:30
:40
:50
1:00

FINISH

45

12
F E B

ONE MINUTE MEMORY

Happy are those who are persecuted because they are good, for the Kingdom of Heaven is theirs.

When you are reviled and persecuted and lied about because you are my followers—wonderful! Be happy about it! Be very glad! for a tremendous reward awaits you up in heaven. And remember, the ancient prophets were persecuted too.

♦ But the Lord stands beside me like a great warrior, and before him, the Mighty, Terrible One, they shall stumble. They cannot defeat me; they shall be shamed and thoroughly humiliated, and they shall have a stigma upon them forever.

♦ Praise the Lord if you are punished for doing right! Of course, you get no credit for being patient if you are beaten for doing wrong; but if you do right and suffer for it, and are patient beneath the blows, God is well pleased.

This suffering is all part of the work God has given you. Christ, who suffered for you, is your example. Follow in his steps.

♦ Since I know it is all for Christ's good, I am quite happy about "the thorn," and about insults and hardships, persecutions and difficulties; for when I am weak, then I am strong—the less I have, the more I depend on him.

Matthew 5:10-12; Jeremiah 20:11; 1 Peter 2:19-21; 2 Corinthians 12:10

:00

:15

:30

:45

:60

done X

For when I am weak, then I am strong– the less I have, the more I depend on Him.

2 Corinthians 12:10b

UNCONDITIONAL LOVE

Who then can ever keep Christ's love from us? When we have trouble or calamity, when we are hunted down or destroyed, is it because he doesn't love us anymore? And if we are hungry or penniless or in danger or threatened with death, has God deserted us?

No,...nothing can ever separate us from his love. Death can't, and life can't. The angels won't, and all the powers of hell itself cannot keep God's love away. Our fears for today, our worries about tomorrow, or where we are—high above the sky, or in the deepest ocean—nothing will ever be able to separate us from the love of God demonstrated by our Lord Jesus Christ when he died for us.

♦ We know how much God loves us because we have felt his love and because we believe him when he tells us that he loves us dearly. God is love, and anyone who lives in love is living with God and God is living in him. And as we live with Christ, our love grows more perfect and complete; so we will not be ashamed and embarrassed at the day of judgment, but can face him with confidence and joy because he loves us and we love him too.

We need have no fear of someone who loves us perfectly; his perfect love for us eliminates all dread of what he might do to us. So you see, our love for him comes as a result of his loving us first.

Romans 8:35, 38-39; 1 John 4:16-18a,19

47

:00
:10
:20
:30
:40
:50
:60
done

Catch T·H·I·S

Unconditional love is the way **God loves you.** God's love for you isn't based on your **grades,** your looks, your athletic performance, your friendships, your personality, or your past. If God loved you for what you did, that would be called "conditional" love. But God's love is "unconditional" because His love has **no strings attached.** There are some things you do that God doesn't like, but He **never stops loving you.**

Nothing you do will distance you from God's love. Believe it or not, there's **no sin** that's **too gross,** no language that's too bad, no action that's too evil to stop God from loving you. Doesn't it seem crazy not to love God in response to His love for you?

Thank Him for His love for you today.

14
F E B

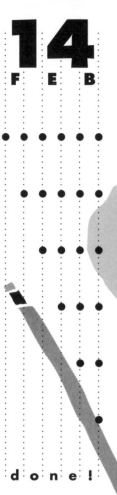

If I had the gift of being able to speak in other languages without learning them and could speak in every language there is in all of heaven and earth, but didn't love others, I would only be making noise. If I had the gift of prophecy and knew all about what is going to happen in the future, knew everything about everything, but didn't love others, what good would it do? Even if I had the gift of faith so that I could speak to a mountain and make it move, I would still be worth nothing at all without love. If I gave everything I have to poor people, and if I were burned alive for preaching the Gospel but didn't love others, it would be of no value whatever.

Love is very patient and kind, never jealous or envious, never boastful or proud, never haughty or selfish or rude. Love does not demand its own way. It is not irritable or touchy. It does not hold grudges and will hardly even notice when others do it wrong. It is never glad about injustice, but rejoices whenever truth wins out. If you love someone, you will be loyal to him no matter what the cost. You will always believe in him, always expect the best of him, and always stand your ground in defending him.

All the special gifts and powers from God will someday come to an end, but love goes on forever. Someday prophecy and speaking in unknown languages and special knowledge—these gifts will disappear.

There are three things that remain—faith, hope, and love—and the greatest of these is love.

1 Corinthians 13:1-8, 13

the greatest is love

done!

Give it a try

Listed below you will find several qualities of love. **Grade** yourself on how you live out each of these qualities (A-F). Next to your lowest grades write a few ideas on how you might **improve** your "love life" with that specific quality.

_____
(your name)

- [ ] is patient
- [ ] is kind
- [ ] rejoices when truth wins
- [ ] doesn't notice when others do wrong
- [ ] is loyal
- [ ] believes in others
- [ ] expects the best of others

Don't let today be the only day of the year when you celebrate love. Work toward being a "lover" every day!

ISRAELITES OPPRESSED

This is the list of the sons of Jacob who accompanied him to Egypt, with their families: Reuben, Simeon, Levi, Judah, Issachar, Zebulun, Benjamin, Dan, Naphtali, Gad, Asher.

So the total number who went with him was seventy (for Joseph was already there). In due season Joseph and each of his brothers died, ending that generation. Meanwhile, their descendants were very fertile, increasing rapidly in numbers; there was a veritable population explosion so that they soon became a large nation, and they filled the land of Goshen.

Then, eventually, a new king came to the throne of Egypt who felt no obligation to the descendants of Joseph.

He told his people, "These Israelis are becoming dangerous to us because there are so many of them. Let's figure out a way to put an end to this. If we don't, and war breaks out, they will join our enemies and fight against us and escape out of the country."

So the Egyptians made slaves of them and put brutal taskmasters over them to wear them down under heavy burdens while building the cities of Pithom and Rameses as supply centers for the king. But the more the Egyptians mistreated and oppressed them, the more the Israelis seemed to multiply! The Egyptians became alarmed and made the Hebrew slavery more bitter still, forcing them to toil long and hard in the fields and to carry heavy loads of mortar and brick.

Then Pharaoh commanded all of his people to throw the newborn Hebrew boys into the Nile River. But the girls, he said, could live.

A taskmaster's job description included torturing the Jewish people (Hebrews) with slave labor. Taskmasters tormented from morning until night so the Hebrews wouldn't have time or strength to have children who might grow up and challenge the Pharaoh's leadership.

It was not uncommon for a taskmaster to beat, even to the point of death, a Hebrew who wasn't working hard. These people became slaves, with no rights under these cruel taskmasters.

Today, those with faith in Jesus are called "Children of God" and are no longer slaves of Pharaoh or slaves to sin. You have freedom from these "masters" through Jesus. Today, thank God for your freedom.

:00
:10
:20
:30
:40
:50
:60

end

personality Plus Moses

Moses is famous for many accomplishments: He **delivered** the Israelites from captivity, with God's **power** he opened the **Red Sea** so the Israelites could escape the Egyptians, and he received God's **Ten Commandments.**

One **interesting** truth about Moses is how God **protected** him as a newborn baby. After Moses' birth, the Pharaoh ordered all newborn Hebrew boys to be killed. Moses' mother created a floatable **basket** and sent him down the **Nile River** hoping he'd remain alive. Pharaoh's daughter found baby Moses floating and adopted him—even though she knew he was a Hebrew baby. An **amazing** story!

When God wants to get something done **He doesn't mess around!** God also has a special purpose for **your** life. Today, trust in Him and **watch** what happens.

:00
:10
:20
:30
:40
:50
:60

the End

There were at this time a Hebrew fellow and girl of the tribe of Levi who married and had a family, and a baby son was born to them. When the baby's mother saw that he was an unusually beautiful baby, she hid him at home for three months. Then, when she could no longer hide him, she made a little boat from papyrus reeds, waterproofed it with tar, put the baby in it, and laid it among the reeds along the river's edge. The baby's sister watched from a distance to see what would happen to him.

Well, this is what happened: A princess, one of Pharaoh's daughters, came down to bathe in the river, and as she and her maids were walking along the riverbank, she spied the little boat among the reeds and sent one of the maids to bring it to her. When she opened it, there was a baby! And he was crying. This touched her heart. "He must be one of the Hebrew children!" she said.

Then the baby's sister approached the princess and asked her, "Shall I go and find one of the Hebrew women to nurse the baby for you?"

"Yes, do!" the princess replied. So the little girl rushed home and called her mother!

"Take this child home and nurse him for me," the princess instructed the baby's mother, "and I will pay you well!" So she took him home and nursed him.

Later, when he was older, she brought him back to the princess and he became her son. She named him Moses (meaning "to draw out") because she had drawn him out of the water.

Exodus 2:1-10

50

Moses Flees from Egypt

One day, many years later when Moses had grown up and become a man, he went out to visit his fellow Hebrews and saw the terrible conditions they were under. During his visit he saw an Egyptian knock a Hebrew to the ground—one of his own Hebrew brothers! Moses looked this way and that to be sure no one was watching, then killed the Egyptian and hid his body in the sand.

The next day as he was out visiting among the Hebrews again, he saw two of them fighting. "What are you doing, hitting your own Hebrew brother like that?" he said to the one in the wrong.

"And who are you?" the man demanded. "I suppose you think you are our prince and judge! And do you plan to kill me as you did that Egyptian yesterday?" When Moses realized that his deed was known, he was frightened. And sure enough, when Pharaoh heard about it he ordered Moses arrested and executed. But Moses ran away into the land of Midian.

Several years later the king of Egypt died. The Israelis were groaning beneath their burdens, in deep trouble because of their slavery, and weeping bitterly before the Lord. He heard their cries from heaven, and remembered his promise to Abraham, Isaac, and Jacob (to bring their descendants back into the land of Canaan). Looking down upon them, he knew that the time had come for their rescue.

Exodus 2:11-15a, 23-25

word

FRIGHTENED

Fright is a **natural** and common reaction. Everyone has a **few** quirks that trigger fear: **spiders,** the dark, speaking to a crowd, **nuclear** war, AIDS, etc. Fright causes physical as well as **emotional** reactions. It's an uncomfortable sensation that puts your entire body on the defense. To constantly live with fear would do terrible **damage** to your body.

Some people allow fears to control their lives and keep them from living and taking risks. Some Christians allow fears to keep them from being all God wants them to be. Do you have any fears holding you back? If your fears are stronger than your faith you'll be in trouble. **Faith** counteracts fear because God is **stronger** than the object of your fear. If you have any fears keeping you from living a vital Christian life, ask God to take **away** those fears **today.**

51

18 FEB

THE LORD APPEARS TO MOSES

CHECK IT OUT

Moses was in the **presence** of God and on **holy** territory. Being in God's presence was **not** to be taken lightly. It still isn't!

This same principle of holiness and respect also applies to **Jesus.** Contrary to many people's beliefs, Jesus is more than JUST a nice man and a good teacher. Jesus is God and worthy of **AWE.**

The Bible informs us that there will be a day when just the **"name"** of **Jesus** will cause respect. Check out Philippians 2:10-11:

"At the name of Jesus every knee shall bow in heaven and on earth and under the earth, and every tongue shall confess that Jesus Christ is Lord to the glory of God the Father."

That's a **powerful** name! How do you respond when you hear it?

:00
:10
:20
:30
:40
:50
:60

One day as Moses was tending the flock of his father-in-law, Jethro, the priest of Midian, out at the edge of the desert near Horeb, the mountain of God, suddenly the Angel of Jehovah appeared to him as a flame of fire in a bush. When Moses saw that the bush was on fire and that it didn't burn up, he went over to investigate. Then God called out to him,

"Moses! Moses!"

"Who is it?" Moses asked.

"Don't come any closer," God told him. "Take off your shoes, for you are standing on holy ground. I am the God of your fathers—the God of Abraham, Isaac, and Jacob." (Moses covered his face with his hands, for he was afraid to look at God.)

Then the Lord told him, "I have seen the deep sorrows of my people in Egypt and have heard their pleas for freedom from their harsh taskmasters. I have come to deliver them from the Egyptians and to take them out of Egypt into a good land, a large land, a land 'flowing with milk and honey'—the land where the Canaanites, Hittites, Amorites, Perizzites, Hivites, and Jebusites live. Now I am going to send you to Pharaoh, to demand that he let you lead my people out of Egypt."

done *Exodus 3:1-8a, 10*

THE LORD REVEALS HIS NAME

WHAT'S it mean

FEB 19

"But I'm not the person for a job like that!" Moses exclaimed.

Then God told him, "I will certainly be with you, and this is the proof that I am the one who is sending you: When you have led the people out of Egypt, you shall worship God here upon this mountain!"

But Moses asked, "If I go to the people of Israel and tell them that their fathers' God has sent me, they will ask, 'Which God are you talking about?' What shall I tell them?"

"'The Sovereign God,'" was the reply. "Just say, 'I Am has sent me!' Yes, tell them, 'Jehovah, the God of your ancestors Abraham, Isaac, and Jacob, has sent me to you.' (This is my eternal name, to be used throughout all generations.)"

♦ "I am Jehovah, the Almighty God who appeared to Abraham, Isaac, and Jacob—though I did not reveal my name, Jehovah, to them."

Exodus 3:11-15; 6:2-3

Ever **wondered** if God has a **name?** God has several different names. In this passage God tells Moses His name is **"I AM."** Seems like an odd name, doesn't it?

I AM is the name God chose for himself. Many believe this name says it all.

"Who's in charge?"
I AM.
"Who's the greatest?"
I AM.
This name—I AM—shows that God is all. There is nothing else but God.

Jesus also said this about himself in John 8:58; He did not say "I was" or "I will be," but He said **"I AM."**

What does all this mean to you today? It means the same thing to you as it did to Moses:

God is everything you need.

DONE

53

FEB

ONE MINUTE MEMORY

All those who know your mercy, Lord, will count on you for help. For you have never yet forsaken those who trust in you.

Psalm 9:10

:00

:15

:30

:45

:60

done

The Names of God: The Lord

All who are oppressed may come to him. He is a refuge for them in their times of trouble. All those who know your mercy, Lord, will count on you for help. For you have never yet forsaken those who trust in you.

♦ You shall not use the name of Jehovah your God irreverently, nor use it to swear to a falsehood. You will not escape punishment if you do.

♦ I will proclaim the greatness of the Lord.
How glorious he is!
He is the Rock. His work is perfect.
Everything he does is just and fair.
He is faithful, without sin.

♦ "Oh, give thanks to the Lord and pray to him," they sang. "Tell the peoples of the world about his mighty doings. Sing to him; yes, sing his praises and tell of his marvelous works. Glory in his holy name; let all rejoice who seek the Lord."

♦ The Lord is a strong fortress. The godly run to him and are safe.

♦ O Lord, there is no other god like you. For you are great, and your name is full of power.

Psalm 9:9-10; Exodus 20:7; Deuteronomy 32:3-4; 1 Chronicles 16:8-10; Proverbs 18:10; Jeremiah 10:6

How great you are, Lord God! We have never heard of any other god like you. And there is no other god. What other nation in all the earth has received such blessings as Israel, your people? For you have rescued your chosen nation in order to bring glory to your name. You have done great miracles to destroy Egypt and its gods. You chose Israel to be your people forever, and you became our God.

♦ He frees us! He rescues us from death.

♦ O Lord, you alone are my hope; I've trusted you from childhood.

♦ Those refusing to worship God will perish, for he destroys those serving other gods. But as for me, I get as close to him as I can! I have chosen him, and I will tell everyone about the wonderful ways he rescues me.

2 Samuel 7:22-24;
Psalms 68:20; 71:5; 73:27-28

IN other words...
SOVEREIGN

The **Lord God** is sovereign. The dictionary defines sovereign as "above" or "superior to all others." It also uses the words "chief" and "one in authority." While these descriptive words may help us understand sovereign, a dictionary doesn't explain why God is sovereign.

God is the one who created all, knows all, controls all, is above all, and is everywhere. There is **nothing** bigger or greater than God. That's why God gets the title "sovereign."

Today, think about God being superior and in complete control of your life. Because God IS sovereign, He's definitely capable of caring for you today.

:00

:10

:20

:30

:40

:50

done :60

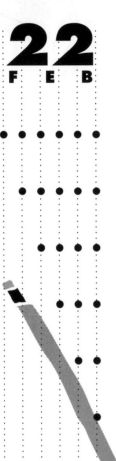

22
F E B

d o n e !

Open up, O ancient gates, and let the King of Glory in. Who is this King of Glory? The Lord, strong and mighty, invincible in battle. Yes, open wide the gates and let the King of Glory in.

Who is this King of Glory? The Commander of all of heaven's armies!

♦ Spread out before me was what seemed to be an ocean of fire and glass, and on it stood all those who had been victorious over the Evil Creature and his statue and his mark and number. All were holding harps of God, and they were singing the song of Moses, the servant of God, and the song of the Lamb:

"Great and marvelous are your doings,
Lord God Almighty.

Just and true are your ways, O King of Ages.

Who shall not fear,
O Lord, and glorify your Name?

For you alone are holy.

All nations will come and worship before you,
For your righteous deeds have been disclosed."

Psalm 24:7-10; Revelation 15:2-4

What are a few **qualities** that a King is traditionally known for?

Give **it a try**

Do these words also **describe God** as you understand Him?

Why do you think **"King"** is a good title for God?

GOD: THE **ALMIGHTY**

WHAT'S **it** mean

Listen to me, you with understanding. Surely everyone knows that God doesn't sin! Rather, he punishes the sinners. There is no truer statement than this: God is never wicked or unjust.

♦ We cannot imagine the power of the Almighty, and yet he is so just and merciful that he does not destroy us. No wonder men everywhere fear him! For he is not impressed by the world's wisest men!

♦ We live within the shadow of the Almighty, sheltered by the God who is above all gods.

This I declare, that he alone is my refuge, my place of safety; he is my God, and I am trusting him. For he rescues you from every trap and protects you from the fatal plague. He will shield you with his wings! They will shelter you. His faithful promises are your armor.

♦ "I am the A and the Z, the Beginning and the Ending of all things," says God, who is the Lord, the All Powerful One who is, and was, and is coming again!

Job 34:10-12; 37:23-24;
Psalm 91:1-4; Revelation 1:8

God uses the **alphabet** to better describe another of His many qualities— "I am the A and the Z." With this analogy, God is reminding us that He is the **beginning** and the **end**.

God was around **before** the earth, before the stars, before your grandparents, and **WAY** before you. God is also the **end** of everything, which means you are somewhere in the middle of His big plan... maybe around the letter "T"...nobody knows.

The only thing we **do** know is His promise to **come back** to us. When that happens, you'll need to know more than just the alphabet. You'll need to **know Jesus.**

Are you ready **for His return?**

57

24 Feb — personality plus LORD

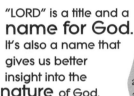

"LORD" is a title and a **name for God.** It's also a name that gives us better insight into the **nature** of God.

A traditional definition of a lord is someone who owned land and ruled over people. If you have a **relationship** with God, He is the Lord and Master **of your life.** He owns you and has authority over you. This means God watches over you and **takes care** of you... you are His creation and His property.

It's a **comforting** way to think of yourself...as the Lord's. You are God's personal possession. **ENJOY that truth today!**

Jehovah your God is God of gods and Lord of lords. He is the great and mighty God, the God of terror who shows no partiality and takes no bribes. He gives justice to the fatherless and widows. He loves foreigners and gives them food and clothing.

✦ O Jehovah, our Lord, the majesty and glory of your name fills the earth.

✦ *A prayer of Moses, the man of God.*
Lord, through all the generations you have been our home! Before the mountains were created, before the earth was formed, you are God without beginning or end.

✦ If you tell others with your own mouth that Jesus Christ is your Lord and believe in your own heart that God has raised him from the dead, you will be saved. For it is by believing in his heart that a man becomes right with God; and with his mouth he tells others of his faith, confirming his salvation.

✦ And now just as you trusted Christ to save you, trust him, too, for each day's problems; live in vital union with him. Let your roots grow down into him and draw up nourishment from him. See that you go on growing in the Lord, and become strong and vigorous in the truth you were taught. Let your lives overflow with joy and thanksgiving for all he has done.

Deuteronomy 10:17-18; Psalms 8:9; 90:1-2; Romans 10:9-10; Colossians 2:6-7

:00
:10
:20
:30
:40
:50
:60

the End

GOD:

God is my shield; he will defend me. He saves those whose hearts and lives are true and right.

♦ God is our refuge and strength, a tested help in times of trouble.

And so we need not fear even if the world blows up and the mountains crumble into the sea. Let the oceans roar and foam; let the mountains tremble!

There is a river of joy flowing through the city of our God—the sacred home of the God above all gods. God himself is living in that city; therefore it stands unmoved despite the turmoil everywhere. He will not delay his help. The nations rant and rave in anger—but when God speaks, the earth melts in submission and kingdoms totter into ruin.

The Commander of the armies of heaven is here among us. He, the God of Jacob, has come to rescue us.

♦ Come, everyone, and clap for joy! Shout triumphant praises to the Lord! For the Lord, the God above all gods, is awesome beyond words; he is the great King of all the earth.

♦ *A song to sing on the Lord's Day.* It is good to say thank you to the Lord, to sing praises to the God who is above all gods.

Every morning tell him, "Thank you for your kindness," and every evening rejoice in all his faithfulness. Sing his praises, accompanied by music from the harp and lute and lyre. You have done so much for me, O Lord. No wonder I am glad! I sing for joy.

O Lord, what miracles you do! And how deep are your thoughts!

Psalms 7:10; 46:1-7; 47:1-2; 92:1-5

2 5

FEB

Just a thought

If God is known to **save** and **protect** the **faithful,** don't you think it's **worth** putting **Him** to the test with **your** life?

:00

:10

:20

:30

:40

:50

1:00

FINISH

CHECK IT OUT

GOD: THE CREATOR

You've **probably** heard it said, "time flies when you're **having fun!**" Well, time flies even if you aren't having fun. Time and life move very quickly. It's easy to waste time and move through life being bored when you don't have the big picture of why you're on this **crazy** playground we call earth. You're here to love God, **celebrate** life, love others, and do good things that will make a **difference** in the world.

Check out the advice from the **Psalmist** regarding our time:
"Teach us to number our days and recognize how few they are; help us to spend them as we should." (Psalm 90:12)

Spend a **minute** today and ask God for His **direction** on how you spend today's time. If God is a part of the day, it's **never** wasted.

:00

:10

:20

:30

:40

:50

:60

d o n e

Don't let the excitement of being young cause you to forget about your Creator. Honor him in your youth before the evil years come—when you'll no longer enjoy living. It will be too late then to try to remember him when the sun and light and moon and stars are dim to your old eyes, and there is no silver lining left among your clouds. For there will come a time when your limbs will tremble with age, your strong legs will become weak, and your teeth will be too few to do their work, and there will be blindness too. Then let your lips be tightly closed while eating when your teeth are gone! And you will waken at dawn with the first note of the birds; but you yourself will be deaf and tuneless, with quavering voice. You will be afraid of heights and of falling—a white-haired, withered old man, dragging himself along: without sexual desire, standing at death's door, and nearing his everlasting home as the mourners go along the streets.

Yes, remember your Creator now while you are young—before the silver cord of life snaps and the gold bowl is broken; before the pitcher is broken at the fountain and the wheel is broken at the cistern; then the dust returns to the earth as it was, and the spirit returns to God who gave it.

Ecclesiastes 12:1-7

O Jacob, O Israel, how can you say that the Lord doesn't see your troubles and isn't being fair? Don't you yet understand? Don't you know by now that the everlasting God, the Creator of the farthest parts of the earth, never grows faint or weary? No one can fathom the depths of his understanding. He gives power to the tired and worn out, and strength to the weak. Even the youths shall be exhausted, and the young men will all give up. But they that wait upon the Lord shall renew their strength. They shall mount up with wings like eagles; they shall run and not be weary; they shall walk and not faint.

♦ How true it is, and how I long that everyone should know it, that Christ Jesus came into the world to save sinners—and I was the greatest of them all. But God had mercy on me so that Christ Jesus could use me as an example to show everyone how patient he is with even the worst sinners, so that others will realize that they, too, can have everlasting life. Glory and honor to God forever and ever. He is the King of the ages, the unseen one who never dies; he alone is God, and full of wisdom. Amen.

Isaiah 40:27-31; 1 Timothy 1:15-17

everlasting God, king of the ages

done!

Give it a try

Record your feelings in the space provided after reading the following verse:

"But they that wait upon the Lord shall renew their strength. They shall mount up with wings like eagles; they shall run and not be weary; they shall walk and not faint."

(Isaiah 40:31)

[SPACE]

The Holy One

word

Holy is a famous religious term given to things associated with God. Something that is holy is **SET APART** from sin. Holiness is **rare** and in a **league of its own.**

Holiness starts with God because **God is holy.** God then calls us and encourages us to be holy–to be SET APART from sin. Since God has given us His Son to redeem us, **holiness** is a **goal** for those wanting to mature and grow in their faith.

Make it a goal...aim at it. Remember the old proverb: **If you aim at nothing** you'll hit it every time.

Take **aim at holiness** today.

You are holy. The praises of our fathers surrounded your throne; they trusted you and you delivered them. You heard their cries for help and saved them; they were never disappointed when they sought your aid.

♦ For the reverence and fear of God are basic to all wisdom. Knowing God results in every other kind of understanding. "I, Wisdom, will make the hours of your day more profitable and the years of your life more fruitful." Wisdom is its own reward, and if you scorn her, you hurt only yourself.

♦ So speaks our Redeemer, who will save Israel from Babylon's mighty power; the Lord Almighty is his name, the Holy One of Israel.

♦ Once as he was teaching in the synagogue, a man possessed by a demon began shouting at Jesus, "Go away! We want nothing to do with you, Jesus from Nazareth. You have come to destroy us. I know who you are—the Holy Son of God."

Jesus cut him short. "Be silent!" he told the demon. "Come out!" The demon threw the man to the floor as the crowd watched, and then left him without hurting him further.

Amazed, the people asked, "What is in this man's words that even demons obey him?"

Psalm 22:3-5; Proverbs 9:10-12; Isaiah 47:4; Luke 4:33-36

The Lord lives on forever; he sits upon his throne to judge justly the nations of the world.

♦ Lord God, to whom vengeance belongs, let your glory shine out. Arise and judge the earth; sentence the proud to the penalties they deserve.

♦ The royal line of David will be cut off, chopped down like a tree; but from the stump will grow a Shoot—yes, a new Branch from the old root. And the Spirit of the Lord shall rest upon him, the Spirit of wisdom, understanding, counsel, and might; the Spirit of knowledge and of the fear of the Lord. His delight will be obedience to the Lord. He will not judge by appearance, false evidence, or hearsay, but will defend the poor and the exploited. He will rule against the wicked who oppress them. For he will be clothed with fairness and with truth.

♦ For the Lord is our Judge, our Lawgiver and our King; he will care for us and save us.

Psalms 9:7-8; 94:1-2; Isaiah 11:1-5; 33:22

:00

:10

:20

:30

:40

:50

:60

In the Old Testament God is seen as the judge. In the New Testament Jesus is given the responsibility of judgment. But since God and Jesus are one, we can assume they will work together and decide the details of judgment. Judgment Day is a mystery day; no one knows when it will come except God. Check out how you can be prepared for that day:

"And all the prophets have written about him, saying that everyone who believes in him [Jesus] will have their sins forgiven through his name."
(Acts 10:43)

It's not always an easy decision to completely trust Jesus, but it's sure an easy choice between eternal life in heaven or eternal life in hell.

What's your choice?

d o n e

No sciences are better attested than the religion of the Bible.

Sir Isaac Newton (1642-1727)
English Scientist

GOD: King

At the Flood the Lord showed his control of all creation. Now he continues to unveil his power. He will give his people strength. He will bless them with peace.

♦ I am the Lord, your Holy One, Israel's Creator and King.

♦ So Pilate asked him, "Are you their Messiah—their King?"

"Yes," Jesus replied, "it is as you say."

♦ Then I saw heaven opened and a white horse standing there; and the one sitting on the horse was named Faithful and True—the one who justly punishes and makes war. His eyes were like flames, and on his head were many crowns. A name was written on his forehead, and only he knew its meaning. He was clothed with garments dipped in blood, and his title was "The Word of God." The armies of heaven, dressed in finest linen, white and clean, followed him on white horses.

In his mouth he held a sharp sword to strike down the nations; he ruled them with an iron grip; and he trod the winepress of the fierceness of the wrath of Almighty God. On his robe and thigh was written this title: "King of Kings and Lord of Lords."

Psalm 29:10-11; Isaiah 43:15; Luke 23:3; Revelation 19:11-16

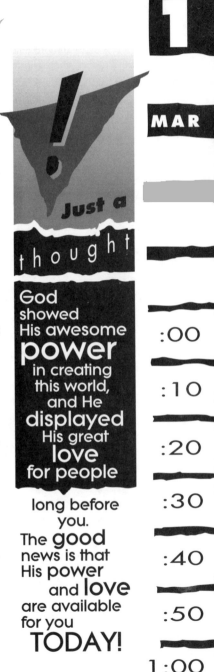

1

MAR

Just a thought

God showed His awesome **power** in creating this world, and He **displayed** His great **love** for people long before you. The **good** news is that His **power** and **love** are available for you **TODAY!**

:OO

:1O

:2O

:3O

:4O

:5O

1:OO

FINISH

67

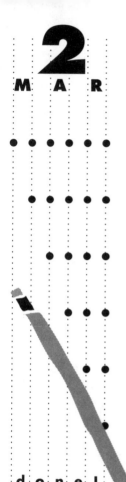

2

M A R

d o n e !

Though once despised and hated and rebuffed by all, you will be beautiful forever, a joy for all the generations of the world, for I will make you so. Powerful kings and mighty nations shall provide you with the choicest of their goods to satisfy your every need, and you will know at last and really understand that I, the Lord, am your Savior and Redeemer, the Mighty One of Israel.

♦ Mary responded, "Oh, how I praise the Lord. How I rejoice in God my Savior! For he took notice of his lowly servant girl, and now generation after generation forever shall call me blest of God. For he, the mighty Holy One, has done great things to me. His mercy goes on from generation to generation, to all who reverence him.

"How powerful is his mighty arm! How he scatters the proud and haughty ones! He has torn princes from their thrones and exalted the lowly. He has satisfied the hungry hearts and sent the rich away with empty hands. And how he has helped his servant Israel! He has not forgotten his promise to be merciful. For he promised our fathers—Abraham and his children—to be merciful to them forever."

Isaiah 60:15-16; Luke 1:46-55

In Mary's joy she said, "God has done great things to me!" What are **four** great things God has done for **you**?

Take a minute to thank Him and give Him praise for the great things He has done in your life.

But as for me, I know that my Redeemer lives, and that he will stand upon the earth at last. And I know that after this body has decayed, this body shall see God! Then he will be on my side! Yes, I shall see him, not as a stranger, but as a friend! What a glorious hope!

♦ How can I ever know what sins are lurking in my heart? Cleanse me from these hidden faults. And keep me from deliberate wrongs; help me to stop doing them. Only then can I be free of guilt and innocent of some great crime.

May my spoken words and unspoken thoughts be pleasing even to you, O Lord my Rock and my Redeemer.

♦ The Lord, the King of Israel, says—yes, it is Israel's Redeemer, the Lord Almighty, who says it—I am the First and Last; there is no other God. Who else can tell you what is going to happen in the days ahead? Let them tell you if they can and prove their power. Let them do as I have done since ancient times. Don't, don't be afraid. Haven't I proclaimed from ages past (that I would save you)? You are my witnesses—is there any other God? No! None that I know about! There is no other Rock!

Job 19:25-27; Psalm 19:12-14; Isaiah 44:6-8

IN other words...

REDEEMER

God is called "Redeemer" because He **saves** people from being prisoners to sin. Since God cannot tolerate sin, we have to be **brought out,** saved, or REDEEMED from being captive to sin. God redeems us through **Jesus' death** on the cross.

Jesus has **paid** for our sins! He bought us back by **dying** for our sins and rescued us (those who believe) from the penalty of sin: death. When you **believe** in Him, you are saved from being a prisoner to sin and experience **salvation.**

Be sure to **ask** questions if you need help understanding this word... it's very important!

:00
:10
:20
:30
:40
:50
done :60

69

GOD: REFUGE

Catch T·H·I·S

These verses are **great** to return to when you feel lonely, hurt, or scared. It's **exciting** to know that God promises to **comfort** you during times of trouble.

A typical move during tough times is to run to **friends**. This can be both **good and bad.** Friends can provide comfort and direction. But friends can also turn their backs or even make things worse (remember **Job's** friends?).

God is **different** than a friend. He's more **consistent** for one thing. But He's also **stronger,** wiser, more **powerful,** and able to provide you with **hope** and strength for your specific hurt.

Allow today's verses to remind you not to overlook God as the source of **comfort.** If you don't think He's strong enough, just **wait** until tomorrow's reading... **you'll see.**

:00 :10 :20 :30 :40 :50 :60 done

All who are oppressed may come to him. He is a refuge for them in their times of trouble. All those who know your mercy, Lord, will count on you for help. For you have never yet forsaken those who trust in you.

♦ O God, listen to me! Hear my prayer! For wherever I am, though far away at the ends of the earth, I will cry to you for help. When my heart is faint and overwhelmed, lead me to the mighty, towering Rock of safety. For you are my refuge, a high tower where my enemies can never reach me. I shall live forever in your tabernacle; oh, to be safe beneath the shelter of your wings!

♦ You are my refuge and my shield, and your promises are my only source of hope.

♦ O Lord, my Strength and Fortress, my Refuge in the day of trouble, nations from around the world will come to you saying, "Our fathers have been foolish, for they have worshiped worthless idols! Can men make God? The gods they made are not real gods at all." And when they come in that spirit, I will show them my power and might and make them understand at last that I alone am God.

Psalms 9:9-10; 61:1-4; 119:114; Jeremiah 16:19-21

GOD: ROCK

5 M A R

CHECK IT OUT

Listen, O heavens and earth! Listen to what I say! My words shall fall upon you like the gentle rain and dew, like rain upon the tender grass, like showers on the hillside.

I will proclaim the greatness of the Lord. How glorious he is! He is the Rock. His work is perfect. Everything he does is just and fair. He is faithful, without sin.

♦ This was Hannah's prayer: "How I rejoice in the Lord! How he has blessed me! Now I have an answer for my enemies, for the Lord has solved my problem. How I rejoice! No one is as holy as the Lord! There is no other God, nor any Rock like our God."

♦ The Lord is my fort where I can enter and be safe; no one can follow me in and slay me. He is a rugged mountain where I hide; he is my Savior, a rock where none can reach me, and a tower of safety. He is my shield. He is like the strong horn of a mighty fighting bull. All I need to do is cry to him—oh, praise the Lord—and I am saved from all my enemies!

Deuteronomy 32:1-4; 1 Samuel 2:1-2; Psalm 18:2-3

:00

:10

:20

:30

:40

:50

:60

In the New Testament, Jesus is also referred to as the **Rock.** Check out 1 Peter 2:4-6 where, in addition to Jesus' being named the "Rock," **you** also receive two names or identities–"living building-stones" and "holy priests." Read the following passage and <u>underline</u> your given identity.

"Come to Christ, who is the living Foundation of Rock upon which God builds; though men have spurned him, he is very precious to God who has chosen him above all others. And now YOU have become living building-stones for God's use in building his house. What's more, you are his holy priests; so come to him and offer to God those things that please him."

Try to live up to your **new identity** today!

d o n e

71

MAR 6

:00
:10
:20
:30
:40
:50
:60 done

IN **other** words...

SALVATION

This word represents one of the main **messages** throughout the Bible. When someone says, "I've been saved," they are saying they have been **saved** from sin's death and **returned to God.**

The only way to experience salvation is by **accepting** Jesus' death as the payment for your sin. There's **no** other way to be saved and **no** other plan or method to get to God. The Bible says in Acts 4:12, "There is **salvation** in no one else [but **Jesus]!** Under all heaven there is no other name for anyone to call upon to **save them.**"

O my soul, don't be discouraged. Don't be upset. Expect God to act! For I know that I shall again have plenty of reason to praise him for all that he will do. He is my help! He is my God!

♦ "But I have witnesses, O Israel," says the Lord. "You are my witnesses and my servants, chosen to know and to believe me and to understand that I alone am God. There is no other God; there never was and never will be. I am the Lord, and there is no other Savior. Whenever you have thrown away your idols, I have shown you my power. With one word I have saved you. You have seen me do it; you are my witnesses that it is true. From eternity to eternity I am God. No one can oppose what I do."

♦ For the free gift of eternal salvation is now being offered to everyone; and along with this gift comes the realization that God wants us to turn from godless living and sinful pleasures and to live good, God-fearing lives day after day, looking forward to that wonderful time we've been expecting, when his glory shall be seen—the glory of our great God and Savior Jesus Christ. He died under God's judgment against our sins so that he could rescue us from constant falling into sin and make us his very own people, with cleansed hearts and real enthusiasm for doing kind things for others.

Psalm 42:11; Isaiah 43:10-13; Titus 2:11-14

72

GOD: shepherd

Because the Lord is my Shepherd, I have everything I need!

✦ Yes, the Lord God is coming with mighty power; he will rule with awesome strength. See, his reward is with him, to each as he has done. He will feed his flock like a shepherd; he will carry the lambs in his arms and gently lead the ewes with young.

✦ Now may the God of peace, who brought again from the dead our Lord Jesus, equip you with all you need for doing his will. May he who became the great Shepherd of the sheep by an everlasting agreement between God and you, signed with his blood, produce in you through the power of Christ all that is pleasing to him. To him be glory forever and ever. Amen.

✦ That is why they are here before the throne of God, serving him day and night in his temple. The one sitting on the throne will shelter them; they will never be hungry again, nor thirsty, and they will be fully protected from the scorching noontime heat. For the Lamb standing in front of the throne will feed them and be their Shepherd and lead them to the springs of the Water of Life. And God will wipe their tears away.

d o n e !

Psalm 23:1; Isaiah 40:10-11;
Hebrews 13:20-21; Revelation 7:15-17

Give it a try

A shepherd's responsibility is to care for his sheep. In the left column you'll find a few qualities that describe a shepherd. Next to those qualities, in the right column, write how God is like a shepherd in your life.

Knows his sheep. **1** _____

Keeps the sheep from danger. **2** _____

Makes sure his sheep are fed. **3** _____

Take a minute to **thank** God for the role He plays as your Shepherd.

73

MAR 8

WHAT'S **it** mean

FRUIT OF THE **SPIRIT**

The fruit of the Spirit is:

love
joy
peace
patience
kindness
goodness
faithfulness
gentleness
self-control

The challenge in these verses is for this fruit to reside in your life. To help you better understand this concept, replace the word **fruit** with the word "actions." Think of them as **"actions** of the spirit."

Look at the three key words just before the listing of the fruit in today's passage: "controls our lives." When you live your life in **faithfulness** and **obedience** to God, His Spirit will energize you to **produce** these actions in how you think, feel, and act.

Read again the listing of bad fruit... it's pretty ugly. Today, **ask** God to begin or continue controlling your life so you'll become a person of **"good fruit."**

But when you follow your own wrong inclinations, your lives will produce these evil results: impure thoughts, eagerness for lustful pleasure, idolatry, spiritism (that is, encouraging the activity of demons), hatred and fighting, jealousy and anger, constant effort to get the best for yourself, complaints and criticisms, the feeling that everyone else is wrong except those in your own little group—and there will be wrong doctrine, envy, murder, drunkenness, wild parties, and all that sort of thing. Let me tell you again, as I have before, that anyone living that sort of life will not inherit the Kingdom of God.

But when the Holy Spirit controls our lives he will produce this kind of fruit in us: love, joy, peace, patience, kindness, goodness, faithfulness, gentleness and self-control; and here there is no conflict with Jewish laws.

✦ For though once your heart was full of darkness, now it is full of light from the Lord, and your behavior should show it! Because of this light within you, you should do only what is good and right and true.

Learn as you go along what pleases the Lord. Take no part in the worthless pleasures of evil and darkness, but instead, rebuke and expose them.

✦ A good man produces good deeds from a good heart. And an evil man produces evil deeds from his hidden wickedness. Whatever is in the heart overflows into speech.

Galatians 5:19-23; Ephesians 5:8-11; Luke 6:45

74

FRUIT OF THE SPIRIT:

Jesus replied, "The [most important commandment is], 'Hear, O Israel! The Lord our God is the one and only God. And you must love him with all your heart and soul and mind and strength.'

"The second is: 'You must love others as much as yourself.' No other commandments are greater than these."

◆ And so I am giving a new commandment to you now—love each other just as much as I love you. Your strong love for each other will prove to the world that you are my disciples.

◆ There is a saying, "Love your friends and hate your enemies." But I say: Love your enemies! Pray for those who persecute you! In that way you will be acting as true sons of your Father in heaven. For he gives his sunlight to both the evil and the good, and sends rain on the just and on the unjust too. If you love only those who love you, what good is that? Even scoundrels do that much.

◆ Since you have been chosen by God who has given you this new kind of life, and because of his deep love and concern for you, you should practice tenderhearted mercy and kindness to others. Don't worry about making a good impression on them, but be ready to suffer quietly and patiently. Be gentle and ready to forgive; never hold grudges. Remember, the Lord forgave you, so you must forgive others.

Most of all, let love guide your life, for then the whole church will stay together in perfect harmony.

Mark 12:29-31; John 13:34-35;
Matthew 5:43-46; Colossians 3:12-14

75

Just a thought

The **secret** to **changing** enemies, friends, parents, teachers, or even little brothers or sisters is to **love them** as Jesus loves **you.**

People can't stay the same when they're **drenched** with the type of **love** Jesus displays.

9
MAR

:00
:10
:20
:30
:40
:50
1:00

FINISH

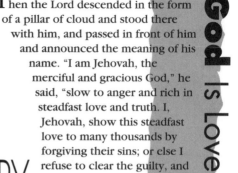

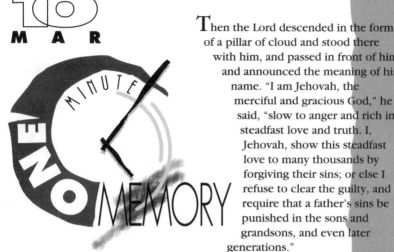

ONE MINUTE MEMORY

Then the Lord descended in the form of a pillar of cloud and stood there with him, and passed in front of him and announced the meaning of his name. "I am Jehovah, the merciful and gracious God," he said, "slow to anger and rich in steadfast love and truth. I, Jehovah, show this steadfast love to many thousands by forgiving their sins; or else I refuse to clear the guilty, and require that a father's sins be punished in the sons and grandsons, and even later generations."

:00
:15
:30
:45
:60

For God loved the world so much that he gave his only Son so that anyone who believes in him shall not perish but have eternal life.

John 3:16

If you already have this verse memorized try the next one.

But God showed his great love for us by sending Christ to die for us while we were still sinners.

Romans 5:8

♦ He loves whatever is just and good; the earth is filled with his tender love.

♦ For God loved the world so much that he gave his only Son so that anyone who believes in him shall not perish but have eternal life.

♦ But God showed his great love for us by sending Christ to die for us while we were still sinners.

♦ For I am convinced that nothing can ever separate us from his love. Death can't, and life can't. The angels won't, and all the powers of hell itself cannot keep God's love away. Our fears for today, our worries about tomorrow, or where we are—high above the sky, or in the deepest ocean—nothing will ever be able to separate us from the love of God demonstrated by our Lord Jesus Christ when he died for us.

♦ We know how much God loves us because we have felt his love and because we believe him when he tells us that he loves us dearly. God is love, and anyone who lives in love is living with God and God is living in him.

Exodus 34:5-7; Psalm 33:5; John 3:16; Romans 5:8; 8:38-39; 1 John 4:16

done

76

FRUIT OF THE SPIRIT:

Let all the joys of the godly well up in praise to the Lord, for it is right to praise him. Play joyous melodies of praise upon the lyre and on the harp. Compose new songs of praise to him, accompanied skillfully on the harp; sing joyfully.

For all God's words are right, and everything he does is worthy of our trust.

◆ Even though the fig trees are all destroyed, and there is neither blossom left nor fruit; though the olive crops all fail, and the fields lie barren; even if the flocks die in the fields and the cattle barns are empty, yet I will rejoice in the Lord; I will be happy in the God of my salvation.

◆ So I pray for you Gentiles that God who gives you hope will keep you happy and full of peace as you believe in him. I pray that God will help you overflow with hope in him through the Holy Spirit's power within you.

◆ Always be full of joy in the Lord; I say it again, rejoice!

◆ Dear friends, don't be bewildered or surprised when you go through the fiery trials ahead, for this is no strange, unusual thing that is going to happen to you. Instead, be really glad—because these trials will make you partners with Christ in his suffering, and afterwards you will have the wonderful joy of sharing in that coming day when it will be displayed.

Psalm 33:1-4; Habakkuk 3:17-18;
Romans 15:13; Philippians 4:4;
1 Peter 4:12-13

77

1 1

MAR

Just a

thought

When you **wake up** tomorrow morning,

try replacing the phrase, **"good God, it's morning"** with a joyful chorus of

"GOOD MORNING, GOD!"

It may **jump-start** your day with a **joyful attitude.**

:00

:10

:20

:30

:40

:50

1:00

FINISH

GOD IS

joyful

BIG time
word

Joy

Did you know that the word **JOY** is different from the word **HAPPINESS?** Happiness is based on some thing or circumstantial happening.

Joy is different. True joy isn't dependent on anything. Joy is an **attitude** that lives within you. Joy doesn't change when situations change.

Even though it may seem impossible, joy can exist in the midst of difficulty. In the Bible, Christians are **encouraged** to be joyful when they encounter problems and to have **joy** during difficult times because **Jesus** has overcome the world.

Pain is unavoidable, and being happy is conditional, but joy is a **fruit of the Spirit** that becomes available when you **depend** on God.

P raise God forever! How he must rejoice in all his work! The earth trembles at his glance; the mountains burst into flame at his touch. I will sing to the Lord as long as I live.

I will praise God to my last breath! May he be pleased by all these thoughts about him, for he is the source of all my joy.

♦ On that day the announcement to Jerusalem will be, "Cheer up, don't be afraid. For the Lord your God has arrived to live among you. He is a mighty Savior. He will give you victory. He will rejoice over you with great gladness; he will love you and not accuse you." Is that a joyous choir I hear? No, it is the Lord himself exulting over you in happy song.

♦ Keep your eyes on Jesus, our leader and instructor. He was willing to die a shameful death on the cross because of the joy he knew would be his afterwards; and now he sits in the place of honor by the throne of God.

If you want to keep from becoming fainthearted and weary, think about his patience as sinful men did such terrible things to him.

Psalm 104:31-34; Zephaniah 3:16-17; Hebrews 12:2-3

Fruit of the Spirit: Peace

13 MAR

ONE MINUTE MEMORY

May the Lord bless and protect you; may the Lord's face radiate with joy because of you; may he be gracious to you, show you his favor, and give you his peace.

♦ Those who love your laws have great peace of heart and mind and do not stumble.

♦ He will keep in perfect peace all those who trust in him, whose thoughts turn often to the Lord! Trust in the Lord God always, for in the Lord Jehovah is your everlasting strength.

♦ I am leaving you with a gift—peace of mind and heart! And the peace I give isn't fragile like the peace the world gives. So don't be troubled or afraid.

♦ Don't worry about anything; instead, pray about everything; tell God your needs, and don't forget to thank him for his answers. If you do this, you will experience God's peace, which is far more wonderful than the human mind can understand. His peace will keep your thoughts and your hearts quiet and at rest as you trust in Christ Jesus.

♦ Let the peace of heart that comes from Christ be always present in your hearts and lives, for this is your responsibility and privilege as members of his body. And always be thankful.

Numbers 6:24-26; Psalm 119:165;
Isaiah 26:3-4; John 14:27;
Philippians 4:6-7; Colossians 3:15

Don't worry about anything; instead, pray about everything; tell God your needs, and don't forget to thank him for his answers.

:00

:15

:30

:45

Philippians 4:6

:60

done

GOD IS PEACEFUL

:00
:10
:20
:30
:40
:50
:60
end

In the Old Testament the Hebrew word for peace is **shalom.** This is the same word you might hear as a **greeting** or closing remark in many present-day **Jewish** temples. Shalom is used to communicate **a blessing** to another person. The meaning of the blessing has its source in God. To withhold shalom is to withhold the blessing and might be interpreted in a similar manner as cursing at someone.

He will give his people strength. He will bless them with peace.

♦ For unto us a child is born; unto us a son is given; and the government shall be upon his shoulder. These will be his royal titles: "Wonderful," "Counselor," "The Mighty God," "The Everlasting Father," "The Prince of Peace." His ever-expanding, peaceful government will never end. He will rule with perfect fairness and justice from the throne of his father David. He will bring true justice and peace to all the nations of the world. This is going to happen because the Lord of heaven's armies has dedicated himself to do it!

♦ So now, since we have been made right in God's sight by faith in his promises, we can have real peace with him because of what Jesus Christ our Lord has done for us. For because of our faith, he has brought us into this place of highest privilege where we now stand, and we confidently and joyfully look forward to actually becoming all that God has had in mind for us to be.

♦ May the God of peace himself make you entirely pure and devoted to God; and may your spirit and soul and body be kept strong and blameless until that day when our Lord Jesus Christ comes back again.

♦ May the Lord of peace himself give you his peace no matter what happens. The Lord be with you all.

Psalm 29:11; Isaiah 9:6-7; Romans 5:1-2;
1 Thessalonians 5:23;
2 Thessalonians 3:16

FRUIT OF THE SPIRIT: PATIENCE

Rest in the Lord; wait patiently for him to act. Don't be envious of evil men who prosper.

Stop your anger! Turn off your wrath. Don't fret and worry—it only leads to harm. For the wicked shall be destroyed, but those who trust the Lord shall be given every blessing.

♦ I waited patiently for God to help me; then he listened and heard my cry. He lifted me out of the pit of despair, out from the bog and the mire, and set my feet on a hard, firm path, and steadied me as I walked along. He has given me a new song to sing, of praises to our God. Now many will hear of the glorious things he did for me, and stand in awe before the Lord, and put their trust in him.

♦ A wise man controls his temper. He knows that anger causes mistakes.

♦ Love is very patient and kind, never jealous or envious, never boastful or proud,

♦ Now as for you, dear brothers who are waiting for the Lord's return, be patient, like a farmer who waits until the autumn for his precious harvest to ripen. Yes, be patient. And take courage, for the coming of the Lord is near.

Psalms 37:7-9; 40:1-3; Proverbs 14:29; 1 Corinthians 13:4; James 5:7-8

Catch T·H·I·S

:00

:10

:20

:30

:40

:50

:60 done

Having **patience** in today's world is **tough!** We live in a time-oriented society where **quick-serve**, getting "in and out," **fast food**, and not waiting in lines have become important values for **survival.**

Have you ever noticed that having patience is really **tough** when you desperately want something to happen? What's even tougher is being **patient** with God's timing. Most of us want God to answer our prayers **NOW.** But whether we like it or not, God answers them **when** He wants to, and His timing is always better than ours... because **He's God.**

Try being patient today. Next time you ask God for something, **accept** His timing. Be **confident** that He hears your prayers. Also, **know** that your patience develops strength of character, which God will use to **build** your **faith.**

:00
:10
:20
:30
:40
:50
1:00

Just a thought

The **greatest** news any of your **friends** could ever hear is that God **loves** them **more** than they love **themselves** and He wants them to have **everlasting** life.

Can you **do** anything to let them **know** this good news **today?**

GOD IS PATIENT

How true it is, and how I long that everyone should know it, that Christ Jesus came into the world to save sinners—and I was the greatest of them all. But God had mercy on me so that Christ Jesus could use me as an example to show everyone how patient he is with even the worst sinners, so that others will realize that they, too, can have everlasting life.

♦ He isn't really being slow about his promised return, even though it sometimes seems that way. But he is waiting, for the good reason that he is not willing that any should perish, and he is giving more time for sinners to repent. The day of the Lord is surely coming, as unexpectedly as a thief, and then the heavens will pass away with a terrible noise, and the heavenly bodies will disappear in fire, and the earth and everything on it will be burned up.

But we are looking forward to God's promise of new heavens and a new earth afterwards, where there will be only goodness.

Dear friends, while you are waiting for these things to happen and for him to come, try hard to live without sinning; and be at peace with everyone so that he will be pleased with you when he returns.

And remember why he is waiting. He is giving us time to get his message of salvation out to others. Our wise and beloved brother Paul has talked about these same things in many of his letters.

1 Timothy 1:15-16; 2 Peter 3:9-10,15

fruit of the spirit: kindness

Honor goes to kind and gracious women, mere money to cruel men.

Your own soul is nourished when you are kind; it is destroyed when you are cruel.

♦ Anyone who oppresses the poor is insulting God who made them. To help the poor is to honor God.

♦ When you help the poor you are lending to the Lord—and he pays wonderful interest on your loan!

♦ Be kind to each other, tenderhearted, forgiving one another, just as God has forgiven you because you belong to Christ.

♦ Since you have been chosen by God who has given you this new kind of life, and because of his deep love and concern for you, you should practice tenderhearted mercy and kindness to others. Don't worry about making a good impression on them, but be ready to suffer quietly and patiently. Be gentle and ready to forgive; never hold grudges. Remember, the Lord forgave you, so you must forgive others.

Most of all, let love guide your life, for then the whole church will stay together in perfect harmony.

Proverbs 11:16-17; 14:31; 19:17;
Ephesians 4:32; Colossians 3:12-14

d o n e !

This is unbelievable!

Try to list 10 specific ways you can help the poor both in your community and around the world.

1 _____

2 _____

3 _____

4 _____

5 _____

6 _____

7 _____

8 _____

9 _____

10 _____

Circle your best idea and **get started** in God's interest-bearing program **today.**

18
MAR

CHECK IT OUT

GOD IS KIND

Prior to the birth of Jesus, prophets foretold God's ultimate act of **kindness.** Check out what was written in **Isaiah 53:4-6** about God's **plan** for Jesus and YOU thousands of years ago:

"Yet it was our grief he bore, our sorrows that weighed him down. And we thought his troubles were a punishment from God, for his own sins! But he was wounded and bruised for our sins. He was chastised that we might have peace; he was lashed—and we were healed! We are the ones who strayed away like sheep! We, who left God's paths to follow our own. Yet God laid on him the guilt and sins of every one of us!"

Go back through the passage and **circle** the words **our** and **we** and then thank God that His ultimate plan included **YOU.**

:00

:10

:20

:30

:40

:50

:60

d o n e

I will tell of the loving-kindnesses of God. I will praise him for all he has done; I will rejoice in his great goodness to Israel, which he has granted in accordance with his mercy and love.

♦ The Lord says: "Let not the wise man bask in his wisdom, nor the mighty man in his might, nor the rich man in his riches. Let them boast in this alone: That they truly know me, and understand that I am the Lord of justice and of righteousness whose love is steadfast; and that I love to be this way."

♦ Once we, too, were foolish and disobedient; we were misled by others and became slaves to many evil pleasures and wicked desires. Our lives were full of resentment and envy. We hated others and they hated us.

But when the time came for the kindness and love of God our Savior to appear, then he saved us—not because we were good enough to be saved but because of his kindness and pity—by washing away our sins and giving us the new joy of the indwelling Holy Spirit.

Isaiah 63:7; Jeremiah 9:23-24; Titus 3:3-5a

84

MAR

Fruit of the Spirit: Goodness

The Lord blesses good men and condemns the wicked.

♦ So I conclude that, first, there is nothing better for a man than to be happy and to enjoy himself as long as he can; and second, that he should eat and drink and enjoy the fruits of his labors, for these are gifts from God.

♦ Let us not get tired of doing what is right, for after a while we will reap a harvest of blessing if we don't get discouraged and give up. That's why whenever we can we should always be kind to everyone, and especially to our Christian brothers.

♦ It is God himself who has made us what we are and given us new lives from Christ Jesus; and long ages ago he planned that we should spend these lives in helping others.

♦ Follow only what is good. Remember that those who do what is right prove that they are God's children; and those who continue in evil prove that they are far from God.

Proverbs 12:2; Ecclesiastes 3:12-13; Galatians 6:9-10; Ephesians 2:10; 3 John 11b

ONE MINUTE MEMORY

It is God himself who has made us what we are and given us new lives from Christ Jesus; and long ages ago he planned that we should spend these lives in helping others.

:00

:15

:30

:45

:60

Ephesians 2:10

done

85

20 MAR

GOD IS GOOD

Catch THIS

God is **good!** You can **see** His goodness, you can **hear** it, you can **touch** His goodness and even **smell** it every single day.

See for yourself!

Experience His goodness with any one of these ideas:

Watch a sunset

Smell a flower

Examine the legs of a centipede

Listen to the waves break on the beach

Ask a Christian to tell you how he or she was saved

Listen to the sounds of nature in a quiet location

Watch a caterpillar turn into a butterfly

Look at the stars on a clear night

Kiss a baby

Look out a window and see God's playground...
called earth.

:00

:10

:20

:30

:40

:50

:60
done

Oh, put God to the test and see how kind he is! See for yourself the way his mercies shower down on all who trust in him.

♦ O Lord, I will praise you forever and ever for your punishment. And I will wait for your mercies—for everyone knows what a merciful God you are.

♦ How good God is to Israel—to those whose hearts are pure.

♦ For the Lord is always good. He is always loving and kind, and his faithfulness goes on and on to each succeeding generation.

♦ Oh, give thanks to the Lord, for he is so good! For his loving-kindness is forever.

♦ You are good and do only good; make me follow your lead.

♦ Praise the Lord because he is so good; sing to his wonderful name.

♦ He is good to everyone, and his compassion is intertwined with everything he does.

Psalms 34:8; 52:9; 73:1; 100:5; 118:29; 119:68; 135:3; 145:9

86

Fruit of the Spirit: Faithfulness

MAR **21**

T rust the Lord and sincerely worship him; think of all the tremendous things he has done for you.

♦ You are merciful to the merciful; you show your perfections to the blameless. To those who are pure, you show yourself pure; but you destroy those who are evil.

You will save those in trouble, but you bring down the haughty; for you watch their every move.

♦ Oh, love the Lord, all of you who are his people; for the Lord protects those who are loyal to him, but harshly punishes all who haughtily reject him. So cheer up! Take courage if you are depending on the Lord.

♦ I am comforted by this truth, that when we suffer and die for Christ it only means that we will begin living with him in heaven. And if we think that our present service for him is hard, just remember that some day we are going to sit with him and rule with him. But if we give up when we suffer, and turn against Christ, then he must turn against us. Even when we are too weak to have any faith left, he remains faithful to us and will help us, for he cannot disown us who are part of himself, and he will always carry out his promises to us.

1 Samuel 12:24; 2 Samuel 22:26-28; Psalm 31:23-24; 2 Timothy 2:11-13

BIG time word

Faithful

Faith is **believing** that an unseen God is big enough to **know** everything about you, to **care** intimately for you, and to provide for all your needs. Being faithful is **living** like you believe in that definition of faith.

It's **easy** to be faithful when everything is going well. It's a lot **tougher** to be faithful when you live with difficult times. **Trusting** that God is going to be God and you're going to be okay is a **process** you'll be working on for years.

Practice being faithful today and don't **worry** about tomorrow until it gets here.

87

22
M A R

Understand, therefore, that the Lord your God is the faithful God who for a thousand generations keeps his promises and constantly loves those who love him and who obey his commands.

♦ Forever and ever I will sing about the tender kindness of the Lord! Young and old shall hear about your blessings. Your love and kindness are forever; your truth is as enduring as the heavens.

♦ Yet there is one ray of hope: his compassion never ends. It is only the Lord's mercies that have kept us from complete destruction. Great is his faithfulness; his loving-kindness begins afresh each day.

♦ So be careful. If you are thinking, "Oh, I would never behave like that"—let this be a warning to you. For you too may fall into sin. But remember this—the wrong desires that come into your life aren't anything new and different. Many others have faced exactly the same problems before you. And no temptation is irresistible. You can trust God to keep the temptation from becoming so strong that you can't stand up against it, for he has promised this and will do what he says. He will show you how to escape temptation's power so that you can bear up patiently against it.

♦ But if we confess our sins to him, he can be depended on to forgive us and to cleanse us from every wrong. (And it is perfectly proper for God to do this for us because Christ died to wash away our sins.)

Deuteronomy 7:9; Psalm 89:1-2; Lamentations 3:21-23; 1 Corinthians 10:12-13; 1 John 1:9

:00
:15
:30
:45
:60

But if we confess our sins to him, he can be depended on to forgive us and to cleanse us from every wrong.

1 John 1:9

Fruit of the Spirit:
Gentleness

A gentle answer turns away wrath, but harsh words cause quarrels.

♦ Be patient and you will finally win, for a soft tongue can break hard bones.

♦ Be humble and gentle. Be patient with each other, making allowance for each other's faults because of your love. Try always to be led along together by the Holy Spirit and so be at peace with one another.

♦ Always be full of joy in the Lord; I say it again, rejoice! Let everyone see that you are unselfish and considerate in all you do. Remember that the Lord is coming soon. Don't worry about anything; instead, pray about everything; tell God your needs, and don't forget to thank him for his answers. If you do this, you will experience God's peace, which is far more wonderful than the human mind can understand. His peace will keep your thoughts and your hearts quiet and at rest as you trust in Christ Jesus.

♦ Usually no one will hurt you for wanting to do good. But even if they should, you are to be envied, for God will reward you for it. Quietly trust yourself to Christ your Lord, and if anybody asks why you believe as you do, be ready to tell him, and do it in a gentle and respectful way.

Do what is right; then if men speak against you, calling you evil names, they will become ashamed of themselves for falsely accusing you when you have only done what is good.

Proverbs 15:1; 25:15; Ephesians 4:2-3; Philippians 4:4-7; 1 Peter 3:13-16

word

gentle

Being **gentle** is a rare quality in today's world. Unfortunately, people who are loud, wild, and obnoxious tend to get most of the attention, while gentle people are often overlooked. But the truth is, **gentleness** is an **important** quality.

Being gentle is often associated with weakness or being soft. But it's actually just the opposite. **Gentleness** is a character quality that denotes **strength.** People who display gentleness have a quiet, controlled **confidence** about themselves and their **faith** in God.

Pray for gentleness today and be **confident** in the person God has **planned** for you to become.

89

24
M A R

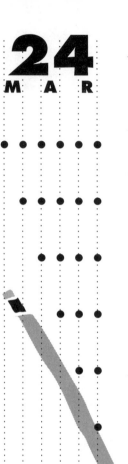

d o n e !

Yes, the Lord God is coming with mighty power; he will rule with awesome strength. See, his reward is with him, to each as he has done. He will feed his flock like a shepherd; he will carry the lambs in his arms and gently lead the ewes with young.

♦ Rejoice greatly, O my people! Shout with joy! For look—your King is coming! He is the Righteous One, the Victor! Yet he is lowly, riding on a donkey's colt!

♦ Come to me and I will give you rest—all of you who work so hard beneath a heavy yoke. Wear my yoke—for it fits perfectly—and let me teach you; for I am gentle and humble, and you shall find rest for your souls; "for I give you only light burdens."

Isaiah 40:10-11; Zechariah 9:9; Matthew 11:28-30

Give it a try

A yoke or a **burden** is something that troubles you or creates hard times in your life.

What burdens or problems are heavy and need to be lightened in your life today?

1 _____

2 _____

3 _____

Ask God for His gentleness to comfort you. He wants to make your burdens light.

90

Fruit of the Spirit:
Self-Control

A man without self-control is as defenseless as a city with broken-down walls.

♦ But as for you, speak up for the right living that goes along with true Christianity. Teach the older men to be serious and unruffled; they must be sensible, knowing and believing the truth and doing everything with love and patience.

Teach the older women to be quiet and respectful in everything they do. They must not go around speaking evil of others and must not be heavy drinkers, but should be teachers of goodness. These older women must train the younger women to live quietly, to love their husbands and their children, and to be sensible and clean minded, spending their time in their own homes, being kind and obedient to their husbands so that the Christian faith can't be spoken against by those who know them.

In the same way, urge the young men to behave carefully, taking life seriously.

♦ But to obtain these gifts, you need more than faith; you must also work hard to be good, and even that is not enough. For then you must learn to know God better and discover what he wants you to do. Next, learn to put aside your own desires so that you will become patient and godly, gladly letting God have his way with you. This will make possible the next step, which is for you to enjoy other people and to like them, and finally you will grow to love them deeply. The more you go on in this way, the more you will grow strong spiritually and become fruitful and useful to our Lord Jesus Christ.

Proverbs 25:28; Titus 2:1-6; 2 Peter 1:5-8

w o r d

SELF-control

c o n t r o l

Self-control has to do with having **power** over yourself. If you have self-control you have the power **not to do** something that might seem natural. For instance, keeping your mouth closed when you want to yell at your little brother for putting hair ointment on your toothbrush. Or **controlling** your sexual urges that tell you to "go all the way"!

Having self-control doesn't mean you will express complete control in all situations. Self-control comes with **maturity**, practice, and **prayer**. It's learned on a daily basis through trial and error. It's worth having.... If you don't have it, ask God for it and begin **trusting** in His **power** today for self-control.

CHECK IT OUT

GOD IS SLOW TO ANGER

God may be slow to anger, but He does give us indication that He will return, in His own time, and express His anger and judgment on those who don't know Jesus. **Check** out what is written in 2 Peter 3:8-10:

"But don't forget this, dear friends, that a day or a thousand years from now is like tomorrow to the Lord. He isn't really being slow about his promised return, even though it sometimes seems that way. But he is waiting, for the good reason that he is not willing that any should perish, and he is giving more time for sinners to repent. The day of the Lord is surely coming, as unexpectedly as a thief...."

Are you **ready** for God to return and show His anger?

:00
:10
:20
:30
:40
:50
:60

done

He is merciful and tender toward those who don't deserve it; he is slow to get angry and full of kindness and love. He never bears a grudge, nor remains angry forever. He has not punished us as we deserve for all our sins, for his mercy toward those who fear and honor him is as great as the height of the heavens above the earth. He has removed our sins as far away from us as the east is from the west.

♦ Jehovah is kind and merciful, slow to get angry, full of love. He is good to everyone, and his compassion is intertwined with everything he does.

♦ God is jealous over those he loves; that is why he takes vengeance on those who hurt them. He furiously destroys their enemies. He is slow in getting angry, but when aroused, his power is incredible, and he does not easily forgive. He shows his power in the terrors of the cyclone and the raging storms; clouds are billowing dust beneath his feet!

Psalms 103:8-12; 145:8-9; Nahum 1:2-3

GOD SENDS MOSES

WHAT'S it mean

"Tell them, 'Jehovah, the God of your ancestors Abraham, Isaac, and Jacob, has sent me to you.' (This is my eternal name, to be used throughout all generations.)

"Call together all the elders of Israel," God instructed him, "and tell them about Jehovah appearing to you here in this burning bush and that he said to you, 'I have visited my people and have seen what is happening to them there in Egypt. I promise to rescue them from the drudgery and humiliation they are undergoing, and to take them to the land now occupied by the Canaanites, Hittites, Amorites, Perizzites, Hivites, and Jebusites, a land "flowing with milk and honey."' The elders of the people of Israel will accept your message. They must go with you to the king of Egypt and tell him, 'Jehovah, the God of the Hebrews, has met with us and instructed us to go three days' journey into the desert to sacrifice to him. Give us your permission.'

"But I know that the king of Egypt will not let you go except under heavy pressure. So I will give him all the pressure he needs! I will destroy Egypt with my miracles, and then at last he will let you go. And I will see to it that the Egyptians load you down with gifts when you leave, so that you will by no means go out empty-handed! Every woman will ask for jewels, silver, gold, and the finest of clothes from her Egyptian master's wife and neighbors. You will clothe your sons and daughters with the best of Egypt!"

Over several hundred years, the Israelites immigrated to Egypt. There they became slaves to the Egyptian people. They had no freedom of their own. For 400 years they suffered hardship and torture and were robbed of their freedom.

God wanted Moses to return to Egypt and free the Israelites because they had suffered long enough. God wanted to deliver them and move them into the Promised Land. This Promised Land was a place for the Israelites to raise their families, prosper, and enjoy their intimate relationship with God. It's a long story, but they eventually get there.

Keep reading and you'll see several illustrations of God's amazing power.

Exodus 3:15-22

93

28 mar

personality Plus Aaron

Aaron was **Moses'** oldest **brother** and his **spokesperson.** God spoke mainly to Moses, but Aaron told others what God said to Moses.

As the people of Israel left Egypt and **wandered** through the **wilderness,** Moses became the **headmaster** and Aaron became the "priest." This was the first "priesthood" of Israel. In this position, Aaron **represented** the people of Israel to Moses and God. Directions for Aaron's service came straight from God.

Aaron is another example of a **faithful** and **normal** person whom God **used** to do great things. Are you ready to be used by God? He uses **ordinary** people to do **extraordinary** things.

You never know what He has **planned** for you **today!**

:00

:10

:20

:30

:40

:50

:60

Jehovah told him, "When you arrive back in Egypt you are to go to Pharaoh and do the miracles I have shown you, but I will make him stubborn so that he will not let the people go. Then you are to tell him, 'Jehovah says, "Israel is my eldest son, and I have commanded you to let him go away and worship me, but you have refused: and now see, I will slay your eldest son."'"

Now Jehovah said to Aaron, "Go into the wilderness to meet Moses." So Aaron traveled to Mount Horeb, the mountain of God, and met Moses there, and they greeted each other warmly. Moses told Aaron what God had said they must do, and what they were to say, and told him about the miracles they must do before Pharaoh.

So Moses and Aaron returned to Egypt and summoned the elders of the people of Israel to a council meeting. Aaron told them what Jehovah had said to Moses, and Moses performed the miracles as they watched. Then the elders believed that God had sent them, and when they heard that Jehovah had visited them and had seen their sorrows, and had decided to rescue them, they all rejoiced and bowed their heads and worshiped.

♦ After this presentation to the elders, Moses and Aaron went to see Pharaoh. They told him, "We bring you a message from Jehovah, the God of Israel. He says, 'Let my people go, for they must make a holy pilgrimage out into the wilderness, for a religious feast, to worship me there.'"

"Is that so?" retorted Pharaoh. "And who is Jehovah, that I should listen to him, and let Israel go? I don't know Jehovah and I will not let Israel go."

Exodus 4:21-23, 27-31; 5:1-2

the End

94

GOD HARDENS
PHARAOH'S HEART

Then the Lord said to Moses, "See, I have appointed you as my ambassador to Pharaoh, and your brother, Aaron, shall be your spokesman. Tell Aaron everything I say to you, and he will announce it to Pharaoh, demanding that the people of Israel be allowed to leave Egypt. But I will cause Pharaoh to stubbornly refuse, and I will multiply my miracles in the land of Egypt. Yet even then Pharaoh won't listen to you; so I will crush Egypt with a final major disaster and then lead my people out. The Egyptians will find out that I am indeed God when I show them my power and force them to let my people go."

Then the Lord said to Moses and Aaron, "Pharaoh will demand that you show him a miracle to prove that God has sent you; when he does, Aaron is to throw down his rod, and it will become a serpent."

So Moses and Aaron went in to see Pharaoh, and performed the miracle, as Jehovah had instructed them—Aaron threw down his rod before Pharaoh and his court, and it became a serpent. Then Pharaoh called in his sorcerers—the magicians of Egypt—and they were able to do the same thing with their magical arts! Their rods became serpents, too! But Aaron's serpent swallowed their serpents! Pharaoh's heart was still hard and stubborn, and he wouldn't listen, just as the Lord had predicted.

Exodus 7:1-5, 8-13

Weird or what

Pharaoh's **magicians** were most likely from a group of Egyptian priests or wise men called **"snake charmers."** The actual illusion of the sticks turning into snakes appears to be quite amazing. The wise men were schooled in magic and the snake charmers were able to put the serpents into a rigid or stiff position, which gave the illusion of snakes being transformed into sticks.

The fact that Moses' staff **ate** the other two snakes demonstrated God's supernatural **power** over the natural or manmade illusion of Pharaoh's snake charmers.

Today, look for God's supernatural power displayed in some event or person's life.

:00 :10 :20 :30 :40 :50 :60 end

95

MAR 30

WHAT'S **it** mean

PLAGUES AGAINST EGYPT

One of the common **securities** of the Egyptian people was the **power** of their gods. The Pharaohs believed their magicians or wise men were a powerful advantage to their kingdom because their gods could perform miracles, or give the **appearance** of miracles.

Every time **Moses** did a miracle, the Pharaoh would summon his magicians to do the same. Because the **Pharaoh's** magicians performed miracles similar to those of Moses, Pharaoh's **heart hardened** and he questioned the power of God.

As you'll read in two days, God's **plague** of death upon the firstborn was something Pharaoh's magicians could not duplicate nor stop. Once again, God showed himself to be the **one** true God.

This **truth** is the same today as it was in the days of Moses.

O my people, listen to my teaching. Open your ears to what I am saying. For I will show you lessons from our history, stories handed down to us from former generations. I will reveal these truths to you so that you can describe these glorious deeds of Jehovah to your children and tell them about the mighty miracles he did. He sent [plagues] upon the Egyptians in Tanis—he turned their rivers into blood so that no one could drink, he sent vast swarms of flies to fill the land, and the frogs covered all of Egypt!

He gave their crops to caterpillars. Their harvest was consumed by locusts. He destroyed their grapevines and their sycamores with hail. Their cattle died in the fields, mortally wounded by huge hailstones from heaven. Their sheep were killed by lightning. He loosed on them the fierceness of his anger, sending sorrow and trouble. He dispatched against them a band of destroying angels. He gave free course to his anger and did not spare the Egyptians' lives, but handed them over to plagues and sickness. Then he killed the eldest son in each Egyptian family—he who was the beginning of its strength and joy.

Psalm 78:1-4, 43-51

DONE

96

Pharaoh personality plus

Then the Lord said to Moses, "I will send just one more disaster on Pharaoh and his land, and after that he will let you go; in fact, he will be so anxious to get rid of you that he will practically throw you out of the country."

Now Moses announced to Pharaoh, "Jehovah says, 'About midnight I will pass through Egypt. And all the oldest sons shall die in every family in Egypt, from the oldest child of Pharaoh, heir to his throne, to the oldest child of his lowliest slave; and even the firstborn of the animals. The wail of death will resound throughout the entire land of Egypt; never before has there been such anguish, and it will never be again.

"'But not a dog shall move his tongue against any of the people of Israel, nor shall any of their animals die. Then you will know that Jehovah makes a distinction between Egyptians and Israelis.' All these officials of yours will come running to me, bowing low and begging, 'Please leave at once, and take all your people with you.' Only then will I go!" Then, red-faced with anger, Moses stomped from the palace.

The Lord had told Moses, "Pharaoh won't listen, and this will give me the opportunity of doing mighty miracles to demonstrate my power." So, although Moses and Aaron did these miracles right before Pharaoh's eyes, the Lord hardened his heart so that he wouldn't let the people leave the land.

Pharaoh is more of a **title** than a name. A Pharaoh is equivalent to a **king** in many countries or similar to the **president** in the United States.

One **difference** between a Pharaoh and other leaders is that a Pharaoh was considered a **god**. He was thought to be a son of the great sun god. It was believed that once a Pharaoh died he would become the sun god **Osiris**. The followers believed that after the Pharaoh died, he became part of the divine gods of the afterworld.

:00

:10

:20

:30

:40

:50

:60

the End

APR

A thorough
knowledge
of the Bible is
worth more
than a college
education.

**Theodore Roosevelt
(1858-1919)**
United States President

THE FIRST PASSOVER

WHAT'S it mean

Then Moses called for all the elders of Israel and said to them, "Go and get lambs from your flocks, a lamb for one or more families depending upon the number of persons in the families, and kill the lamb so that God will pass over you and not destroy you. Drain the lamb's blood into a basin, and then take a cluster of hyssop branches and dip them into the lamb's blood, and strike the hyssop against the lintel above the door and against the two side panels, so that there will be blood upon them, and none of you shall go outside all night.

"For Jehovah will pass through the land and kill the Egyptians; but when he sees the blood upon the panel at the top of the door and on the two side pieces, he will pass over that home and not permit the Destroyer to enter and kill your firstborn. And remember, this is a permanent law for you and your posterity. And when you come into the land that the Lord will give you, just as he promised, and when you are celebrating the Passover, and your children ask, 'What does all this mean? What is this ceremony about?' you will reply, 'It is the celebration of Jehovah's passing over us, for he passed over the homes of the people of Israel, though he killed the Egyptians; he passed over our houses and did not come in to destroy us.'"

Exodus 12:21-27

The history of **Passover** starts with the tenth **plague** God sent to the people of Egypt–death to the firstborn. The Israelites were given **special** instructions to save their firstborn from death. They were told to smear blood from a lamb over their front door. This blood was a sign to the "Destroyer," or the "Angel of Death," to pass over those homes. Those who didn't put blood over their door, mostly Egyptians, experienced **massive** death throughout the passover night.

Passover is a **tragic** story of death but a **beautiful** story of God's **saving** power and promise to save the Israelite people from Egyptian captivity.

God keeps His promises!

ONE MINUTE MEMORY

We–every one
of us–have
strayed away
like sheep!
We, who left
God's paths to
follow our own.
Yet God laid
on him
the guilt and
sins of every
one of us!

Isaiah 53:6

:00

:15

:30

:45

:60

The Prophecy of the Suffering Servant

See, my Servant shall prosper; he shall be highly exalted.

♦ We despised him and rejected him—a man of sorrows, acquainted with bitterest grief. We turned our backs on him and looked the other way when he went by. He was despised, and we didn't care.

Yet it was our grief he bore, our sorrows that weighed him down. And we thought his troubles were a punishment from God, for his own sins! But he was wounded and bruised for our sins. He was beaten that we might have peace; he was lashed—and we were healed! We—every one of us—have strayed away like sheep! We, who left God's paths to follow our own. Yet God laid on him the guilt and sins of every one of us!

He was oppressed and he was afflicted, yet he never said a word. He was brought as a lamb to the slaughter; and as a sheep before her shearers is dumb, so he stood silent before the ones condemning him.

But it was the Lord's good plan to bruise him and fill him with grief. However, when his soul has been made an offering for sin, then he shall have a multitude of children, many heirs. He shall live again, and God's program shall prosper in his hands.

Isaiah 52:13; 53:3-7, 10

John the Baptist

The next day John saw Jesus coming toward him and said, "Look! There is the Lamb of God who takes away the world's sin! He is the one I was talking about when I said, 'Soon a man far greater than I am is coming, who existed long before me!' I didn't know he was the one, but I am here baptizing with water in order to point him out to the nation of Israel."

Then John told about seeing the Holy Spirit in the form of a dove descending from heaven and resting upon Jesus.

"I didn't know he was the one," John said again, "but at the time God sent me to baptize he told me, 'When you see the Holy Spirit descending and resting upon someone—he is the one you are looking for. He is the one who baptizes with the Holy Spirit.' I saw it happen to this man, and I therefore testify that he is the Son of God."

♦ Then in my vision I heard the singing of millions of angels surrounding the throne and the Living Beings and the Elders: "The Lamb is worthy" (loudly they sang it!) "—the Lamb who was slain. He is worthy to receive the power, and the riches, and the wisdom, and the strength, and the honor, and the glory, and the blessing."

John 1:29-34; Revelation 5:11-12

John the Baptist wasn't a representative from the Baptist church. He lived long before church denominations came into existence. John was a preacher who spoke of **forgiveness** and **salvation.** While preaching one day, John spotted Jesus and said, **"This is the one** [referring to the person of Jesus] I was talking about when I said, 'Someone is coming who is greater by far than I am—for he existed long before I did!'"** (John 1:15) God used John the Baptist to "roll out the red carpet" for Jesus to begin His public ministry.

Sounds as if we have something in common with John the Baptist—to **prepare** people for the coming of Jesus. How can you do this **today?**

:00

:10

:20

:30

:40

:50

:60

the End

4

:OO

:1O

:2O

:3O

:4O

:5O

1:OO

FINISH

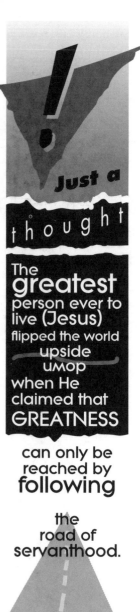

Just a

thought

The **greatest** person ever to live (Jesus) flipped the world upside down when He claimed that **GREATNESS**

can only be reached by **following**

the road of servanthood.

JESUS PREDICTS HIS RESURRECTION

So Jesus called them to him and said, "As you know, the kings and great men of the earth lord it over the people; but among you it is different. Whoever wants to be great among you must be your servant. And whoever wants to be greatest of all must be the slave of all. For even I, the Messiah, am not here to be served, but to help others, and to give my life as a ransom for many."

♦ One day as he was alone, praying, with his disciples nearby, he came over and asked them, "Who are the people saying I am?"

"John the Baptist," they told him, "or perhaps Elijah or one of the other ancient prophets risen from the dead."

Then he asked them, "Who do you think I am?"

Peter replied, "The Messiah—the Christ of God!"

He gave them strict orders not to speak of this to anyone. "For I, the Messiah, must suffer much," he said, "and be rejected by the Jewish leaders—the elders, chief priests, and teachers of the Law—and be killed; and three days later I will come back to life again!"

Mark 10:42-45; Luke 9:18-22

104

JESUS' TRIUMPHAL ENTRY

As Jesus and the disciples approached Jerusalem, and were near the town of Bethphage on the Mount of Olives, Jesus sent two of them into the village ahead.

"Just as you enter," he said, "you will see a donkey tied there, with its colt beside it. Untie them and bring them here. If anyone asks you what you are doing, just say, 'The Master needs them,' and there will be no trouble."

This was done to fulfill the ancient prophecy, "Tell Jerusalem her King is coming to her, riding humbly on a donkey's colt!"

The two disciples did as Jesus said, and brought the animals to him and threw their garments over the colt for him to ride on. And some in the crowd threw down their coats along the road ahead of him, and others cut branches from the trees and spread them out before him.

Then the crowds surged on ahead and pressed along behind, shouting, "God bless King David's Son!" . . . "God's Man is here!". . . Bless him, Lord!" . . . "Praise God in highest heaven!"

The entire city of Jerusalem was stirred as he entered. "Who is this?" they asked.

And the crowds replied, "It's Jesus, the prophet from Nazareth up in Galilee."

Matthew 21:1-11

:00
:10
:20
:30
:40
:50
:60
done

Catch T·H·I·S

When you learn about the **person** of Jesus you'll see how **different** He is from the rest in the world. For one thing, He isn't selfish, He is a **servant.** His entire life models this truth; He was born in a barn instead of a palace, He entered Jerusalem on a donkey instead of a large horse, and He washed His followers' feet saying, "I have **given** you an example to follow: do as I have done to you." Jesus gave us a model to follow.

The **model** is called **servanthood.** It's not about being first, the biggest, or the best. Servanthood is about serving others. Jesus said, "Whoever wants to be great among you must be your servant." It's as easy or as tough as this: if you want to be great in God's eyes you need to serve.

Think about how you might be a **servant** today. Give it a try and see if you find God's **reward** of **greatness.**

WHAT'S it ? mean

JESUS CLEANSES THE TEMPLE

You can get a **feel** for the **anger** of Jesus by reading this story. He was **mad!** His anger was directed at the people who had turned the Temple into a market for profit. These people were more concerned about **selling** their over-priced doves and other sacrificial animals than they were concerned for the **House of God.**

Jesus **continually** expresses concern for our **motives** and heart. The merchants and money-changers around the Temple didn't have the motive to please God with their business. They intended to make a quick buck by cheating the worshipers into buying unfit animals at high prices.

This is a great **illustration** to keep in mind today. What would Jesus **clean** out of your life if you gave Him the chance?

Keep checking **those inner motives!**

As they came closer to Jerusalem and he saw the city ahead, he began to cry. "Eternal peace was within your reach and you turned it down," he wept, "and now it is too late. Your enemies will pile up earth against your walls and encircle you and close in on you, and crush you to the ground, and your children within you; your enemies will not leave one stone upon another—for you have rejected the opportunity God offered you."

♦Jesus went into the Temple, drove out the merchants, and knocked over the moneychangers' tables and the stalls of those selling doves.

"The Scriptures say my Temple is a place of prayer," he declared, "but you have turned it into a den of thieves."

And now the blind and crippled came to him, and he healed them there in the Temple. But when the chief priests and other Jewish leaders saw these wonderful miracles and heard even the little children in the Temple shouting, "God bless the Son of David," they were disturbed and indignant and asked him, "Do you hear what these children are saying?"

"Yes," Jesus replied. "Didn't you ever read the Scriptures? For they say, 'Even little babies shall praise him!'"

Luke 19:41-44; Matthew 21:12-16

106

Then, surrounded by the Pharisees, he asked them a question: "What about the Messiah? Whose son is he?"

"The son of David," they replied.

"Then why does David, speaking under the inspiration of the Holy Spirit, call him 'Lord'?" Jesus asked. "For David said,

'God said to my Lord, Sit at my right hand until I put your enemies beneath your feet.'
Since David called him 'Lord,' how can he be merely his son?"

They had no answer. And after that no one dared ask him any more questions.

♦ Six days later Jesus took Peter, James and John to the top of a mountain. No one else was there.

Suddenly his face began to shine with glory, and his clothing became dazzling white, far more glorious than any earthly process could ever make it. A cloud covered them, blotting out the sun, and a voice from the cloud said, "This is my beloved Son. Listen to him."

Matthew 22:41-46; Mark 9:2,3,7

IN other words...

TRANSFIGURATION

This is a **big** word to describe the bodily **change** that happened to Jesus in the story you just read. On the top of the mountain, Jesus' appearance was **transformed** or changed into a likeness of God's presence. It was evident to Peter, James, and John that when Jesus was transfigured, His presence became like a **radiant light** that they believed to be God. For a brief moment, Jesus' radiant deity was allowed to shine through in the presence of His Father.

Unlike Jesus, you can't be transfigured into God. But with His **power** you can **change** your ways to become more like God **wants** you to become.

:00
:10
:20
:30
:40
:50

done :60

107

APR

8

IN **other** words...

LAST SUPPER

Since the death of Jesus, Christians have followed a **model** He left us called the Lord's Supper or **communion**. It's intended to **remind** us of Jesus' death on the cross. The cracker or **bread** used during communion represents the **body** of Jesus that was broken on the cross, while the wine or grape **juice** represents Jesus' **blood** shed on the cross for us.

Communion helps us remember what Jesus did on the cross two thousand years ago. He died for us. More specifically, His death was for YOU! Remember Jesus' death and **celebrate** your new life!

:00

:10

:20

:30

:40

:50

:60 **done**

Now the day of the Passover celebration arrived, when the Passover lamb was killed and eaten with the unleavened bread. Jesus sent Peter and John ahead to find a place to prepare their Passover meal.

Then Jesus and the others arrived, and at the proper time all sat down together at the table; and he said, "I have looked forward to this hour with deep longing, anxious to eat this Passover meal with you before my suffering begins. For I tell you now that I won't eat it again until what it represents has occurred in the Kingdom of God."

Then he took a glass of wine, and when he had given thanks for it, he said, "Take this and share it among yourselves. For I will not drink wine again until the Kingdom of God has come."

Then he took a loaf of bread; and when he had thanked God for it, he broke it apart and gave it to them, saying, "This is my body, given for you. Eat it in remembrance of me."

After supper he gave them another glass of wine, saying, "This wine is the token of God's new agreement to save you—an agreement sealed with the blood I shall pour out to purchase back your souls. But here at this table, sitting among us as a friend, is the man who will betray me. I must die. It is part of God's plan. But, oh, the horror awaiting that man who betrays me."

Luke 22:7-8, 14-22

Judas personality plus

After saying these things Jesus crossed the Kidron ravine with his disciples and entered a grove of olive trees. Judas, the betrayer, knew this place, for Jesus had gone there many times with his disciples.

The chief priests and Pharisees had given Judas a squad of soldiers and police to accompany him. Now with blazing torches, lanterns, and weapons they arrived at the olive grove.

Jesus fully realized all that was going to happen to him. Stepping forward to meet them he asked, "Whom are you looking for?"

"Jesus of Nazareth," they replied.

"I am he," Jesus said. And as he said it, they all fell backwards to the ground!

Once more he asked them, "Whom are you searching for?"

And again they replied, "Jesus of Nazareth."

"I told you I am he," Jesus said; "and since I am the one you are after, let these others go." He did this to carry out the prophecy he had just made, "I have not lost a single one of those you gave me...."

John 18:1-9

Judas (also known as Judas Iscariot) was one of the main **disciples** of Jesus. His job was to oversee the **money,** but he's best known for his deception and **betrayal** of Jesus.

He was a **greedy** man who deserted his commitment to Jesus. Judas led a crowd of officers to arrest Jesus for thirty pieces of **silver.** After Jesus was crucified, Judas **repented,** gave back all the money, but later hanged himself.

Unfortunately, even those closest to Jesus didn't completely follow Him and change their ways. **Watch** yourself so you don't get **"bribed"** into betraying Jesus in your life.

:00

:10

:20

:30

:40

:50

:60

the End

APR 10

IN other words...

BLASPHEMY

"Blasphemy" is a word used to describe an **abusive** comment or action directed at something **sacred** or holy. Blasphemy is **more** than cussing with God's name, it's total disrespect for God or godliness in general.

:00

:10

The high priest shouted, "Blasphemy!" because Jesus claimed to be God's Son. He thought Jesus was crazy because of this claim. The priests said Jesus' claim to be God's Son was blasphemous, a religious crime.

:20

:30

:40

Because Jesus proved who He claimed to be, His words weren't blasphemous. Take a minute to **thank** God for this truth.

:50

:60 **done**

The chief priests and, in fact, the entire Jewish Supreme Court assembled there and looked for witnesses who would lie about Jesus, in order to build a case against him that would result in a death sentence. But even though they found many who agreed to be false witnesses, these always contradicted each other.

Finally two men were found who declared, "This man said, 'I am able to destroy the Temple of God and rebuild it in three days.'"

Then the High Priest stood up and said to Jesus, "Well, what about it? Did you say that, or didn't you?" But Jesus remained silent.

Then the High Priest said to him, "I demand in the name of the living God that you tell us whether you claim to be the Messiah, the Son of God."

"Yes," Jesus said, "I am. And in the future you will see me, the Messiah, sitting at the right hand of God and returning on the clouds of heaven."

Then the High Priest tore at his own clothing, shouting, "Blasphemy! What need have we for other witnesses? You have all heard him say it! What is your verdict?"

They shouted, "Death!—Death!—Death!" Then they spat in his face and struck him and some slapped him, saying, "Prophesy to us, you Messiah! Who struck you that time?"

Matthew 26:59-68

JESUS IS CRUCIFIED

It was about nine o'clock in the morning when the crucifixion took place.

A signboard was fastened to the cross above his head, announcing his crime. It read, "The King of the Jews."

Two robbers were also crucified that morning, their crosses on either side of his. And so the Scripture was fulfilled that said, "He was counted among evil men."

The people jeered at him as they walked by, and wagged their heads in mockery.

"Ha! Look at you now!" they yelled at him. "Sure, you can destroy the Temple and rebuild it in three days! If you're so wonderful, save yourself and come down from the cross."

The chief priests and religious leaders were also standing around joking about Jesus.

"He's quite clever at 'saving' others," they said, "but he can't save himself!"

"Hey there, Messiah!" they yelled at him. "You 'King of Israel'! Come on down from the cross and we'll believe you!"

And even the two robbers dying with him cursed him.

Then Jesus uttered another loud cry and dismissed his spirit.

And the curtain in the Temple was split apart from top to bottom.

When the Roman officer standing beside his cross saw how he dismissed his spirit, he exclaimed, "Truly, this was the Son of God!"

Mark 15:25-32, 37-39 111

Weird or What

Crucifying someone on a cross was one of the most abusive **punishments** ever devised because of its slow, torturous death of suffocation.

The inscription that was put over Jesus' head was not unusual. These inscriptions informed visitors of the crimes worthy of this brutal death. Typically, criminals were crucified immediately outside the city gates so everyone could see the consequences of their crime. Jesus was crucified for being "King of the Jews."

Jesus died a **real** and **painful** death. He died so that you might have **new life** today.

 :00
 :10
 :20
 :30
 :40
 :50
 :60

end

:00
:10
:20
:30
:40
:50
1:00

Just a

t h o u g h t

He's
alive!
He has
risen
from the dead
He's
alive!
Shout it out...
"He's
alive!"

Celebrate
this Easter with
Jesus alive in
your life...
tell a friend...
He's alive!

ALIVE

Early on Sunday morning, as the new day was dawning, Mary Magdalene and the other Mary went out to the tomb.

Suddenly there was a great earthquake; for an angel of the Lord came down from heaven and rolled aside the stone and sat on it. His face shone like lightning and his clothing was a brilliant white. The guards shook with fear when they saw him, and fell into a dead faint.

Then the angel spoke to the women. "Don't be frightened!" he said. "I know you are looking for Jesus, who was crucified, but he isn't here! For he has come back to life again, just as he said he would. Come in and see where his body was lying. . . . And now, go quickly and tell his disciples that he has risen from the dead, and that he is going to Galilee to meet them there. That is my message to them."

The women ran from the tomb, badly frightened, but also filled with joy, and rushed to find the disciples to give them the angel's message. And as they were running, suddenly Jesus was there in front of them!

"Good morning!" he said. And they fell to the ground before him, holding his feet and worshiping him.

Then Jesus said to them, "Don't be frightened! Go tell my brothers to leave at once for Galilee, to meet me there."

Matthew 28:1-10

ALL-IMPORTANCE OF THE RESURRECTION

RESURRECTION
RESURRECTION
RESURRECTION

But tell me this! Since you believe what we preach, that Christ rose from the dead, why are some of you saying that dead people will never come back to life again? For if there is no resurrection of the dead, then Christ must still be dead. And if he is still dead, then all our preaching is useless and your trust in God is empty, worthless, hopeless; and we apostles are all liars because we have said that God raised Christ from the grave, and of course that isn't true if the dead do not come back to life again. If they don't, then Christ is still dead, and you are very foolish to keep on trusting God to save you, and you are still under condemnation for your sins; in that case, all Christians who have died are lost! And if being a Christian is of value to us only now in this life, we are the most miserable of creatures.

But the fact is that Christ did actually rise from the dead and has become the first of millions who will come back to life again someday. Death came into the world because of what one man (Adam) did, and it is because of what this other man (Christ) has done that now there is the resurrection from the dead. Everyone dies because all of us are related to Adam, being members of his sinful race, and wherever there is sin, death results. But all who are related to Christ will rise again.

1 Corinthians 15:12-22

113

1 3

APR

Just a thought

Belief in the **resurrection** of Jesus is the **backbone** of the Christian **faith.**

If Jesus **didn't** rise from the dead, then He'd be a **liar** and just another man in a grave.

Who would **worship** a dead guy?

:00
:10
:20
:30
:40
:50
1:00

FINISH

14
APR

CHECK IT OUT

JESUS CHRIST: OUR PASSOVER

Not only did Jesus **die** in our place and **save** us from eternal death, but He also brought us into a **NEW** family.

Check out Hebrews 2:11:
"We who have been made holy by Jesus, now have the same Father he has. That is why Jesus is not ashamed to call us brothers."

You're **part** of God's family. Congratulations, and don't forget to **talk** to your Heavenly Father **today**.

:00

:10

:20

:30

:40

:50

:60

What a terrible thing it is that you are boasting about your purity and yet you let this sort of thing go on. Don't you realize that if even one person is allowed to go on sinning, soon all will be affected? Remove this evil cancer—this wicked person—from among you, so that you can stay pure. Christ, God's Lamb, has been slain for us. So let us feast upon him and grow strong in the Christian life, leaving entirely behind us the cancerous old life with all its hatreds and wickedness. Let us feast instead upon the pure bread of honor and sincerity and truth.

♦ And remember that your heavenly Father to whom you pray has no favorites when he judges. He will judge you with perfect justice for everything you do; so act in reverent fear of him from now on until you get to heaven. God paid a ransom to save you from the impossible road to heaven which your fathers tried to take, and the ransom he paid was not mere gold or silver as you very well know. But he paid for you with the precious lifeblood of Christ, the sinless, spotless Lamb of God. God chose him for this purpose long before the world began, but only recently was he brought into public view, in these last days, as a blessing to you.

1 Corinthians 5:6-8; 1 Peter 1:17-20

d o n e

114

ISRAELITES LEAVE EGYPT

WHAT'S it mean

That night, at midnight, Jehovah killed all the firstborn sons in the land of Egypt, from Pharaoh's oldest son to the oldest son of the captive in the dungeon; also all the firstborn of the cattle. Then Pharaoh and his officials and all the people of Egypt got up in the night; and there was bitter crying throughout all the land of Egypt, for there was not a house where there was not one dead.

And Pharaoh summoned Moses and Aaron during the night and said, "Leave us; please go away, all of you; go and serve Jehovah as you said. Take your flocks and herds and be gone; and oh, give me a blessing as you go." And the Egyptians were urgent upon the people of Israel, to get them out of the land as quickly as possible. For they said, "We are as good as dead."

The Israelis took with them their bread dough without yeast, and bound their kneading troughs into their spare clothes, and carried them on their shoulders. And the people of Israel did as Moses said and asked the Egyptians for silver and gold jewelry and for clothing. And the Lord gave the Israelis favor with the Egyptians, so that they gave them whatever they wanted. And the Egyptians were practically stripped of everything they owned!

Exodus 12:29-36

The **release** of the Israelites is another example of how God remains **faithful** to His promises! No doubt the Israelites wanted God's help a lot earlier. They screamed, cried, and **prayed** like crazy. But God had His own plans and demonstrated His **goodness** by protecting the Israelite's release from Egypt. He proved that He is God and His timing is **perfect**.

These same **principles** can be applied today. Most of us want God to move **faster** than He does. BUT, He is God, He is faithful, and His timing is always **perfect**. That's plenty of reason to trust Him and give Him your praise today...
don't you think?

16

A P R

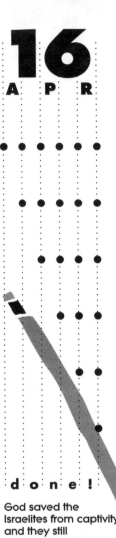

done!

Pharaoh's entire cavalry—horses, chariots, and charioteers—was used in the chase; and the Egyptian army overtook the people of Israel as they were camped beside the shore near Piha-hiroth, across from Baal-zephon.

As the Egyptian army approached, the people of Israel saw them far in the distance, speeding after them, and they were terribly frightened and cried out to the Lord to help them.

And they turned against Moses, whining, "Have you brought us out here to die in the desert because there were not enough graves for us in Egypt? Why did you make us leave Egypt? Isn't this what we told you, while we were slaves, to leave us alone? We said it would be better to be slaves to the Egyptians than dead in the wilderness."

But Moses told the people, "Don't be afraid. Just stand where you are and watch, and you will see the wonderful way the Lord will rescue you today. The Egyptians you are looking at—you will never see them again. The Lord will fight for you, and you won't need to lift a finger!"

Then the Lord said to Moses, "Quit praying and get the people moving! Forward, march! Use your rod—hold it out over the water, and the sea will open up a path before you, and all the people of Israel shall walk through on dry ground! I will harden the hearts of the Egyptians, and they will go in after you and you will see the honor I will get in defeating Pharaoh and all his armies, chariots, and horsemen. And all Egypt shall know that I am Jehovah."

Exodus 14:9-18

Pharaoh pursues the Israelites

God saved the Israelites from captivity and they still complained. Write down three **complaints** you have about your life. Next to each complaint list what you can **do** to change each complaint. Next, express your thankfulness to God for saving you from the bondage of sin.

Give it a try

1 _____ _____

2 _____ _____

3 _____ _____

CROSSING
THE RED SEA

Moses stretched his rod over the sea, and the Lord opened up a path through the sea, with walls of water on each side; and a strong east wind blew all that night, drying the sea bottom. So the people of Israel walked through the sea on dry ground! Then the Egyptians followed them between the walls of water along the bottom of the sea—all of Pharaoh's horses, chariots, and horsemen. But in the early morning Jehovah looked down from the cloud of fire upon the array of the Egyptians, and began to harass them. Their chariot wheels began coming off, so that their chariots scraped along the dry ground. "Let's get out of here," the Egyptians yelled. "Jehovah is fighting for them and against us."

When all the Israelites were on the other side, the Lord said to Moses, "Stretch out your hand again over the sea, so that the waters will come back over the Egyptians and their chariots and horsemen." Moses did, and the sea returned to normal beneath the morning light. The Egyptians tried to flee, but the Lord drowned them in the sea. The water covered the path and the chariots and horsemen. And of all the army of Pharaoh that chased after Israel through the sea, not one remained alive.

Exodus 14:21-28

:00

:10

Today, the Red Sea is known to have a total **length** of **1,200** miles and range between 230 miles wide in the south to 130 miles wide in the north. The greatest **depth** of the Red Sea is about **7,200** feet. This doesn't describe a little puddle! God performed a **major** miracle when He opened the sea for the Israelites to cross.

:20

:30

:40

God **loves** you so much that He's willing to part seas and open mountains to **express** His love and fulfill His promises. **Count** on that **today!**

:50

:60

end

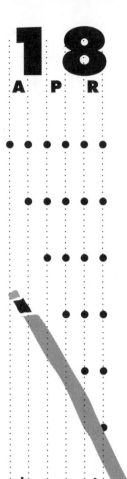

18 APR

• • • • • •

• • • • •

• • • •

• •

• •

d o n e !

^Thus Jehovah saved Israel that day from the Egyptians; and the people of Israel saw the Egyptians dead, washed up on the seashore. When the people of Israel saw the mighty miracle the Lord had done for them against the Egyptians, they were afraid and revered the Lord, and believed in him and in his servant Moses.

♦ Then Moses and the people of Israel sang this song to the Lord:

> I will sing to the Lord,
> for he has triumphed gloriously;
> He has thrown both horse and rider
> into the sea.
> The Lord is my strength, my song,
> and my salvation.
> He is my God, and I will praise him.
> He is my father's God—I will exalt him.
> The Lord is a warrior— Yes, Jehovah is his name.
> He has overthrown Pharaoh's chariots
> and armies,
> drowning them in the sea.
> The famous Egyptian captains are
> dead beneath the waves.
> Who else is like the Lord among the gods?
> Who is glorious in holiness like him?
> Who is so awesome in splendor,
> a wonder-working God?
> You have led the people you redeemed.
> But in your loving-kindness
> You have guided them wonderfully
> to your holy land.
> Jehovah shall reign forever and forever.

Exodus 14:30-31; 15:1-4, 11, 13, 18

the Lord is a warrior

Give it a try

Try writing a song or poem of praise describing the incredible saving power of God.

(If you need help getting started, use some of the words from today's reading.)

God's care in the desert

19
APR

Thank the Lord for all the glorious things he does; proclaim them to the nations. Sing his praises and tell everyone about his miracles. Glory in the Lord; O worshipers of God, rejoice.

Search for him and for his strength, and keep on searching!

Think of the mighty deeds he did for us, his chosen ones—descendants of God's servant Abraham, and of Jacob. Remember how he destroyed our enemies and brought his people safely out from Egypt, loaded with silver and gold; there were no sick and feeble folk among them then. Egypt was glad when they were gone, for the dread of them was great.

He spread out a cloud above them to shield them from the burning sun and gave them a pillar of flame at night to give them light. They asked for meat, and he sent them quail and gave them manna—bread from heaven. He opened up a rock, and water gushed out to form a river through the dry and barren land; for he remembered his sacred promises to Abraham his servant.

So he brought his chosen ones singing into the Promised Land. He gave them the lands of the Gentiles, complete with their growing crops; they ate what others planted. This was done to make them faithful and obedient to his laws. Hallelujah!

done!

Psalm 105:1-6, 37-45

Give it a try

Yesterday, you wrote a song or poem of praise describing God's **power.**

Today, list one specific area in your life where you need God's saving power.

How can God **provide** for this need?

"Search for him and for his strength, and keep on searching!" (Psalm 105:4)

119

WHAT'S it 2 mean

GOD'S COVENANT WITH ISRAEL

On this **mountain,** Moses received from God what we know as the Ten Commandments. Over the next ten days you will read these commandments. It's important for you to notice that the first four commandments give us directions about loving God. The next six commandments provide us with instructions on how to live with and relate to one another.

This is why Jesus summed up the Ten Commandments by saying,

"Love God with all your heart, soul, and mind (1-4). And love your neighbor as you love yourself" (5-10).

Look for **opportunities** you have today to love God, your friends (neighbors), and yourself.

The Israelis arrived in the Sinai peninsula three months after the night of their departure from Egypt. After breaking camp at Rephidim, they came to the base of Mt. Sinai and set up camp there. Moses climbed the rugged mountain to meet with God, and from somewhere in the mountain God called to him and said,

"Give these instructions to the people of Israel. Tell them, 'You have seen what I did to the Egyptians, and how I brought you to myself as though on eagle's wings. Now if you will obey me and keep your part of my contract with you, you shall be my own little flock from among all the nations of the earth; for all the earth is mine. And you shall be a kingdom of priests to God, a holy nation.'"

Moses returned from the mountain and called together the leaders of the people and told them what the Lord had said.

They all responded in unison, "We will certainly do everything he asks of us." Moses reported the words of the people to the Lord.

Then he said to Moses, "I am going to come to you in the form of a dark cloud, so that the people themselves can hear me when I talk with you, and then they will always believe you."

Exodus 19:1-9

NO OTHER GODS

I am Jehovah your God who liberated you from your slavery in Egypt.

You may worship no other god than me.

♦ Sing to the Lord, O earth, declare each day that he is the one who saves! Show his glory to the nations! Tell everyone about his miracles. For the Lord is great and should be highly praised; he is to be held in awe above all gods. The other so-called gods are demons, but the Lord made the heavens. Majesty and honor march before him, strength and gladness walk beside him.

O people of all nations of the earth, ascribe great strength and glory to his name! Yes, ascribe to the Lord the glory due his name! Bring an offering and come before him; worship the Lord when clothed with holiness! Tremble before him, all the earth! The world stands unmoved. Let the heavens be glad, the earth rejoice; let all the nations say, "It is the Lord who reigns."

Exodus 20:2-3; 1 Chronicles 16:23-31

Idols were viewed as having god-like power. People believed the power of gods could be contained in an idol. This is one reason why God **refused** to allow any images to be made of Him.

God cannot be limited to an idol. Idols have no power and can be stolen or destroyed. He can't be captured in any human-made image. He is a God who is living: One who can't be bound by a church, a temple, a golden calf, or even the Bible.

You'd search **forever** to find any book, person, or crystal that has anything like God's power. Today, tell a friend this truth.

end

121

word

IDOL

During biblical times, an idol was a **handmade** item that became the object of **worship.** People may have worshiped a wooden pigeon, a golden calf, or a ceramic armadillo. The important thing wasn't what they worshiped, but that they worshiped something **other** than the true God.

Is idol worship even an issue today? No and yes. No, because you probably don't have friends bowing before foreign objects. But, yes it's an issue, when you see the different things people value and worship that take their eyes off God.

How about you?

Do you have any **modern-day** idols? Television? Clothes? **Music?** Boyfriend or girlfriend? Do you have other "gods" that are more important than God? If so, you may want to **reread** the last sentence in today's reading!

You shall not make yourselves any idols: no images of animals, birds, or fish. You must never bow or worship it in any way; for I, the Lord your God, am very possessive. I will not share your affection with any other god!

And when I punish people for their sins, the punishment continues upon the children, grandchildren, and great-grandchildren of those who hate me; but I lavish my love upon thousands of those who love me and obey my commandments.

♦ Glorify your name, not ours, O Lord! Cause everyone to praise your loving-kindness and your truth. Why let the nations say, "Their God is dead!"

For he is in the heavens and does as he wishes. Their gods are merely manmade things of silver and of gold. They can't talk or see, despite their eyes and mouths! Nor can they hear, nor smell, nor use their hands or feet, nor speak! And those who make and worship them are just as foolish as their idols are.

Exodus 20:4-6; Psalm 115:1-8

122

The Ten Commandments: God's Name

Y ou shall not use the name of Jehovah your God irreverently, nor use it to swear to a falsehood. You will not escape punishment if you do.

♦ Out in the camp one day, a young man whose mother was an Israelite and whose father was an Egyptian, got into a fight with one of the men of Israel. During the fight the Egyptian man's son cursed God, and was brought to Moses for judgment. (His mother's name was Shelomith, daughter of Dibri of the tribe of Dan.) He was put in jail until the Lord would indicate what to do with him.

And the Lord said to Moses, "Take him outside the camp and tell all who heard him to lay their hands upon his head; then all the people are to execute him by stoning. And tell the people of Israel that anyone who curses his God must pay the penalty: he must die. All the congregation shall stone him; this law applies to the foreigner as well as to the Israelite who blasphemes the name of Jehovah. He must die."

♦ The Lord is a strong fortress. The godly run to him and are safe.

Exodus 20:7; Leviticus 24:10-16; Proverbs 18:10

The Lord is a strong fortress. The godly run to him and are safe.

Proverbs 18:10

APR 24

The Ten Commandments:
THE SABBATH

:00

:10 For those **faithful** to Judaism, the Sabbath is a day when **all work stops.** During Old Testament times, if someone **broke** Sabbath rules, that person was judged and **:20** put to **death** (see Numbers 15:32-36).

:30 **Today,** there is a problem with the Sabbath **rule** prohibiting anyone to **:40** make a **fire.** Turning on a light switch in a modern home is a non-combustive type of burning that is **:50** labeled as starting a fire. Those faithful to Judaism are prohibited from turning on **any** electrical device. The only electrical **:60** appliance that can be left **on** is the refrigerator.

end

Remember to observe the Sabbath as a holy day. Six days a week are for your daily duties and your regular work, but the seventh day is a day of Sabbath rest before the Lord your God. On that day you are to do no work of any kind, nor shall your son, daughter, or slaves—whether men or women—or your cattle or your house guests. For in six days the Lord made the heaven, earth, and sea, and everything in them, and rested the seventh day; so he blessed the Sabbath day and set it aside for rest.

♦ Then he went over to the synagogue and noticed there a man with a deformed hand. The Pharisees asked Jesus, "Is it legal to work by healing on the Sabbath day?" (They were, of course, hoping he would say yes, so they could arrest him!) This was his answer: "If you had just one sheep, and it fell into a well on the Sabbath, would you work to rescue it that day? Of course you would. And how much more valuable is a person than a sheep! Yes, it is right to do good on the Sabbath." Then he said to the man, "Stretch out your arm." And as he did, his hand became normal, just like the other one!

Exodus 20:8-11; Matthew 12:9-13

THE TEN COMMANDMENTS: PARENTS

Honor your father and mother, that you may have a long, good life in the land the Lord your God will give you.

♦ Anyone who strikes his father or mother shall surely be put to death.

♦ Anyone who curses his father or mother shall surely be put to death—for he has cursed his own flesh and blood.

♦ Happy is the man with a level-headed son; sad the mother of a rebel.

♦ Listen to your father's advice and don't despise an old mother's experience. Get the facts at any price, and hold on tightly to all the good sense you can get. The father of a godly man has cause for joy—what pleasure a wise son is! So give your parents joy!

♦ Children, obey your parents; this is the right thing to do because God has placed them in authority over you. Honor your father and mother. This is the first of God's Ten Commandments that ends with a promise. And this is the promise: that if you honor your father and mother, yours will be a long life, full of blessing.

Exodus 20:12; 21:15; Leviticus 20:9; Proverbs 10:1; 23:22-25; Ephesians 6:1-3

:00
:10
:20
:30
:40
:50
:60
done

Catch THIS

There is no **perfect** family and there are no perfect parents. Parents don't have an easy job; it's one of the toughest **responsibilities** ever created. Parents didn't receive a college degree in parenting, and there's no such thing as a professional parent. Parents live with a lot of **pressure** to care for their children, their careers, and their own personal life. In case you've forgotten, parents are also human, which means they've got real feelings and pain **just like we do.**

One of the ways in which you can **HONOR** your parents is to allow them the freedom to fail. Like you, they're not perfect and they need your love, forgiveness, and acceptance. Many parents are so accustomed to their child's greed—always wanting something—that they'll be shocked when greed is **replaced** with **caring** behavior. Give it a try. Honor your parents and watch for God's **blessing** on your life.

The Ten Commandments: Murder

Murder is bad. Anger isn't bad. **Resentment is bad.** Anger isn't bad. **Hate is bad.** Anger isn't bad. **Revenge is bad.** Anger isn't bad. **Bitterness is bad.** Anger isn't bad.

Get the point?

Anger comes and goes as a quick and natural emotion. Anger becomes negative when we allow it to stay in our life, our thoughts, and our heart. When anger remains, it transforms into resentment, which then can lead to bitterness, hate, and revenge.

Be careful your anger doesn't lead to sin. The Bible instructs us to deal with our anger before the sun goes down. Deal with your anger today so it doesn't become resentment... you'll **sleep** a lot better.

Y ou must not murder.

♦ Any man who murders shall be killed; for to kill a man is to kill one made like God.

♦ Under the laws of Moses the rule was, "If you murder, you must die." But I have added to that rule and tell you that if you are only angry, even in your own home, you are in danger of judgment! If you call your friend an idiot, you are in danger of being brought before the court. And if you curse him, you are in danger of the fires of hell.

♦ The message to us from the beginning has been that we should love one another.

We are not to be like Cain, who belonged to Satan and killed his brother. Why did he kill him? Because Cain had been doing wrong and he knew very well that his brother's life was better than his. So don't be surprised, dear friends, if the world hates you.

If we love other Christians, it proves that we have been delivered from hell and given eternal life. But a person who doesn't have love for others is headed for eternal death. Anyone who hates his Christian brother is really a murderer at heart; and you know that no one wanting to murder has eternal life within. We know what real love is from Christ's example in dying for us. And so we also ought to lay down our lives for our Christian brothers.

Exodus 20:13; Genesis 9:6;
Matthew 5:21-22; 1 John 3:11-16

THE TEN COMMANDMENTS: ADULTERY

You must not commit adultery.

♦ Why delight yourself with prostitutes, embracing what isn't yours? For God is closely watching you, and he weighs carefully everything you do.

♦ The laws of Moses said, "You shall not commit adultery." But I say: Anyone who even looks at a woman with lust in his eye has already committed adultery with her in his heart.

♦ Don't you know that those doing such things have no share in the Kingdom of God? Don't fool yourselves. Those who live immoral lives, who are idol worshipers, adulterers or homosexuals—will have no share in his Kingdom. Neither will thieves or greedy people, drunkards, slanderers, or robbers. There was a time when some of you were just like that but now your sins are washed away, and you are set apart for God; and he has accepted you because of what the Lord Jesus Christ and the Spirit of our God have done for you.

♦ Honor your marriage and its vows, and be pure; for God will surely punish all those who are immoral or commit adultery.

Exodus 20:14; Proverbs 5:20-21;
Matthew 5:27-28; 1 Corinthians 6:9-11;
Hebrews 13:4

Catch THIS

God **wasn't big** on setting up rules to **frustrate** people. A lot of people believe God is a "cosmic kill-joy" who lives in heaven trying to discover ways to quench our joy. This couldn't be **further** from the truth! God created rules and **guidelines** to help us live life to its **fullest**.

When it comes to adultery or sex outside of marriage, God established this rule for our **own** good. God isn't down on sex, He created it. GOD IS DOWN ON PAIN! And the pain from adultery is intense. Adultery usually ends up with broken families, destroyed lives, and terrible lifelong memories.

God wants His people to be sexually **pure** for the health, happiness, and goodness of His children. Sex is a beautiful gift from God, and He created it to be shared and experienced **between** a husband and wife. God gets really excited when life is lived as He created it to be lived. Keep following Him and you'll continue to discover how rich and full life was **intended** to be.

:00 :10 :20 :30 :40 :50 :60 done

127

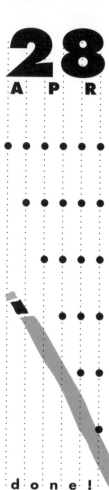

28

APR

• • • • • •

• • • • •

• • • •

• • •

• •

•

d o n e !

You must not steal.

♦ Don't become rich by extortion and robbery; if your riches increase, don't be proud. God has said it many times, that power belongs to him (and also, O Lord, steadfast love belongs to you). He rewards each one of us according to what our works deserve.

♦ Tell those who are rich not to be proud and not to trust in their money, which will soon be gone, but their pride and trust should be in the living God who always richly gives us all we need for our enjoyment. Tell them to use their money to do good. They should be rich in good works and should give happily to those in need, always being ready to share with others whatever God has given them. By doing this they will be storing up real treasure for themselves in heaven—it is the only safe investment for eternity! And they will be living a fruitful Christian life down here as well.

♦ If anyone is stealing he must stop it and begin using those hands of his for honest work so he can give to others in need.

Exodus 20:15; Psalm 62:10-12;
1 Timothy 6:17-19; Ephesians 4:28

Give it a try

What would you say to your very best friend if you caught him or her stealing?

_____

_____

_____

You must not lie.

♦ If anyone gives false witness, claiming he has seen someone do wrong when he hasn't, both men shall be brought before the priests and judges on duty before the Lord at the time. They must be closely questioned, and if the witness is lying, his penalty shall be the punishment he thought the other man would get. In this way you will purge out evil from among you. Then those who hear about it will be afraid to tell lies on the witness stand.

♦ Lord, who may go and find refuge and shelter in your tabernacle up on your holy hill?

Anyone who leads a blameless life and is truly sincere. Anyone who refuses to slander others, does not listen to gossip, never harms his neighbor, speaks out against sin, criticizes those committing it, commends the faithful followers of the Lord, keeps a promise even if it ruins him, does not crush his debtors with high interest rates, and refuses to testify against the innocent despite the bribes offered him—such a man shall stand firm forever.

Exodus 20:16; Deuteronomy 19:16-20; Psalm 15

:00

:10

:20

:30

:40

:50

:60

The Book of **Proverbs** is an incredible book filled with wisdom, common sense, and good old-fashioned values. Here are a few verses on telling the truth:

"Lies will get any man into trouble, but honesty is its own defense."
(12:13)

"A good man is known by his truthfulness; a false man by deceit and lies."
(12:17)

d o n e

MEMORY

:00

:15

:30

:45

:60

done

The Ten Commandments: Coveting

You must not be envious of your neighbor's house, or want to sleep with his wife, or want to own his slaves, oxen, donkeys, or anything else he has.

♦ Pay all your debts except the debt of love for others—never finish paying that! For if you love them, you will be obeying all of God's laws, fulfilling all his requirements. If you love your neighbor as much as you love yourself you will not want to harm or cheat him, or kill him or steal from him. And you won't sin with his wife or want what is his, or do anything else the Ten Commandments say is wrong. All ten are wrapped up in this one, to love your neighbor as you love yourself. Love does no wrong to anyone. That's why it fully satisfies all of God's requirements. It is the only law you need.

♦ Do you want to be truly rich? You already are if you are happy and good. After all, we didn't bring any money with us when we came into the world, and we can't carry away a single penny when we die. So we should be well satisfied without money if we have enough food and clothing.

♦ Stay away from the love of money; be satisfied with what you have. For God has said, "I will never, never fail you nor forsake you."

Exodus 20:17; Romans 13:8-10;
1 Timothy 6:6-8; Hebrews 13:5

Stay away from the LOVE of money; be satisfied with what you have. For God has said, "I will never, never fail you nor forsake you."

Hebrews 13:5

MAY

The Bible is the greatest benefit which the human race has ever experienced. A single line in the Bible has consoled me more than all the books I ever read besides.

**Immanuel Kant
(1724-1804)**
German Philosopher

the greatest commandment

O Israel, listen: Jehovah is our God, Jehovah alone. You must love him with all your heart, soul, and might. And you must think constantly about these commandments I am giving you today. You must teach them to your children and talk about them when you are at home or out for a walk; at bedtime and the first thing in the morning. Tie them on your finger, wear them on your forehead, and write them on the doorposts of your house!

♦ "Sir, which is the most important command in the laws of Moses?"

Jesus replied, "'Love the Lord your God with all your heart, soul, and mind.' This is the first and greatest commandment. The second most important is similar: 'Love your neighbor as much as you love yourself.' All the other commandments and all the demands of the prophets stem from these two laws and are fulfilled if you obey them. Keep only these and you will find that you are obeying all the others."

Deuteronomy 6:4-9; Matthew 22:36-40

MAY 1

• • • • •

• • • •

• • •

• •

•

done!

Give it a try

What does the following sentence mean to you, **"Love your neighbor as much as you love yourself"?**

_____

_____

_____

What can you do today to bring the second greatest commandment into action?

:00

:10

:20

:30

:40

:50

1:00

Just a thought

God's presence will be evident **in your life** when you go out of your way to care for **orphans** and **widows.**

Do you know someone like this?

Delight **God** by loving that person **today.**

WIDOWS, ORPHANS, AND FOREIGNERS

You must not exploit widows or orphans; if you do so in any way, and they cry to me for my help, I will surely give it. And my anger shall flame out against you, and I will kill you with enemy armies, so that your wives will be widows and your children fatherless.

♦ Justice must be given to migrants and orphans, and you must never accept a widow's garment in pledge of her debt. Always remember that you were slaves in Egypt, and that the Lord your God rescued you; that is why I have given you this command. If, when reaping your harvest, you forget to bring in a sheaf from the field, don't go back after it. Leave it for the migrants, orphans, and widows; then the Lord your God will bless and prosper all you do. When you beat the olives from your olive trees, don't go over the boughs twice; leave anything remaining for the migrants, orphans, and widows. It is the same for the grapes in your vineyard; don't glean the vines after they are picked, but leave what's left for those in need. Remember that you were slaves in the land of Egypt—that is why I am giving you this command.

♦ The Christian who is pure and without fault, from God the Father's point of view, is the one who takes care of orphans and widows, and who remains true to the Lord—not soiled and dirtied by his contacts with the world.

Exodus 22:22-24; Deuteronomy 24:17-22; James 1:27

134

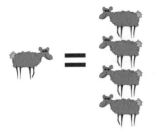

If a man steals an ox or sheep and then kills or sells it, he shall pay a fine of five to one—five oxen shall be returned for each stolen ox. For sheep, the fine shall be four to one—four sheep returned for each sheep stolen.

If a thief is captured, he must make full restitution; if he can't, then he must be sold as a slave for his debt.

If he is caught in the act of stealing a live ox or donkey or sheep or whatever it is, he shall pay double value as his fine.

If someone deliberately lets his animal loose and it gets into another man's vineyard; or if he turns it into another man's field to graze, he must pay for all damages by giving the owner of the field or vineyard an equal amount of the best of his own crop.

In every case in which an ox, donkey, sheep, clothing, or anything else is lost, and the owner believes he has found it in the possession of someone else who denies it, both parties to the dispute shall come before God for a decision, and the one whom God declares guilty shall pay double to the other.

Exodus 22:1, 3-5, 9

IN other words...
RESTITUTION

Restitution means to **pay back** or to make right. For example, if you stole something you would need to pay the person you stole from in order to **restore** his or her property and the relationship.

The theme of restoration, or bringing people back together, is biblical. Jesus taught His followers to **restore** relationships. He told them to leave church if they must and find the friend who has something against them and apologize in order to be reconciled.

The Bible doesn't give instructions so our joy might be stolen. The opposite is true; instructions **help us live** right and enjoy the friendships God has given us. Do you have any friends you need to **forgive** or be forgiven by today? Reconcile with them and you'll find yourself a **happier** person.

:00

:10

:20

:30

:40

:50

done :60

4 MAY

The Law: Eye for Eye

word

REVENGE

During Old Testament times, **controlled** revenge was allowed—you smack Tom in the face and he gets to hit you back. **But** in the New Testament, Jesus explains the essential meaning of the Law. He tells us **not** to strike back. He wants us to live without seeking revenge. He said, "Love your enemies and pray for those that persecute you...if you love only those who love you, what good is that? Even scoundrels do that much. If you are friendly to your friends, how are you different from anyone else?" (Matthew 5:44, 46, 47)

Jesus wants us to be **different!** Next time you pass someone you don't like, **pray** for him or her... see what happens.

If two men are fighting, and in the process hurt a pregnant woman so that she has a miscarriage, but she lives, then the man who injured her shall be fined whatever amount the woman's husband shall demand, and as the judges approve. But if any harm comes to the woman and she dies, he shall be executed.

If her eye is injured, injure his; if her tooth is knocked out, knock out his; and so on—hand for hand, foot for foot, burn for burn, wound for wound, lash for lash.

♦ Also, all murderers must be executed. Anyone who kills an animal (that isn't his) shall replace it. The penalty for injuring anyone is to be injured in exactly the same way: fracture for fracture, eye for eye, tooth for tooth. Whatever anyone does to another shall be done to him.

To repeat, whoever kills an animal must replace it, and whoever kills a man must die. You shall have the same law for the foreigner as for the home-born citizen, for I am Jehovah your God.

♦ The law of Moses says, "If a man gouges out another's eye, he must pay with his own eye. If a tooth gets knocked out, knock out the tooth of the one who did it." But I say: Don't resist violence! If you are slapped on one cheek, turn the other too.

Exodus 21:22-25; Leviticus 24:17-22; Matthew 5:38-39

136

The Law: Capital Punishment

Anyone who hits a man so hard that he dies shall surely be put to death.

Anyone who strikes his father or mother shall surely be put to death. A kidnapper must be killed, whether he is caught in possession of his victim or has already sold him as a slave.

♦ A sorceress shall be put to death. Anyone having sexual relations with an animal shall certainly be executed. Anyone sacrificing to any other god than Jehovah shall be executed.

♦ Rest on the Sabbath, for it is holy. Anyone who does not obey this command must die; anyone who does any work on that day shall be killed.

♦ Anyone who curses his father or mother shall surely be put to death—for he has cursed his own flesh and blood.

If a man commits adultery with another man's wife, both the man and woman shall be put to death. If a man sleeps with his father's wife, he has defiled what is his father's; both the man and the woman must die, for it is their own fault. And if a man has sexual intercourse with his daughter-in-law, both shall be executed: they have brought it upon themselves by defiling each other. The penalty for homosexual acts is death to both parties. They have brought it upon themselves.

Exodus 21:12, 15-16; 22:18-20; 31:14; Leviticus 20:9-13

BIG time word

CAPITAL PUNISHMENT

It's fairly clear from these Old Testament passages that there was a stronger cultural view on the death penalty than we have today. Now, capital punishment is more a political than religious issue.

Though the death penalty isn't always enforced for killing someone, there is usually a "price" for crime. This price is better defined by the word "consequence."

The decisions you make today probably won't result in the death penalty, but the consequences may result in pain, broken relations, negative memories, and other difficulties.

Life was created to be lived. Today, think through your decisions and their consequences so you can live a full life.

personality plus Israelites

The Israelites were **descendants** of Abraham and called God's **chosen** people. They were His special group because of God's promise to Abraham. Because of Abraham's faithfulness, God promised Abraham that his **descendants** would be blessed.

:00

:10

:20

The Israelites' **journey** is an up and down one. They lived in slavery for **400 years** before God delivered them from Egyptian bondage. God **promised** them a new home. But before they got there, they rebelled against God. God **punished** them by allowing them to wander in the desert for 40 years before fulfilling His promise to Abraham and allowing them to **enter** into the Promised Land.

:30

Through the Israelites' journey we can learn a lot about God's character.
1. God is faithful to His promises.
2. God loves His people.
3. God hates sin.
4. God wants us to be faithful in our relationship with Him.
Which of these four truths do **you** need to learn **today?**

:40

:50

:60

the End

Then the Lord said to Moses and Aaron, "Tell the people of Israel that the animals which may be used for food include any animal with cloven hooves which chews its cud.

As to fish, you may eat whatever has fins and scales, whether taken from rivers or from the sea; but all other water creatures are strictly forbidden to you. You mustn't eat their meat or even touch their dead bodies.

No insects may be eaten, with the exception of those that jump; locusts of all varieties—ordinary locusts, bald locusts, crickets, and grasshoppers—may be eaten.

I am the Lord your God. Keep yourselves pure concerning these things, and be holy, for I am holy; therefore do not defile yourselves by touching any of these things that crawl upon the earth. For I am the Lord who brought you out of the land of Egypt to be your God. You must therefore be holy, for I am holy."

Leviticus 11:1-3, 9-11, 20-21, 44-45

THE FESTIVALS

Always remember to celebrate the Passover during the month of April, for that was when Jehovah your God brought you out of Egypt by night. Your Passover sacrifice shall be either a lamb or an ox, sacrificed to the Lord your God at his sanctuary.

For the following six days you shall eat no bread made with yeast. On the seventh day there shall be a quiet gathering of the people of each city before the Lord your God. Don't do any work that day.

Seven weeks after the harvest begins, there shall be another festival before the Lord your God called the Festival of Weeks. At that time bring to him a free-will offering proportionate in size to his blessing upon you as judged by the amount of your harvest.

Another celebration, the Festival of Shelters, must be observed for seven days at the end of the harvest season, after the grain is threshed and the grapes have been pressed.

This feast will be held at the sanctuary, which will be located at the place the Lord will designate. It is a time of deep thanksgiving to the Lord for blessing you with a good harvest and in so many other ways; it shall be a time of great joy.

Every man in Israel shall appear before the Lord your God three times a year at the sanctuary for these festivals: The Festival of Unleavened Bread, The Festival of Weeks, The Festival of Shelters.

On each of these occasions bring a gift to the Lord. Give as you are able, according as the Lord has blessed you.

Deuteronomy 16:1-2, 8-10, 13, 15-17

139

Catch THIS

The **names** of these festivals might seem a bit **bizarre** to us, but they were very important to the people of Israel. The word "festival" is taken from a Hebrew word that means "to **celebrate**." These festivals were commanded by God for the Israelites to take time from their busy schedules and give thanks to Him.

Unfortunately, we have an absence of celebration in our world today. We have lots of parties but not true celebration. Most of today's parties don't **honor** God; they honor the god of alcohol. They're celebrations in disguise–they give momentary happiness. Once the party is over and the buzz wears off, the people start to look for a new high the next day.

You can **celebrate** in a new way. Celebration is giving thanks for all God has done in your life. Create your own festivals and wake up each morning thanking God for all He is and all He has done in your life. You'll be a **different** person if you learn how to celebrate at the party that never ends.

:00
:10
:20
:30
:40
:50
:60
done

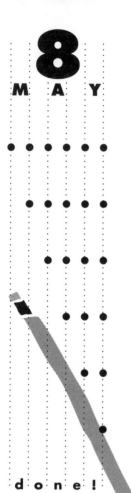

8

MAY

• • • • • •

• • • • •

• • • •

• • •

• •

•

done!

Honor your father and mother (remember, this is a commandment of the Lord your God); if you do so, you shall have a long, prosperous life in the land he is giving you.

♦ Some Pharisees and other Jewish leaders now arrived from Jerusalem to interview Jesus.

"Why do your disciples disobey the ancient Jewish traditions?" they demanded. "For they ignore our ritual of ceremonial handwashing before they eat." He replied, "And why do your traditions violate the direct commandments of God? For instance, God's law is 'Honor your father and mother; anyone who reviles his parents must die.' But you say, 'Even if your parents are in need, you may give their support money to the church instead.' And so, by your man-made rule, you nullify the direct command of God to honor and care for your parents. You hypocrites! Well did Isaiah prophesy of you, 'These people say they honor me, but their hearts are far away. Their worship is worthless, for they teach their man-made laws instead of those from God.'"

Deuteronomy 5:16; Matthew 15:1-9

honor your mother

Give it a try

What are four qualities you like about your mother?

1 _____

2 _____

3 _____

4 _____

You can show her great **honor** by taking the time to let her know what you like about her. Through words or a letter you can give her a better gift than money could buy.

COMPASSION

Sing for joy, O heavens; shout, O earth. Break forth with song, O mountains, for the Lord has comforted his people and will have compassion upon them in their sorrow.

Yet they say, "My Lord deserted us; he has forgotten us."

Never! Can a mother forget her little child and not have love for her own son? Yet even if that should be, I will not forget you. See, I have tattooed your name upon my palm, and ever before me is a picture of Jerusalem's walls in ruins. Soon your rebuilders shall come and chase away all those destroying you. Look and see, for the Lord has vowed that all your enemies shall come and be your slaves. They will be as jewels to display, as bridal ornaments.

Even the most desolate parts of your abandoned land shall soon be crowded with your people, and your enemies who enslaved you shall be far away.

Isaiah 49:13-19

Just a thought

Moms are **famous** for the **incredible** love they show their children. Since **all** love originates with **God**, just think how much **more** God loves **you...**

"for love comes from God and those who are loving and kind show that they are the children of God." (1 John 4:7)

:00

:10

:20

:30

:40

:50

1:00

FINISH

141

A HAPPY MOTHER

WEIRD or what

:00

:10 Did you know that the **Psalms** were written to be **sung?** Music was both popular and **powerful** during biblical times. Moses **sang** and taught his followers to sing. The Israelites sang on their way to the **Promised** Land. Jesus sang with His disciples. Paul sang in jail. And you can just imagine how great the singing will be in **heaven.**

:20

:30

:40

:50 Since God isn't **concerned** about the quality of your voice, try singing a song of thanksgiving to God for giving you another day to **enjoy** His love.

:60

 end

Hallelujah! O servants of Jehovah, praise his name. Blessed is his name forever and forever. Praise him from sunrise to sunset! For he is high above the nations; his glory is far greater than the heavens.

Who can be compared with God enthroned on high? Far below him are the heavens and the earth; he stoops to look, and lifts the poor from the dirt and the hungry from the garbage dump, and sets them among princes! He gives children to the childless wife, so that she becomes a happy mother.

Hallelujah! Praise the Lord.

Psalm 113

142

A Mother's Teaching

Listen to your father and mother. What you learn from them will stand you in good stead; it will gain you many honors.

• These are the wise sayings of King Lemuel of Massa, taught to him at his mother's knee:

O my son, whom I have dedicated to the Lord, do not spend your time with women—the royal pathway to destruction.

And it is not for kings, O Lemuel, to drink wine and whiskey. For if they drink they may forget their duties and be unable to give justice to those who are oppressed. Hard liquor is for sick men at the brink of death, and wine for those in deep depression. Let them drink to forget their poverty and misery.

You should defend those who cannot help themselves. Yes, speak up for the poor and helpless, and see that they get justice.

Proverbs 1:8-9; 31:1-9

ONE MINUTE MEMORY

Listen to your father and mother. What you learn from them will stand you in good stead; it will gain you many honors.

Proverbs 1:8-9

:00

:15

:30

:45

:60

done

:OO

:1O

:2O

:3O

:4O

:5O

1:OO

FINISH

THE NOBLE WIFE: PART 1

A worthy wife is her husband's joy and crown; the other kind corrodes his strength and tears down everything he does.

♦ If you can find a truly good wife, she is worth more than precious gems! Her husband can trust her, and she will richly satisfy his needs. She will not hinder him but help him all her life. She finds wool and flax and busily spins it. She buys imported foods brought by ship from distant ports. She gets up before dawn to prepare breakfast for her household and plans the day's work for her servant girls. She goes out to inspect a field and buys it; with her own hands she plants a vineyard. She is energetic, a hard worker, and watches for bargains. She works far into the night!

She sews for the poor and generously helps those in need.

Proverbs 12:4; 31:10-20

the noble wife: part 2

If you can find a truly good wife, she is worth more than precious gems!

She has no fear of winter for her household, for she has made warm clothes for all of them. She also upholsters with finest tapestry; her own clothing is beautifully made—a purple gown of pure linen. Her husband is well known, for he sits in the council chamber with the other civic leaders. She makes belted linen garments to sell to the merchants.

She is a woman of strength and dignity and has no fear of old age. When she speaks, her words are wise, and kindness is the rule for everything she says. She watches carefully all that goes on throughout her household and is never lazy. Her children stand and bless her; so does her husband. He praises her with these words: "There are many fine women in the world, but you are the best of them all!" Charm can be deceptive and beauty doesn't last, but a woman who fears and reverences God shall be greatly praised. Praise her for the many fine things she does. These good deeds of hers shall bring her honor and recognition from people of importance.

♦ The man who finds a wife finds a good thing; she is a blessing to him from the Lord.

Proverbs 31:10, 21-31; 18:22

13
M A Y

d o n e !

These verses describe a woman who possesses godly qualities that make her shine with a new type of beauty.

If you are a **female**, write down three qualities from the passage that you would like to own in your life. Next to each quality write one goal that will help you develop that quality.

1 _____

2 _____

3 _____

If you are a **male**, write down three qualities you would like to see in the woman you marry. Then ask God to prepare you to be the kind of man who will bring out the inner beauty in your future wife.

CHECK IT OUT

YOUR MAKER IS YOUR HUSBAND

While we are alive we will **experience** times of pain, emptiness and sadness–everyone does. In the midst of pain, there is **hope** for those who have been promised eternal life. Check out the description of heaven from Revelation 21:2-4: "It was a **glorious** sight, beautiful as a bride at her wedding. I heard a loud shout from the throne saying, 'Look, the home of God is now among men, and he will live with them and they will be his people; yes, God himself will be among them. He will wipe away all tears from their eyes, and there shall be no more death, nor sorrow, nor crying, nor pain. All of that has gone forever.'"

God will be your husband, your wife, your everything. May this give you **hope** to keep living every day with the faith that you'll be in God's presence someday!

:00

:10

:20

:30

:40

:50

:60

d o n e

"Sing, O childless woman! Break out into loud and joyful song, Jerusalem, for she who was abandoned has more blessings now than she whose husband stayed! Enlarge your house; build on additions; spread out your home!

Fear not; you will no longer live in shame. The shame of your youth and the sorrows of widowhood will be remembered no more, for your Creator will be your "husband." The Lord Almighty is his name; he is your Redeemer, the Holy One of Israel, the God of all the earth. For the Lord has called you back from your grief—a young wife abandoned by her husband. For a brief moment I abandoned you. But with great compassion I will take you back. In a moment of anger I turned my face a little while; but with everlasting love I will have pity on you," says the Lord, your Redeemer.

Isaiah 54:1-2, 4-8

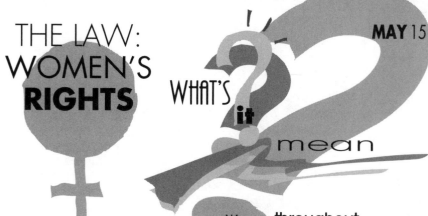

THE LAW: WOMEN'S **RIGHTS**

WHAT'S **it** 2 mean

If a man sells his daughter as a slave, she shall not be freed at the end of six years as the men are. If she does not please the man who bought her, then he shall let her be bought back again; but he has no power to sell her to foreigners, since he has wronged her by no longer wanting her after marrying her. And if he arranges an engagement between a Hebrew slave-girl and his son, then he may no longer treat her as a slave-girl, but must treat her as a daughter. If he himself marries her and then takes another wife, he may not reduce her food or clothing, or fail to sleep with her as his wife. If he fails in any of these three things, then she may leave freely without any payment.

♦ Do not violate your daughter's sanctity by making her a prostitute, lest the land become full of enormous wickedness.

♦ If a man's brother dies without a son, his widow must not marry outside the family; instead, her husband's brother must marry her and sleep with her. The first son she bears to him shall be counted as the son of the dead brother, so that his name will not be forgotten.

Exodus 21:7-11; Leviticus 19:29; Deuteronomy 25:5-6

Women **throughout** the Bible are found in **many** different roles and situations. During Old Testament times women weren't considered as important as men, so God made **laws** that sound very **strange** today to protect women. Both culture and family models were very male-centered. The woman's place was in the fields and home working long and hard hours cooking, grinding grain, and drawing water. The Law **shielded** women from the abuse ancient society often subjected them to.

The Old Testament Law is not the Bible's final word on women. Within the Bible we are blessed with some **incredible** exceptions to the ancient world's stereotype of women. Exceptional women such as **Miriam, Deborah, Huldah,** and **Esther** were political and religious **leaders** who led, served, and guided the nation as well as any man.

DONE

MAY

16

The Tabernacle

IN other words...

HIGH PRIEST

In the Old Testament, the high priest was the **greatest** of all priests and performed **sacrifices** to God on behalf of the people. In the New Testament, **Jesus** is given the title "High Priest" because He sacrificed His life on behalf of all people.

By understanding the **meaning** of this title, you can better appreciate that Jesus destroyed the power of sin in your life by dying on the cross. You can never thank God too many times for that ultimate sacrifice on your behalf. Go ahead, thank Him **one more time.**

:00

:10

:20

:30

:40

:50

:60   done

Now in that first agreement between God and his people there were rules for worship and there was a sacred tent down here on earth. Inside this place of worship there were two rooms. The first one contained the golden candlestick and a table with special loaves of holy bread upon it; this part was called the Holy Place. Then there was a curtain, and behind the curtain was a room called the Holy of Holies. In that room there were a golden incense-altar and the golden chest, called the ark of the covenant, completely covered on all sides with pure gold.

Well, when all was ready, the priests went in and out of the first room whenever they wanted to, doing their work. But only the high priest went into the inner room, and then only once a year, all alone, and always with blood that he sprinkled on the mercy seat as an offering to God to cover his own mistakes and sins and the mistakes and sins of all the people.

He came as High Priest of this better system that we now have. He went into that greater, perfect tabernacle in heaven, not made by men nor part of this world, and once for all took blood into that inner room, the Holy of Holies, and sprinkled it on the mercy seat; but it was not the blood of goats and calves. No, he took his own blood, and with it he, by himself, made sure of our eternal salvation.

Hebrews 9:1-4a, 6-7, 11-12

The Lord now spoke to Aaron: "You and your sons and your family are responsible for any desecration of the sanctuary," he said, "and will be held liable for any impropriety in your priestly work.

"Your kinsmen, the tribe of Levi, are your assistants; but only you and your sons may perform the sacred duties in the Tabernacle itself.

"Remember, only the priests are to perform the sacred duties within the sanctuary and at the altar. If you follow these instructions, the wrath of God will never again fall upon any of the people of Israel for violating this law. I say it again—your kinsmen the Levites are your assistants for the work of the Tabernacle. They are a gift to you from the Lord. But you and your sons, the priests, shall personally handle all the sacred service, including the altar and all that is within the veil, for the priesthood is your special gift of service. Anyone else who attempts to perform these duties shall die.

"Yes, I have given to you all of these 'wave offerings' brought by the people of Israel to the Lord; they are for you and your families as food; this is a permanent contract between the Lord and you and your descendants.

"You priests may own no property nor have any other income, for I am all that you need."

Numbers 18:1-2, 5-7, 19-20

:00 One of the **duties** of the high priest was to present **sacrifices.** Today, Christians are **also** called high priests because we

:10 also present sacrifices. Christians are called to give their **life** as a **living** sacrifice.

Check out Romans 12:1:

:20 "...I plead with you to give your bodies to God. Let them be a living sacrifice, holy–the kind

:30 he can accept."

This type of sacrifice **requires** us to present to God all that

:40 we are, into all that we know about God. This type of living sacrifice **shows** God that He is top priority in our lives.

:50 It's not the easiest sacrifice to make, but it sure pleases God.

Today, think about what a living sacrifice

:60 would mean with **your** life.

d o n e

149

WHAT'S it mean

DRIVING OUT THE NATIONS

When you read these types of Bible passages it's hard to imagine God possessing **mercy,** compassion, and love. But consider this: other nations served other gods–just like today. (For example: Japan serves Buddha; Palestine serves Allah, etc.) Israel traveled through nations that served other gods. When one nation conquered another, it was proof their nation's god was more **powerful.** War was common and if Israel didn't kill other nations they would have been killed or taken as slaves.

Today, those of us who believe in Jesus are a nation. There will come a day when we will be raised to **heaven** and made like Jesus. We are God's **children,** we are God's **army.** God is a God of love, mercy, and compassion, but there will come a time when He will **destroy** all who are not His nation.

What **nation** are you a citizen of?

When the Lord brings you into the Promised Land, as he soon will, he will destroy the following seven nations, all greater and mightier than you are: the Hittites, the Girgashites, the Amorites, the Canaanites, the Perizzites, the Hivites, the Jebusites.

When the Lord your God delivers them over to you to be destroyed, do a complete job of it—don't make any treaties or show them mercy; utterly wipe them out. Do not intermarry with them, nor let your sons and daughters marry their sons and daughters. That would surely result in your young people's beginning to worship their gods. Then the anger of the Lord would be hot against you, and he would surely destroy you.

You must break down the heathen altars and shatter the obelisks and cut up the shameful images and burn the idols.

For you are a holy people, dedicated to the Lord your God. He has chosen you from all the people on the face of the whole earth to be his own chosen ones. He didn't choose you and pour out his love upon you because you were a larger nation than any other, for you were the smallest of all! It was just because he loves you, and because he kept his promise to your ancestors. That is why he brought you out of slavery in Egypt with such amazing power and mighty miracles.

Deuteronomy 7:1-8

The Law: Not Too Difficult

ONE MINUTE MEMORY

Obeying these commandments is not something beyond your strength and reach; for these laws are not in the far heavens, so distant that you can't hear and obey them, and with no one to bring them down to you; nor are they beyond the ocean, so far that no one can bring you their message; but they are very close at hand—in your hearts and on your lips—so obey them.

Look, today I have set before you life and death, depending on whether you obey or disobey. I have commanded you today to love the Lord your God and to follow his paths and to keep his laws, so that you will live and become a great nation, and so that the Lord your God will bless you and the land you are about to possess. But if your hearts turn away and you won't listen—if you are drawn away to worship other gods— then I declare to you this day that you shall surely perish; you will not have a long, good life in the land you are going in to possess.

I call heaven and earth to witness against you that today I have set before you life or death, blessing or curse. Oh, that you would choose life; that you and your children might live! Choose to love the Lord your God and to obey him and to cling to him, for he is your life and the length of your days. You will then be able to live safely in the land the Lord promised your ancestors, Abraham, Isaac, and Jacob.

Deuteronomy 30:11-20

Choose to love the Lord your God and to obey him and to cling to him, for he is your life and the length of your days.

Deuteronomy 30:20a

:00

:15

:30

:45

:60

done

151

20 MAY

Sermon on the Mount: the Beatitudes

word

humble

Humble people have a proper perspective of themselves before God and other people. Humble people are **secure** in who they were created to be and don't need to bring attention to themselves. Unfortunately, a living example of humility is difficult to find.

The Bible says humble people are **fortunate.** They are fortunate because they're secure with themselves, and they understand the true greatness of God and don't **NEED** attention from others.

You'll never hear **humble** people tell you they're humble, but you would give them a great compliment if you appreciated their humility. Do this today and keep **watching** for humble examples, and be ready to learn from them.

One day as the crowds were gathering, he went up the hillside with his disciples and sat down and taught them there.

"Humble men are very fortunate!" he told them, "for the Kingdom of Heaven is given to them. Those who mourn are fortunate! for they shall be comforted. The meek and lowly are fortunate! for the whole wide world belongs to them.

Happy are those who long to be just and good, for they shall be completely satisfied. Happy are the kind and merciful, for they shall be shown mercy. Happy are those whose hearts are pure, for they shall see God. Happy are those who strive for peace—they shall be called the sons of God. Happy are those who are persecuted because they are good, for the Kingdom of Heaven is theirs."

Matthew 5:1-10

SALT & LIGHT

When you are reviled and persecuted and lied about because you are my followers—wonderful! Be happy about it! Be very glad! for a tremendous reward awaits you up in heaven. And remember, the ancient prophets were persecuted too.

You are the world's seasoning, to make it tolerable. If you lose your flavor, what will happen to the world? And you yourselves will be thrown out and trampled underfoot as worthless. You are the world's light—a city on a hill, glowing in the night for all to see. Don't hide your light! Let it shine for all; let your good deeds glow for all to see, so that they will praise your heavenly Father.

◆ For though once your heart was full of darkness, now it is full of light from the Lord, and your behavior should show it! Because of this light within you, you should do only what is good and right and true. Learn as you go along what pleases the Lord.

Matthew 5:11-16; Ephesians 5:8-10

Just a thought

Don't **hide** it! Let your **life shine!**

The world is filled with **darkness** and needs **you** to be a bright light **today.**

:00

:10

:20

:30

:40

:50

1:00

FINISH

153

personality Plus Pharisee

22 may

The Pharisees were a **very** respected and **influential** group of religious men. They were known for their **strict** commitment to following the Law **exactly** as it was written.

:00

:10

:20

They focused so much on **right** behavior that they missed the Scripture's revelation of Jesus as the Messiah. They started with good **intentions** but they became blind to what Jesus had to say. Jesus focused on the **heart** and they focused on actions. Jesus constantly battled with them and even called them **"painted tombs"** because they looked good on the outside (by doing the right actions), but they were dead on the inside (heart in the wrong place).

:30

:40

:50

:60

You can fool anyone with your spirituality... anyone **except** for God. God knows your heart and He knows the **real** you. If you're a modern-day Pharisee, take off your mask, get your **heart** right with God, and start **living**.

Don't misunderstand why I have come—it isn't to cancel the laws of Moses and the warnings of the prophets. No, I came to fulfill them and to make them all come true. With all the earnestness I have I say: Every law in the Book will continue until its purpose is achieved. And so if anyone breaks the least commandment and teaches others to, he shall be the least in the Kingdom of Heaven. But those who teach God's laws and obey them shall be great in the Kingdom of Heaven.

But I warn you—unless your goodness is greater than that of the Pharisees and other Jewish leaders, you can't get into the Kingdom of Heaven at all!

♦ So there is now no condemnation awaiting those who belong to Christ Jesus. For the power of the life-giving Spirit—and this power is mine through Christ Jesus—has freed me from the vicious circle of sin and death. We aren't saved from sin's grasp by knowing the commandments of God because we can't and don't keep them, but God put into effect a different plan to save us. He sent his own Son in a human body like ours—except that ours are sinful—and destroyed sin's control over us by giving himself as a sacrifice for our sins. So now we can obey God's laws if we follow after the Holy Spirit and no longer obey the old evil nature within us.

Matthew 5:17-20; Romans 8:1-4

the End

154

Sermon on the Mount: murder and hate

Under the laws of Moses the rule was, "If you murder, you must die." But I have added to that rule and tell you that if you are only angry, even in your own home, you are in danger of judgment! If you call your friend an idiot, you are in danger of being brought before the court. And if you curse him, you are in danger of the fires of hell.

So if you are standing before the altar in the Temple, offering a sacrifice to God, and suddenly remember that a friend has something against you, leave your sacrifice there beside the altar and go and apologize and be reconciled to him, and then come and offer your sacrifice to God. Come to terms quickly with your enemy before it is too late and he drags you into court and you are thrown into a debtor's cell, for you will stay there until you have paid the last penny.

♦ Anyone who says he is walking in the light of Christ but dislikes his fellow man is still in darkness. But whoever loves his fellow man is "walking in the light" and can see his way without stumbling around in darkness and sin. For he who dislikes his brother is wandering in spiritual darkness and doesn't know where he is going, for the darkness has made him blind so that he cannot see the way.

Matthew 5:21-26; 1 John 2:9-11

d o n e !

Give it a try

If you were to try to follow the teachings in today's reading, what should you do with your enemies or those you don't like?

_____

_____

What are the results of disliking another person according to 1 John 2:9-11?

_____

_____

:00

:10 The Old Testament was written in the **Hebrew** language. The Hebrew word used to describe sex outside of the marriage relationship (fornication) is **Zanah.** This word is used ninety-three times in the Old Testament. In the New Testament that same word is translated in the **Greek** language as **porneia,** which is the root word for pornography.

:20

:30

:40 The Bible has a lot to say about **sex.** Whether it's in Hebrew, Greek, or translated into English, it still says God **created** it, He sees it as good, and it's intended for **marriage.** Love in any language says the same thing...**wait** until you're married.

:50

:60

○ **end**

The laws of Moses said, "You shall not commit adultery." But I say: Anyone who even looks at a woman with lust in his eye has already committed adultery with her in his heart. So if your eye—even if it is your best eye! —causes you to lust, gouge it out and throw it away. Better for part of you to be destroyed than for all of you to be cast into hell. And if your hand—even your right hand—causes you to sin, cut it off and throw it away. Better that than find yourself in hell.

The law of Moses says, "If anyone wants to be rid of his wife, he can divorce her merely by giving her a letter of dismissal." But I say that a man who divorces his wife, except for fornication, causes her to commit adultery if she marries again. And he who marries her commits adultery.

♦ For God wants you to be holy and pure and to keep clear of all sexual sin so that each of you will marry in holiness and honor—not in lustful passion as the heathen do, in their ignorance of God and his ways.

And this also is God's will: that you never cheat in this matter by taking another man's wife because the Lord will punish you terribly for this, as we have solemnly told you before. For God has not called us to be dirty-minded and full of lust but to be holy and clean. If anyone refuses to live by these rules, he is not disobeying the rules of men but of God who gives his Holy Spirit to you.

Matthew 5:27-32; 1 Thessalonians 4:3-8

LOVE, NOT REVENGE

WHAT'S **it**
mean

The law of Moses says, "If a man gouges out another's eye, he must pay with his own eye. If a tooth gets knocked out, knock out the tooth of the one who did it." But I say: Don't resist violence! If you are slapped on one cheek, turn the other too. If you are ordered to court, and your shirt is taken from you, give your coat too. If the military demand that you carry their gear for a mile, carry it two. Give to those who ask, and don't turn away from those who want to borrow.

There is a saying, "Love your friends and hate your enemies." But I say: Love your enemies! Pray for those who persecute you! In that way you will be acting as true sons of your Father in heaven. For he gives his sunlight to both the evil and the good, and sends rain on the just and on the unjust too. If you love only those who love you, what good is that? Even scoundrels do that much. If you are friendly only to your friends, how are you different from anyone else? Even the heathen do that. But you are to be perfect, even as your Father in heaven is perfect.

♦ Dear friends, let us practice loving each other, for love comes from God and those who are loving and kind show that they are the children of God, and that they are getting to know him better. But if a person isn't loving and kind, it shows that he doesn't know God—for God is love.

Matthew 5:38-48; 1 John 4:7-8

During the **Sermon** on the Mount, Jesus brings some additions to the Old Testament Law. He **challenges** people to take the Law one step further. These steps are no "baby steps," they are huge jumps! He does this six times in the fifth chapter of Matthew. Here are two examples in addition to the two in today's reading:

Old Law #1:
If you kill you die (v. 21)

New Law #1:
But I say: if you are angry you are in danger of judgment (v. 22)

Old Law #2:
You shall not commit adultery (v. 27)

New Law #2:
But I say: anyone who lusts has already committed adultery in his heart (v. 28)

Jesus is concerned about your heart. Actions without proper **motives** in the **heart** are empty actions. Check yourself today and if you need a little help, ask God to perform "heart surgery" on you.

DONE

TREASURE IN HEAVEN

Churches, various ministries, and Christian service organizations wouldn't have to waste their time raising money if God's people would give. These **ministries** could spend their fundraising time trying to change the world. But the world is filled with more takers than givers and, unfortunately, not all Christians are free from this selfish attitude.

During Old Testament times, people were **required** by law to give a tenth (called a tithe) of their money to God's work. But, in the New Testament, Jesus is more concerned about the **attitude** of our heart when we give than He is with the amount. The Bible teaches that the cheerful givers are the ones God appreciates (2 Corinthians 9:7).

Giving demonstrates obedience to God. Be guaranteed that God will **honor** your giving, your faithfulness, and your heart. He will take care of you...**put Him to the test.**

:00
:10
:20
:30
:40
:50
:60
done

Take care! Don't do your good deeds publicly, to be admired, for then you will lose the reward from your Father in heaven. When you give a gift to a beggar, don't shout about it as the hypocrites do—blowing trumpets in the synagogues and streets to call attention to their acts of charity! I tell you in all earnestness, they have received all the reward they will ever get. But when you do a kindness to someone, do it secretly—don't tell your left hand what your right hand is doing. And your Father, who knows all secrets, will reward you.

Don't store up treasures here on earth where they can erode away or may be stolen. Store them in heaven where they will never lose their value and are safe from thieves. If your profits are in heaven, your heart will be there too.

If your eye is pure, there will be sunshine in your soul. But if your eye is clouded with evil thoughts and desires, you are in deep spiritual darkness. And oh, how deep that darkness can be!

You cannot serve two masters: God and money. For you will hate one and love the other, or else the other way around.

Matthew 6:1-4, 19-24

PRAYER

Just a thought

Αnd now about prayer. When you pray, don't be like the hypocrites who pretend piety by praying publicly on street corners and in the synagogues where everyone can see them. Truly, that is all the reward they will ever get. But when you pray, go away by yourself, all alone, and shut the door behind you and pray to your Father secretly, and your Father, who knows your secrets, will reward you.

Don't recite the same prayer over and over as the heathen do, who think prayers are answered only by repeating them again and again. Remember, your Father knows exactly what you need even before you ask him!

Pray along these lines: "Our Father in heaven, we honor your holy name. We ask that your kingdom will come now. May your will be done here on earth, just as it is in heaven. Give us our food again today, as usual, and forgive us our sins, just as we have forgiven those who have sinned against us. Don't bring us into temptation, but deliver us from the Evil One. Amen." Your heavenly Father will forgive you if you forgive those who sin against you; but if you refuse to forgive them, he will not forgive you.

Matthew 6:5-15

If you don't know what to **say** or how to **pray,** don't worry. Talk to God **like a friend.**

He **hears** your prayers, and He doesn't give you a grade on how "good" it is. Your words directed toward God will **always** make **sense** to Him.

:00

:10

:20

:30

:40

:50

1:00

FINISH

WHAT'S **it** mean

FASTING
FASTING
FASTING

Fasting is going **without** food or drink for a period of time. During biblical times, fasting was done for a variety of reasons. Today, the most **common** description of fasting is related to a spiritual discipline. The discipline is to spend extra time **focusing** on God and giving Him priority over food. People who fast may spend time in prayer during the times they would normally eat.

Before you try to fast, discuss it further with your parents or pastor to better understand the **spiritual** reasoning as well as the **health** precautions. Whether you fast or not, be reminded that Jesus is focusing on the **motives** of your heart. He knows your heart...He knows the **real you!**

And now about fasting. When you fast, declining your food for a spiritual purpose, don't do it publicly, as the hypocrites do, who try to look wan and disheveled so people will feel sorry for them. Truly, that is the only reward they will ever get. But when you fast, put on festive clothing, so that no one will suspect you are hungry, except your Father who knows every secret. And he will reward you.

♦ John's disciples and the Jewish leaders sometimes fasted, that is, went without food as part of their religion. One day some people came to Jesus and asked why his disciples didn't do this too.

Jesus replied, "Do friends of the bridegroom refuse to eat at the wedding feast? Should they be sad while he is with them? But some day he will be taken away from them, and then they will mourn. (Besides, going without food is part of the old way of doing things.) It is like patching an old garment with unshrunk cloth! What happens? The patch pulls away and leaves the hole worse than before. You know better than to put new wine into old wineskins. They would burst. The wine would be spilled out and the wineskins ruined. New wine needs fresh wineskins."

Matthew 6:16-18; Mark 2:18-22

160

Sermon on the Mount: Why Worry?

So my counsel is: Don't worry about things—food, drink, and clothes. For you already have life and a body—and they are far more important than what to eat and wear. Look at the birds! They don't worry about what to eat—they don't need to sow or reap or store up food—for your heavenly Father feeds them. And you are far more valuable to him than they are. Will all your worries add a single moment to your life?

And why worry about your clothes? Look at the field lilies! They don't worry about theirs. Yet King Solomon in all his glory was not clothed as beautifully as they. And if God cares so wonderfully for flowers that are here today and gone tomorrow, won't he more surely care for you, O men of little faith?

So don't worry at all about having enough food and clothing. Why be like the heathen? For they take pride in all these things and are deeply concerned about them. But your heavenly Father already knows perfectly well that you need them, and he will give them to you if you give him first place in your life and live as he wants you to.

So don't be anxious about tomorrow. God will take care of your tomorrow too. Live one day at a time.

Matthew 6:25-34

So don't be anxious about tomorrow. God will take care of your tomorrow too. Live one day at a time.

Matthew 6:34

:00

:15

:30

:45

:60

161

MAY
30

JUDGING
AND
ASKING

:00

:10 The word **"hypocrite"** **once** meant to "act out the part of a **character** in a play." During ancient times, actors covered their faces with masks

:20 representing the character they were playing.

:30 In **today's** world, a hypocrite is one who covers his real self and "acts" as a different person. This person is better known as a **fake.**

:40 You can always fool an audience, but God wrote the script, created the characters, and knows **everything** about the

:50 play. God created you just as He wants you to be. If you're wearing a mask, try taking it off. You'll enjoy life

:60 a lot better when you show **the real you.**

end

Don't criticize, and then you won't be criticized. For others will treat you as you treat them. And why worry about a speck in the eye of a brother when you have a board in your own? Should you say, "Friend, let me help you get that speck out of your eye," when you can't even see because of the board in your own? Hypocrite! First get rid of the board. Then you can see to help your brother.

Don't give holy things to depraved men. Don't give pearls to swine! They will trample the pearls and turn and attack you.

Ask, and you will be given what you ask for. Seek, and you will find. Knock, and the door will be opened. For everyone who asks, receives. Anyone who seeks, finds. If only you will knock, the door will open. If a child asks his father for a loaf of bread, will he be given a stone instead? If he asks for fish, will he be given a poisonous snake? Of course not! And if you hardhearted, sinful men know how to give good gifts to your children, won't your Father in heaven even more certainly give good gifts to those who ask him for them?

Do for others what you want them to do for you. This is the teaching of the laws of Moses in a nutshell.

Matthew 7:1-12

162

THE TWO WAYS

Heaven can be entered only through the narrow gate! The highway to hell is broad, and its gate is wide enough for all the multitudes who choose its easy way. But the Gateway to Life is small, and the road is narrow, and only a few ever find it.

Not all who sound religious are really godly people. They may refer to me as "Lord," but still won't get to heaven. For the decisive question is whether they obey my Father in heaven. At the Judgment many will tell me, "Lord, Lord, we told others about you and used your name to cast out demons and to do many other great miracles." But I will reply, "You have never been mine. Go away, for your deeds are evil."

All who listen to my instructions and follow them are wise, like a man who builds his house on solid rock. Though the rain comes in torrents, and the floods rise and the storm winds beat against his house, it won't collapse, for it is built on rock.

But those who hear my instructions and ignore them are foolish, like a man who builds his house on sand. For when the rains and floods come, and storm winds beat against his house, it will fall with a mighty crash.

The crowds were amazed at Jesus' sermons, for he taught as one who had great authority, and not as their Jewish leaders.

Matthew 7:13-14, 21-29

Just a thought

When **Jesus** finished speaking, the **crowds** were **amazed!** People came from **everywhere** to hear Him speak, and He **continually** amazed them.

Now, as God, **He amazes** those of us who remain on **earth.**

:00
:10
:20
:30
:40
:50
1:00

FINISH

JUN

When you read God's word, you must constantly be saying to yourself, "It is talking to me, and about me."

**Soren Kierkegaard
(1813-1855)**
Danish Philosopher

THE GOLDEN CALF

Catch T·H·I·S

When Moses didn't come back down the mountain right away, the people went to Aaron. "Look," they said, "make us a god to lead us, for this fellow Moses who brought us here from Egypt has disappeared; something must have happened to him."

"Give me your gold earrings," Aaron replied.

So they all did—men and women, boys and girls. Aaron melted the gold, then molded and tooled it into the form of a calf. The people exclaimed, "O Israel, this is the god that brought you out of Egypt!"

When Aaron saw how happy the people were about it, he built an altar before the calf and announced, "Tomorrow there will be a feast to Jehovah!"

So they were up early the next morning and began offering burnt offerings and peace offerings to the calf-idol; afterwards they sat down to feast and drink at a wild party, followed by sexual immorality.

Then the Lord told Moses, "Quick! Go on down, for your people that you brought from Egypt have defiled themselves, and have quickly abandoned all my laws. They have molded themselves a calf, and worshiped it, and sacrificed to it, and said, 'This is your god, O Israel, that brought you out of Egypt.'"

Then the Lord said, "I have seen what a stubborn, rebellious lot these people are. Now let me alone and my anger shall blaze out against them and destroy them all; and I will make you, Moses, into a great nation instead of them."

Exodus 32:1-10

:00
:10
:20
:30
:40
:50
:60
done

Moses was a great leader! He accomplished amazing things with a group of people who weren't good at following.

Today, our world is in desperate need of quality leaders but, unfortunately, we have a misunderstanding about leadership. We believe that effective leaders must have charisma. This description only fits one type of leader.

You can be a leader and stay completely "behind the scenes." The "unsung" leaders in your church may set up chairs, straighten the church building, or cut out paper figurines for the Sunday school class. These people are leaders because they're used by God to do His work.

Jesus gave us a new standard for leadership when He came into the world. He showed us the true heart of leadership: **servanthood.** When you serve others you are displaying leadership gifts. God's work needs all kinds of leaders, especially servant-leaders. One of those leaders looks **just like you.**

2 JUN

Moses Pleads
for the Israelites

BIG time
word

INTERCESSORY
PRAYER

When Moses **begged** God on behalf of the Israelites, he was **praying** or pleading for their own good. Today, this type of prayer is called **intercessory prayer.** You perform intercessory prayer when you pray for someone else.

Also, the Holy Spirit intercedes on your behalf. Check it out:

"The Holy Spirit prays for us with such feeling that it cannot be expressed in words. And the Father who knows all hearts knows, of course, what the Spirit is saying as he pleads for us in harmony with God's own will."
(Romans 8:26b-27)

God **hears** your prayers on behalf of the people that you pray for, and God hears the prayers of the Holy Spirit who pleads for you. Put God's **ears** to the test today on behalf of someone you know and care for.

But Moses begged God not to do it. "Lord," he pleaded, "why is your anger so hot against your own people whom you brought from the land of Egypt with such great power and mighty miracles? Do you want the Egyptians to say, 'God tricked them into coming to the mountains so that he could slay them, destroying them from off the face of the earth'? Turn back from your fierce wrath. Turn away from this terrible evil you are planning against your people! Remember your promise to your servants—to Abraham, Isaac, and Israel. For you swore by your own self, 'I will multiply your posterity as the stars of heaven, and I will give them all of this land I have promised to your descendants, and they shall inherit it forever.'"

So the Lord changed his mind and spared them.

Then Moses went down the mountain, holding in his hands the Ten Commandments written on both sides of two stone tablets. (God himself had written the commandments on the tablets.)

When they came near the camp, Moses saw the calf and the dancing, and in terrible anger he threw the tablets to the ground, and they lay broken at the foot of the mountain. He took the calf and melted it in the fire, and when the metal cooled, he ground it into powder and spread it upon the water and made the people drink it.

Exodus 32:11-16, 19-20

168

ONE MINUTE MEMORY

Israel's History Is Our Warning

For we must never forget, dear brothers, what happened to our people in the wilderness long ago. God guided them by sending a cloud that moved along ahead of them; and he brought them all safely through the waters of the Red Sea. And by a miracle God sent them food to eat and water to drink there in the desert; they drank the water that Christ gave them. He was there with them as a mighty Rock of spiritual refreshment. Yet after all this most of them did not obey God, and he destroyed them in the wilderness.

All these things happened to them as examples—as object lessons to us—to warn us against doing the same things; they were written down so that we could read about them and learn from them in these last days as the world nears its end.

So be careful. If you are thinking, "Oh, I would never behave like that"—let this be a warning to you. For you too may fall into sin. But remember this—the wrong desires that come into your life aren't anything new and different. Many others have faced exactly the same problems before you. And no temptation is irresistible. You can trust God to keep the temptation from becoming so strong that you can't stand up against it, for he has promised this and will do what he says. He will show you how to escape temptation's power so that you can bear up patiently against it.

1 Corinthians 10:1, 3-5, 11-13

> You can trust God to keep the temptation from becoming so strong that you can't stand up against it, for he has promised this and will do what he says. He will show you how to escape temptation's power so that you can bear up patiently against it.
>
> 1 Corinthians 10:13b

:00

:15

:30

:45

:60

done

IN other words...

REPENT

The word "repent" means to **confess** to God that you've **sinned** and then change your mind so you won't do that sin again. Repentance is more than confession, it means to **change** the direction of your life and to **STOP PRACTICING** the sins you've confessed.

Jesus **forgave** a woman who was caught in adultery. As she left His presence, Jesus said to her, "Go and sin no more." Her repentance required **more** than simply receiving forgiveness; it also included a radical **change** in her life.

Do **you** have an area of your life where you need to repent? Remember, it's "confess" and "change." Be sorry enough about your sin to **stop sinning!**

:00
:10
:20
:30
:40
:50
:60   **done**

The Lord told Moses, "Prepare two stone tablets like the first ones, and I will write upon them the same commands that were on the tablets you broke.

So Moses took two tablets of stone like the first ones, and was up early and climbed Mount Sinai, as the Lord had told him to, taking the two stone tablets in his hands.

Then the Lord descended in the form of a pillar of cloud and stood there with him, and passed in front of him and announced the meaning of his name. "I am Jehovah, the merciful and gracious God," he said, "slow to anger and rich in steadfast love and truth. I, Jehovah, show this steadfast love to many thousands by forgiving their sins; or else I refuse to clear the guilty, and require that a father's sins be punished in the sons and grandsons, and even later generations."

Moses fell down before the Lord and worshiped. And he said, "If it is true that I have found favor in your sight, O Lord, then please go with us to the Promised Land; yes, it is an unruly, stubborn people, but pardon our iniquity and our sins, and accept us as your own."

The Lord replied, "All right, this is the contract I am going to make with you. I will do miracles such as have never been done before anywhere in all the earth, and all the people of Israel shall see the power of the Lord—the terrible power I will display through you."

Exodus 34:1, 4-10

170

GOD IS COMPASSIONATE

Do not be like your fathers and brothers who sinned against the Lord God of their fathers and were destroyed. Do not be stubborn, as they were, but yield yourselves to the Lord and come to his Temple which he has sanctified forever, and worship the Lord your God so that his fierce anger will turn away from you. For if you turn to the Lord again, your brothers and your children will be treated mercifully by their captors, and they will be able to return to this land. For the Lord your God is full of kindness and mercy and will not continue to turn away his face from you if you return to him.

♦ Jehovah is kind and merciful, slow to get angry, full of love. He is good to everyone, and his compassion is intertwined with everything he does.

♦ What a wonderful God we have—he is the Father of our Lord Jesus Christ, the source of every mercy, and the one who so wonderfully comforts and strengthens us in our hardships and trials. And why does he do this? So that when others are troubled, needing our sympathy and encouragement, we can pass on to them this same help and comfort God has given us. You can be sure that the more we undergo sufferings for Christ, the more he will shower us with his comfort and encouragement.

2 Chronicles 30:7-9; Psalm 145:8-9;
2 Corinthians 1:3-5

5

JUN

Just a thought

God won't allow more to be put **"on you"** than He puts **"in you"** to deal with the **temptation** that comes your way.

:00

:10

:20

:30

:40

:50

1:00

FINISH

Catch
T·H·I·S

GOD IS FORGIVING

There are few things more **mind-blowing** than God's forgiveness. God **forgives** us over and over. Do you ever wonder why He doesn't get tired of forgiving just you? Well, add the times He's forgiven you to the times He's forgiven 40 billion other people...that's **a lot** of **forgiveness**.

In **addition** to God's forgiveness, He instructs us to forgive and **keep** forgiving. We can't expect God to forgive us if we aren't willing to forgive others. Jesus said, "Your heavenly Father will forgive you if you forgive those who sin against you; but if you refuse to forgive them, he will not forgive you." It's clear cut! If we want to be forgiven, **we must forgive others**.

After you've confessed your sins to God, **rest** in the truth that He delights in forgiving and forgetting your sins. He's absent-minded when it comes to your confessed sins. There's great **freedom** and hope in that truth...as long as you've forgiven others. Do you have any forgiving you need to do **today**?

:00

:10

:20

:30

:40

:50

:60
done

Where is another God like you, who pardons the sins of the survivors among his people? You cannot stay angry with your people, for you love to be merciful. Once again you will have compassion on us. You will tread our sins beneath your feet; you will throw them into the depths of the ocean! You will bless us as you promised Jacob long ago. You will set your love upon us, as you promised our father Abraham!

◆ This is the message God has given us to pass on to you: that God is Light and in him is no darkness at all. So if we say we are his friends but go on living in spiritual darkness and sin, we are lying. But if we are living in the light of God's presence, just as Christ does, then we have wonderful fellowship and joy with each other, and the blood of Jesus his Son cleanses us from every sin.

If we say that we have no sin, we are only fooling ourselves and refusing to accept the truth. But if we confess our sins to him, he can be depended on to forgive us and to cleanse us from every wrong. (And it is perfectly proper for God to do this for us because Christ died to wash away our sins.) If we claim we have not sinned, we are lying and calling God a liar, for he says we have sinned.

Micah 7:18-20; 1 John 1:5-10

172

How kind he is! How good he is! So merciful, this God of ours! The Lord protects the simple and the childlike; I was facing death, and then he saved me. Now I can relax. For the Lord has done this wonderful miracle for me.

◆ But God is so rich in mercy; he loved us so much that even though we were spiritually dead and doomed by our sins, he gave us back our lives again when he raised Christ from the dead—only by his undeserved favor have we ever been saved—and lifted us up from the grave into glory along with Christ, where we sit with him in the heavenly realms—all because of what Christ Jesus did. And now God can always point to us as examples of how very, very rich his kindness is, as shown in all he has done for us through Jesus Christ.

Because of his kindness, you have been saved through trusting Christ. And even trusting is not of yourselves; it too is a gift from God. Salvation is not a reward for the good we have done, so none of us can take any credit for it.

Psalm 116:5-7; Ephesians 2:4-9

IN other words...
GRACE

The word "grace" is one of the greatest words you could ever learn within the Christian faith. Grace is best defined by the words undeserved favor. The gift is God's love. His love never stops! This gift keeps giving.

There is nothing you have done or can do to deserve God's grace. You can't work for it, earn it, achieve it, or buy it. All you can do is receive it. It's free! What a gift!

When you sense God's love today, stop for a moment and thank Him for His free gift of grace.

:00

:10

:20

:30

:40

:50

done :60

WHAT'S it mean 2

GOD IS HOLY

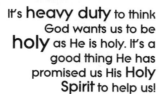

For I am the Lord who brought you out of the land of Egypt to be your God. You must therefore be holy, for I am holy.

♦ The year King Uzziah died I saw the Lord! He was sitting on a lofty throne, and the Temple was filled with his glory. Hovering about him were mighty, six-winged angels of fire. With two of their wings they covered their faces with two others they covered their feet, and with two they flew. In a great antiphonal chorus they sang, "Holy, holy, holy is the Lord Almighty; the whole earth is filled with his glory."

It's **heavy duty** to think God wants us to be **holy** as He is holy. It's a good thing He has promised us His **Holy Spirit** to help us!

God calls us to be holy or **"set apart."** Being "set apart" means to be **"different"** than the things of the world. For example, if your friends plan on doing something bad, and you're trying to be holy, you wouldn't be a part of their bad plans. You would set yourself apart from them and you would **be** different.

Holiness is hating that which is evil and trying to live a life pleasing to God. **Ask** God to help you **live** a life that is set apart **today.**

♦ The high and lofty One who inhabits eternity, the Holy One, says this: I live in that high and holy place where those with contrite, humble spirits dwell; and I refresh the humble and give new courage to those with repentant hearts. For I will not fight against you forever, nor always show my wrath; if I did, all mankind would perish—the very souls that I have made.

♦ Obey God because you are his children; don't slip back into your old ways—doing evil because you knew no better. But be holy now in everything you do, just as the Lord is holy, who invited you to be his child. He himself has said, "You must be holy, for I am holy."

Leviticus 11:45; Isaiah 6:1-3; 57:15-16; 1 Peter 1:14-16

Jehovah personality plus

O God enthroned in heaven, I lift my eyes to you.

We look to Jehovah our God for his mercy and kindness just as a servant keeps his eyes upon his master or a slave girl watches her mistress for the slightest signal.

Have mercy on us, Lord, have mercy. For we have had our fill of contempt and of the scoffing of the rich and proud.

♦ Once you were under God's curse, doomed forever for your sins. You went along with the crowd and were just like all the others, full of sin, obeying Satan, the mighty prince of the power of the air, who is at work right now in the hearts of those who are against the Lord. All of us used to be just as they are, our lives expressing the evil within us, doing every wicked thing that our passions or our evil thoughts might lead us into. We started out bad, being born with evil natures, and were under God's anger just like everyone else.

But God is so rich in mercy; he loved us so much that even though we were spiritually dead and doomed by our sins, he gave us back our lives again when he raised Christ from the dead—only by his undeserved favor have we ever been saved.

Psalm 123:1-4; Ephesians 2:1-5

Jehovah is one of the **common** names of God during the Old Testament times. Jehovah was most commonly referred to as God's **personal** name. The name Jehovah is really an **English** word used to translate and pronounce God's Hebrew name: JHWH. The word JHWH has no **vowels** and probably could be better enunciated as **Yahweh** rather than Jehovah.

God is given **several** different names throughout the Bible. Though His names may have changed, His character, His abilities, and the way in which He loves His creation has stayed consistent. That's **news** worthy of your celebration **today!**

:00

:10

:20

:30

:40

:50

:60

the End

10

Then Job replied to God:
"I know that you can do anything and that no one can stop you."

♦ Power belongs to God! His majesty shines down on Israel; his strength is mighty in the heavens. What awe we feel, kneeling here before him in the sanctuary. The God of Israel gives strength and mighty power to his people. Blessed be God!

♦ O Lord God! You have made the heavens and earth by your great power; nothing is too hard for you! You are loving and kind to thousands, yet children suffer for their fathers' sins; you are the great and mighty God, the Lord Almighty. You have all wisdom and do great and mighty miracles; for your eyes are open to all the ways of men, and you reward everyone according to his life and deeds.

♦ O Lord, you are worthy to receive the glory and the honor and the power, for you have created all things. They were created and called into being by your act of will.

Job 42:1-2; Psalm 68:34-35; Jeremiah 32:17-19; Revelation 4:11

God is all-powerful

done!

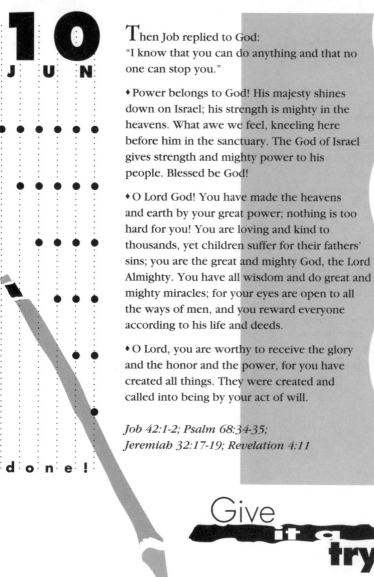

Give it a try

God is worthy of your honor and praise. List **five** creations of God that you are thankful for.

1
2
3
4
5

176

GOD IS EVERYWHERE

I can never be lost to your Spirit! I can never get away from my God! If I go up to heaven, you are there; if I go down to the place of the dead, you are there. If I ride the morning winds to the farthest oceans, even there your hand will guide me, your strength will support me. If I try to hide in the darkness, the night becomes light around me. For even darkness cannot hide from God; to you the night shines as bright as day. Darkness and light are both alike to you.

♦ Am I a God who is only in one place and cannot see what they are doing? Can anyone hide from me? Am I not everywhere in all of heaven and earth?

♦ He told his disciples, "I have been given all authority in heaven and earth. Therefore go and make disciples in all the nations, baptizing them into the name of the Father and of the Son and of the Holy Spirit, and then teach these new disciples to obey all the commands I have given you; and be sure of this—that I am with you always, even to the end of the world."

Psalm 139:7-12; Jeremiah 23:23-24; Matthew 28:18-20

Just a thought

Have you ever played hide-and-seek and hid so well that your friends gave up looking for you?

Well, there is nowhere you could go to hide from the love of God.

:00
:10
:20
:30
:40
:50
1:00
FINISH

177

JUN

O Lord, you have examined my heart and know everything about me. You know when I sit or stand. When far away you know my every thought. You chart the path ahead of me and tell me where to stop and rest. Every moment you know where I am. You know what I am going to say before I even say it. You both precede and follow me and place your hand of blessing on my head.

This is too glorious, too wonderful to believe!

For whatever God says to us is full of living power: it is sharper than the sharpest dagger, cutting swift and deep into our innermost thoughts and desires with all their parts, exposing us for what we really are.

Hebrews 4:12

:00

:15

:30

:45

:60

♦ Oh, what a wonderful God we have! How great are his wisdom and knowledge and riches! How impossible it is for us to understand his decisions and his methods! For who among us can know the mind of the Lord? Everything lives by his power, and everything is for his glory. To him be glory evermore.

♦ For whatever God says to us is full of living power: it is sharper than the sharpest dagger, cutting swift and deep into our innermost thoughts and desires with all their parts, exposing us for what we really are. He knows about everyone, everywhere. Everything about us is bare and wide open to the all-seeing eyes of our living God; nothing can be hidden from him to whom we must explain all that we have done.

Psalm 139:1-6;
Romans 11:33-34a, 36b;
Hebrews 4:12-13

178

O Israel, listen: Jehovah is our God, Jehovah alone.

♦ The Lord shall be King over all the earth. In that day there shall be one Lord—his name alone will be worshiped.

♦ And does God save only the Jews in this way? No, the Gentiles, too, may come to him in this same manner. God treats us all the same; all, whether Jews or Gentiles, are acquitted if they have faith.

♦ According to some people, there are a great many gods, both in heaven and on earth. But we know that there is only one God, the Father, who created all things and made us to be his own; and one Lord Jesus Christ, who made everything and gives us life.

♦ We are all parts of one body, we have the same Spirit, and we have all been called to the same glorious future. For us there is only one Lord, one faith, one baptism, and we all have the same God and Father who is over us all and in us all, and living through every part of us.

Deuteronomy 6:4; Zechariah 14:9; Romans 3:29-30; 1 Corinthians 8:5-6; Ephesians 4:4-6

:00 When Jesus was asked which of the Ten Commandments was the most important He said,

"The one that says, The Lord our God is the one and only God. And you must love him with all your heart and soul and mind and strength" (Mark 12:29-30).

:10

:20

There's no question as to the importance of loving God and God only. This truth may come into opposition with friends from other religions who worship other gods. The Bible is **clear** about loving only God. Check out Isaiah 44:6, 8:

:30

:40

"I am the First and Last; there is no other God...You are my witnesses–is there any other God? No! None that I know about!"

:50

:60 This is an important truth for our faith. Talk to God today as your only God.

d o n e

personality plus King David

David was a man with great **strengths** who made some serious **mistakes**.

David's **strengths** were numerous: he was used by God to kill Goliath and claim victory for Israel; he displayed great acts of **friendship** with Jonathan; he was the most-loved **King** of Israel, and he wrote many of the Psalms in the Bible.

Opposing David's strengths was a weakness that involved obvious disobedience to God. David had sex with Bathsheba, the wife of one of his soldiers. Afterward, he arranged her husband's death so Bathsheba could become his own.

Though David's life was not perfect, God chose to use David's family line. When you hear about Jesus being born of the **Davidic line,** let it be a reminder of God's mercy in allowing David to be an **ancestor** of Jesus.

Demand justice for me, Lord! Gather all peoples before you; sit high above them, judging their sins. But justify me publicly; establish my honor and truth before them all. End all wickedness, O Lord, and bless all who truly worship God; for you, the righteous God, look deep within the hearts of men and examine all their motives and their thoughts.

♦ "For the time is coming," says the Lord, "when I will place a righteous Branch upon King David's throne. He shall be a King who shall rule with wisdom and justice and cause righteousness to prevail everywhere throughout the earth. And this is his name: The Lord Our Righteousness. At that time Judah will be saved and Israel will live in peace.

♦ My little children, I am telling you this so that you will stay away from sin. But if you sin, there is someone to plead for you before the Father. His name is Jesus Christ, the one who is all that is good and who pleases God completely. He is the one who took God's wrath against our sins upon himself and brought us into fellowship with God; and he is the forgiveness for our sins, and not only ours but all the world's.

Psalm 7:6b-9; Jeremiah 23:5-6; 1 John 2:1-2

:00

:10

:20

:30

:40

:50

:60

the End

180

OUR HEAVENLY
FATHER

For now we are all children of God through faith in Jesus Christ, and we who have been baptized into union with Christ are enveloped by him. We are no longer Jews or Greeks or slaves or free men or even merely men or women, but we are all the same—we are Christians; we are one in Christ Jesus. And now that we are Christ's we are the true descendants of Abraham, and all of God's promises to him belong to us.

♦ We were slaves to Jewish laws and rituals, for we thought they could save us. But when the right time came, the time God decided on, he sent his Son, born of a woman, born as a Jew, to buy freedom for us who were slaves to the law so that he could adopt us as his very own sons. And because we are his sons, God has sent the Spirit of his Son into our hearts, so now we can rightly speak of God as our dear Father. Now we are no longer slaves but God's own sons. And since we are his sons, everything he has belongs to us, for that is the way God planned.

♦ See how very much our heavenly Father loves us, for he allows us to be called his children—think of it—and we really are! But since most people don't know God, naturally they don't understand that we are his children. Yes, dear friends, we are already God's children, right now, and we can't even imagine what it is going to be like later on.

Galatians 3:26-29; 4:2-7; 1 John 3:1-2a

Just a thought

Every day can be **Father's Day** when you focus on **God** as your **Heavenly Father** and **rejoice** over the fact that He **loves** you and accepts you **just** as **you are.**

15 JUN

:00

:10

:20

:30

:40

:50

1:00

FINISH

HONOR YOUR FATHER

Catch T·H·I·S

There is a way to celebrate Father's Day every day. It's a different type of celebration, for it doesn't celebrate our earthly fathers but rather God our Father.

We can...

1. CELEBRATE God the Father as our CREATOR. God made the delicate, inner parts of our body and knit us together in our mother's womb.
2. CELEBRATE God the Father as our COMFORTER. God will never let us down. People will always let us down, but God promises to comfort and care for us in every situation.
3. CELEBRATE God the Father as our CHALLENGER. God doesn't want us to "get stuck." He wants us to grow, change, and mature.

We can do this every day...

1. REJOICE in our CREATION by thanking God for our unique design and accepting ourselves as He created us.
2. RELAX in God's COMFORT. God loves us more than we love ourselves.
3. RUN with the CHALLENGE by taking "baby steps" toward maturity.

Celebrate this week by rejoicing, relaxing, and running. You'll get there!

:00

:10

:20

:30

:40

:50

:60
done

Honor your father and mother, that you may have a long, good life in the land the Lord your God will give you.

♦ It's no fun to be a rebel's father.

♦ My son, how I will rejoice if you become a man of common sense. Yes, my heart will thrill to your thoughtful, wise words.

O my son, be wise and stay in God's paths.

♦ Remember what Christ taught, and let his words enrich your lives and make you wise; teach them to each other and sing them out in psalms and hymns and spiritual songs, singing to the Lord with thankful hearts. And whatever you do or say, let it be as a representative of the Lord Jesus, and come with him into the presence of God the Father to give him your thanks.

You wives, submit yourselves to your husbands, for that is what the Lord has planned for you. And you husbands must be loving and kind to your wives and not bitter against them nor harsh.

You children must always obey your fathers and mothers, for that pleases the Lord. Fathers, don't scold your children so much that they become discouraged and quit trying.

Exodus 20:12;
Proverbs 17:21; 23:15-16, 19;
Colossians 3:16-21

A FATHER'S INSTRUCTION

CHECK IT OUT

17 JUN

Young men, listen to me as you would to your father. Listen, and grow wise, for I speak the truth—don't turn away. For I, too, was once a son, tenderly loved by my mother as an only child, and the companion of my father. He told me never to forget his words. "If you follow them," he said, "you will have a long and happy life. Learn to be wise," he said, "and develop good judgment and common sense! I cannot overemphasize this point." Cling to wisdom—she will protect you. Love her—she will guard you.

Getting wisdom is the most important thing you can do! And with your wisdom, develop common sense and good judgment. If you exalt wisdom, she will exalt you. Hold her fast, and she will lead you to great honor; she will place a beautiful crown upon your head. My son, listen to me and do as I say, and you will have a long, good life.

I would have you learn this great fact: that a life of doing right is the wisest life there is. If you live that kind of life, you'll not limp or stumble as you run.

Proverbs 4:1-12

:00

:10

:20

:30

:40

:50

:60

The Proverbs are filled with common sense wisdom. The following two selections from Proverbs have to do with the wisdom your parents will bring you: "Only fools refuse to be taught. Listen to your father and mother. What you learn from them will stand you in good stead; it will gain you many honors." (1:8-9)

"Obey your father and your mother. Take to heart all of their advice. Every day and all night long their counsel will lead you and save you from harm; when you wake up in the morning, let their instructions guide you into the new day." (6:20-22)

You may not like to hear this, but God gave you **parents** to guide and direct you. They'll never be perfect, but you'll please God and honor your parents when you hear their wisdom. **Keep listening.**

d o n e

A Father's Discipline

word

DIS**CIPLINE**

The word used in today's selection is **"punish."** Another word commonly used in this context is "correct." God corrects or disciplines those He loves. Discipline means **CORRECTION.**

God's discipline is to move us toward maturity, to correct us so we might be holier. Proverbs 10:17 says,

"Anyone willing to be corrected is on the pathway to life. Anyone refusing has lost his chance."

God **loves** us so much that He wants us to gain understanding and **celebrate** life. Be open to God's correction through **reading** the Bible, listening to the Holy Spirit, and learning from other Christians. Don't turn your back on correction. **Here's why:**

"If you refuse criticism you will end in poverty and disgrace; if you accept criticism you are on the road to fame." (Proverbs 13:18)

After all, you have never yet struggled against sin and temptation until you sweat great drops of blood.

And have you quite forgotten the encouraging words God spoke to you, his child? He said, "My son, don't be angry when the Lord punishes you. Don't be discouraged when he has to show you where you are wrong. For when he punishes you, it proves that he loves you. When he whips you, it proves you are really his child."

Let God train you, for he is doing what any loving father does for his children. Whoever heard of a son who was never corrected? If God doesn't punish you when you need it, as other fathers punish their sons, then it means that you aren't really God's son at all—that you don't really belong in his family. Since we respect our fathers here on earth, though they punish us, should we not all the more cheerfully submit to God's training so that we can begin really to live?

Our earthly fathers trained us for a few brief years, doing the best for us that they knew how, but God's correction is always right and for our best good, that we may share his holiness. Being punished isn't enjoyable while it is happening—it hurts! But afterwards we can see the result, a quiet growth in grace and character.

Hebrews 12:4-11

184

a faithful husband

Listen to me, my son! I know what I am saying; listen! Watch yourself, lest you be indiscreet and betray some vital information. For the lips of a prostitute are as sweet as honey, and smooth flattery is her stock in trade. But afterwards only a bitter conscience is left to you, sharp as a double-edged sword.

Drink from your own well, my son—be faithful and true to your wife. Why should you beget children with women of the street? Why share your children with those outside your home? Be happy, yes, rejoice in the wife of your youth. Let her breasts and tender embrace satisfy you. Let her love alone fill you with delight. Why delight yourself with prostitutes, embracing what isn't yours? For God is closely watching you, and he weighs carefully everything you do.

The wicked man is doomed by his own sins; they are ropes that catch and hold him. He shall die because he will not listen to the truth; he has let himself be led away into incredible folly.

Proverbs 5:1-4, 15-23

19 JUN

done!

These verses include a father's wisdom to his son. The father advises his son to be careful and faithful in his relationship to his wife.

Give it a try

If you are a **male,** write down three **qualities** you would like to have in your life before you are a husband. Next to each quality write one goal that will help you develop that quality.

1 _____
2 _____
3 _____

If you are a **female,** write down three qualities you would like to see in the **man** you marry. Then ask God to prepare you to be the kind of woman who will love and be faithful to her future husband.

185

LOVE SONG TO A HUSBAND

:00

:10

:20

:30

:40

:50

:60

end

Song of Songs is one of the most **confusing** and diversely interpreted **books** in the Bible. It contains sexual **lyrics**, a mysterious religious meaning, and an **intriguing** plot.

Song of Songs illustrates the **power** of human love. This love is a special gift from God. The book is filled with **a lot** of sexual allegories that will definitely grab your attention. Read it with an open mind and a heart to experience God's radical, yet **tender** love.

The Girl: "My lover is an apple tree, the finest in the orchard as compared with any of the other youths. I am seated in his much-desired shade and his fruit is lovely to eat. He brings me to the banquet hall, and everyone can see how much he loves me. Oh, feed me with your love—your 'raisins' and your 'apples'—for I am utterly lovesick. His left hand is under my head and with his right hand he embraces me."

The Girl: "Ah, I hear him—my beloved! Here he comes, leaping upon the mountains and bounding over the hills. My beloved is like a gazelle or young deer. Look, there he is behind the wall, now looking in at the windows.

"My beloved said to me, 'Rise up, my love, my fair one, and come away. For the winter is past, the rain is over and gone. The flowers are springing up and the time of the singing of birds has come. Yes, spring is here. The leaves are coming out, and the grapevines are in blossom. How delicious they smell! Arise, my love, my fair one, and come away.'"

Song of Songs 2:3-6, 8-13

HUSBANDS, LOVE YOUR WIVES

Husbands, show the same kind of love to your wives as Christ showed to the Church when he died for her, to make her holy and clean, washed by baptism and God's Word; so that he could give her to himself as a glorious Church without a single spot or wrinkle or any other blemish, being holy and without a single fault. That is how husbands should treat their wives, loving them as parts of themselves. For since a man and his wife are now one, a man is really doing himself a favor and loving himself when he loves his wife! No one hates his own body but lovingly cares for it, just as Christ cares for his body the Church, of which we are parts.

So again I say, a man must love his wife as a part of himself; and the wife must see to it that she deeply respects her husband—obeying, praising, and honoring him.

♦ You husbands must be careful of your wives, being thoughtful of their needs and honoring them as the weaker sex. Remember that you and your wife are partners in receiving God's blessings, and if you don't treat her as you should, your prayers will not get ready answers.

Ephesians 5:25-30, 33; 1 Peter 3:7

Just a thought

Imagine what families would be like if husbands and wives loved each other as much as Jesus loves His children.

:00

:10

:20

:30

:40

:50

1:00

FINISH

WHAT'S it mean

GOD'S DAILY GUIDANCE

The **tabernacle** was a portable sanctuary. Its purpose was to provide a place where the Israelites could **worship** God, make **sacrifices,** and store the **ark** containing the Ten Commandments.

In Exodus 25:8 God said, "For I want the people of Israel to make me a sacred Temple where I can live among them." The tabernacle became a visual **symbol** of God's presence for the Israelites. The cloud and fire described in today's reading were a physical testimony to the Israelites that God was with them.

Today, God has given us His **Holy Spirit** to express His presence in our lives. The clouds and fire aren't used these days, but God's **presence** is available in a portable sanctuary...your body. Spend time today thinking about **yourself** as God's temple.

On the day the Tabernacle was raised the Cloud covered it; and that evening the Cloud changed to the appearance of fire, and stayed that way throughout the night. It was always so—the daytime Cloud changing to the appearance of fire at night. When the Cloud lifted, the people of Israel moved on to wherever it stopped, and camped there. In this way they journeyed at the command of the Lord and stopped where he told them to, then remained there as long as the Cloud stayed. If it stayed a long time, then they stayed a long time. But if it stayed only a few days, then they remained only a few days; for so the Lord had instructed them.

Sometimes the fire-cloud stayed only during the night and moved on the next morning. But day or night, when it moved, the people broke camp and followed. If the Cloud stayed above the Tabernacle two days, a month, or a year, that is how long the people of Israel stayed; but as soon as it moved, they moved. So it was that they camped or traveled at the commandment of the Lord; and whatever the Lord told Moses they should do, they did.

Numbers 9:15-23

They murmured and complained, demanding other food than God was giving them. They even spoke against God himself. "Why can't he give us decent food as well as water?" they grumbled. Jehovah heard them and was angry; the fire of his wrath burned against Israel because they didn't believe in God or trust in him to care for them, even though he commanded the skies to open—he opened the windows of heaven—and rained down manna for their food. He gave them bread from heaven! They ate angels' food! He gave them all they could hold.

And he led forth the east wind and guided the south wind by his mighty power. He rained down birds as thick as dust, clouds of them like sands along the shore! He caused the birds to fall to the ground among the tents. The people ate their fill. He gave them what they asked for. But they had hardly finished eating, and the meat was yet in their mouths, when the anger of the Lord rose against them and killed the finest of Israel's young men. Yet even so the people kept on sinning and refused to believe in miracles.

Psalm 78:18-32

:00

:10

:20

:30

:40

:50

:60

done

This **attitude** of unthankfulness, unfaithfulness, and complaining wasn't **only** an Israelite problem. Thousands of years later, James wrote to Christians about the same type of problem. Check out James 4:2-3:

"And yet the reason you don't have what you want is that you don't ask God for it. And even when you do ask you don't get it because your whole aim is wrong–you want only what will give you pleasure."

Today, this attitude is **still** a problem. Though God continues to show himself faithful, we **complain** about things we don't have.

Be thankful God has given you what you have...it's more than most of the world will **ever** have.

189

24 JUN

ISRAEL REJECTS THE PROMISED LAND

Catch T·H·I·S

God gave the **Israelites** a leader–**Moses.** God saved them from slavery–in Egypt. God directed them to a new place to live–the Promised Land. With all of God's provisions, you wouldn't think that the Israelites would **whine** and complain. How quickly they forgot His blessings.

Can you **relate** to the Israelites' feelings? We can sit back and read about the Israelites and make fun of how unfaithful they were, but in reality, **we're** a lot like them. God has provided for us over and over, and yet we still complain when we don't get what we want.

Being **faithful** is tough, but it's not impossible! Spend time **today** thinking of all the different ways God has shown himself faithful to you. Then promise to trust Him a little **more** today than you did yesterday.

:00
:10
:20
:30
:40
:50
:60
done

Jehovah now instructed Moses, "Send spies into the land of Canaan—the land I am giving to Israel; send one leader from each tribe."

After forty days of exploration they returned from their tour. They made their report to Moses, Aaron, and all the people of Israel in the wilderness of Paran at Kadesh, and they showed the fruit they had brought with them.

This was their report: "We arrived in the land you sent us to see, and it is indeed a magnificent country—a land 'flowing with milk and honey.' Here is some fruit we have brought as proof. But the people living there are powerful, and their cities are fortified and very large.

But Caleb reassured the people as they stood before Moses. "Let us go up at once and possess it," he said, "for we are well able to conquer it!"

"Not against people as strong as they are!" the other spies said. "They would crush us!"

Then all the people began weeping aloud, and they carried on all night. Their voices rose in a great chorus of complaint against Moses and Aaron.

"We wish we had died in Egypt," they wailed, "or even here in the wilderness, rather than be taken into this country ahead of us. Jehovah will kill us there, and our wives and little ones will become slaves. Let's get out of here and return to Egypt!"

The idea swept the camp. "Let's elect a leader to take us back to Egypt!" they shouted.

Numbers 13:1-2, 25-28a, 30-31; 14:1-4

190

J U N

Forty Years in the Desert

40 39 38 ... 20 ... 11 10 9 8 7 6 5 4 3 2 1

ONE MINUTE MEMORY

Then Moses and Aaron fell face downward on the ground before the people of Israel. Two of the spies, Joshua (the son of Nun), and Caleb (the son of Jephunneh), ripped their clothing and said to all the people, "It is a wonderful country ahead, and the Lord loves us. He will bring us safely into the land and give it to us. It is very fertile, a land 'flowing with milk and honey'! Oh, do not rebel against the Lord, and do not fear the people of the land. For they are but bread for us to eat! The Lord is with us and he has removed his protection from them! Don't be afraid of them!"

Then the Lord said to Moses and to Aaron, "How long will this wicked nation complain about me? For I have heard all that they have been saying. Tell them, 'The Lord vows to do to you what you feared: You will all die here in this wilderness! Not a single one of you twenty years old and older, who has complained against me, shall enter the Promised Land. Only Caleb (son of Jephunneh) and Joshua (son of Nun) are permitted to enter it.

"Since the spies were in the land for forty days, you must wander in the wilderness for forty years—a year for each day, bearing the burden of your sins. I will teach you what it means to reject me."

♦ What can we ever say to such wonderful things as these? If God is on our side, who can ever be against us?

Numbers 14:5-9, 26-30, 34;
Romans 8:31

If God is on our side, who can ever be against us?

Romans 8:31

:00

:15

:30

:45

:60

done

191

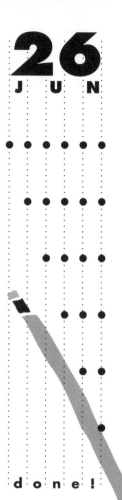

26
JUN

done!

Since Christ is so much superior, the Holy Spirit warns us to listen to him, to be careful to hear his voice today and not let our hearts become set against him, as the people of Israel did. They steeled themselves against his love and complained against him in the desert while he was testing them. But God was patient with them forty years, though they tried his patience sorely; he kept right on doing his mighty miracles for them to see. "But," God says, "I was very angry with them, for their hearts were always looking somewhere else instead of up to me, and they never found the paths I wanted them to follow."

Then God, full of this anger against them, bound himself with an oath that he would never let them come to his place of rest.

Beware then of your own hearts, dear brothers, lest you find that they, too, are evil and unbelieving and are leading you away from the living God. Speak to each other about these things every day while there is still time so that none of you will become hardened against God, being blinded by the glamor of sin. For if we are faithful to the end, trusting God just as we did when we first became Christians, we will share in all that belongs to Christ.

But now is the time. Never forget the warning, "Today if you hear God's voice speaking to you, do not harden your hearts against him, as the people of Israel did when they rebelled against him in the desert."

Hebrews 3:7-15

listen to God's voice

Give it a try

A person with a hardened heart has become **closed** to the truth, teachings, and ways of God. What are three **things** you can **do** today to ensure your heart doesn't become hardened, but that you continue to **grow?**

1 _____
2 _____
3 _____

192

GOD CRUSHES REBELLION

One day Korah (son of Izhar, grandson of Kohath, and a descendant of Levi) conspired with Dathan and Abiram (the sons of Eliab) and On (the son of Peleth), all three from the tribe of Reuben, to incite a rebellion against Moses. Two hundred and fifty popular leaders, all members of the Assembly, were involved.

They went to Moses and Aaron and said, "We have had enough of your presumption; you are no better than anyone else; everyone in Israel has been chosen of the Lord, and he is with all of us. What right do you have to put yourselves forward, claiming that we must obey you, and acting as though you were greater than anyone else among all these people of the Lord?"

When Moses heard what they were saying he fell face downward to the ground. Then he said to Korah and to those who were with him, "In the morning the Lord will show you who are his, and who is holy, and whom he has chosen as his priest."

Meanwhile, Korah had stirred up the entire nation against Moses and Aaron, and they all assembled to watch.

Then the glory of Jehovah appeared to all the people, and a great fissure swallowed them up, along with their tents and families and the friends who were standing with them, and everything they owned. So they went down alive into Sheol and the earth closed upon them, and they perished.

Numbers 16:1-5, 19, 32-33

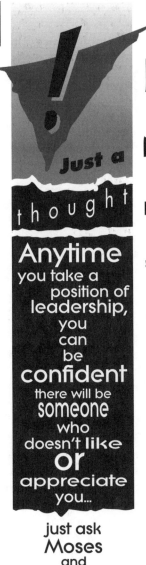

Just a thought

Anytime you take a position of **leadership,** you can be **confident** there will be **someone** who doesn't **like** **or** appreciate you...

just ask **Moses** and **Aaron.**

:00

:10

:20

:30

:40

:50

1:00

FINISH

MOSES DISOBEYS GOD

The people of Israel arrived in the wilderness of Zin in April and camped at Kadesh. There was not enough water to drink at that place, so the people again rebelled against Moses and Aaron.

"Would that we too had died with our dear brothers the Lord killed!" they shouted at Moses. "You have deliberately brought us into this wilderness to get rid of us, along with our flocks and herds. Why did you ever make us leave Egypt and bring us here to this evil place?"

Moses and Aaron turned away and went to the entrance of the Tabernacle, where they fell face downward before the Lord; and the glory of Jehovah appeared to them.

And he said to Moses, "Get Aaron's rod; then you and Aaron must summon the people. As they watch, speak to that rock over there and tell it to pour out its water! You will give them water from a rock, enough for all the people and all their cattle!"

So Moses did as instructed. He took the rod from the place where it was kept before the Lord; then Moses and Aaron summoned the people to come and gather at the rock; and he said to them, "Listen, you rebels! Must we bring you water from this rock?"

Then Moses lifted the rod and struck the rock twice, and water gushed out; and the people and their cattle drank.

But the Lord said to Moses and Aaron, "Because you did not believe me and did not sanctify me in the eyes of the people of Israel, you shall not bring them into the land I have promised them!"

Numbers 20:1a, 2, 4-5a,12

Weird or what

:00
:10 It seems **strange** that after all Moses and Aaron had done, they wouldn't be allowed to enter and
:20 **enjoy** the Promised Land. But when Moses and Aaron brought water from the rock by striking it and
:30 then took credit for the miracle, they tried to improve on God's **unimprovable** plan. God could not reward
:40 them for failing to believe in and honor Him. Moses and Aaron learned a hard lesson that day: **No one**
:50 is exempt from obeying God.

Being **faithful** is an on-going, everyday battle. Try
:60 to win that battle today and God will be **pleased** with

end

194

Look Up and Live

29 JUN

ONE MINUTE MEMORY

Then the people of Israel returned to Mount Hor, and from there continued southward along the road to the Red Sea in order to go around the land of Edom. The people were very discouraged; they began to murmur against God and to complain against Moses. "Why have you brought us out of Egypt to die here in the wilderness?" they whined. "There is nothing to eat here, and nothing to drink, and we hate this insipid manna."

So the Lord sent poisonous snakes among them to punish them, and many of them were bitten and died.

Then the people came to Moses and cried out, "We have sinned, for we have spoken against Jehovah and against you. Pray to him to take away the snakes." So Moses prayed for the people.

Then the Lord told him, "Make a bronze replica of one of these snakes and attach it to the top of a pole; anyone who is bitten shall live if he simply looks at it!"

So Moses made the replica, and whenever anyone who had been bitten looked at the bronze snake, he recovered!

♦ And as Moses in the wilderness lifted up the bronze image of a serpent on a pole, even so I must be lifted up upon a pole, so that anyone who believes in me will have eternal life. For God loved the world so much that he gave his only Son so that anyone who believes in him shall not perish but have eternal life. God did not send his Son into the world to condemn it, but to save it.

Numbers 21:4-9; John 3:14-17

> **God did not send his Son into the world to condemn it, but to save it.**
>
> John 3:17

:00

:15

:30

:45

:60

done

195

30 jun

personality plus Balaam

Balaam is an interesting character because of the **strange** way God got his attention.

One day, Balaam was riding a **donkey** and an angel appeared before them. Balaam didn't see the angel but the donkey went **crazy.** Three times the donkey went wild and all three times Balaam beat the animal. God then caused the donkey to **speak,** saying, "What have I done that deserves your beating me these three times?" Now, **Balaam** went crazy.

God was trying to **stop** Balaam's direction by speaking **through** a donkey. Balaam responded with **repentance.**

Does God have **your** full attention? Today, ask Him if you're going in the **right** direction.

:00

:10

:20

:30

:40

:50

:60

the End

The people of Israel now traveled to the plains of Moab and camped east of the Jordan River opposite Jericho. When King Balak of Moab (the son of Zippor) realized how many of them there were, and when he learned what they had done to the Amorites, he and his people were terrified. They quickly consulted with the leaders of Midian.

"This mob will eat us like an ox eats grass," they exclaimed.

So King Balak sent messengers to Balaam (son of Beor) who was living in his native land of Pethor, near the Euphrates River. He begged Balaam to come and help him.

"A vast horde of people has arrived from Egypt, and they cover the face of the earth and are headed toward me," he frantically explained. "Please come and curse them for me, so that I can drive them out of my land; for I know what fantastic blessings fall on those whom you bless, and I also know that those whom you curse are doomed."

♦ No Ammonite or Moabite may ever enter the sanctuary, even after the tenth generation. The reason for this law is that these nations did not welcome you with food and water when you came out of Egypt; they even tried to hire Balaam, the son of Beor from Pethor, Mesopotamia, to curse you. But the Lord wouldn't listen to Balaam; instead, he turned the intended curse into a blessing for you because the Lord loves you.

Numbers 22:1-3, 4-6; Deuteronomy 23:3-5

196

JUL

After more than sixty years of almost daily reading of the Bible, I never fail to find it always new and marvelously in tune with the changing needs of every day.

Cecil B. DeMille
(1881-1959)
American Movie Producer

Balaam...went at once and looked out toward the camp of Israel which stretched away across the plains, divided by tribal areas.

Then the Spirit of God came upon him, and he spoke this prophecy concerning them:

"Balaam the son of Beor says—
The man whose eyes are open says—
'I have listened to the word of God,
I have seen what God Almighty
   showed me;
I fell, and my eyes were opened:
Oh, the joys awaiting Israel,
Joys in the homes of Jacob.
I see them spread before me as
   green valleys,
And fruitful gardens by the riverside;
As aloes planted by the Lord himself;
As cedar trees beside the waters.
They shall be blessed with an
   abundance of water,
And they shall live in many places.
Their king will be greater than Agag;
Their kingdom is exalted.
God has brought them from Egypt.
Israel has the strength of a wild ox,
And shall eat up the nations that
   oppose him;
He shall break their bones in pieces,
And shall shoot them with
   many arrows.
Israel sleeps as a lion or a lioness—
Who dares arouse him?
Blessed is everyone who blesses you,
   O Israel,
And curses shall fall upon everyone
   who curses you.'"

Numbers 24:1-9

IN other words...
PROPHECY

Prophecy is a word used to describe a **vision,** a truth, a burden, or a word from **God** spoken by a person called a prophet. Prophets were **messengers** who were authorized to **speak** for God.

The prophecies in the **Bible** have been coming true for thousands of years. One book in the Bible filled with prophecy is Revelation. If you read those prophecies, you can be confident God is **unfolding** history in His own time. God will fulfill all prophecies! This is good news for those who believe. Go ahead and thank God for your **future** that He already knows.

:00
:10
:20
:30
:40
:50
done :60

199

2
J U L

ONE MINUTE MEMORY

Judgment for Immortality

:00
:15
:30
:45
:60

For God has bought you with a great price. So use every part of your body to give glory back to God because he owns it.

1 Corinthians 6:20

done

W hile Israel was camped at Acacia, some of the young men began going to wild parties with the local Moabite girls. These girls also invited them to attend the sacrifices to their gods, and soon the men were not only attending the feasts, but also bowing down and worshiping the idols. Before long all Israel was joining freely in the worship of Baal, the god of Moab; and the anger of the Lord was hot against his people.

He issued the following command to Moses:

"Execute all the tribal leaders of Israel. Hang them up before the Lord in broad daylight, so that his fierce anger will turn away from the people."

So Moses ordered the judges to execute all who had worshiped Baal.

✦ That is why I say to run from sex sin. No other sin affects the body as this one does. When you sin this sin it is against your own body. Haven't you yet learned that your body is the home of the Holy Spirit God gave you, and that he lives within you? Your own body does not belong to you. For God has bought you with a great price. So use every part of your body to give glory back to God because he owns it.

Numbers 25:1-5; 1 Corinthians 6:18-20

CHECK IT OUT

Then the Lord said to Moses, "Take vengeance on the Midianites for leading you into idolatry, and then you must die."

Moses said to the people, "Some of you must take arms to wage Jehovah's war against Midian. Conscript 1,000 men from each tribe." So this was done; and out of the many thousands of Israel, 12,000 armed men were sent to battle by Moses.

And every man of Midian was killed. Among those killed were all five of the Midianite kings—Evi, Rekem, Zur, Hur, and Reba. Balaam, the son of Beor, was also killed.

Then the Israeli army took as captives all the women and children, and seized the cattle and flocks and a lot of miscellaneous booty.

Moses and Eleazar the priest and all the leaders of the people went out to meet the victorious army, but Moses was very angry with the army officers and battalion leaders.

"Why have you let all the women live?" he demanded. "These are the very ones who followed Balaam's advice and caused the people of Israel to worship idols on Mount Peor, and they are the cause of the plague that destroyed us."

Numbers 31:1-5, 7-10, 13-16

:00

:10

:20

:30

:40

:50

:60

As we've already learned, the **battles** between the nations were **necessary** in order for the Israelites to occupy the Promised Land. The victorious battles proved God was the only God.

The New Testament teaches us to take a **different** position on killing and revenge. Check out the teaching in Romans 12:17-18: "Never pay back evil for evil. Do things in such a way that everyone can see you are honest clear through. Don't quarrel with anyone. Be at peace with everyone, just as much as possible."

The key words are "**as much as possible.**" It's tough not to fight and quarrel, but try doing less of it today than you did yesterday. Then **celebrate** your **progress.**

d o n e

201

LOVE THE LORD YOUR GOD

Catch THIS

If you've been reading this book for a while, you've noticed that God is **serious** when He asks us to love Him and follow His instructions. Today's passage gives the benefit of doing this: "You will have long, prosperous years ahead of you." That's worth underlining! God gave us instructions so we might live better and longer. These instructions are in God's love letter to us...the Bible.

Think about this; if you built a house you would know everything about it. You'd know the location of all the wires, the minor flaws, the strong areas, the depth of the foundation...you'd know it all! With this knowledge, you could inform the homeowners how to best live in it. This same principle works with God and His creations. God built us. He knows His creations best. He knows our hearts, thoughts, and plans. If we follow His instructions, we'll live life to its **fullest.**

Choose today to live your life the way **God** built you to live it. **There's no better plan!**

:00
:10
:20
:30
:40
:50
:60
done

The Lord your God told me to give you all these commandments which you are to obey in the land you will soon be entering, where you will live. The purpose of these laws is to cause you, your sons, and your grandsons to reverence the Lord your God by obeying all of his instructions as long as you live; if you do, you will have long, prosperous years ahead of you. Therefore, O Israel, listen closely to each command and be careful to obey it, so that all will go well with you, and so that you will have many children. If you obey these commands, you will become a great nation in a glorious land 'flowing with milk and honey,' even as the God of your fathers promised you.

O Israel, listen: Jehovah is our God, Jehovah alone. You must love him with all your heart, soul, and might. And you must think constantly about these commandments I am giving you today. You must teach them to your children and talk about them when you are at home or out for a walk; at bedtime and the first thing in the morning. Tie them on your finger, wear them on your forehead, and write them on the doorposts of your house!

♦ Nothing is perfect except your words. Oh, how I love them. I think about them all day long.

Deuteronomy 6:1-9; Psalm 119:96,97

202

Joshua personality plus

After Moses had said all these things to the people of Israel, he told them, "I am now 120 years old! I am no longer able to lead you, for the Lord has told me that I shall not cross the Jordan River. But the Lord himself will lead you and will destroy the nations living there, and you shall overcome them. Joshua is your new commander, as the Lord has instructed. The Lord will destroy the nations living in the land, just as he destroyed Sihon and Og, the kings of the Amorites. The Lord will deliver over to you the people living there, and you shall destroy them as I have commanded you. Be strong! Be courageous! Do not be afraid of them! For the Lord your God will be with you. He will neither fail you nor forsake you."

Then Moses called for Joshua and said to him, as all Israel watched, "Be strong! Be courageous! For you shall lead these people into the land promised by the Lord to their ancestors; see to it that they conquer it. Don't be afraid, for the Lord will go before you and will be with you; he will not fail nor forsake you."

Then Moses wrote out the laws he had already delivered to the people and gave them to the priests, the sons of Levi, who carried the Ark containing the Ten Commandments of the Lord. Moses also gave copies of the laws to the elders of Israel.

Deuteronomy 31:1-9

Moses sent twelve **spies** into the Promised Land to evaluate the land's occupants. Joshua was one of the two who returned with a **positive** outlook and faith that God would lead the Israelites into the Promised Land.

In addition to Joshua's **confidence** in God, he was a leader. Such a strong leader that God appointed him to replace Moses. His leadership proved **capable** as he conquered the enemies and led the Israelites into their inheritance.

Joshua's **faithfulness** allowed him to be used to fulfill God's prophecy and promise. There's that word again... **faithfulness.** Does the word faithfulness belong next to **your** name?

:00
:10
:20
:30
:40
:50
:60

the End

203

6 JUL

Be Strong and Brave

BIG time word

BRAVE

Being brave is **tough!** It's easy to be a coward and hide your feelings and beliefs and go along with the crowd. But brave people **"stand their ground"** and accept comments directed at them. Brave people are willing to tell someone **no** even when their friends are saying **yes.** Brave people aren't afraid of the jeers, laughter, or put-downs they might receive. Being brave doesn't mean they enjoy the attacks, rather they aren't AFRAID of receiving them.

It takes bravery to be a Christian in today's world. Try being brave for God **today** and be willing to stand up for what you **believe** is **right.**

After the death of Moses, the Lord's disciple, God spoke to Moses' assistant, whose name was Joshua (the son of Nun), and said to him, "Now that my disciple is dead, [you are the new leader of Israel]. Lead my people across the Jordan River into the Promised Land. I say to you what I said to Moses: 'Wherever you go will be part of the land of Israel—all the way from the Negeb desert in the south to the Lebanon mountains in the north, and from the Mediterranean Sea in the west to the Euphrates River in the east, including all the land of the Hittites.' No one will be able to oppose you as long as you live, for I will be with you just as I was with Moses; I will not abandon you or fail to help you.

"Be strong and brave, for you will be a successful leader of my people; and they shall conquer all the land I promised to their ancestors. You need only to be strong and courageous and to obey to the letter every law Moses gave you, for if you are careful to obey every one of them, you will be successful in everything you do. Constantly remind the people about these laws, and you yourself must think about them every day and every night so that you will be sure to obey all of them. For only then will you succeed. Yes, be bold and strong! Banish fear and doubt! For remember, the Lord your God is with you wherever you go."

Joshua 1:1-9

RAHAB HIDES
THE ISRAELITE SPIES

Then Joshua sent two spies from the Israeli camp at Acacia to cross the river and check out the situation on the other side, especially at Jericho. They arrived at an inn operated by a woman named Rahab, who was a prostitute. They were planning to spend the night there, but someone informed the king of Jericho that two Israelis who were suspected of being spies had arrived in the city that evening. He dispatched a police squadron to Rahab's home, demanding that she surrender them.

"They are spies," he explained. "They have been sent by the Israeli leaders to discover the best way to attack us."

But she had hidden them, so she told the officer in charge, "The men were here earlier, but I didn't know they were spies. They left the city at dusk as the city gates were about to close, and I don't know where they went. If you hurry, you can probably catch up with them!"

But actually she had taken them up to the roof and hidden them beneath piles of flax that were drying there.

The spies went up into the mountains and stayed there three days, until the men who were chasing them had returned to the city after searching everywhere along the road without success. Then the two spies came down from the mountain and crossed the river and reported to Joshua all that had happened to them.

"The Lord will certainly give us the entire land," they said, "for all the people over there are scared to death of us."

Joshua 2:1-6, 22-24

7

JUL

Just a
t h o u g h t

If God is
willing
to use a
prostitute
to help
others,

don't you
think
He can
use you to do
great things
as well?

:OO

:1O

:2O

:3O

:4O

:5O

1:OO

FINISH

ISRAELITES CONQUER JERICHO

atch T·H·I·S

This story of how God wanted Israel to **attack** Jericho reminds us that God's plans are often **different** than ours.

Imagine the Israelites' military headquarters. The trained soldiers were reviewing their plan on how to attack and conquer Jericho. Then their leader, Joshua, tells them to march around the city, play their **trumpets,** and shout so the city walls will fall down. Can you imagine the soldiers' response? "Yeah, right, Joshua. That will never work." His plan would have seemed **ridiculous** if God wasn't in control.

When God is in **charge** of your life, you may find His plans are different than yours. Next time you're faced with a problem, ask God to **reveal** His plan to you. It's amazing how God accomplishes His plan. And don't be **surprised** if His plan doesn't happen as you thought it would. Go grab your **trumpet** and **get ready** for God to work!

:00
:10
:20
:30
:40
:50
:60
done

The gates of Jericho were kept tightly shut because the people were afraid of the Israelis; no one was allowed to go in or out.

But the Lord said to Joshua, "Jericho and its king and all its mighty warriors are already defeated, for I have given them to you! Your entire army is to walk around the city once a day for six days, followed by seven priests walking ahead of the Ark, each carrying a trumpet made from a ram's horn. On the seventh day you are to walk around the city seven times, with the priests blowing their trumpets. Then, when they give one long, loud blast, all the people are to give a mighty shout, and the walls of the city will fall down; then move in upon the city from every direction."

So when the people heard the trumpet blast, they shouted as loud as they could. And suddenly the walls of Jericho crumbled and fell before them, and the people of Israel poured into the city from every side and captured it! They destroyed everything in it—men and women, young and old; oxen; sheep; donkeys—everything.

Joshua saved Rahab the prostitute and her relatives who were with her in the house, and they still live among the Israelites because she hid the spies sent to Jericho by Joshua.

Joshua 6:1-5, 20-21, 25

206

Joshua conquers the land of Canaan

The Lord had commanded his disciple Moses [to take the land]; and Moses had passed the commandment on to Joshua, who did as he had been told: he carefully obeyed all of the Lord's instructions to Moses.

So Joshua conquered the entire land—the hill country, the Negeb, the land of Goshen, the lowlands, the Arabah, and the hills and lowlands of Israel. The Israeli territory now extended all the way from Mount Halak, near Seir, to Baal-gad in the valley of Lebanon, at the foot of Mount Hermon. And Joshua killed all the kings of those territories. It took seven years of war to accomplish all of this. None of the cities was given a peace treaty except the Hivites of Gibeon; all of the others were destroyed. For the Lord made the enemy kings want to fight the Israelis instead of asking for peace; so they were mercilessly killed, as the Lord had commanded Moses.

So Joshua took the entire land just as the Lord had instructed Moses; and he gave it to the people of Israel as their inheritance, dividing the land among the tribes. So the land finally rested from its war.

Joshua 11:15-20, 23

done!

Give it a try

God is faithful!
Does God's faithfulness mean anything to you?

If yes, **what does it mean?**

The Israelites went through a lot of pain, suffering, wandering, and disobedience before **reaching** the **Promised** Land. God proved himself faithful by fulfilling His promise to the Israelites. He brought them into their **inheritance!**

Can God rely on **your** faithfulness?

JOSHUA'S FAREWELL ADDRESS

Catch
T·H·I·S

Before Joshua's death he repeatedly challenged the Israelites to turn from their idols and love God. Doesn't it seem **crazy** that after all God had done for the Israelites they **still** worshiped idols and other gods?

When we take a look at ourselves, we see we're a lot like the Israelites. God has done a lot for us. He sent Jesus to die in our place. What more could He do? And yet we are unfaithful when we turn our backs on Him and make other "gods" higher priorities. We can point to the Israelites and say, "How could you be so **stupid?**" Unfortunately, they could probably make the **same** comments about our **unfaithfulness.**

Don't allow the day to end without taking a reflective **journey** of your faith and your commitment to God. God has **proven** himself to be faithful over and over. Can you say the same thing the Israelites eventually said..."We choose the Lord"? If so, let God know **right away.**

:00
:10
:20
:30
:40
:50
:60
done

[Joshua said,] "Revere Jehovah and serve him in sincerity and truth. Put away forever the idols your ancestors worshiped when they lived beyond the Euphrates River and in Egypt. Worship the Lord alone. But if you are unwilling to obey the Lord, then decide today whom you will obey. Will it be the gods of your ancestors beyond the Euphrates or the gods of the Amorites here in this land? But as for me and my family, we will serve the Lord."

And the people replied, "We would never forsake the Lord and worship other gods! For the Lord our God is the one who rescued our fathers from their slavery in the land of Egypt. He is the God who did mighty miracles before the eyes of Israel, as we traveled through the wilderness, and preserved us from our enemies when we passed through their land. It was the Lord who drove out the Amorites and the other nations living here in the land. Yes, we choose the Lord, for he alone is our God."

But Joshua replied to the people, "You can't worship the Lord God, for he is holy and jealous; he will not forgive your rebellion and sins. If you forsake him and worship other gods, he will turn upon you and destroy you, even though he has taken care of you for such a long time."

But the people answered, "We choose the Lord!"

Joshua 24:14-21

THE DAYS OF THE JUDGES

WHAT'S it mean

Joshua, the man of God, died at the age of 110. The people had remained true to the Lord throughout Joshua's lifetime, and as long afterward as the old men of his generation were still living—those who had seen the mighty miracles the Lord had done for Israel.

But finally all that generation died; and the next generation did not worship Jehovah as their God and did not care about the mighty miracles he had done for Israel. They did many things that the Lord had expressly forbidden, including the worshiping of heathen gods. The anger of the Lord flamed out against all Israel. He left them to the mercy of their enemies, for they had departed from Jehovah and were worshiping Baal and the Ashtaroth idols. But when the people were in this terrible plight, the Lord raised up judges to save them from their enemies.

Each judge rescued the people of Israel from their enemies throughout his lifetime, for the Lord was moved to pity by the groaning of his people under their crushing oppressions; so he helped them as long as that judge lived. But when the judge died, the people turned from doing right and behaved even worse than their ancestors had. They prayed to heathen gods again, throwing themselves to the ground in humble worship. They stubbornly returned to the evil customs of the nations around them.

Judges 2:7-11, 14, 16, 18-19

Judges during Old Testament times were very different than our present-day court judges. Old Testament judges were **leaders** that God appointed after the Israelites occupied the Promised Land. They helped create laws, judge disputes, and provide spiritual and military leadership.

Even though the Israelites had a designated person to act as judge, God was and is the **ultimate** and only qualified Judge. It's written in James 4:12:

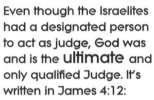

"Only he who made the law [God] can rightly judge among us. He alone decides to save us or destroy. So what right do you have to judge or criticize others?"

Don't play judge today and see if it makes any difference in your life. It's best to let **God** be the one to judge others. You won't miss a thing if you **stop** judging.

DONE

personality Plus Deborah

Deborah was a **woman** judge who's best known for leading a **victorious** battle over Sisera. Prior to this battle, she was **confident** God had already planned and **prepared** the victory. When she told one of her military leaders to begin the battle, he requested her presence by saying, "I'll go, but only if you go with me!" Deborah's faith in God gave her the confidence to say, "Now is the time for action! The Lord leads on! He has already delivered Sisera into your hand!"

Deborah is another **example of** someone who was **faithful** and possessed confidence that God was who He claimed to be. How can **you** become more **confident** that God will **provide?**

:00
:10
:20
:30
:40
:50
:60

After Ehud's death the people of Israel again sinned against the Lord, so the Lord let them be conquered by King Jabin of Hazor, in Canaan. The commander-in-chief of his army was Sisera, who lived in Harosheth-hagoiim. He had nine hundred iron chariots and made life unbearable for the Israelis for twenty years. But finally they begged the Lord for help.

Israel's leader at that time, the one who was responsible for bringing the people back to God, was Deborah, a prophetess, the wife of Lappidoth. She held court at a place now called "Deborah's Palm Tree," between Ramah and Bethel, in the hill country of Ephraim; and the Israelites came to her to decide their disputes.

One day she summoned Barak (son of Abinoam), who lived in Kedesh, in the land of Naphtali, and said to him, "The Lord God of Israel has commanded you to mobilize ten thousand men from the tribes of Naphtali and Zebulun. Lead them to Mount Tabor to fight King Jabin's mighty army with all his chariots, under General Sisera's command. The Lord says, 'I will draw them to the Kishon River, and you will defeat them there.'"

"I'll go, but only if you go with me!" Barak told her.

"All right," she replied, "I'll go with you; but I'm warning you now that the honor of conquering Sisera will go to a woman instead of to you!" So she went with him to Kedesh.

Judges 4:1-9a

the End

JAEL KILLS THE CANAANITE GENERAL

Then Deborah said to Barak, "Now is the time for action! The Lord leads on! He has already delivered Sisera into your hand!"

So Barak led his ten thousand men down the slopes of Mount Tabor into battle.

Then the Lord threw the enemy into a panic, both the soldiers and the charioteers, and Sisera leaped from his chariot and escaped on foot. Barak and his men chased the enemy and the chariots as far as Harosheth-ha-goiim, until all of Sisera's army was destroyed; not one man was left alive. Meanwhile, Sisera had escaped to the tent of Jael, the wife of Heber the Kenite, for there was a mutual-assistance agreement between King Jabin of Hazor and the clan of Heber.

Jael went out to meet Sisera and said to him, "Come into my tent, sir. You will be safe here in our protection. Don't be afraid." So he went into her tent, and she covered him with a blanket.

"Please give me some water," he said, "for I am very thirsty." So she gave him some milk and covered him again.

"Stand in the door of the tent," he told her, "and if anyone comes by, looking for me, tell them that no one is here."

Then Jael took a sharp tent peg and a hammer and, quietly creeping up to him as he slept, she drove the peg through his temples and into the ground; and so he died, for he was fast asleep from weariness.

Judges 4:14-21

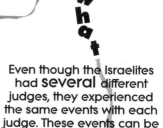

Even though the Israelites had **several** different judges, they experienced the same events with each judge. These events can be seen in five stages:

Stage 1: SIN–
when the Israelites left God and returned to worship idols.
Stage 2: OPPRESSION–
because of their sin, God allowed surrounding nations to rule over the Israelites.
Stage 3: REPENTANCE–
because of the oppression and pain, the Israelites would repent and turn back to God.
Stage 4: SALVATION–
after they repented God would provide a judge to save them from the ruling nations.
Stage 5: PEACE–
then there was a time of peace when the Israelites would worship God and stay out of trouble.

But before long the cycle would start again with SIN.

Do you have any **destructive** cycles that begin with sin? If so, is there anyone who can help you **break** that cycle?

:00
:10
:20
:30
:40
:50
:60

end

CHECK IT OUT

THE BIRTH OF SAMSON

When an **angel** appeared to Samson's mother and told her she was going to have a special son, it wasn't the last time God used an angel to **announce** a coming birth. Hundreds of years later, an angel told the virgin Mary she was going to have a child unlike anyone the world had ever seen. God used Mary to bring His Son into this world.

Check out
Luke 1:30-32a:
"Don't be frightened, Mary," the angel told her, "for God has decided to wonderfully bless you! Very soon now, you will become pregnant and have a baby boy, and you are to name him 'Jesus.' He shall be very great and shall be called the Son of God."

Our world hasn't been the same since that historic moment. There's a **big** difference between Samson and Jesus. One was only a man, the other a God-man. Take a minute to **thank** God for entering the world as a person just like you.

:00

:10

:20

:30

:40

:50

:60

d o n e

Once again Israel sinned by worshiping other gods, so the Lord let them be conquered by the Philistines, who kept them in subjection for forty years.

Then one day the Angel of the Lord appeared to the wife of Manoah, of the tribe of Dan, who lived in the city of Zorah. She had no children, but the Angel said to her, "Even though you have been barren so long, you will soon conceive and have a son! Don't drink any wine or beer and don't eat any food that isn't kosher. Your son's hair must never be cut, for he shall be a Nazirite, a special servant of God from the time of his birth; and he will begin to rescue Israel from the Philistines."

When her son was born they named him Samson, and the Lord blessed him as he grew up. And the Spirit of the Lord began to excite him whenever he visited the parade grounds of the army of the tribe of Dan, located between the cities of Zorah and Eshtaol.

♦ Samson was Israel's leader for the next twenty years, but the Philistines still controlled the land.

Judges 13:1-5, 24-25; 15:20

Samson personality Plus

Samson fell in love with a girl named Delilah over in the valley of Sorek. The five heads of the Philistine nation went personally to her and demanded that she find out from Samson what made him so strong, so that they would know how to overpower and subdue him and put him in chains.

"Each of us will give you a thousand dollars for this job," they promised.

So Delilah begged Samson to tell her his secret. "Please tell me, Samson, why you are so strong," she pleaded. "I don't think anyone could ever capture you!"

"Well," Samson replied, "if I were tied with seven raw-leather bowstrings, I would become as weak as anyone else."

So they brought her the seven bowstrings, and while he slept she tied him with them. Some men were hiding in the next room, so as soon as she had tied him up she exclaimed,

"Samson! The Philistines are here!"

Then he snapped the bowstrings like cotton thread, and so his secret was not discovered.

Judges 16:4-9

Samson is known for being a man with **great** strength and **unique** abilities. Why God chose to bless his **strength** by the length of his hair is a mystery. But God works in **strange** ways.

As you read today and will read tomorrow, Samson hung around and confided in the wrong person. Delilah broke his trust and Samson **lost** his hair, his strength, and his **leadership**.

Samson's life can provide us a learning **example**. God gave him many gifts with a potential for great things. But Samson made **bad** decisions and aligned himself with the **wrong** people. Think about who you hang around with today and what kind of influence they have on your life. Are they keeping you from using God's gift in **your** life?

:00

:10

:20

:30

:40

:50

:60

the End

PHILISTINES BLIND SAMSON

Catch T·H·I·S

After reading about Delilah's manipulation, it sure doesn't seem like the **tactics** have changed very much over a few thousand years. Today, her **line** is still famous: "If you love me you'll...." What seems to be an **obvious** and manipulating line sure has caused a lot of **pain** over the years.

Unfortunately, the line may "win" for the manipulator, but the person who gives in usually **looses.** Samson lost "big time." You will too if you feel pressured to do something you don't want to do. If you hear this, "If you really love me you'll...have sex with me...steal for me...lie for me...etcetera," be **aware!** True love for another person doesn't take selfish advantage. If someone really loves you, he or she will respect and honor your feelings. Being used is **no** fun. Evaluate your relationships. Are you being **used?** Are you using anyone? What can you do to put a **stop** to it **today?**

:00
:10
:20
:30
:40
:50
:60
done

"How can you say you love me when you don't confide in me?" she whined. "You've made fun of me three times now, and you still haven't told me what makes you so strong!" She nagged at him every day until he couldn't stand it any longer and finally told her his secret.

"My hair has never been cut," he confessed, "for I've been a Nazirite to God since before my birth. If my hair were cut, my strength would leave me, and I would become as weak as anyone else."

Delilah realized that he had finally told her the truth, so she sent for the five Philistine leaders.

"Come just this once more," she said, "for this time he has told me everything."

So they brought the money with them. She lulled him to sleep with his head in her lap, and they brought in a barber and cut off his hair. Delilah began to hit him, but she could see that his strength was leaving him.

Then she screamed, "The Philistines are here to capture you, Samson!"

And he woke up and thought, "I will do as before; I'll just shake myself free." But he didn't realize that the Lord had left him. So the Philistines captured him and gouged out his eyes and took him to Gaza, where he was bound with bronze chains and made to grind grain in the prison.

Judges 16:15-21

SAMSON'S REVENGE

The Philistine leaders declared a great festival to celebrate the capture of Samson. The people made sacrifices to their god Dagon and excitedly praised him.

Half drunk by now, the people demanded, "Bring out Samson so we can have some fun with him!"

So he was brought from the prison and made to stand at the center of the temple, between the two pillars supporting the roof. Samson said to the boy who was leading him by the hand, "Place my hands against the two pillars. I want to rest against them."

By then the temple was completely filled with people. The five Philistine leaders were there as well as three thousand people in the balconies who were watching Samson and making fun of him.

Then Samson prayed to the Lord and said, "O Lord Jehovah, remember me again—please strengthen me one more time, so that I may pay back the Philistines for the loss of at least one of my eyes."

Then Samson pushed against the pillars with all his might.

"Let me die with the Philistines," he prayed.

And the temple crashed down upon the Philistine leaders and all the people. So those he killed at the moment of his death were more than those he had killed during his entire lifetime.

WEIRD or what

Samson is written about in the Bible **more** than any of the other judges, but he is the **least** likely of all judges to be morally qualified for his leadership position. Also, he is the only judge who **didn't** bring the Israelites any lasting relief from their **oppressed** condition.

So why does Samson get so much **attention?** It's not known why you know more about Samson than you do Judge Ibzan, but it's good to know God uses people who **don't** have it all together. Does that sound like **you?** You're not perfect either, but God can **still** do great things in and **through** your life.

Judges 16:23, 25-30

18

JUL

:00

:10

:20

:30

:40

:50

1:00

FINISH

Just a thought

Be on the **look-out** for God's **reward** in **your** life.

He rewards **faithfulness** to himself **and to His creations** (others).

NAOMI AND RUTH:

Long ago when judges ruled in Israel, a man named Elimelech, from Bethlehem, left the country because of a famine and moved to the land of Moab. With him were his wife, Naomi, and his two sons, Mahlon and Chilion. During the time of their residence there, Elimelech died and Naomi was left with her two sons.

These young men, Mahlon and Chilion, married girls of Moab, Orpah and Ruth. But later, both men died, so that Naomi was left alone, without her husband or sons. She decided to return to Israel with her daughters-in-law, for she heard that the Lord had blessed his people by giving them good crops again.

But after they had begun their homeward journey, she changed her mind and said to her two daughters-in-law, "Why don't you return to your parents' homes instead of coming with me? And may the Lord reward you for your faithfulness to your husbands and to me. And may he bless you with another happy marriage." Then she kissed them, and they all broke down and cried.

But Ruth replied, "Don't make me leave you, for I want to go wherever you go and to live wherever you live; your people shall be my people, and your God shall be my God; I want to die where you die and be buried there. May the Lord do terrible things to me if I allow anything but death to separate us."

(Their return from Moab and arrival in Bethlehem was at the beginning of the barley harvest.)

Ruth 1:1-9, 16-17, 22

216

RUTH MEETS BOAZ

Now Naomi had an in-law there in Bethlehem who was a very wealthy man. His name was Boaz.

One day Ruth said to Naomi, "Perhaps I can go out into the fields of some kind man to glean the free grain behind his reapers."

And Naomi said, "All right, dear daughter. Go ahead."

So she did. And as it happened, the field where she found herself belonged to Boaz, this relative of Naomi's husband.

Boaz went over and talked to her. "Listen, my child," he said to her. "Stay right here with us to glean; don't think of going to any other fields."

She thanked him warmly. "How can you be so kind to me?" she asked. "You must know I am only a foreigner."

"Yes, I know," Boaz replied, "and I also know about all the love and kindness you have shown your mother-in-law since the death of your husband, and how you left your father and mother in your own land and have come here to live among strangers. May the Lord God of Israel, under whose wings you have come to take refuge, bless you for it."

Ruth 2:1-3, 8, 10-12

Gleaning was the act of gathering food left from a harvest. Gleaners would **follow** the field workers and pick up dropped or leftover food. It was a **law** that the poor and visiting travelers could glean the fallen food or grain from a field. God always wanted provisions made for those who were less fortunate or didn't have the availability to own or buy.

God has given you many **gifts** and **abilities** that you could share with people in need. How can you distribute some of your excess to those who are not as fortunate as you?

:00
:10
:20
:30
:40
:50
:60

end

personality plus Ruth

As you can tell by your reading, Ruth was a **true** friend. She was unselfish and deeply **committed** to staying with Naomi. She obviously **loved** Naomi and enjoyed her company. Their relationship is a **great** example of what friendship means.

As you read about Ruth and Naomi, you might think about **your** relationships and the commitments you and your friends make to one another. Is there strength **beyond** the fun you have? Would pain devastate your relationship? Take an **inventory** of your friendships and see what you need from a friend and how **you** can be a better one **yourself**.

.00

:10

:20

:30

:40

:50

:60

One day Naomi said to Ruth, "My dear, isn't it time that I try to find a husband for you and get you happily married again? The man I'm thinking of is Boaz! He has been so kind to us and is a close relative. I happen to know that he will be winnowing barley tonight out on the threshing-floor. Now do what I tell you—bathe and put on some perfume and some nice clothes and go on down to the threshing-floor, but don't let him see you until he has finished his supper. Notice where he lies down to sleep; then go and lift the cover off his feet and lie down there, and he will tell you what to do concerning marriage."

After Boaz had finished a good meal, he lay down very contentedly beside a heap of grain and went to sleep. Then Ruth came quietly and lifted the covering off his feet and lay there. Suddenly, around midnight, he wakened and sat up, startled. There was a woman lying at his feet!

"Who are you?" he demanded.

"It's I, sir—Ruth," she replied. "Make me your wife according to God's law, for you are my close relative."

"Thank God for a girl like you!" he exclaimed. "For you are being even kinder to Naomi now than before. Naturally you'd prefer a younger man, even though poor. But you have put aside your personal desires. Now don't worry about a thing, my child; I'll handle all the details, for everyone knows what a wonderful person you are."

Ruth 3:1-4, 7-11

the End

Ruth marries Boaz

21 JUL

Then Boaz said to the witnesses and to the crowd standing around, "You have seen that today I have bought all the property of Elimelech, Chilion, and Mahlon, from Naomi, and that with it I have purchased Ruth the Moabitess, the widow of Mahlon, to be my wife, so that she can have a son to carry on the family name of her dead husband."

And all the people standing there and the witnesses replied, "We are witnesses. May the Lord make this woman, who has now come into your home, as fertile as Rachel and Leah, from whom all the nation of Israel descended! May you be a great and successful man in Bethlehem, and may the descendants the Lord will give you from this young woman be as numerous and honorable as those of our ancestor Perez, the son of Tamar and Judah."

So Boaz married Ruth, and when he slept with her, the Lord gave her a son.

And the women of the city said to Naomi, "Bless the Lord who has given you this little grandson; may he be famous in Israel. May he restore your youth and take care of you in your old age; for he is the son of your daughter-in-law who loves you so much, and who has been kinder to you than seven sons!"

Ruth 4:9-15

done!

Give it a try

Ruth was a woman who expressed kindness. This quality of kindness is **rare** in today's world. **List three** specific acts of **kindness** you can do **today** to make a difference in someone's life.

1 _____

2 _____

3 _____

I Am: The Bread of Life

JUL 22

IN other words...

ETERNAL LIFE

Eternal life is life **beyond** our body. Eternal is timeless and has no beginning and no end. God is eternal. God created the earth and human beings, both of which had a beginning and will have an end.

Eternal **life** is the life with God after ours ends. This life is **promised** to those who, by faith, believe Jesus' death paid for their sins and made them **right** with God. Those made right will have eternal life while the unrighteous will have eternal punishment. Basically, eternal life is **longer** than you could ever imagine. The question for those who don't believe isn't "How long is eternal?" but, "Doesn't eternal life in heaven sound a lot better than eternal life in hell?" **What do you say?**

:00
:10
:20
:30
:40
:50
:60   done

[The people told Jesus,] "You must show us more miracles if you want us to believe you are the Messiah. Give us free bread every day, like our fathers had while they journeyed through the wilderness! As the Scriptures say, 'Moses gave them bread from heaven.'"

Jesus said, "Moses didn't give it to them. My Father did. And now he offers you true Bread from heaven. The true Bread is a Person—the one sent by God from heaven, and he gives life to the world."

"Sir," they said, "give us that bread every day of our lives!"

Jesus replied, "I am the Bread of Life. No one coming to me will ever be hungry again. Those believing in me will never thirst. But the trouble is, as I have told you before, you haven't believed even though you have seen me. But some will come to me—those the Father has given me—and I will never, never reject them. For I have come here from heaven to do the will of God who sent me, not to have my own way. And this is the will of God, that I should not lose even one of all those he has given me, but that I should raise them to eternal life at the Last Day. For it is my Father's will that everyone who sees his Son and believes on him should have eternal life—that I should raise him at the Last Day."

John 6:30-40

220

I AM: THE LIGHT OF THE WORLD

In one of his talks, Jesus said to the people, "I am the Light of the world. So if you follow me, you won't be stumbling through the darkness, for living light will flood your path."

♦ As he was walking along, he saw a man blind from birth.

"Master," his disciples asked him, "why was this man born blind? Was it a result of his own sins or those of his parents?"

"Neither," Jesus answered. "But to demonstrate the power of God. All of us must quickly carry out the tasks assigned us by the one who sent me, for there is little time left before the night falls and all work comes to an end. But while I am still here in the world, I give it my light."

Then he spat on the ground and made mud from the spittle and smoothed the mud over the blind man's eyes, and told him, "Go and wash in the Pool of Siloam" (the word Siloam means "Sent"). So the man went where he was sent and washed and came back seeing!

♦ Eternal life is in him, and this life gives light to all mankind. His life is the light that shines through the darkness—and the darkness can never extinguish it.

John 8:12; 9:1-7; 1:4-5

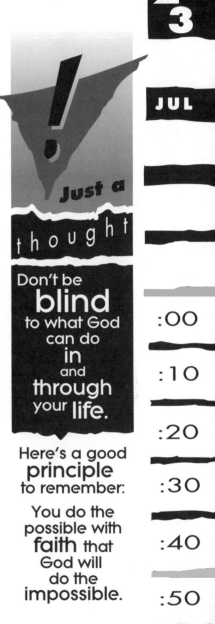

Just a thought

Don't be **blind** to what God can do **in** and **through** your **life.**

Here's a good **principle** to remember:

You do the possible with **faith** that God will do the **impossible.**

23

JUL

:00

:10

:20

:30

:40

:50

1:00

FINISH

24 JUL

ONE MINUTE MEMORY

[Jesus said,] "Anyone refusing to walk through the gate into a sheepfold, who sneaks over the wall, must surely be a thief! For a shepherd comes through the gate. The gatekeeper opens the gate for him, and the sheep hear his voice and come to him; and he calls his own sheep by name and leads them out. He walks ahead of them; and they follow him, for they recognize his voice. They won't follow a stranger but will run from him, for they don't recognize his voice."

Those who heard Jesus use this illustration didn't understand what he meant, so he explained it to them.

"I am the Gate for the sheep," he said. "All others who came before me were thieves and robbers. But the true sheep did not listen to them. Yes, I am the Gate. Those who come in by way of the Gate will be saved and will go in and out and find green pastures. The thief's purpose is to steal, kill and destroy. My purpose is to give life in all its fullness."

John 10:1-10

:00
:15
:30
:45
:60
done X

The thief's purpose is to steal, kill and destroy. My purpose is to give life in all its fullness.

John 10:10

I AM: THE GOOD SHEPHERD

[Jesus said,] "I am the Good Shepherd. The Good Shepherd lays down his life for the sheep. A hired man will run when he sees a wolf coming and will leave the sheep, for they aren't his and he isn't their shepherd. And so the wolf leaps on them and scatters the flock. The hired man runs because he is hired and has no real concern for the sheep.

"I am the Good Shepherd and know my own sheep, and they know me, just as my Father knows me and I know the Father; and I lay down my life for the sheep. I have other sheep, too, in another fold. I must bring them also, and they will heed my voice; and there will be one flock with one Shepherd.

"The Father loves me because I lay down my life that I may have it back again. No one can kill me without my consent—I lay down my life voluntarily. For I have the right and power to lay it down when I want to and also the right and power to take it again. For the Father has given me this right."

• He personally carried the load of our sins in his own body when he died on the cross so that we can be finished with sin and live a good life from now on. For his wounds have healed ours! Like sheep you wandered away from God, but now you have returned to your Shepherd, the Guardian of your souls who keeps you safe from all attacks.

John 10:11-18; 1 Peter 2:24-25

WEIRD or what

There are over **80** animals mentioned throughout the Bible. Sheep appear more frequently than any other animal, over **700** times.

Sheep are **not** smart animals. Have you ever seen one doing tricks in a circus? Probably not. They are **helpless** animals in need of a shepherd to lead them to water and food. **We** are a lot **like** sheep. Sometimes we're dumb and get into trouble. We also have a need for a shepherd. That's why Jesus described himself as the **"Good Shepherd."** He takes care of His sheep...that means **ewe**...which isn't **baaaad** news. You're a whole lot smarter than sheep if you **follow** the Shepherd **today**.

:00
:10
:20
:30
:40
:50
:60

end

JUL 26

WHAT'S it mean

I AM: THE RESURRECTION AND THE LIFE

In today's reading you'll see the word **"Messiah."** During the Old Testament times, it was believed that God would send Israel a **deliverer** who would rule as king, restore the divided kingdom, and explain God's plan. This person would be called the Messiah.

Today, Christians accept **Jesus** as God's Son and the promised **Messiah.** But during Jesus' time, people didn't believe He fit the prophesied description of the Messiah. Jesus was charged with blasphemy, **rejected** by the Jewish leaders, and hung **on a cross.**

One of the main differences between present-day Jews and Christians is that many Jewish people **still** don't believe Jesus was the Messiah. They are still waiting for a Messiah. **How about you?** What are you waiting for? Do you **believe** Jesus was who He claimed to be? **God's Son? The Messiah?**

[M ary's] brother Lazarus, who lived in Bethany with Mary and her sister Martha, was sick.

But when Jesus heard about it he said, "The purpose of his illness is not death, but for the glory of God. I, the Son of God, will receive glory from this situation."

When they arrived at Bethany, they were told that Lazarus had already been in his tomb for four days.

Martha said to Jesus, "Sir, if you had been here, my brother wouldn't have died. And even now it's not too late, for I know that God will bring my brother back to life again, if you will only ask him to."

Jesus told her, "Your brother will come back to life again."

"Yes," Martha said, "when everyone else does, on Resurrection Day."

Jesus told her, "I am the one who raises the dead and gives them life again. Anyone who believes in me, even though he dies like anyone else, shall live again. He is given eternal life for believing in me and shall never perish. Do you believe this, Martha?"

"Yes, Master," she told him. "I believe you are the Messiah, the Son of God, the one we have so long awaited."

Then he shouted, "Lazarus, come out!" And Lazarus came—bound up in the gravecloth, his face muffled in a head swath. Jesus told them, "Unwrap him and let him go!"

John 11:1, 4, 17, 21-27, 43-44

DONE

224

I Am: The Way and the Truth and the Life

[Jesus said,] "Let not your heart be troubled. You are trusting God, now trust in me. There are many homes up there where my Father lives, and I am going to prepare them for your coming. When everything is ready, then I will come and get you, so that you can always be with me where I am. If this weren't so, I would tell you plainly. And you know where I am going and how to get there."

"No, we don't," Thomas said. "We haven't any idea where you are going, so how can we know the way?"

Jesus told him, "I am the Way—yes, and the Truth and the Life. No one can get to the Father except by means of me. If you had known who I am, then you would have known who my Father is. From now on you know him—and have seen him!"

Philip said, "Sir, show us the Father and we will be satisfied."

Jesus replied, "Don't you even yet know who I am, Philip, even after all this time I have been with you? Anyone who has seen me has seen the Father!"

John 14:1-9

ONE MINUTE MEMORY

I am the
Way–yes,
and the Truth
and the Life.
No one can
get to the Father
except by
means of me.

John 14:6

:00

:15

:30

:45

:60

done

225

OBEY

This book is filled with **incredible** examples of people who obeyed God. The **Israelites,** as unfaithful as they were, were God's **special** nation because their ancestor Abraham **obeyed** God. Biblical heros, like Abraham, weren't perfect but they obeyed.

God **loves** obedience. Obedience helps us to live according to God's plans. God is delighted when we **choose** to obey Him. Obeying God is **more** than knowing the Bible; it's **living** every day by faith that God is ultimately in control and **knows** what's best for your life. Try **pleasing** God today by obeying **one** of His instructions.

[Jesus said,] "I am the true Vine, and my Father is the Gardener. He lops off every branch that doesn't produce. And he prunes those branches that bear fruit for even larger crops. He has already tended you by pruning you back for greater strength and usefulness by means of the commands I gave you. Take care to live in me, and let me live in you. For a branch can't produce fruit when severed from the vine. Nor can you be fruitful apart from me.

"Yes, I am the Vine; you are the branches. Whoever lives in me and I in him shall produce a large crop of fruit. For apart from me you can't do a thing. If anyone separates from me, he is thrown away like a useless branch, withers, and is gathered into a pile with all the others and burned. But if you stay in me and obey my commands, you may ask any request you like, and it will be granted! My true disciples produce bountiful harvests. This brings great glory to my Father.

"I have loved you even as the Father has loved me. Live within my love. When you obey me you are living in my love, just as I obey my Father and live in his love. I have told you this so that you will be filled with my joy. Yes, your cup of joy will overflow!"

John 15:1-11

Hannah prays for a son

This is the story of Elkanah, a man of the tribe of Ephraim who lived in Ramathaim-zophim, in the hills of Ephraim.
His father's name was Jeroham,
His grandfather was Elihu,
His great-grandfather was Tohu,
His great-great-grandfather was Zuph.
He had two wives, Hannah and Peninnah. Peninnah had some children, but Hannah didn't.

Each year Elkanah and his families journeyed to the Tabernacle at Shiloh to worship the Lord of the heavens and to sacrifice to him. (The priests on duty at that time were the two sons of Eli—Hophni and Phinehas.) On the day he presented his sacrifice, Elkanah would celebrate the happy occasion by giving presents to Peninnah and her children; but although he loved Hannah very much, he could give her only one present, for the Lord had sealed her womb; so she had no children to give presents to. Peninnah made matters worse by taunting Hannah because of her barrenness.

One evening after supper, when they were at Shiloh, Hannah went over to the Tabernacle. She was in deep anguish and was crying bitterly as she prayed to the Lord.

And she made this vow: "O Lord of heaven, if you will look down upon my sorrow and answer my prayer and give me a son, then I will give him back to you, and he'll be yours for his entire lifetime, and his hair shall never be cut."

1 Samuel 1:1-6, 9a-11

29 JUL

d o n e !

Give it a try

Hannah asked God for something that seemed **impossible**. Write **one** prayer request that might seem impossible for God to answer. Let God know the **desires** within your heart.

It seems impossible but, God, please...

30

J U L

d o n e !

It's not uncommon for us to ask God for something and then not thank Him for answering our prayers. Hannah expressed her thankfulness by giving Samuel back to God for His service.

If any of your prayers have been answered, thank God for hearing your prayers and responding. **Express** your thanksgiving in a **letter** to God.

228

The entire family was up early the next morning and went to the Tabernacle to worship the Lord once more. Then they returned home to Ramah, and when Elkanah slept with Hannah, the Lord remembered her petition; in the process of time, a baby boy was born to her. She named him Samuel (meaning "asked of God") because, as she said, "I asked the Lord for him."

The next year Elkanah and Peninnah and her children went on the annual trip to the Tabernacle without Hannah, for she told her husband, "Wait until the baby is weaned, and then I will take him to the Tabernacle and leave him there."

So she stayed home until the baby was weaned. Then, though he was still so small, they took him to the Tabernacle in Shiloh, along with a three-year-old bull for the sacrifice, and a bushel of flour and some wine. After the sacrifice they took the child to Eli.

"Sir, do you remember me?" Hannah asked him. "I am the woman who stood here that time praying to the Lord! I asked him to give me this child, and he has given me my request; and now I am giving him to the Lord for as long as he lives." So she left him there at the Tabernacle for the Lord to use.

1 Samuel 1:19-22, 23b-28

Samuel: Hannah's firstborn

Give
it a
try

Dear God

Love,

SAMUEL: PROPHET AND JUDGE

Now the sons of Eli were evil men who didn't love the Lord.

Samuel, though only a child, was the Lord's helper and wore a little linen robe just like the priest's. Each year his mother made a little coat for him and brought it to him when she came with her husband for the sacrifice. Before they returned home Eli would bless Elkanah and Hannah and ask God to give them other children to take the place of this one they had given to the Lord. And the Lord gave Hannah three sons and two daughters. Meanwhile Samuel grew up in the service of the Lord.

♦ As Samuel grew, the Lord was with him and people listened carefully to his advice. And all Israel from one end of the land to the other knew that Samuel was going to be a prophet of the Lord. Then the Lord began to give messages to him there at the Tabernacle in Shiloh, and he passed them on to the people of Israel.

♦ Samuel continued as Israel's judge for the remainder of his life. He rode circuit annually, setting up his court first at Bethel, then Gilgal, and then Mizpah, and cases of dispute were brought to him in each of those three cities from all the surrounding territory. Then he would come back to Ramah, for his home was there, and he would hear cases there too. And he built an altar to the Lord at Ramah.

1 Samuel 2:12, 18-21; 3:19-21; 7:15-17

Just a thought

You're **never** too **young** to love **GOD** and grow up in **His** ways.

:00

:10

:20

:30

:40

:50

1:00

FINISH

229

AUG

This book...is the best gift God has given to man.... But for it we could not know right from wrong.

**Abraham Lincoln
(1809-1865)**
United States President

Israel Asks for a King

BIG time
w o r d

In his old age, Samuel retired and appointed his sons as judges in his place. Joel and Abijah, his oldest sons, held court in Beer-sheba; but they were not like their father, for they were greedy for money. They accepted bribes and were very corrupt in the administration of justice. Finally the leaders of Israel met in Ramah to discuss the matter with Samuel. They told him that since his retirement things hadn't been the same, for his sons were not good men.

"Give us a king like all the other nations have," they pleaded. Samuel was terribly upset and went to the Lord for advice.

"Do as they say," the Lord replied, "for I am the one they are rejecting, not you—they don't want me to be their king any longer. Ever since I brought them from Egypt they have continually forsaken me and followed other gods. And now they are giving you the same treatment. Do as they ask, but warn them about what it will be like to have a king!"

So Samuel told the people what the Lord had said.

But the people refused to listen to Samuel's warning.

"Even so, we still want a king," they said, "for we want to be like the nations around us. He will govern us and lead us to battle."

So Samuel told the Lord what the people had said, and the Lord replied again, "Then do as they say and give them a king."

So Samuel agreed and sent the men home again.

1 Samuel 8:1-10, 19-22a

GREED

Throughout the Bible we see greed hurting people and keeping them from godliness. Greed takes our heart away from God and puts our eyes, thoughts, and desires on the object of the greed. If we are greedy for money, we will think more about money and how to get it than we will think about God.

We can replace greed with confidence that God has a plan for our lives and will provide for us. Right now, identify the object of your greed. Realize how worthless it's going to be when you're with God. The object of your greed will eventually burn...no matter how great it is, it's not worth taking your eyes off God.

233

personality plus Samuel

2 aug

Samuel was the **last** of the judges of Israel and the **first** of the prophets. His birth was a **gift** from God to Hannah who asked Him for a child. Samuel's name actually means **"asked of God."**

As a young child, Samuel was in God's presence. It was **obvious** God wanted to use him in great ways, and He used Eli the priest to help him learn God's standards for living.

It's good to see an **example** of God preparing a child to do His work. **Allow** Samuel to remind you that you're **never** too young for God to begin working in your life. Spend a **minute** and ask God to send the right person (like Eli) to train and help you grow **stronger** in your **faith.**

:00
:10
:20
:30
:40
:50
:60

the End

Samuel now called a convocation of all Israel at Mizpah and gave them this message from the Lord God: "I brought you from Egypt and rescued you from the Egyptians and from all of the nations that were torturing you. But although I have done so much for you, you have rejected me and have said, 'We want a king instead!' All right, then, present yourselves before the Lord by tribes and clans."

So Samuel called the tribal leaders together before the Lord, and the tribe of Benjamin was chosen by sacred lot. Then he brought each family of the tribe of Benjamin before the Lord, and the family of the Matrites was chosen. And finally the sacred lot selected Saul, the son of Kish. But when they looked for him, he had disappeared!

So they asked the Lord, "Where is he? Is he here among us?"

And the Lord replied, "He is hiding in the baggage."

So they found him and brought him out, and he stood head and shoulders above anyone else.

Then Samuel said to all the people, "This is the man the Lord has chosen as your king. There isn't his equal in all of Israel!"

And all the people shouted, "Long live the king!"

Then Samuel told the people again what the rights and duties of a king were; he wrote them in a book and put it in a special place before the Lord. Then Samuel sent the people home again.

1 Samuel 10:17-25

THE LORD REJECTS SAUL AS KING

One day Samuel said to Saul, "I crowned you king of Israel because God told me to. Now be sure that you obey him. Here is his commandment to you: 'I have decided to settle accounts with the nation of Amalek for refusing to allow my people to cross their territory when Israel came from Egypt. Now go and completely destroy the entire Amalek nation—men, women, babies, little children, oxen, sheep, camels, and donkeys.'"

Then Saul butchered the Amalekites from Havilah all the way to Shur, east of Egypt. However, Saul and his men kept the best of the sheep and oxen and the fattest of the lambs—everything, in fact, that appealed to them. They destroyed only what was worthless or of poor quality.

Then the Lord said to Samuel,

"I am sorry that I ever made Saul king, for he has again refused to obey me."

When Samuel finally found him, Saul greeted him cheerfully.

"Hello there," he said. "Well, I have carried out the Lord's command!"

Samuel replied, "Has the Lord as much pleasure in your burnt offerings and sacrifices as in your obedience? Obedience is far better than sacrifice. He is much more interested in your listening to him than in your offering the fat of rams to him. For rebellion is as bad as the sin of witchcraft, and stubbornness is as bad as worshiping idols. And now because you have rejected the word of Jehovah, he has rejected you from being king."

1 Samuel 15:1-3a, 7, 9-11a, 13, 22-23

:00
:10
:20
:30
:40
:50
:60
done

Catch T·H·I·S

God has placed a **higher** level of moral responsibility on **Christian** leaders. Don't misunderstand, God wants all His followers to live right and follow Him, but He wants His leaders to set godly **examples**. God doesn't expect leaders to be perfect; He knows better. But leaders are **watched** by those who **follow**.

Saul, whom God **chose** to be king and leader, made God angry because he disobeyed Him and lied to Samuel. These are not the qualities expressed by godly leaders. A strong leader sets his heart to obey and **please** God.

The Good News of God's love is **confusing** to others if Christian leaders aren't living godly lives. If you are a leader in your youth group or church, be reminded that you are **modeling** Christianity. Whether you like it or not, people judge Christianity by its leaders. God asks you to be a faithful leader today. You're **not too young** to be serving God.

AUG 4

ONE MINUTE MEMORY

Samuel Anoints David as King

:00

:15

:30

:45

:60

done

Men judge by outward appearance, but I look at a man's thoughts and intentions.

1 Samuel 16:7a

The Lord said to Samuel, "You have mourned long enough for Saul, for I have rejected him as king of Israel. Now take a vial of olive oil and go to Bethlehem and find a man named Jesse, for I have selected one of his sons to be the new king."

When they arrived, Samuel took one look at Eliab and thought, "Surely this is the man the Lord has chosen!"

But the Lord said to Samuel, "Don't judge by a man's face or height, for this is not the one. I don't make decisions the way you do! Men judge by outward appearance, but I look at a man's thoughts and intentions."

In the same way all seven of his sons presented themselves to Samuel and were rejected. "The Lord has not chosen any of them," Samuel told Jesse. "Are these all there are?"

"Well, there is the youngest," Jesse replied. "But he's out in the fields watching the sheep."

"Send for him at once," Samuel said, "for we will not sit down to eat until he arrives."

So Jesse sent for him. He was a fine looking boy, ruddy-faced, and with pleasant eyes. And the Lord said, "This is the one; anoint him."

So as David stood there among his brothers, Samuel took the olive oil he had brought and poured it upon David's head; and the Spirit of Jehovah came upon him and gave him great power from that day onward. Then Samuel returned to Ramah.

1 Samuel 16:1, 6-7, 9-13

GOLIATH
CHALLENGES THE ARMIES OF
ISRAEL

The Philistines now mustered their army for battle and camped between Socoh in Judah and Azekah in Ephes-dammim. Saul countered with a buildup of forces at Elah Valley. So the Philistines and Israelis faced each other on opposite hills, with the valley between them.

Then Goliath, a Philistine champion from Gath, came out of the Philistine ranks to face the forces of Israel. He was a giant of a man, measuring over nine feet tall! He wore a bronze helmet, a two-hundred-pound coat of mail, bronze leggings, and carried a bronze javelin several inches thick, tipped with a twenty-five-pound iron spearhead, and his armor-bearer walked ahead of him with a huge shield.

He stood and shouted across to the Israelis, "Do you need a whole army to settle this? I will represent the Philistines, and you choose someone to represent you, and we will settle this in single combat! If your man is able to kill me, then we will be your slaves. But if I kill him, then you must be our slaves! I defy the armies of Israel! Send me a man who will fight with me!"

When Saul and the Israeli army heard this, they were dismayed and frightened.

1 Samuel 17:1-11

The **armor** that Goliath wore **weighed more** than David's entire body. David's **victory** over the giant is just another example of how **huge** obstacles can be **overcome** when God is involved.

237

CHECK IT OUT

DAVID ACCEPTS GOLIATH'S CHALLENGE

A lot of people want to tell students that they are the "church of **tomorrow**." They believe God will use you when you're older. That's **not** true. You're the church of **today** and God can use you **now!** God never gives a command to follow Him tomorrow or when you reach a specific age. God has used **young** people in the past, like David, and He will continue to use them. Check out what Paul told young Timothy in 1 Timothy 4:12:

"Don't let anyone think little of you because you are young. Be their ideal; let them follow the way you teach and live; be a pattern for them in your love, your faith, and your clean thoughts."

Your **age** may be a problem for some, but not for God. **Thank** Him for your age and ask Him to do something **great** with your life **today.**

:00

:10

:20

:30

:40

:50

:60

"**D**on't worry about a thing," David told [Saul]. "I'll take care of this Philistine!"

"Don't be ridiculous!" Saul replied. "How can a kid like you fight with a man like him? You are only a boy, and he has been in the army since he was a boy!"

But David persisted. "When I am taking care of my father's sheep," he said, "and a lion or a bear comes and grabs a lamb from the flock, I go after it with a club and take the lamb from its mouth. If it turns on me, I catch it by the jaw and club it to death. I have done this to both lions and bears, and I'll do it to this heathen Philistine too, for he has defied the armies of the living God! The Lord who saved me from the claws and teeth of the lion and the bear will save me from this Philistine!"

Saul finally consented, "All right, go ahead," he said, "and may the Lord be with you!"

Then he picked up five smooth stones from a stream and put them in his shepherd's bag and, armed only with his shepherd's staff and sling, started across to Goliath.

1 Samuel 17:32-37, 40

d o n e

238

DAVID KILLS GOLIATH

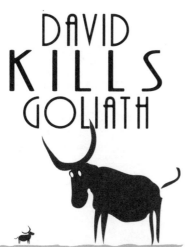

Goliath walked out toward David with his shield-bearer ahead of him, sneering in contempt at this nice little red-cheeked boy!

"Am I a dog," he roared at David, "that you come at me with a stick?" And he cursed David by the names of his gods.

David shouted in reply, "You come to me with a sword and a spear, but I come to you in the name of the Lord of the armies of heaven and of Israel—the very God whom you have defied. Today the Lord will conquer you, and I will kill you and cut off your head; and then I will give the dead bodies of your men to the birds and wild animals, and the whole world will know that there is a God in Israel! And Israel will learn that the Lord does not depend on weapons to fulfill his plans—he works without regard to human means! He will give you to us!"

As Goliath approached, David ran out to meet him and, reaching into his shepherd's bag, took out a stone, hurled it from his sling, and hit the Philistine in the forehead. The stone sank in, and the man fell on his face to the ground. So David conquered the Philistine giant with a sling and a stone.

1 Samuel 17:41-43, 45-49

Just a thought

A little stone with **big** faith can conquer a big giant with a little god.

:00

:10

:20

:30

:40

:50

1:00

FINISH

239

8
aug

personality Plus Jonathan

Jonathan was **loyal** to God and his friends. His friendship with David is one of the great **models** for friendship found within the Bible. Jonathan's **ultimate** loyalty started with God. Because of his strong relationship with God, Jonathan was able to gain God's **wisdom** when he was caught in a **terrible** spot between his father and David.

Jonathan is a **strong** example for us to follow. He was an **unselfish** and true friend. Friends like Jonathan are difficult to find. If you have a friend who isn't selfish and is **loyal** to your relationship, make sure you go out of your way to **express** your appreciation today. Friendships like this are **definitely** worth keeping!

:00

:10

:20

:30

:40

:50

:60

After King Saul had finished his conversation with David, David met Jonathan, the king's son, and there was an immediate bond of love between them. Jonathan swore to be his blood brother, and sealed the pact by giving him his robe, sword, bow, and belt.

King Saul now kept David with him and wouldn't let him return home any more. He was Saul's special assistant, and he always carried out his assignments successfully. So Saul made him commander of his troops, an appointment that was applauded by the army and general public alike. But something had happened when the victorious Israeli army was returning home after David had killed Goliath. Women came out from all the towns along the way to celebrate and to cheer for King Saul, and were singing and dancing for joy with tambourines and cymbals.

However, this was their song: "Saul has slain his thousands, and David his ten thousands!"

Of course Saul was very angry. "What's this?" he said to himself. "They credit David with ten thousands and me with only thousands. Next they'll be making him their king!"

So from that time on King Saul kept a jealous watch on David.

1 Samuel 18:1-9

the End

Saul tries to kill David

Saul now urged his aides and his son Jonathan to assassinate David. But Jonathan, because of his close friendship with David, told him what his father was planning. "Tomorrow morning," he warned him, "you must find a hiding place out in the fields. I'll ask my father to go out there with me, and I'll talk to him about you; then I'll tell you everything I can find out."

The next morning as Jonathan and his father were talking together, he spoke well of David and begged him not to be against David. "He's never done anything to harm you," Jonathan pleaded. "He has always helped you in any way he could. Have you forgotten about the time he risked his life to kill Goliath, and how the Lord brought a great victory to Israel as a result? You were certainly happy about it then. Why should you now murder an innocent man? There is no reason for it at all!"

Finally Saul agreed and vowed, "As the Lord lives, he shall not be killed."

Afterwards Jonathan called David and told him what had happened. Then he took David to Saul and everything was as it had been before.

But one day as Saul was sitting at home, listening to David playing the harp, suddenly the tormenting spirit from the Lord attacked him. He had his spear in his hand and hurled it at David in an attempt to kill him. But David dodged out of the way and fled into the night, leaving the spear imbedded in the timber of the wall.

1 Samuel 19:1-7, 9-10

AUG 9

done!

Give it a try

List **three** qualities you look for in a friend. **Next** to each of the qualities come up with an action **plan** for improving those qualities in your own life. Make **specific** plans and start working on them **now!**

qualities   plan

1 _____   _____

2 _____   _____

3 _____   _____

If you expect those qualities in others, you should have them in your own life as well.

241

10

AUG

:00

:10

:20

:30

:40

:50

1:00

FINISH

! Just a thought

In **Saul's** situation, his disobedience **resulted** in a quick **death...**

what are the consequences of **disobedience** in **your** life?

THE DEATH OF SAUL AND HIS SONS

The Philistines attacked and defeated the Israeli troops, who turned and fled and were slaughtered on the slopes of Mount Gilboa. They caught up with Saul and his three sons, Jonathan, Abinadab, and Malchishua, and killed them all. Saul had been hard pressed with heavy fighting all around him, when the Philistine archers shot and wounded him.

He cried out to his bodyguard, "Quick, kill me with your sword before these uncircumcised heathen capture and torture me."

But the man was afraid to do it, so Saul took his own sword and fell against its point; and it pierced his body. Then his bodyguard, seeing that Saul was dead, killed himself in the same way. So Saul and his three sons died together; the entire family was wiped out in one day.

When the Israelis in the valley below the mountain heard that their troops had been routed and that Saul and his sons were dead, they abandoned their cities and fled. And the Philistines came and lived in them.

Saul died for his disobedience to the Lord and because he had consulted a medium, and did not ask the Lord for guidance. So the Lord killed him and gave the kingdom to David, the son of Jesse.

1 Chronicles 10:1-7, 13-14

242

THE LORD'S COVENANT w/DAVID

WHAT'S it ? mean

When the Lord finally sent peace upon the land, and Israel was no longer at war with the surrounding nations, David said to Nathan the prophet, "Look! Here I am living in this beautiful cedar palace while the Ark of God is out in a tent!"

"Go ahead with what you have in mind," Nathan replied, "for the Lord is with you."

But that night the Lord said to Nathan, "Now go and give this message to David from the Lord of heaven: 'I chose you to be the leader of my people Israel when you were a mere shepherd, tending your sheep in the pastureland. I have been with you wherever you have gone and have destroyed your enemies. And I will make your name greater yet, so that you will be one of the most famous men in the world!

"'There will be no more wars against you; and your descendants shall rule this land for generations to come! For when you die, I will put one of your sons upon your throne, and I will make his kingdom strong. He is the one who shall build me a temple. And I will continue his kingdom into eternity. I will be his father and he shall be my son. If he sins, I will use other nations to punish him, but my love and kindness shall not leave him as I took it from Saul, your predecessor. Your family shall rule my kingdom forever.'"

2 Samuel 7:1-4, 8-9, 11b-16

In today's reading we see God **promising** great things through David's family. This is one of the prophecies that addresses the **birth of Jesus.** God promised a great king to be born through David's family who will live forever and build an **eternal** kingdom.

The Bible has recorded this specific prophecy through several different prophets and time periods. Hundreds of years later, God used **Mary,** who was from the family of David, to give birth to Jesus and **fulfill** this **prophecy.**

God's plan has worked out and will continue to work out as He intended. Take a **minute** to thank God for His plan and let Him know you want to be a part of the **eternal kingdom** if you haven't already.

He has room for you!

12

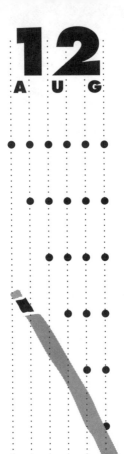

d o n e !

Because the Lord is my Shepherd, I have everything I need!

He lets me rest in the meadow grass and leads me beside the quiet streams. He gives me new strength. He helps me do what honors him the most.

Even when walking through the dark valley of death I will not be afraid, for you are close beside me, guarding, guiding all the way.

You provide delicious food for me in the presence of my enemies. You have welcomed me as your guest; blessings overflow!

Your goodness and unfailing kindness shall be with me all of my life, and afterwards I will live with you forever in your home.

♦ I am the Good Shepherd. The Good Shepherd lays down his life for the sheep.

Psalm 23:1-6; John 10:11

the Lord is my shepherd

Give it a try

Rewrite and paraphrase Psalm 23 in your own words. **Personalize** this Psalm by using specific examples of how God is **your** Shepherd.

244

DAVID COMMITS ADULTERY WITH BATHSHEBA

In the spring of the following year, at the time when wars begin, David sent Joab and the Israeli army to destroy the Ammonites. They began by laying siege to the city of Rabbah. But David stayed in Jerusalem.

One night he couldn't get to sleep and went for a stroll on the roof of the palace. As he looked out over the city, he noticed a woman of unusual beauty taking her evening bath. He sent to find out who she was and was told that she was Bathsheba, the daughter of Eliam and the wife of Uriah. Then David sent for her and when she came he slept with her. (She had just completed the purification rites after menstruation.) Then she returned home. When she found that he had gotten her pregnant she sent a message to inform him.

So David dispatched a memo to Joab: "Send me Uriah the Hittite." When he arrived, David asked him how Joab and the army were getting along and how the war was prospering. Then he told him to go home and relax, and he sent a present to him at his home. But Uriah didn't go there. He stayed that night at the gateway of the palace with the other servants of the king.

2 Samuel 11:1-9

245

Catch T·H·I·S

:00

David was **tempted** when he saw Bathsheba bathing. This temptation was not a sin. David's sin was **acting** upon his temptation. He sinned again when he attempted to cover up his first sin. Basically, he **blew it!**

:10

It's not uncommon for us to be sexually tempted. Sex is everywhere and it is tempting! But we have something in common with David. We can **control** our sexual urges. Even though David didn't control his, he could have. God knows we will be tempted so He created us with self-control.

:20

:30

David was a great king, but he should have left the roof and ran from his temptation. The devil uses temptation to take our eyes off God and put them on things that are pleasing to ourselves and not to God.

:40

Today, think of the tempting situations you need to run from. And remember, God has given you the **strength** to have **control** over any temptation.

:50

:60
done

Just a

thought

Another way to **identify** sin is

"the wrong use of a right thing."

:OO

:1O

:2O

:3O

:4O

:5O

1:OO

FINISH

DAVID ARRANGES URIAH'S DEATH

The next morning David wrote a letter to Joab and gave it to Uriah to deliver. The letter instructed Joab to put Uriah at the front of the hottest part of the battle—and then pull back and leave him there to die! So Joab assigned Uriah to a spot close to the besieged city where he knew that the enemies' best men were fighting; and Uriah was killed along with several other Israeli soldiers.

When Bathsheba heard that her husband was dead, she mourned for him; then, when the period of mourning was over, David sent for her and brought her to the palace and she became one of his wives; and she gave birth to his son. But the Lord was very displeased with what David had done.

♦ "I have sinned against the Lord," David confessed to Nathan.

Then Nathan replied, "Yes, but the Lord has forgiven you, and you won't die for this sin. But you have given great opportunity to the enemies of the Lord to despise and blaspheme him, so your child shall die."

♦ For the wages of sin is death, but the free gift of God is eternal life through Jesus Christ our Lord.

2 Samuel 11:14-17, 26-27; 12:13-14; Romans 6:23

David's prayer of repentance

Written after Nathan the prophet had come to inform David of God's judgment against him because of his adultery with Bathsheba, and his murder of Uriah, her husband.

O loving and kind God, have mercy. Have pity upon me and take away the awful stain of my transgressions. Oh, wash me, cleanse me from this guilt. Let me be pure again. For I admit my shameful deed—it haunts me day and night. It is against you and you alone I sinned and did this terrible thing. You saw it all, and your sentence against me is just. But I was born a sinner, yes, from the moment my mother conceived me. You deserve honesty from the heart; yes, utter sincerity and truthfulness. Oh, give me this wisdom.

Sprinkle me with the cleansing blood and I shall be clean again. Wash me and I shall be whiter than snow. And after you have punished me, give me back my joy again. Don't keep looking at my sins—erase them from your sight. Create in me a new, clean heart, O God, filled with clean thoughts and right desires. Don't toss me aside, banished forever from your presence. Don't take your Holy Spirit from me. Restore to me again the joy of your salvation, and make me willing to obey you. Then I will teach your ways to other sinners, and they—guilty like me—will repent and return to you.

Psalm 51:1-13

done!

After reading David's prayer of forgiveness, write God a **letter** asking Him to **create** in you a new and **clean** heart.

Dear God,

Love,

AUG

ONE MINUTE MEMORY

:00

:15

:30

:45

:60

done

**In everything
you do,
put God first,
and he will
direct you and
crown your
efforts with
success.**

Proverbs 3:6

David Appoints Solomon as King

As the time of King David's death approached, he gave this charge to his son Solomon:

"I am going where every man on earth must some day go. I am counting on you to be a strong and worthy successor. Obey the laws of God and follow all his ways; keep each of his commands written in the law of Moses so that you will prosper in everything you do, wherever you turn. If you do this, then the Lord will fulfill the promise he gave me, that if my children and their descendants watch their step and are faithful to God, one of them shall always be the king of Israel—my dynasty will never end."

✦ So God appointed Solomon to take the throne of his father David; and he prospered greatly, and all Israel obeyed him. The national leaders, the army officers, and his brothers all pledged their allegiance to King Solomon. And the Lord gave him great popularity with all the people of Israel, and he amassed even greater wealth and honor than his father.

✦ In everything you do, put God first, and he will direct you and crown your efforts with success.

1 Kings 2:1-4; 1 Chronicles 29:23-25; Proverbs 3:6

Solomon Asks for Wisdom

The Lord appeared to him in a dream that night and told him to ask for anything he wanted, and it would be given to him!

[Solomon answered,] "O Lord my God, now you have made me the king instead of my father David, but I am as a little child who doesn't know his way around. And here I am among your own chosen people, a nation so great that there are almost too many people to count! Give me an understanding mind so that I can govern your people well and know the difference between what is right and what is wrong. For who by himself is able to carry such a heavy responsibility?"

The Lord was pleased with his reply and was glad that Solomon had asked for wisdom. So he replied, "Because you have asked for wisdom in governing my people and haven't asked for a long life, or riches for yourself, or the defeat of your enemies—yes, I'll give you what you asked for! I will give you a wiser mind than anyone else has ever had or ever will have! And I will also give you what you didn't ask for—riches and honor! And no one in all the world will be as rich and famous as you for the rest of your life! And I will give you a long life if you follow me and obey my laws as your father David did."

1 Kings 3:5, 7-14

WISDOM

Wisdom has nothing to do with your **grade** point average or your achievement test scores. Wisdom comes from God. Another biblical word used for wisdom is **understanding.** Solomon asked God for an understanding mind so he could **know** the difference between right and wrong (1 Kings 3:9). This understanding is one of the essential elements of wisdom.

If you **DON'T** have wisdom you'll...

- struggle between knowing right from wrong,
- follow the crowd rather than lead,
- be confused on what to do in and with your life,
- be unsure of God's plan for your life, and
- conform to others' standards.

Ask God to give you His **wisdom** for the decisions you need to make **today.**

249

THE WISDOM OF SOLOMON

AUG 18

:00

:10 Did you know Solomon was a **multi-millionaire?** The Bible tells us that he received $250,000,000 worth of **gold** each year from the kings of Arabia.

:20 He also sold horses and exotic goods as well as copper and bronze that were manufactured in his

:30 mines. He would be considered a **very** wealthy person in today's economy, so there's no

:40 question he was one of the **richest** men alive. But with all his wealth and fame Solomon still asked

:50 God for **wisdom.** He knew money couldn't buy what God offered.

:60 Try to live today without concern over your financial situation and **ask** God for the things money **can't** buy.

end

Israel and Judah were a wealthy, populous, contented nation at this time. King Solomon ruled the whole area from the Euphrates River to the land of the Philistines and down to the borders of Egypt. The conquered peoples of those lands sent taxes to Solomon and continued to serve him throughout his lifetime.

God gave Solomon great wisdom and understanding, and a mind with broad interests. In fact, his wisdom excelled that of any of the wise men of the East, including those in Egypt. He was wiser than Ethan the Ezrahite and Heman, Calcol, and Darda, the sons of Mahol; and he was famous among all the surrounding nations. He was the author of 3,000 proverbs and wrote 1,005 songs. He was a great naturalist, with interest in animals, birds, snakes, fish, and trees—from the great cedars of Lebanon down to the tiny hyssop which grows in cracks in the wall. And kings from many lands sent their ambassadors to him for his advice.

1 Kings 4:20-21, 29-34

Solomon personality plus

These are the proverbs of King Solomon of Israel, David's son:

He wrote them to teach his people how to live—how to act in every circumstance, for he wanted them to be understanding, just and fair in everything they did. "I want to make the simpleminded wise!" he said. "I want to warn young men about some problems they will face. I want those already wise to become the wiser and become leaders by exploring the depths of meaning in these nuggets of truth."

How does a man become wise? The first step is to trust and reverence the Lord!

Only fools refuse to be taught.

✦ As the crowd pressed in upon him, he preached them this sermon: "These are evil times, with evil people. They keep asking for some strange happening in the skies (to prove I am the Messiah), but the only proof I will give them is a miracle like that of Jonah, whose experiences proved to the people of Nineveh that God had sent him. My similar experience will prove that God has sent me to these people.

"And at the Judgment Day the Queen of Sheba shall arise and point her finger at this generation, condemning it, for she went on a long, hard journey to listen to the wisdom of Solomon; but one far greater than Solomon is here (and few pay any attention)."

Proverbs 1:1-7; Luke 11:29-31

Solomon was the son of **David** and **Bathsheba.** He followed his family line and became **king** of Israel. He had great wealth, wisdom, and respect. But he also had problems like any other person. Though he appeared to "have it all," he made some **bad** decisions by marrying ungodly women and allowing them to **weaken** his commitment to God.

We **all** lack wisdom at times and must be ready to **pay** for the **consequences.** Try reading through the Proverbs and see if you can find **any** advice that could have **helped** Solomon with his relationships.

:00
:10
:20
:30
:40
:50
:60

the End

251

AUG 20

IN other words...

PARABLE

A parable was usually a **story** or a verbal **illustration**. Jesus didn't have the technology of using a slide-show or a video presentation to make His message more clear, so He told **parables.**

They're **great** parables, and if you don't know any you might read: The Good Samaritan (Luke 10:30-37), The Lost Coin (Luke 15:8-10), or The Ten Virgins (Matthew 25:1-13). There are several more... **check** them out and allow God's Word to take root in your life so you'll **never** forget His incredible message.

:00

:10

:20

:30

:40

:50

:60   **done**

One day he gave this illustration to a large crowd that was gathering to hear him—while many others were still on the way, coming from other towns.

"A farmer went out to his field to sow grain. As he scattered the seed on the ground, some of it fell on a footpath and was trampled on; and the birds came and ate it as it lay exposed. Other seed fell on shallow soil with rock beneath. This seed began to grow, but soon withered and died for lack of moisture. Other seed landed in thistle patches, and the young grain stalks were soon choked out. Still other fell on fertile soil; this seed grew and produced a crop one hundred times as large as he had planted." (As he was giving this illustration he said, "If anyone has listening ears, use them now!")

His apostles asked him what the story meant.

He replied, "God has granted you to know the meaning of these parables, for they tell a great deal about the Kingdom of God. But these crowds hear the words and do not understand, just as the ancient prophets predicted."

Luke 8:4-10

"This is its meaning: The seed is God's message to men. The hard path where some seed fell represents the hard hearts of those who hear the words of God, but then the devil comes and steals the words away and prevents people from believing and being saved. The stony ground represents those who enjoy listening to sermons, but somehow the message never really gets through to them and doesn't take root and grow. They know the message is true, and sort of believe for awhile; but when the hot winds of persecution blow, they lose interest. The seed among the thorns represents those who listen and believe God's words but whose faith afterwards is choked out by worry and riches and the responsibilities and pleasures of life. And so they are never able to help anyone else to believe the Good News.

"But the good soil represents honest, good-hearted people. They listen to God's words and cling to them and steadily spread them to others who also soon believe."

(Another time he asked,) "Who ever heard of someone lighting a lamp and then covering it up to keep it from shining? No, lamps are mounted in the open where they can be seen. This illustrates the fact that someday everything (in men's hearts) shall be brought to light and made plain to all. So be careful how you listen; for whoever has, to him shall be given more; and whoever does not have, even what he thinks he has shall be taken away from him."

Luke 8:11-18

IN **other** words...

GOOD NEWS

When "good" and "news" are used together ["Good News"], they refer to what we know as the Bible. The writers of the New Testament Books referred to God's Word as "Scriptures" or the "Good News."

The Bible is God's love letter to us. As you know, this book in your hands is filled with sections of the Good News, but it isn't the complete Bible. If you don't have a Bible, ask a friend, parent, or pastor to help get you one.* The Good News is one of the ways God chooses to speak to us. Open it, read it, and begin to see what God wants for your life. It's a lot like what you've been reading in this book...only more...and in this case, more is better.

*Look in the back of this book for a list of some good student Bibles.

:00 :10 :20 :30 :40 :50 done :60

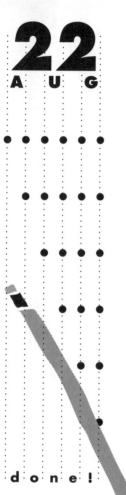

22
A U G

Here is another of his illustrations: "The Kingdom of Heaven is like a tiny mustard seed planted in a field. "It is the smallest of all seeds but becomes the largest of plants, and grows into a tree where birds can come and find shelter."

He also used this example:

"The Kingdom of Heaven can be compared to a woman making bread. She takes a measure of flour and mixes in the yeast until it permeates every part of the dough."

"The Kingdom of Heaven is like a treasure a man discovered in a field. In his excitement, he sold everything he owned to get enough money to buy the field—and get the treasure, too!

"Again, the Kingdom of Heaven is like a pearl merchant on the lookout for choice pearls. He discovered a real bargain—a pearl of great value—and sold everything he owned to purchase it!

"Again, the Kingdom of Heaven can be illustrated by a fisherman—he casts a net into the water and gathers in fish of every kind, valuable and worthless. When the net is full, he drags it up onto the beach and sits down and sorts out the edible ones into crates and throws the others away. That is the way it will be at the end of the world—the angels will come and separate the wicked people from the godly, casting the wicked into the fire; there shall be weeping and gnashing of teeth."

Matthew 13:31-33, 44-50

d o n e !

After reading today's selection, **write** what you believe **heaven** will be like.

Give it a try

254

LOST AND FOUND

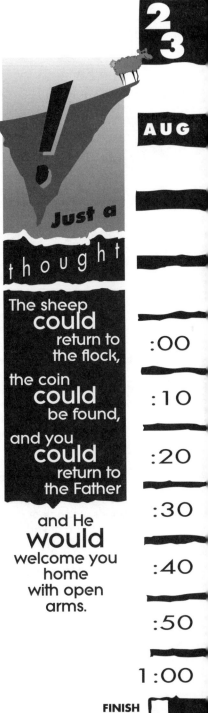

Dishonest tax collectors and other notorious sinners often came to listen to Jesus' sermons; but this caused complaints from the Jewish religious leaders and the experts on Jewish law because he was associating with such despicable people—even eating with them!

So Jesus used this illustration: "If you had a hundred sheep and one of them strayed away and was lost in the wilderness, wouldn't you leave the ninety-nine others to go and search for the lost one until you found it? And then you would joyfully carry it home on your shoulders. When you arrived you would call together your friends and neighbors to rejoice with you because your lost sheep was found.

"Well, in the same way heaven will be happier over one lost sinner who returns to God than over ninety-nine others who haven't strayed away!

"Or take another illustration: A woman has ten valuable silver coins and loses one. Won't she light a lamp and look in every corner of the house and sweep every nook and cranny until she finds it? And then won't she call in her friends and neighbors to rejoice with her? In the same way there is joy in the presence of the angels of God when one sinner repents."

Luke 15:1-10

2 3 AUG

Just a thought

The sheep **could** return to the flock, the coin **could** be found, and you **could** return to the Father and He **would** welcome you home with open arms.

:00
:10
:20
:30
:40
:50
1:00

FINISH

AUG 24

WHAT'S **it** mean

PRODIGAL SON:
PART 1

The **son** goes his own way, **blows** all he was given, and then returns to his father's home with the hope of **simply** being hired for a job. The father accepts him back, not as an employee, but as his **son**.

This parable is an **incredible** story of God's love for us. When we go our own way and turn our back on God, He is **waiting** to welcome us home. When we return home, God doesn't accept us as sinners, but He forgives us and brings us in as His sons or daughters. **Wow,** what an awesome God!

Right now, write in your notebook or on the palm of your hand **something** that will remind you of this truth all day...God **loves** you **as** His **child.**

[Jesus] told them this story: "A man had two sons. When the younger told his father, 'I want my share of your estate now, instead of waiting until you die!' his father agreed to divide his wealth between his sons.

"A few days later this younger son packed all his belongings and took a trip to a distant land, and there wasted all his money on parties and prostitutes. About the time his money was gone a great famine swept over the land, and he began to starve. He persuaded a local farmer to hire him to feed his pigs. The boy became so hungry that even the pods he was feeding the swine looked good to him. And no one gave him anything.

"When he finally came to his senses, he said to himself, 'At home even the hired men have food enough and to spare, and here I am, dying of hunger! I will go home to my father and say, "Father, I have sinned against both heaven and you, and am no longer worthy of being called your son. Please take me on as a hired man."'

"So he returned home to his father. And while he was still a long distance away, his father saw him coming, and was filled with loving pity and ran and embraced him and kissed him.

"His son said to him, 'Father, I have sinned against heaven and you, and am not worthy of being called your son—'"

Luke 15:11-21

256

PRODIGAL SON: PART 2

"But his father said to the slaves, 'Quick! Bring the finest robe in the house and put it on him. And a jeweled ring for his finger; and shoes! And kill the calf we have in the fattening pen. We must celebrate with a feast, for this son of mine was dead and has returned to life. He was lost and is found.' So the party began.

"Meanwhile, the older son was in the fields working; when he returned home, he heard dance music coming from the house, and he asked one of the servants what was going on.

"'Your brother is back,' he was told, 'and your father has killed the calf we were fattening and has prepared a great feast to celebrate his coming home again unharmed.'

"The older brother was angry and wouldn't go in. His father came out and begged him, but he replied, 'All these years I've worked hard for you and never once refused to do a single thing you told me to; and in all that time you never gave me even one young goat for a feast with my friends. Yet when this son of yours comes back after spending your money on prostitutes, you celebrate by killing the finest calf we have on the place.'

"'Look, dear son,' his father said to him, 'you and I are very close, and everything I have is yours. But it is right to celebrate. For he is your brother; and he was dead and has come back to life! He was lost and is found!'"

Luke 15:22-32

257

2 5

AUG

Just a thought

If you're **away** from God and in need of a **real** party, return to Him and He'll give **you** a **celebration** you'll **never** forget.

:00

:10

:20

:30

:40

:50

1:00

FINISH

WHAT'S it ? mean

SOLOMON BUILDS THE **TEMPLE**

Do you remember the **Tabernacle?** The Tabernacle was a **portable** place of worship that traveled with the Israelites during their years prior to entering the Promised Land. The Temple that Solomon built was like the Tabernacle **except** it wasn't portable. The Temple was a meeting place between God and His people where **worship** and **sacrifice** took place.

This Temple was not built to house or contain God. Solomon said, "Why, even the skies and the highest heavens cannot contain you, much less this Temple I have built!" (1 Kings 8:27)

Today, God is building a "holy temple" in the **lives** of His followers. If you're a follower, what condition is **your** temple in?

King Hiram of Tyre had always been a great admirer of David, so when he learned that David's son Solomon was the new king of Israel, he sent ambassadors to extend congratulations and good wishes. Solomon replied with a proposal about the Temple of the Lord he wanted to build. His father David, Solomon pointed out to Hiram, had not been able to build it because of the numerous wars going on, and he had been waiting for the Lord to give him peace.

"But now," Solomon said to Hiram, "the Lord my God has given Israel peace on every side; I have no foreign enemies or internal rebellions. So I am planning to build a Temple for the Lord my God, just as he instructed my father that I should do. For the Lord told him, 'Your son, whom I will place upon your throne, shall build me a Temple.' Now please assist me with this project. Send your woodsmen to the mountains of Lebanon to cut cedar timber for me, and I will send my men to work beside them, and I will pay your men whatever wages you ask; for as you know, no one in Israel can cut timber like you Sidonians!"

Hiram was very pleased with the message from Solomon. "Praise God for giving David a wise son to be king of the great nation of Israel," he said.

1 Kings 5:1-7

I, the Preacher, was king of Israel, living in Jerusalem. And I applied myself to search for understanding about everything in the universe. I discovered that the lot of man, which God has dealt to him, is not a happy one. It is all foolishness, chasing the wind.

♦ There is a right time for everything:
  A time to be born; a time to die;
  A time to plant; a time to harvest;
  A time to kill; a time to heal;
  A time to destroy; a time to rebuild;
  A time to cry; a time to laugh;
  A time to grieve; a time to dance;
  A time for scattering stones; a time for
    gathering stones;
  A time to hug; a time not to hug;
  A time to find; a time to lose;
  A time for keeping; a time for
    throwing away;
  A time to tear; a time to repair;
  A time to be quiet; a time to speak up;
  A time for loving; a time for hating;
  A time for war; a time for peace.

Ecclesiastes 1:12-14; 3:1-8

:00

:10

:20

:30

:40

:50

:60

Time has become a **precious** possession in today's world. We are a time-conscious generation. We all have the same **amount** of time–24 hours a day. And God is in **complete** control of all time. He began the world according to His timing, and He will return to take over the world in His time. Because God is God, He knew **exactly** when to send Jesus to the world. Check out Galatians 4:4-5:

"But when the right time came, the time God decided on, he sent his Son, born of a woman, born as a Jew, to buy freedom for us who were slaves to the law so that he could adopt us as his very own sons."

Take a **minute** to give God your time. Ask Him to direct how you **spend** it today.

d o n e

259

28 AUG

ONE MINUTE MEMORY

The Teacher's Proverbs and Conclusion

Two can accomplish more than twice as much as one, for the results can be much better. If one falls, the other pulls him up; but if a man falls when he is alone, he's in trouble.

Also, on a cold night, two under the same blanket gain warmth from each other, but how can one be warm alone? And one standing alone can be attacked and defeated, but two can stand back-to-back and conquer; three is even better, for a triple-braided cord is not easily broken.

♦ Because the Preacher was wise, he went on teaching the people all he knew; and he collected proverbs and classified them. For the Preacher was not only a wise man but a good teacher; he not only taught what he knew to the people, but taught them in an interesting manner.

The wise man's words are like goads that spur to action. They nail down important truths. Students are wise who master what their teachers tell them.

But, my son, be warned: there is no end of opinions ready to be expressed. Studying them can go on forever and become very exhausting!

Here is my final conclusion: fear God and obey his commandments, for this is the entire duty of man. For God will judge us for everything we do, including every hidden thing, good or bad.

Ecclesiastes 4:9-12; 12:9-14

:00
:15
:30
:45
:60

And one standing alone can be attacked and defeated, but two can stand back-to-back and conquer; three is even better, for a triple braided cord is not easily broken.

Ecclesiastes 4:12

done

THE SINS OF
SOLOMON

King Solomon married many other girls besides the Egyptian princess. Many of them came from nations where idols were worshiped—Moab, Ammon, Edom, Sidon, and from the Hittites—even though the Lord had clearly instructed his people not to marry into those nations, because the women they married would get them started worshiping their gods. Yet Solomon did it anyway.

Sure enough, they turned his heart away from the Lord, especially in his old age. They encouraged him to worship their gods instead of trusting completely in the Lord as his father David had done.

Jehovah was very angry with Solomon about this, for now Solomon was no longer interested in the Lord God of Israel who had appeared to him twice to warn him specifically against worshiping other gods. But he hadn't listened, so now the Lord said to him, "Since you have not kept our agreement and have not obeyed my laws, I will tear the kingdom away from you and your family and give it to someone else. However, for the sake of your father David, I won't do this while you are still alive. I will take the kingdom away from your son. And even so I will let him be king of one tribe, for David's sake and for the sake of Jerusalem, my chosen city."

1 Kings 11:1-2, 3b-4, 9-13

It seems **weird** that Solomon could be so wise and yet make such **dumb** mistakes. The law **forbade** kings to have multiple wives and **prohibited** taking wives from other nations. Solomon married foreign women to be **"politically correct"** and gain other nations' loyalty. This move turned out to be **unwise** and led Solomon to be unloyal to God.

We can **learn** from Solomon's mistake. It is better to **please** God first and then others rather than the other way around. Take note and be wise **today**.

end

261

THE KINGDOM DIVIDES

Catch T·H·I·S

Rehoboam didn't take the advice of the older men. No one knows how history would have been different if he had. Instead, he followed the advice of the younger men and the results split the nation in half.

One of the most attractive qualities a person can possess is the ability to take advice from others. When we are open to advice, we communicate humility and leadership.

If you have the opportunity to get advice, take it. Evaluate the advice against the Bible before making your decisions. If you can get older people to give you advice, accept it even more readily. Why? Because your peers or friends may have a tendency to tell you what you want to hear, which isn't advice but confirmation.

It's wise to realize that many people are quick to give advice but slow to take it. Try turning that around in your own life–be slow to give it and quick to take it.

:00

:10

:20

:30

:40

:50

:60
done

[Solomon] ruled in Jerusalem for forty years, and then died and was buried in the city of his father David; and his son Rehoboam reigned in his place.

✦ Rehoboam's inauguration was at Shechem, and all Israel came for the coronation ceremony. Jeroboam, who was still in Egypt where he had fled from King Solomon, heard about the plans from his friends. They urged him to attend, so he joined the rest of Israel at Shechem and was the ringleader in getting the people to make certain demands upon Rehoboam.

"Your father was a hard master," they told Rehoboam. "We don't want you as our king unless you promise to treat us better than he did."

When Jeroboam and the people returned three days later, the new king answered them roughly. He ignored the old men's advice and followed that of the young men.

When the people realized that the king meant what he said and was refusing to listen to them, they began shouting, "Down with David and all his relatives! Let's go home! Let Rehoboam be king of his own family!"

And they all deserted him except for the tribe of Judah, who remained loyal and accepted Rehoboam as their king.

When the people of Israel learned of Jeroboam's return from Egypt, he was asked to come before an open meeting of all the people; and there he was made king of Israel. Only the tribe of Judah continued under the kingship of the family of David.

1 Kings 11:42-43; 12:1-4, 12-14, 16-17, 20

262

THE SINS OF **JEROBOAM**

Jeroboam now built the city of Shechem in the hill country of Ephraim, and it became his capital. Later he built Penuel. Jeroboam thought, "Unless I'm careful, the people will want a descendant of David as their king. When they go to Jerusalem to offer sacrifices at the Temple, they will become friendly with King Rehoboam; then they will kill me and ask him to be their king instead."

So on the advice of his counselors, the king had two gold calf-idols made and told the people, "It's too much trouble to go to Jerusalem to worship; from now on these will be your gods—they rescued you from your captivity in Egypt!"

One of these calf-idols was placed in Bethel and the other in Dan. This was of course a great sin, for the people worshiped them. He also made shrines on the hills and ordained priests from the rank and file of the people—even those who were not from the priest-tribe of Levi.

♦ This was a great sin and resulted in the destruction of Jeroboam's kingdom and the death of all of his family.

1 Kings 12:25-31; 13:34

WHAT'S it mean

For over **100** years three kings ruled the Israelites: Saul, David, and Solomon. When Solomon died, his son, Rehoboam, became king. Immediately, he started a national **rebellion** because he promised to increase the Israelites' pain. His peers told him, "Tell them, if you think my father was hard on you, well, I'll be harder!" (1 Kings 12:10). When the Israelites heard those words, ten of the twelve kingdoms revolted and formed a new nation. The new nation became the northern kingdom called Israel. King Rehoboam maintained control of the southern nation, which was called **Judah.**

The northern kingdom had a new king named Jeroboam. He was **worse** than Rehoboam because he tried to replace God with two golden calves.

You should receive **hope** when you see how God patiently cared for the Israelites even after they **continually** messed up.

Pray a prayer of **thanksgiving** today, thanking God for His **patience** with you.

263

SEP

The Bible is alive,
it speaks to me.

**Martin Luther
(1483-1546)**
German Theologian and
Reformer

King Asa of Judah had been on the throne thirty-eight years when Ahab became the king of Israel; and Ahab reigned for twenty-two years. But he was even more wicked than his father Omri; he was worse than any other king of Israel! And as though that were not enough, he married Jezebel, the daughter of King Ethbaal of the Sidonians, and then began worshiping Baal. First he built a temple and an altar for Baal in Samaria. Then he made other idols and did more to anger the Lord God of Israel than any of the other kings of Israel before him.

♦ Then Elijah, the prophet from Tishbe in Gilead, told King Ahab, "As surely as the Lord God of Israel lives—the God whom I worship and serve—there won't be any dew or rain for several years until I say the word!"

Then the Lord said to Elijah, "Go to the east and hide by Cherith Brook at a place east of where it enters the Jordan River. Drink from the brook and eat what the ravens bring you, for I have commanded them to feed you."

So he did as the Lord had told him to and camped beside the brook. The ravens brought him bread and meat each morning and evening, and he drank from the brook.

♦ If I shut up the heavens so that there is no rain, or if I command the locust swarms to eat up all of your crops, or if I send an epidemic among you, then if my people will humble themselves and pray, and search for me, and turn from their wicked ways, I will hear them from heaven and forgive their sins and heal their land.

1 Kings 16:29-33; 17:1-6; 2 Chronicles 7:13-14

IN **other** words...
KING

The reign of kings **replaced** Israel's period of judges. God was **slow** to give the Israelites a king because He wanted to be the King of the Israelites. Only He could be a totally wise and just king. The Israelites wanted to be ruled by a king just as the surrounding nations were. Because the Israelites wanted to be like other nations, they rejected God as their true King.

Many people want to be like **others** so much that they reject God's ways and go the ways of their friends. Have you rejected God so you can be like others? Ask God to **show** you His way and try to **honor** Him as King of **your** life.

:00
:10
:20
:30
:40
:50
done :60

267

SEP 2
ELIJAH CHALLENGES
THE PROPHETS OF BAAL

:00

:10

Elijah called on God to **consume** a sacrifice with **fire** because He was known as a God of Fire. For

:20

example, a cherub with a flaming sword guarded the Garden of Eden; a burning bush spoke to Moses; Isaiah saw a

:30

throne with "fiery" beings flying around when he was taken into God's presence.

:40

The author of Hebrews calls God a **"consuming fire"** (See 12:24). Fire is a purifier. In heaven, our bodies will

:50

be **purified** because of Jesus. Are you ready to be tested by **God's** fire?

:60

end

It was three years later that the Lord said to Elijah, "Go and tell King Ahab that I will soon send rain again!"

"So it's you, is it?—the man who brought this disaster upon Israel!" Ahab exclaimed when he saw him.

"You're talking about yourself," Elijah answered. "For you and your family have refused to obey the Lord and have worshiped Baal instead. Now bring all the people of Israel to Mount Carmel, with all 450 prophets of Baal and the 400 prophets of Asherah who are supported by Jezebel."

So Ahab summoned all the people and the prophets to Mount Carmel.

Then Elijah talked to them. "How long are you going to waver between two opinions?" he asked the people. "If the Lord is God, follow him! But if Baal is God, then follow him!"

Then Elijah spoke again. "I am the only prophet of the Lord who is left," he told them, "but Baal has 450 prophets. Now bring two young bulls. The prophets of Baal may choose whichever one they wish and cut it into pieces and lay it on the wood of their altar, but without putting any fire under the wood; and I will prepare the other young bull and lay it on the wood on the Lord's altar, with no fire under it. Then pray to your god, and I will pray to the Lord; and the god who answers by sending fire to light the wood is the true God!" And all the people agreed to this test.

1 Kings 18:1, 17-24

268

Elijah

personality plus

Then Elijah turned to the prophets of Baal. "You first," he said, "for there are many of you; choose one of the bulls and prepare it and call to your god; but don't put any fire under the wood."

So they prepared one of the young bulls and placed it on the altar; and they called to Baal all morning, shouting, "O Baal, hear us!" But there was no reply of any kind. Then they began to dance around the altar.

They raved all afternoon until the time of the evening sacrifice, but there was no reply, no voice, no answer.

At the customary time for offering the evening sacrifice, Elijah walked up to the altar and prayed, "O Lord God of Abraham, Isaac, and Israel, prove today that you are the God of Israel and that I am your servant; prove that I have done all this at your command. O Lord, answer me! Answer me so these people will know that you are God and that you have brought them back to yourself."

Then, suddenly, fire flashed down from heaven and burned up the young bull, the wood, the stones, the dust, and even evaporated all the water in the ditch!

And when the people saw it, they fell to their faces upon the ground shouting, "Jehovah is God! Jehovah is God!"

Then Elijah told them to grab the prophets of Baal. "Don't let a single one escape," he commanded.

So they seized them all, and Elijah took them to Kishon Brook and killed them there.

1 Kings 18:25-26, 29, 36-40

Elijah was the **most famous** of the prophets. God used him in **mighty** ways. As you read today, you learned how he showed others that idols were no match for God.

Although Elijah was a **great** prophet, he did get tired and frustrated while working for God. He became depressed because he didn't believe people were responding to his message. During this "down time," God reminded Elijah that He was the mighty God–big enough to **understand** Elijah's discouragement and to care for his prophetic ministry.

Doing ministry can get tiring. But **BEING** God's person will help you survive the **DOING.** Be God's person today and allow Him to **give** you the **strength** to do His work.

:00

:10

:20

:30

:40

:50

:60

the End

4

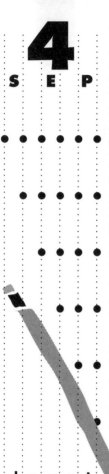

The Lord sent this message to Jonah, the son of Amittai: "Go to the great city of Nineveh, and give them this announcement from the Lord: 'I am going to destroy you, for your wickedness rises before me; it smells to highest heaven.'"

But Jonah was afraid to go and ran away from the Lord. He went down to the seacoast, to the port of Joppa, where he found a ship leaving for Tarshish. He bought a ticket, went on board, and climbed down into the dark hold of the ship to hide there from the Lord.

But as the ship was sailing along, suddenly the Lord flung a terrific wind over the sea, causing a great storm that threatened to send them to the bottom. Fearing for their lives, the desperate sailors shouted to their gods for help and threw the cargo overboard to lighten the ship.

Then the crew decided to draw straws to see which of them had offended the gods and caused this terrible storm; and Jonah drew the short one.

"Throw me out into the sea," [Jonah] said, "and it will become calm again. For I know this terrible storm has come because of me."

Then they picked up Jonah and threw him overboard into the raging sea—and the storm stopped!

The men stood there in awe before Jehovah, and they sacrificed to him and vowed to serve him.

Now the Lord had arranged for a great fish to swallow Jonah. And Jonah was inside the fish three days and three nights.

Jonah 1:1-5a, 7, 12, 15-17

done!

Jonah disobeys the Lord

Give it a try

We are often like Jonah:

1 We run from good things.

2 We think we can hide from God.

3 We keep truth from people.

Write a few thoughts about how one of these three statements **most** relates to your life.

Jonah Prays from the Belly of a Fish

Then Jonah prayed to the Lord his God from inside the fish:

"In my great trouble I cried to the Lord and he answered me; from the depths of death I called, and Lord, you heard me! You threw me into the ocean depths; I sank down into the floods of waters and was covered by your wild and stormy waves. Then I said, 'O Lord, you have rejected me and cast me away. How shall I ever again see your holy Temple?'

"I sank beneath the waves, and death was very near. The waters closed above me; the seaweed wrapped itself around my head. I went down to the bottoms of the mountains that rise from off the ocean floor. I was locked out of life and imprisoned in the land of death. But, O Lord my God, you have snatched me from the yawning jaws of death!

"When I had lost all hope, I turned my thoughts once more to the Lord. And my earnest prayer went to you in your holy Temple. (Those who worship false gods have turned their backs on all the mercies waiting for them from the Lord!)

"I will never worship anyone but you! For how can I thank you enough for all you have done? I will surely fulfill my promises. For my deliverance comes from the Lord alone."

And the Lord ordered the fish to spit up Jonah on the beach, and it did.

Jonah 2

ONE MINUTE MEMORY

I will never worship anyone but you! For how can I thank you enough for all you have done? I will surely fulfill my promises. For my deliverance comes from the Lord alone.

Jonah 2:9

:00

:15

:30

:45

:60

done

271

THE LORD RELENTS FROM SENDING DISASTER

Catch T·H·I·S

God has **proven** Himself to be a God of second chances, **forgiveness,** and grace. The Ninevites turned from their evil ways, and God spared them from destruction. Then they were **thankful** people!

God has also **promised** not to destroy Christians. If you are a Christian, this is good news! God is worthy of your **praise** and worship.

Today, **thank** God for his **unconditional** love for you and spend some time identifying an area of your life that needs to be changed. God **graciously** gives second chances, but He prefers our obedience.

:00
:10
:20
:30
:40
:50
:60
done

Then the Lord spoke to Jonah again: "Go to that great city, Nineveh," he said, "and warn them of their doom, as I told you to before!"

So Jonah obeyed and went to Nineveh. Now Nineveh was a very large city with many villages around it—so large that it would take three days to walk through it.

But the very first day when Jonah entered the city and began to preach, the people repented. Jonah shouted to the crowds that gathered around him, "Forty days from now Nineveh will be destroyed!" And they believed him and declared a fast; from the king on down, everyone put on sackcloth—the rough, coarse garments worn at times of mourning.

For when the king of Nineveh heard what Jonah was saying, he stepped down from his throne, laid aside his royal robes, put on sackcloth, and sat in ashes. And the king and his nobles sent this message throughout the city: "Let no one, not even the animals, eat anything at all, nor even drink any water. Everyone must wear sackcloth and cry mightily to God, and let everyone turn from his evil ways, from his violence and robbing. Who can tell? Perhaps even yet God will decide to let us live and will hold back his fierce anger from destroying us."

And when God saw that they had put a stop to their evil ways, he abandoned his plan to destroy them and didn't carry it through.

Jonah 3

That is why the Lord says, "Turn to me now, while there is time. Give me all your hearts. Come with fasting, weeping, mourning. Let your remorse tear at your hearts and not your garments." Return to the Lord your God, for he is gracious and merciful. He is not easily angered; he is full of kindness and anxious not to punish you.

Who knows? Perhaps even yet he will decide to let you alone and give you a blessing instead of his terrible curse. Perhaps he will give you so much that you can offer your grain and wine to the Lord as before!

Sound the trumpet in Zion! Call a fast and gather all the people together for a solemn meeting. Bring everyone—the elders, the children, and even the babies. Call the bridegroom from his quarters and the bride from her privacy.

The priests, the ministers of God, will stand between the people and the altar, weeping; and they will pray, "Spare your people, O our God; don't let the heathen rule them, for they belong to you. Don't let them be disgraced by the taunts of the heathen who say, 'Where is this God of theirs? How weak and helpless he must be!'"

Then the Lord will pity his people and be indignant for the honor of his land!

Joel 2:12-18

:00

:10

:20

:30

:40

:50

:60

In today's reading Joel called Judah to repent from her sinfulness. Prior to this, God had sent His judgment on the Judeans in the form of locusts, or **grasshoppers.** Millions of locusts invaded them, darkened the skies, and **devastated** the land.

Revelation 9:3-4 describes an even more destructive plague of locusts that will come on the Day of the Lord:

"Then locusts came from the smoke and descended onto the earth and were given power to sting like scorpions. They were told not to hurt the grass or plants or trees, but to attack those people who did not have the mark of God on their foreheads."

There's no reason to be scared if you are a Christian. Thank God for His **protection** today.

d o n e

273

IN **other** words...

"SAYS THE LORD YOUR GOD"

Amos finished his **prophecy** with the key words "says the Lord your God." These words were his **guarantee** that his spoken vision would be fulfilled by the God of creation, the God of Abraham, the God of Moses, etc. He wanted the people to know that his prophetic words weren't his own words but **God's** words and vision for His chosen people.

The Bible you read isn't filled with words of men. The Bible is filled with God's words. These words are life-changing because they're from the Lord your God. Read these words, **learn** from them, **memorize** them, and you'll never be the same.

:00

:10

:20

:30

:40

:50

:60 **done**

"The eyes of the Lord God are watching Israel, that sinful nation, and I will root her up and scatter her across the world. Yet I have promised that this rooting out will not be permanent.

"But all these sinners who say, 'God will not touch us,' will die by the sword.

"Then, at that time I will rebuild the City of David, which is now lying in ruins, and return it to its former glory, and Israel will possess what is left of Edom and of all the nations that belong to me." For so the Lord, who plans it all, has said.

"The time will come when there will be such abundance of crops that the harvest time will scarcely end before the farmer starts again to sow another crop, and the terraces of grapes upon the hills of Israel will drip sweet wine! I will restore the fortunes of my people Israel, and they will rebuild their ruined cities and live in them again; they will plant vineyards and gardens; they will eat their crops and drink their wine. I will firmly plant them there upon the land that I have given them; they shall not be pulled up again," says the Lord your God.

Amos 9:8, 10-15

HOSEA:
THE LORD'S ANGER AND COMPASSION

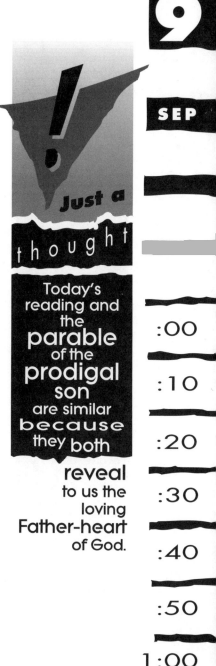

When Israel was a child I loved him as a son and brought him out of Egypt. But the more I called to him, the more he rebelled, sacrificing to Baal and burning incense to idols. I trained him from infancy, I taught him to walk, I held him in my arms. But he doesn't know or even care that it was I who raised him.

As a man would lead his favorite ox, so I led Israel with my ropes of love. I loosened his muzzle so he could eat. I myself have stooped and fed him. But my people shall return to Egypt and Assyria because they won't return to me.

Oh, how can I give you up, my Ephraim? How can I let you go? How can I forsake you like Admah and Zeboiim? My heart cries out within me; how I long to help you! No, I will not punish you as much as my fierce anger tells me to. This is the last time I will destroy Ephraim. For I am God and not man; I am the Holy One living among you, and I did not come to destroy.

For the people shall walk after the Lord. I shall roar as a lion (at their enemies) and my people shall return trembling from the west. Like a flock of birds, they will come from Egypt—like doves flying from Assyria. And I will bring them home again; it is a promise from the Lord.

Hosea 11:1-5, 8-11

9

SEP

Just a

thought

Today's reading and the **parable** of the **prodigal son** are similar because they both **reveal** to us the loving **Father-heart** of God.

:00

:10

:20

:30

:40

:50

1:00

FINISH

ISAIAH
SEES
THE LORD

Catch T·H·I·S

God spoke and His people didn't hear. He **repeated** miracles and the people didn't know what they meant. God **continually** revealed Himself to the Israelites, and yet they continued to worship idols instead of worshiping Him. People reacted the same way when Jesus entered the world's scene hundreds of years later. Jesus **spoke** and some people didn't respond.

You may run into a **similar** reaction when you're trying to reach your friends for God. You may show them Christian love, invite them to church, help them with problems, and provide them with examples of God's love and they still may not respond. If this happens, **realize** you're in good company–it happened to God AND to Jesus.

Understand that you can't make decisions for your friends. They all make their **own** decisions. A Christian's responsibility is to be an **example** of God's love and remain faithful. Do the possible today and allow God to do the impossible with **your** friends.

:00

:10

:20

:30

:40

:50

:60 done

The year King Uzziah died I saw the Lord! He was sitting on a lofty throne, and the Temple was filled with his glory. Hovering about him were mighty, six-winged angels of fire. With two of their wings they covered their faces with two others they covered their feet, and with two they flew. In a great antiphonal chorus they sang, "Holy, holy, holy is the Lord Almighty; the whole earth is filled with his glory."

Then I said, "My doom is sealed, for I am a foul-mouthed sinner, a member of a sinful, foul-mouthed race; and I have looked upon the King, the Lord of heaven's armies."

Then one of the mighty angels flew over to the altar and with a pair of tongs picked out a burning coal. He touched my lips with it and said, "Now you are pronounced 'not guilty' because this coal has touched your lips. Your sins are all forgiven."

Then I heard the Lord asking, "Whom shall I send as a messenger to my people? Who will go?"

And I said, "Lord, I'll go! Send me."

And he said, "Yes, go. But tell my people this: 'Though you hear my words repeatedly, you won't understand them. Though you watch and watch as I perform my miracles, still you won't know what they mean.' Dull their understanding, close their ears, and shut their eyes. I don't want them to see or to hear or to understand, or to turn to me to heal them."

Isaiah 6:1-3, 5-10

MICAH: THE SINS OF ISRAEL

WHAT'S it mean?

These are messages from the Lord to Micah, who lived in the town of Moresheth during the reigns of King Jotham, King Ahaz, and King Hezekiah, all kings of Judah. The messages were addressed to both Samaria and Judah and came to Micah in the form of visions.

Attention! Let all the peoples of the world listen. For the Lord in his holy Temple has made accusations against you!

Look! He is coming! He leaves his throne in heaven and comes to earth, walking on the mountaintops. They melt beneath his feet and flow into the valleys like wax in fire, like water pouring down a hill.

And why is this happening? Because of the sins of Israel and Judah. What sins? The idolatry and oppression centering in the capital cities, Samaria and Jerusalem!

Therefore, the entire city of Samaria will crumble into a heap of rubble and become an open field, her streets plowed up for planting grapes! The Lord will tear down her wall and her forts, exposing their foundations, and pour their stones into the valleys below. All her carved images will be smashed to pieces; her ornate idol temples, built with the gifts of worshipers, will all be burned.

Micah 1:1-7

Samaria was the capital of the Northern Kingdom. The leaders of this kingdom led people **away** from God and into idol worship. All the people of Judah were going to pay for their leader's mistakes. God sent Elijah, Elisha, and Amos in an attempt to get them to turn from their idols. But there was no change. Then Micah came along and prophesied their future destruction as God's judgment for their unfaithfulness.

One **famous** verse in Micah reminds the Israelites of what God wants from them..."to be fair, just, merciful, and to walk humbly with [their] God." These words are a good reminder for us today. Circle one of these words and try to work on it in your life (fair, just, merciful, walk humbly with God).

BIG time word

STUBBORN

What's the **first** thing that comes to your mind when someone says, "Don't be so stubborn"? Do you get defensive? **Angry?** Being stubborn is usually a negative quality displayed by a selfish person who is unwilling to move from a strongly held position or belief. A stubborn person rarely compromises.

If you're known to be stubborn, try **changing** a negative into a positive and become **"stubborn"** for God. Being stubborn for God means you **won't** compromise your beliefs, and you **won't** give in to the distractions that can turn your thoughts, actions, and focus from God.

Finally, in the ninth year of King Hoshea's reign, Samaria fell and the people of Israel were exiled to Assyria. They were placed in colonies in the city of Halah and along the banks of the Habor River in Gozan, and among the cities of the Medes.

This disaster came upon the nation of Israel because the people worshiped other gods, thus sinning against the Lord their God who had brought them safely out of their slavery in Egypt. They had followed the evil customs of the nations which the Lord had cast out from before them. The people of Israel had also secretly done many things that were wrong, and they had built altars to other gods throughout the land. They had placed obelisks and idols at the top of every hill and under every green tree; and they had burned incense to the gods of the very nations which the Lord had cleared out of the land when Israel came in. So the people of Israel had done many evil things, and the Lord was very angry. Yes, they worshiped idols, despite the Lord's specific and repeated warnings.

Again and again the Lord had sent prophets to warn both Israel and Judah to turn from their evil ways; he had warned them to obey his commandments which he had given to their ancestors through these prophets, but Israel wouldn't listen. The people were as stubborn as their ancestors and refused to believe in the Lord their God.

2 Kings 17:6-14

GOOD KING HEZEKIAH

[H]ezekiah] removed the shrines on the hills, broke down the obelisks, knocked down the shameful idols of Asherah, and broke up the bronze serpent that Moses had made, because the people of Israel had begun to worship it by burning incense to it; even though, as King Hezekiah pointed out to them, it was merely a piece of bronze. He trusted very strongly in the Lord God of Israel. In fact, none of the kings before or after him were as close to God as he was. For he followed the Lord in everything, and carefully obeyed all of God's commands to Moses. So the Lord was with him and prospered everything he did. Then he rebelled against the king of Assyria and refused to pay tribute any longer. He also conquered the Philistines as far distant as Gaza and its suburbs, destroying cities both large and small.

It was during the fourth year of his reign (which was the seventh year of the reign of King Hoshea in Israel) that King Shalmaneser of Assyria attacked Israel and began a siege on the city of Samaria. Three years later (during the sixth year of the reign of King Hezekiah and the ninth year of the reign of King Hoshea of Israel) Samaria fell.

2 Kings 18:4-10

Catch T·H·I·S

King Hezekiah is a **rare** example of someone who followed God during a time of sin and rebellion. Today's reading explains that God **blessed** King Hezekiah because he **obeyed** God. God was with him so he prospered in everything he did. Those are great results for following God!

If you follow God you should **stand out** as being unique. Following God doesn't mean you will prosper financially, but it does mean you will have a relationship with God that causes you to live a **different** life.

The Bible tells us that those who don't follow God live in the darkness, and those who do walk in the light. Following God won't mean you'll have a easy or perfect life, but being in God's light will make life **worth** living and you will experience His **rewards** for all eternity.

:00
:10
:20
:30
:40
:50
:60
done

Prayers of **trouble**

need to be followed by

prayers of **praise.**

:OO

:1O

:2O

:3O

:4O

:5O

1:OO

FINISH

THE LORD DELIVERS JUDAH FROM ASSYRIA

During the fourteenth year of the reign of King Hezekiah, King Sennacherib of Assyria besieged and captured all the fortified cities of Judah.

♦ Then [Hezekiah] prayed this prayer: "O Lord God of Israel, sitting on your throne high above the angels, you alone are the God of all the kingdoms of the earth. You created the heavens and the earth. Bend low, O Lord, and listen. Open your eyes, O Lord, and see. Listen to this man's defiance of the living God. Lord, it is true that the kings of Assyria have destroyed all those nations and have burned their idol-gods. But they weren't gods at all; they were destroyed because they were only things that men had made of wood and stone. O Lord our God, we plead with you to save us from his power; then all the kingdoms of the earth will know that you alone are God."

Then Isaiah sent this message to Hezekiah: "The Lord God of Israel says, 'I have heard you!'"

♦ That very night the angel of the Lord killed 185,000 Assyrian troops, and dead bodies were seen all across the landscape in the morning.

Then King Sennacherib returned to Nineveh.

2 Kings 18:13; 19:15-20, 35-36

CHECK IT OUT

God is jealous over those he loves; that is why he takes vengeance on those who hurt them. He furiously destroys their enemies. He is slow in getting angry, but when aroused, his power is incredible, and he does not easily forgive. He shows his power in the terrors of the cyclone and the raging storms; clouds are billowing dust beneath his feet!

Who can stand before an angry God? His fury is like fire; the mountains tumble down before his anger.

The Lord is good. When trouble comes, he is the place to go! And he knows everyone who trusts in him! But he sweeps away his enemies with an overwhelming flood; he pursues them all night long.

What are you thinking of, Nineveh, to defy the Lord? He will stop you with one blow; he won't need to strike again.

♦ O Assyrian king, your princes lie dead in the dust; your people are scattered across the mountains; there is no shepherd now to gather them. There is no healing for your wound—it is far too deep to cure. All who hear your fate will clap their hands for joy, for where can one be found who has not suffered from your cruelty?

Nahum 1:2-3, 6-9; 3:18-19

:00
:10
:20
:30
:40
:50
:60

In many Old Testament passages, we have seen God's anger and **disappointment** directed at both individuals and nations. In the New Testament, God's anger is aimed at those who push away His truth. Check out Romans 1:18-20:
"But God shows his anger from heaven against all sinful, evil men who push away the truth from them. For the truth about God is known to them instinctively; God has put this knowledge in their hearts. Since earliest times men have seen the earth and sky and all God made, and have known of his existence and great eternal power. So they will have no excuse [when standing before God at Judgment Day]."

We can **avoid** God's **anger** by following the truth He has revealed to us.
His truth sets us free.

d o n e

281

SEP

ONE MINUTE MEMORY

:00

:15

:30

:45

:60

done

For the Lord your God has arrived to live among you. He is a mighty Savior. He will give you victory. He will rejoice over you with great gladness; he will love you and not accuse you.

Zephaniah 3:17

Woe to filthy, sinful Jerusalem, city of violence and crime. In her pride she won't listen even to the voice of God. No one can tell her anything; she refuses all correction. She does not trust the Lord nor seek for God.

Her leaders are like roaring lions hunting for their victims—out for everything that they can get. Her judges are like ravenous wolves at evening time, who by dawn have left no trace of their prey.

Her "prophets" are liars seeking their own gain; her priests defile the Temple by their disobedience to God's laws.

But the Lord is there within the city, and he does no wrong. Day by day his justice is more evident, but no one heeds—the wicked know no shame.

Sing, O daughter of Zion; shout, O Israel; be glad and rejoice with all your heart, O daughter of Jerusalem. For the Lord will remove his hand of judgment and disperse the armies of your enemy. And the Lord himself, the King of Israel, will live among you! At last your troubles will be over—you need fear no more.

On that day the announcement to Jerusalem will be, "Cheer up, don't be afraid. For the Lord your God has arrived to live among you. He is a mighty Savior. He will give you victory. He will rejoice over you with great gladness; he will love you and not accuse you." Is that a joyous choir I hear? No, it is the Lord himself exulting over you in happy song.

Zephaniah 3:1-5, 14-17

Zephaniah: Jerusalem's Correction

282

THE CALL OF JEREMIAH: PART 1

These are God's messages to Jeremiah the priest (the son of Hilkiah) who lived in the town of Anathoth in the land of Benjamin. The first of these messages came to him in the thirteenth year of the reign of Amon's son Josiah, king of Judah. Others came during the reign of Josiah's son Jehoiakim, king of Judah, and at various other times until July of the eleventh year of the reign of Josiah's son Zedekiah, king of Judah, when Jerusalem was captured and the people were taken away as slaves.

The Lord said to me, "I knew you before you were formed within your mother's womb; before you were born I sanctified you and appointed you as my spokesman to the world."

"O Lord God," I said, "I can't do that! I'm far too young! I'm only a youth!"

"Don't say that," he replied, "for you will go wherever I send you and speak whatever I tell you to. And don't be afraid of the people, for I, the Lord, will be with you and see you through."

Then he touched my mouth and said, "See, I have put my words in your mouth! Today your work begins, to warn the nations and the kingdoms of the world. In accord with my words spoken through your mouth I will tear down some and destroy them, and plant others, nurture them, and make them strong and great."

Jeremiah 1:1-10

:00 :10 :20 :30 :40 :50 :60 done

Catch T·H·I·S

When God **wants** to use someone, He doesn't respond to excuses like Jeremiah used: "I can't do that! I'm far too young! I'm only a youth!" Jeremiah may not have felt qualified because he lacked training and experience. But that didn't matter to God. God overruled his excuses and let him know that His authority and presence didn't depend on Jeremiah's training or experience. God was **present** in the prophet's life.

Excuses don't limit God when He wants to get a hold of your life. So **get rid** of your excuses and **prepare** yourself to be used by God. Preparing yourself means being **open** to God and **faithful** to living the Christian life. If you have any excuses, go ahead and list them, share them with a friend or youth pastor, and then **throw** them away. Remember, it's not you anyway–it's **God** working in you.

283

:00
:10
:20
:30
:40
:50
1:00

Just a
thought

Where
God
leads

He will
provide
for your
needs!

THE CALL OF
JEREMIAH:
PART 2

Then the Lord asked me, "What do you see now?"

And I replied, "I see a pot of boiling water, tipping southward, spilling over Judah."

"Yes," he said, "for terror from the north will boil out upon all the people of this land. I am calling the armies of the kingdoms of the north to come to Jerusalem and set their thrones at the gates of the city and all along its walls, and in all the other cities of Judah. This is the way I will punish my people for deserting me and for worshiping other gods—yes, idols they themselves have made! Get up and dress and go out and tell them whatever I tell you to say. Don't be afraid of them, or else I will make a fool of you in front of them. For see, today I have made you impervious to their attacks. They cannot harm you. You are strong like a fortified city that cannot be captured, like an iron pillar and heavy gates of brass. All the kings of Judah, its officers, priests, and people will not be able to prevail against you. They will try, but they will fail. For I am with you," says the Lord. "I will deliver you."

Jeremiah 1:13-19

JEREMIAH
SAVED BY MICAH'S
PROPHECY

This message came to Jeremiah from the Lord during the first year of the reign of Jehoiakim (son of Josiah), king of Judah:

Tell them the Lord says: "If you will not listen to me and obey the laws I have given you, and if you will not listen to my servants, the prophets—for I sent them again and again to warn you, but you would not listen to them— then I will destroy this Temple as I destroyed the Tabernacle at Shiloh, and I will make Jerusalem a curse word in every nation of the earth."

When Jeremiah had finished his message, saying everything the Lord had told him to, the priests and false prophets and all the people in the Temple mobbed him, shouting, "Kill him! Kill Him!"

Then some of the wise old men stood and spoke to all the people standing around and said:

"The decision is right; for back in the days when Micah the Morasthite prophesied in the days of King Hezekiah of Judah, he told the people that God said: 'This hill shall be plowed like an open field and this city of Jerusalem razed into heaps of stone, and a forest shall grow at the top where the great Temple now stands!' But did King Hezekiah and the people kill him for saying this? No, they turned from their wickedness and worshiped the Lord and begged the Lord to have mercy upon them; and the Lord held back the terrible punishment he had pronounced against them. If we kill Jeremiah for giving us the messages of God, who knows what God will do to us!"

Jeremiah 26:1, 4-6, 7-8, 17-19

 :00

Although being a prophet was a **"big-time"** responsibility, holding that job had nothing to do with who the parents were. Being a king or priest was a hereditary position which parents passed down the family line. Prophets were unique because they came from different backgrounds and life experiences. It was a special calling from God.

 :10
 :20
 :30

Again and again we see the Bible filled with **ordinary** people doing extraordinary things. Let that be an encouragement to you today. And remember that if you're a Christian, you're part of an **incredible** family line, and eternal life is passed on to you from Jesus.

 :40
 :50
 :60

end

285

WHAT'S it mean

JUDAH GOES INTO EXILE

Jeremiah had **warned** the Israelites that their Temple would be **destroyed.** Today's reading describes this destruction that was the result of their **sin,** for they had taken God out of their Temple. God tried to show great compassion to the Israelites by warning them through the prophets. The Babylonians, however, showed no compassion at all and even killed them in the Temple itself. God's presence had left the Temple. The Babylonians burned the Temple and plundered its treasures.

Your church building allows people to gather for **worship,** but God doesn't live in your church. The Bible informs us that Christians are God's **temple** because His presence lives in people. Are you doing anything to your body or life that might be destroying God's temple? If so, what can you do **today** to **stop** the **destruction?**

Zedekiah was twenty-one years old when he became king and he reigned eleven years in Jerusalem. His reign, too, was evil so far as the Lord was concerned, for he refused to take the counsel of Jeremiah the prophet, who gave him messages from the Lord.

Jehovah the God of their fathers sent his prophets again and again to warn them, for he had compassion on his people and on his Temple. But the people mocked these messengers of God and despised their words, scoffing at the prophets until the anger of the Lord could no longer be restrained, and there was no longer any remedy.

Then the Lord brought the king of Babylon against them and killed their young men, even going after them right into the Temple, and had no pity upon them, killing even young girls and old men. The Lord used the king of Babylon to destroy them completely. He also took home with him all the items, great and small, used in the Temple, and treasures from both the Temple and the palace, and took with him all the royal princes. Then his army burned the Temple and broke down the walls of Jerusalem and burned all the palaces and destroyed all the valuable Temple utensils. Those who survived were taken away to Babylon as slaves to the king and his sons until the kingdom of Persia conquered Babylon.

Thus the word of the Lord spoken through Jeremiah came true, that the land must rest for seventy years to make up for the years when the people refused to observe the Sabbath.

2 Chronicles 36:11-12, 15-21

286

Lament Over Fallen Jerusalem

Jerusalem's streets, once thronged with people, are silent now. Like a widow broken with grief, she sits alone in her mourning.

She, once queen of nations, is now a slave. She sobs through the night; tears run down her cheeks. Among all her lovers, there is none to help her. All her friends are now her enemies.

♦ All hope is gone; my strength has turned to water, for the Lord has left me. Oh, remember the bitterness and suffering you have dealt to me! For I can never forget these awful years; always my soul will live in utter shame.

Yet there is one ray of hope: his compassion never ends. It is only the Lord's mercies that have kept us from complete destruction. Great is his faithfulness; his loving-kindness begins afresh each day. My soul claims the Lord as my inheritance; therefore I will hope in him. The Lord is wonderfully good to those who wait for him, to those who seek for him. It is good both to hope and wait quietly for the salvation of the Lord.

Lamentations 1:1-2; 3:18-26

ONE MINUTE MEMORY

The Lord is wonderfully good to those who wait for him, to those who seek him.

Lamentations 3:25

:00

:15

:30

:45

:60

done

287

CHECK IT OUT

THE LORD PROMISES VENGEANCE ON BABYLON

Obadiah **describes** God's punishment on Edom for helping Babylon invade and conquer Israel. He **prophesied** that God would destroy the Edomites **because** of their actions.

In many places throughout the Bible it has been prophesied that God will punish and destroy all those who have not **repented** from their sin. Check out Peter's description of what this future will look like:
"The day of the Lord is surely coming...and the heavenly bodies will disappear in fire, and the earth and everything on it will be burned up. But we are looking forward to God's promise of new heavens and a new earth afterwards, where there will be only goodness."
(2 Peter 3:10, 12)

It's **good** advice to be on God's side. God is **compassionate** and slow to anger but his final judgement against the godless will be severe. Read the rest of 2 Peter chapter three and see how you are called to prepare **yourself**.

:00

:10

:20

:30

:40

:50

:60

done

Note this: Wicked men trust themselves alone (as these Chaldeans do), and fail; but the righteous man trusts in me and lives! What's more, these arrogant Chaldeans are betrayed by all their wine, for it is treacherous. In their greed they have collected many nations, but like death and hell, they are never satisfied. The time is coming when all their captives will taunt them, saying: "You robbers! At last justice has caught up with you! Now you will get your just deserts for your oppression and extortion!"

• I tremble when I hear all this; my lips quiver with fear. My legs give way beneath me, and I shake in terror. I will quietly wait for the day of trouble to come upon the people who invade us.

Even though the fig trees are all destroyed, and there is neither blossom left nor fruit; though the olive crops all fail, and the fields lie barren; even if the flocks die in the fields and the cattle barns are empty, yet I will rejoice in the Lord; I will be happy in the God of my salvation. The Lord God is my strength; he will give me the speed of a deer and bring me safely over the mountains.

Habakkuk 2:4-6; 3:16-19a

288

OBADIAH: THE DAY OF THE LORD

"In that day not one wise man will be left in all of Edom!" says the Lord. "For I will fill the wise men of Edom with stupidity.

"And why? Because of what you did to your brother Israel. Now your sins will be exposed for all to see; ashamed and defenseless, you will be cut off forever. For you deserted Israel in his time of need. You stood aloof, refusing to lift a finger to help him when invaders carried off his wealth and divided Jerusalem among them by lot; you were as one of his enemies.

"You should not have done it. You should not have gloated when they took him far away to foreign lands; you should not have rejoiced in the day of his misfortune; you should not have mocked in his time of need.

"The Lord's vengeance will soon fall upon all Gentile nations. As you have done to Israel, so will it be done to you. Your acts will boomerang upon your heads. You drank my cup of punishment upon my holy mountain, and the nations round about will drink it too; yes, they will drink and stagger back and disappear from history, no longer nations any more.

"But Jerusalem will become a refuge, a way of escape. Israel will reoccupy the land."

Obadiah 1:8, 10-12, 15-17

Obadiah is the **shortest** of the 39 Old Testament books. In only **21** verses the prophet Obadiah expresses **nothing** but bad news. His words are directed at the Edomites who rejoiced at the destruction of Jerusalem. Edom was a neighboring nation who **always** opposed Israel. God **loved** the Israelites, His chosen children, and promised to deal forcefully with the nations that went against them. As a Christian, **you** are one of God's children...He will **protect** you...count on it.

:00

:10

:20

:30

:40

:50

:60

end

SEP 24

WHAT'S it ? mean

EZEKIEL SEES
THE RESTORATION
OF ISRAEL

Ezekiel's **vision** is an example of something that **only** God could accomplish. The scattered bones refer to the nation of Israel who seemed to be spiritually dead and hopeless. Only God could **restore** this nation. It was God's **promise!**

Today, there are nations, churches, and people that are spiritually dead and hopeless. Like the nation of Israel, only God can **restore** them. Our responsibility is to **pray** for them. If your church or youth group is a graveyard of scattered bones, you should pray that God would **breathe** life into it. It may appear hopeless, but it's not impossible for God. Begin praying **today** for those "dead bones" that only God can **raise up.**

The power of the Lord was upon me and I was carried away by the Spirit of the Lord to a valley full of old, dry bones that were scattered everywhere across the ground.

Then he told me to speak to the bones and say: "O dry bones, listen to the words of God, for the Lord God says, 'See! I am going to make you live and breathe again! I will replace the flesh and muscles on you and cover you with skin. I will put breath into you, and you shall live and know I am the Lord.'"

So I spoke these words from God, just as he told me to; and suddenly there was a rattling noise from all across the valley, and the bones of each body came together and attached to each other as they used to be.

Then he told me to call to the wind and say: "The Lord God says: Come from the four winds, O Spirit, and breathe upon these slain bodies, that they may live again." So I spoke to the winds as he commanded me, and the bodies began breathing; they lived and stood up—a very great army.

Then he told me what the vision meant: "These bones," he said, "represent all the people of Israel. They say: 'We have become a heap of dried-out bones—all hope is gone.' But tell them, 'The Lord God says: My people, I will open your graves of exile and cause you to rise again and return to the land of Israel. I will put my Spirit into you, and you shall live and return home again to your own land. Then you will know that I, the Lord, have done just what I promised you.'"

Ezekiel 37:1-2a, 4-7, 9-12, 14

290

Daniel

Belshazzar the king invited a thousand of his officers to a great feast where the wine flowed freely. While Belshazzar was drinking, he was reminded of the gold and silver cups taken long before from the Temple in Jerusalem during Nebuchadnezzar's reign and brought to Babylon. Belshazzar ordered that these sacred cups be brought in to the feast, and when they arrived he and his princes, wives, and concubines drank toasts from them to their idols made of gold and silver, brass and iron, wood and stone.

Suddenly, as they were drinking from these cups, they saw the fingers of a man's hand writing on the plaster of the wall opposite the lampstand. The king himself saw the fingers as they wrote. His face blanched with fear, and such terror gripped him that his knees knocked together and his legs gave way beneath him.

But when the queen-mother heard what was happening, she rushed to the banquet hall and said to Belshazzar, "Calm yourself, Your Majesty, don't be so pale and frightened over this. For there is a man in your kingdom who has within him the spirit of the holy gods. In the days of your father this man was found to be as full of wisdom and understanding as though he were himself a god. And in the reign of King Nebuchadnezzar, he was made chief of all the magicians, astrologers, Chaldeans, and soothsayers of Babylon. Call for this man, Daniel—or Belteshazzar, as the king called him—for his mind is filled with divine knowledge and understanding. He can interpret dreams, explain riddles, and solve knotty problems. He will tell you what the writing means."

Daniel 5:1-2, 4-6, 10-12

Daniel was born in **Israel** but was taken **captive** in 605 B.C. by the Babylonians. He became a **servant** of the Babylonian king, **Nebuchadnezzar.** In an attempt to brainwash and take away Daniel's identity, he was given the name Belteshazaar. But Daniel had an unwavering, deep-rooted faith in God. Because of this **faith,** God granted him gifts of exceptional **wisdom** and understanding. As you read about Daniel, you'll see his **godliness** expressed in his **courage.**

:00

:10

:20

:30

:40

:50

:60

the End

291

:00

:10

:20

:30

:40

:50

1:00

FINISH

It's much **easier** to keep your **mouth closed** and your hand **open** for gifts

than it is to **reject** rewards and speak **against** the wickedness of the **gift-giver!**

DANIEL
INTERPRETS
THE WRITING

So Daniel was rushed in to see the king. The king asked him, "Are you the Daniel brought from Israel as a captive by King Nebuchadnezzar? I am told you can solve all kinds of mysteries. If you can tell me the meaning of those words, I will clothe you in purple robes, with a gold chain around your neck, and make you the third ruler in the kingdom."

Daniel answered, "Keep your gifts or give them to someone else, but I will tell you what the writing means.

"You have defied the Lord of Heaven and brought here these cups from his Temple; and you and your officers and wives and concubines have been drinking wine from them while praising gods of silver, gold, brass, iron, wood, and stone—gods that neither see nor hear nor know anything at all. But you have not praised the God who gives you the breath of life and controls your destiny! And so God sent those fingers to write this message:
'Mene,' 'Mene,' 'Tekel,' 'Parsin.'

"This is what it means:

"*Mene* means 'numbered'—God has numbered the days of your reign, and they are ended.

"*Tekel* means 'weighed'—you have been weighed in God's balances and have failed the test.

"*Parsin* means 'divided'—your kingdom will be divided and given to the Medes and Persians."

That very night Belshazzar, the Chaldean king, was killed, and Darius the Mede entered the city and began reigning at the age of sixty-two.

Daniel 5:13, 16-17, 23-28, 30-31

292

Cyrus Sends Israel Home

During the first year of the reign of King Cyrus of Persia, the Lord fulfilled Jeremiah's prophecy by giving King Cyrus the desire to send this proclamation throughout his empire (he also put it into the permanent records of the realm):

"Cyrus, king of Persia, hereby announces that Jehovah, the God of heaven who gave me my vast empire, has now given me the responsibility of building him a Temple in Jerusalem, in the land of Judah. All Jews throughout the kingdom may now return to Jerusalem to rebuild this Temple of Jehovah, who is the God of Israel and of Jerusalem. May his blessings rest upon you. Those Jews who do not go should contribute toward the expenses of those who do and also supply them with clothing, transportation, supplies for the journey, and a freewill offering for the Temple."

Then God gave a great desire to the leaders of the tribes of Judah and Benjamin, and to the priests and Levites, to return to Jerusalem at once to rebuild the Temple. And all the Jewish exiles who chose to remain in Persia gave them whatever assistance they could, as well as gifts for the Temple.

King Cyrus himself donated the gold bowls and other valuable items, which King Nebuchadnezzar had taken from the Temple at Jerusalem and had placed in the temple of his own gods.

Ezra 1:1-7

BIG time word

CON TRIB UTE

In the **rebuilding** of the Temple, the Israelites needed to help out with the work load or **contribute** to the finances.

When we think of contributing, we usually think of **donating** money to church or to a worthy organization. But you can contribute **more** than your money. In addition to money, God can use your work and your **time**. There are thousands of churches and ministries outside the church that **need** your contribution to help **build** and **rebuild** their ministry.

Make a **contribution** today! Your contribution may not seem like much to you, but it may be a **treasure** to another.

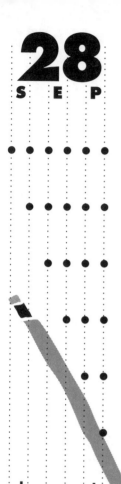

28
S E P

d o n e !

"Why is everyone saying it is not the right time for rebuilding my Temple?" asks the Lord.

His reply to them is this: "Is it then the right time for you to live in luxurious homes, when the Temple lies in ruins?

"Think it over," says the Lord Almighty. "Consider how you have acted and what has happened as a result! Then go up into the mountains, bring down timber, and rebuild my Temple, and I will be pleased with it and appear there in my glory," says the Lord.

"You hope for much but get so little. And when you bring it home, I blow it away—it doesn't last at all. Why? Because my Temple lies in ruins, and you don't care. Your only concern is your own fine homes. That is why I am holding back the rains from heaven and giving you such scant crops. In fact, I have called for a drought upon the land, yes, and in the highlands too—a drought to wither the grain and grapes and olives and all your other crops, a drought to starve both you and all your cattle and ruin everything you have worked so hard to get."

Then Zerubbabel (son of Shealtiel), the governor of Judah, and Joshua (son of Josedech), the High Priest, and the few people remaining in the land obeyed Haggai's message from the Lord their God; they began to worship him in earnest.

Haggai 1:2-4, 7-12

Haggai: rebuild the temple

God withheld His blessing from the people because of their selfish hearts.

What are **two** things in your life that **cause** you to have a **selfish heart?**

Give it a try

1 _____

2 _____

Today, ask God to change the selfish areas in your life.

ZECHARIAH ENCOURAGES THE EXILES

The following February, still in the second year of the reign of King Darius, another message from the Lord came to Zechariah (son of Berechiah and grandson of Iddo the prophet), in a vision in the night: I saw a Man sitting on a red horse that was standing among the myrtle trees beside a river. Behind him were other horses, red and bay and white, each with its rider.

Then the other riders reported to the Angel of the Lord, "We have patrolled the whole earth, and everywhere there is prosperity and peace."

Upon hearing this, the Angel of the Lord prayed this prayer: "O Lord Almighty, for seventy years your anger has raged against Jerusalem and the cities of Judah. How long will it be until you again show mercy to them?"

And the Lord answered the angel who stood beside me, speaking words of comfort and assurance.

Then the angel said, "Shout out this message from the Lord Almighty: 'Don't you think I care about what has happened to Judah and Jerusalem? I am as jealous as a husband for his captive wife. I am very angry with the heathen nations sitting around at ease, for I was only a little displeased with my people, but the nations afflicted them far beyond my intentions.' Therefore the Lord declares: 'I have returned to Jerusalem filled with mercy; my Temple will be rebuilt,' says the Lord Almighty, 'and so will all Jerusalem.' Say it again: 'The Lord Almighty declares that the cities of Israel will again overflow with prosperity, and the Lord will again comfort Jerusalem and bless her and live in her.'"

Zechariah 1:7-8, 11-17

295

:00
:10
:20
:30
:40
:50
:60
done

Catch THIS

The Israelites **suffered** great pain and defeat. While God directed His anger toward the nations that beat up the Israelites, He also expressed **compassion** for the Israelites' pain.

In the New Testament we read that God expresses compassion to suffering Christians. Check out 2 Corinthians 1:3-4: "What a wonderful God we have—he is the Father of our Lord Jesus Christ, the source of every mercy, and the one who so wonderfully comforts and strengthens us in our hardships and trials. And why does he do this? So that when others are troubled, needing our sympathy and encouragement, we can pass on to them this same help and comfort God has given us."

Rest in the promise that God continues to give **encouragement** and support to those in need.

:00

:10

:20

:30

:40

:50

1:00

Just a

t h o u g h t

Discouragement and **f e a r** are two tactics the devil uses to **stop** God's work.

Don't let them get in **your** way!

THE EXILES
REBUILD
THE TEMPLE

When the enemies of Judah and Benjamin heard that the exiles had returned and were rebuilding the Temple, they approached Zerubbabel and the other leaders and suggested, "Let us work with you, for we are just as interested in your God as you are; we have sacrificed to him ever since King Esar-haddon of Assyria brought us here."

But Zerubbabel and Jeshua and the other Jewish leaders replied, "No, you may have no part in this work. The Temple of the God of Israel must be built by the Israelis, just as King Cyrus has commanded."

Then the local residents tried to discourage and frighten them by sending agents to tell lies about them to King Cyrus. This went on during his entire reign and lasted until King Darius took the throne.

♦ Governors Tattenai and Shethar-bozenai, and their companions complied at once with the command of King Darius.

So the Jewish leaders continued in their work, and they were greatly encouraged by the preaching of the prophets Haggai and Zechariah (son of Iddo).

The Temple was finally finished, as had been commanded by God and decreed by Cyrus, Darius, and Artaxerxes, the kings of Persia. The completion date was February 18 in the sixth year of the reign of King Darius II.

Ezra 4:1-5; 6:13-15

OCT

I feel that a comprehensive study of the Bible is a liberal education for anyone. Nearly all of the great men of our country have been well versed in the teachings of the Bible.

Franklin D. Roosevelt (1882-1945)
United States President

Nehemiah personality Plus

The autobiography of Nehemiah, the son of Hecaliah:

In December of the twentieth year of the reign of King Artaxerxes of Persia, when I was at the palace at Shushan, one of my fellow Jews named Hanani came to visit me with some men who had arrived from Judah. I took the opportunity to inquire about how things were going in Jerusalem.

"How are they getting along—," I asked, "the Jews who returned to Jerusalem from their exile here?"

"Well," they replied, "things are not good; the wall of Jerusalem is still torn down, and the gates are burned."

When I heard this, I sat down and cried. In fact, I refused to eat for several days, for I spent the time in prayer to the God of heaven.

"O Lord God," I cried out; "O great and awesome God who keeps his promises and is so loving and kind to those who love and obey him! Hear my prayer! Listen carefully to what I say! Look down and see me praying night and day for your people Israel. I confess that we have sinned against you; yes, I and my people have committed the horrible sin of not obeying the commandments you gave us through your servant Moses. Oh, please remember what you told Moses! You said,

"'If you sin, I will scatter you among the nations; but if you return to me and obey my laws, even though you are exiled to the farthest corners of the universe, I will bring you back to Jerusalem. For Jerusalem is the place in which I have chosen to live.'"

Nehemiah 1:1-9

Nehemiah is an example of a **great** leader. He had to provide the necessary leadership to rebuild the **wall** of Jerusalem. This was no easy job! He faced one obstacle after another. But his **vision,** courage, and **faith** were much stronger than any of the problems that came his way.

Nehemiah's **prayer** life is one leadership quality worth studying. He knew his strongest **defense** against the enemy was to be on his knees and in conversation with God.

Check out Nehemiah, **copy** his character qualities, **begin** praying about everything, and ask God to **bless** your leadership.

:00

:10

:20

:30

:40

:50

:60

the End

CHECK IT OUT

Being a Christian isn't easy. Trying to follow God and keeping His commandments will bring opposition, frustration, and trials. But Jesus **understands** these struggles and reminds Christians that problems are only **temporary.** Check out the good news in John 16:33:

"I have told you all this so that you will have peace of heart and mind. Here on earth you will have many trials and sorrows; but cheer up, for I have overcome the world."

This is a **great** verse to remember when you're struggling. Pain is temporary. Trials will clear up. Problems will pass away. Christians will have an **eternity** to rejoice and **celebrate** because Jesus has overcome the world. **Praise** Him **today.**

:00

:10

:20

:30

:40

:50

:60

At last the wall was completed to half its original height around the entire city—for the workers worked hard.

But when Sanballat and Tobiah and the Arabians, Ammonites, and Ashdodites heard that the work was going right ahead and that the breaks in the wall were being repaired, they became furious. They plotted to lead an army against Jerusalem to bring about riots and confusion. But we prayed to our God and guarded the city day and night to protect ourselves.

From then on, only half worked while the other half stood guard behind them. And the masons and laborers worked with weapons within easy reach beside them or with swords belted to their sides. The trumpeter stayed with me to sound the alarm.

♦ The wall was finally finished in early September—just fifty-two days after we had begun!

When our enemies and the surrounding nations heard about it, they were frightened and humiliated, and they realized that the work had been done with the help of our God.

Nehemiah 4:6-9, 16-18a; 6:15-16

d o n e

word

peace

I was glad for the suggestion of going to Jerusalem, to the Temple of the Lord. Now we are standing here inside the crowded city. All Israel—Jehovah's people—have come to worship as the law requires, to thank and praise the Lord. Look! There are the judges holding court beside the city gates, deciding all the people's arguments.

Pray for the peace of Jerusalem. May all who love this city prosper. O Jerusalem, may there be peace within your walls and prosperity in your palaces. This I ask for the sake of all my brothers and my friends who live here; and may there be peace as a protection to the Temple of the Lord.

Psalm 122

"Peace" is an **important** word for Christians. Those without a relationship with God really can't understand or experience the peace **God** offers. This peace comes from being in **harmony** with God and with other people and brings a **confidence** that conquers worry. It's a peace that can't be quenched. God used Jesus to bring this type of **peace** into the world. Those that rejected Jesus, rejected His peace. If you're a Christian and you don't feel peace, then talk to someone who can provide you wise counsel and help you **experience** this peace. It's worth the risk of asking someone for help...go for it **today!**

4
oct

personality Ezra
plus

Ezra was a **priest** known for his **diligent** study of the Scriptures. While in Babylonian captivity, he took advantage of a **negative** situation and made it **positive** for himself as well as for the Israelites. Ezra's work **strengthened** the Israelite's faith and helped them keep **focused** on God.

:00

:10

Are you a man or woman of God who **knows** the Scriptures and can use this God-given knowledge to **influence** others spiritually? If you're not, try putting together an **action** plan of how you might become this **type** of person.

:20

:30

:40

:50

:60

Ezra the priest brought out to them the scroll of Moses' laws. He stood on a wooden stand made especially for the occasion so that everyone could see him as he read. He faced the square in front of the Water Gate and read from early morning until noon. To his right stood Mattithiah, Shema, Anaiah, Uriah, Hilkiah, and Maaseiah. To his left were Pedaiah, Mishael, Malchijah, Hashum, Hash-baddenah, Zechariah, and Meshullam.

Then Ezra blessed the Lord, the great God, and all the people said, "Amen," and lifted their hands toward heaven; then they bowed and worshiped the Lord with their faces toward the ground.

As Ezra read from the scroll, Jeshua, Bani, Sherebiah, Jamin, Akkub, Shabbethai, Hodiah, Maaseiah, Kelita, Azariah, Jozabad, Hanan, Pelaiah, and the Levites went among the people and explained the meaning of the passage that was being read. All the people began sobbing when they heard the commands of the law.

Then Ezra the priest, and I as governor, and the Levites who were assisting me, said to them, "Don't cry on such a day as this! For today is a sacred day before the Lord your God—it is a time to celebrate with a hearty meal and to send presents to those in need, for the joy of the Lord is your strength. You must not be dejected and sad!"

Nehemiah 8:2-3, 5-10

the End

302

PERSIA
NEEDS A NEW
QUEEN

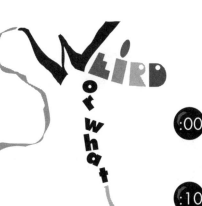

It was the third year of the reign of King Ahasuerus, emperor of vast Media-Persia, with its 127 provinces stretching from India to Ethiopia. This was the year of the great celebration at Shushan Palace, to which the emperor invited all his governors, aides, and army officers, bringing them in from every part of Media-Persia for the occasion.

On the final day when the king was feeling high, half drunk from wine, he told the seven eunuchs who were his personal aides—Mehuman, Biztha, Harbona, Bigtha, Abagtha, Zethar, and Carkas—to bring Queen Vashti to him with the royal crown upon her head so that all the men could gaze upon her beauty—for she was a very beautiful woman. But when they conveyed the emperor's order to Queen Vashti, she refused to come. The king was furious

Memucan answered for the others, "Queen Vashti has wronged not only the king but every official and citizen of your empire. We suggest that, subject to your agreement, you issue a royal edict, a law of the Medes and Persians that can never be changed, that Queen Vashti be forever banished from your presence and that you choose another queen more worthy than she. When this decree is published throughout your great kingdom, husbands everywhere, whatever their rank, will be respected by their wives!"

Esther 1:1-3, 10-12, 16, 19-20

:00

:10

God is never explicitly mentioned in the entire Book of Esther. Nevertheless, the book's 167 verses **definitely** show the **hand** of God working in people's lives. The Book of Esther is a story of God's **love** for the Israelites and His **protection** for them.
:20

:30

God is **always** loving and protecting...even when you're not aware of it. Today, look for ways God is working in **your** life that you normally wouldn't notice. His work doesn't stop even when His name isn't mentioned.
:40

:50

:60

end

personality Plus Esther

Esther was a Jewish **orphan** raised in Persia by her uncle Mordecai. She became the **Queen** of Persia when the previous queen refused to appear at a banquet hosted by her husband. Her absence offended the King and he immediately **chose** Esther to replace her.

:00

:10

As Queen, Esther initially kept her **Jewish** identity a secret. When a madman attempted to destroy the Jewish people, however, she foiled his evil plot by **revealing** her heritage to the king.

:20

:30

Over and **over** we see God using unlikely people like Esther to do **great** things. Sometimes God uses men, other times He uses women. You never know when He's going to use you. **Prepare** yourself to be used by God **today.**

:40

:50

:60

Nₒw there was a certain Jew at the palace named Mordecai (son of Jair, son of Shimei, son of Kish, a Benjaminite). He had been captured when Jerusalem was destroyed by King Nebuchadnezzar and had been exiled to Babylon along with King Jeconiah of Judah and many others. This man had a beautiful and lovely young cousin, Hadassah (also called Esther), whose father and mother were dead, and whom he had adopted into his family and raised as his own daughter. So now, as a result of the king's decree, Esther was brought to the king's harem at Shushan Palace along with many other young girls. Hegai, who was responsible for the harem, was very much impressed with her and did his best to make her happy; he ordered a special menu for her, favored her for the beauty treatments, gave her seven girls from the palace as her maids, and gave her the most luxurious apartment in the harem. Esther hadn't told anyone that she was a Jewess, for Mordecai had said not to.

Well, the king loved Esther more than any of the other girls. He was so delighted with her that he set the royal crown on her head and declared her queen instead of Vashti.

Esther 2:5-10, 17

the End

HAMAN PLOTS TO KILL **THE JEWS**

WHAT'S it mean

Soon afterwards King Ahasuerus appointed Haman (son of Hammedatha the Agagite) as prime minister. He was the most powerful official in the empire next to the king himself. Now all the king's officials bowed before him in deep reverence whenever he passed by, for so the king had commanded. But Mordecai refused to bow.

Haman was furious but decided not to lay hands on Mordecai alone, but to move against all of Mordecai's people, the Jews, and destroy all of them throughout the whole kingdom of Ahasuerus.

Haman now approached the king about the matter. "There is a certain race of people scattered through all the provinces of your kingdom," he began, "and their laws are different from those of any other nation, and they refuse to obey the king's laws; therefore, it is not in the king's interest to let them live. If it please the king, issue a decree that they be destroyed, and I will pay $20,000,000 into the royal treasury for the expenses involved in this purge."

The king agreed, confirming his decision by removing his ring from his finger and giving it to Haman, telling him, "Keep the money, but go ahead and do as you like with these people—whatever you think best."

Esther 3:1-2, 5-6, 8-11

Haman was a **madman** full of pride who became **outraged** when Mordecai didn't bow to him. Rather than confronting Mordecai with his anger, he made an oath to kill the **entire** race of Jewish people. But God thwarted his plans and used Esther to save the Jewish people. Haman was then killed as a result of his evil plans.

Throughout thousands of years, Haman has been followed by others who have expressed rage and hatred by committing crimes on innocent victims. We need to **pray** daily for these angry people and do whatever we can to **stamp** out hatred. Today, ask God to give you a **sensitive** heart that mourns over hatred. **Walk** in love today and be an example for others to **follow**.

:00

:10

:20

:30

:40

:50

1:00

Just a thought

When a **situation** seems **hopeless**, remind yourself of God's **power** and ask Him to turn things **around**.

He has done it **before** and can do it **again**.

HAMAN'S DOWNFALL

So the king and Haman came to Esther's banquet. Again, during the wine course, the king asked her, "What is your petition, Queen Esther? What do you wish? Whatever it is, I will give it to you, even if it is half of my kingdom!"

And at last Queen Esther replied, "If I have won your favor, O king, and if it please Your Majesty, save my life and the lives of my people. For I and my people have been sold to those who will destroy us. We are doomed to destruction and slaughter. If we were only to be sold as slaves, perhaps I could remain quiet, though even then there would be incalculable damage to the king that no amount of money could begin to cover."

"What are you talking about?" King Ahasuerus demanded. "Who would dare touch you?"

Esther replied, "This wicked Haman is our enemy."

Then Haman grew pale with fright before the king and queen.

Then Harbona, one of the king's aides, said, "Sir, Haman has just ordered a 75-foot gallows constructed, to hang Mordecai, the man who saved the king from assassination! It stands in Haman's courtyard."

"Hang Haman on it," the king ordered.

So they did, and the king's wrath was pacified.

Esther 7:1-6, 9-10

306

MALACHI:
MESSENGER OF THE COVENANT

"Listen: I will send my messenger before me to prepare the way. And then the One you are looking for will come suddenly to his Temple—the Messenger of God's promises, to bring you great joy. Yes, he is surely coming," says the Lord Almighty. "But who can live when he appears? Who can endure his coming? For he is like a blazing fire refining precious metal, and he can bleach the dirtiest garments! Like a refiner of silver he will sit and closely watch as the dross is burned away. He will purify the Levites, the ministers of God, refining them like gold or silver, so that they will do their work for God with pure hearts. Then once more the Lord will enjoy the offerings brought to him by the people of Judah and Jerusalem, as he did before."

♦ "Watch now," the Lord Almighty declares, "the day of judgment is coming, burning like a furnace. The proud and wicked will be burned up like straw; like a tree, they will be consumed—roots and all.

"But for you who fear my name, the Sun of Righteousness will rise with healing in his wings. And you will go free, leaping with joy like calves let out to pasture. Then you will tread upon the wicked as ashes underfoot," says the Lord Almighty.

"See, I will send you another prophet like Elijah before the coming of the great and dreadful judgment day of God. His preaching will bring fathers and children together again, to be of one mind and heart, for they will know that if they do not repent, I will come and utterly destroy their land."

Malachi 3:1-4; 4:1-3, 5-6

:00

:10

Malachi is the **last** of the Old Testament prophets. We know **nothing** about the person of Malachi. All we have are his written words. But by these words we can sense his **dynamic** love for God and a **strong** faith in God's plan.

:30

What would **your** words tell the world about your **love** for God and **faith** in Him?

:40

:50

:60

end

307

CHECK IT OUT

THE PROMISE OF JESUS' COMING

To **"be commissioned"** means to receive the authority, permission, and **support** to be sent out. Churches throughout the country commission missionaries, with prayer and other types of support, to serve God in foreign nations.

In Matthew 28:19-20, Jesus commissions His followers by saying, "Therefore GO and make disciples in all the nations, baptizing them into the name of the Father and of the Son and of the Holy Spirit, and then teach these new disciples to obey all the commands I have given you and be sure of this—that I am with you always, even to the end of the world."

Today, pray for a missionary you might know. Also, ask God how you might be commissioned to make **disciples** in **your** "nations" (school, neighborhood, church, etc.).

:00

:10

:20

:30

:40

:50

:60

d o n e

" And now," said the Lord—the Lord who formed me from my mother's womb to serve him who commissioned me to restore to him his people Israel, who has given me the strength to perform this task and honored me for doing it!—"you shall do more than restore Israel to me. I will make you a Light to the nations of the world to bring my salvation to them too."

♦ "O Bethlehem Ephrathah, you are but a small Judean village, yet you will be the birthplace of my King who is alive from everlasting ages past!" God will abandon his people to their enemies until she who is to give birth has her son; then at last his fellow countrymen—the exile remnants of Israel—will rejoin their brethren in their own land.

And he shall stand and feed his flock in the strength of the Lord, in the majesty of the name of the Lord his God, and his people shall remain there undisturbed, for he will be greatly honored all around the world. He will be our Peace.

Isaiah 49:5-6; Micah 5:2-5a

308

Jesus: Son of God, Son of Man

Next I saw the arrival of a Man—or so he seemed to be—brought there on clouds from heaven; he approached the Ancient of Days and was presented to him. He was given the ruling power and glory over all the nations of the world, so that all people of every language must obey him. His power is eternal—it will never end; his government shall never fall.

♦ Long ago God spoke in many different ways to our fathers through the prophets (in visions, dreams, and even face to face), telling them little by little about his plans.

But now in these days he has spoken to us through his Son to whom he has given everything and through whom he made the world and everything there is.

God's Son shines out with God's glory, and all that God's Son is and does marks him as God. He regulates the universe by the mighty power of his command. He is the one who died to cleanse us and clear our record of all sin, and then sat down in highest honor beside the great God of heaven.

Thus he became far greater than the angels, as proved by the fact that his name "Son of God," which was passed on to him from his Father, is far greater than the names and titles of the angels. For God never said to any angel, "You are my Son, and today I have given you the honor that goes with that name." But God said it about Jesus. Another time he said, "I am his Father and he is my Son."

Daniel 7:13-14; Hebrews 1:1-5

ONE MINUTE MEMORY

> God's Son shines out with God's glory, and all that God's Son is and does marks him as God.

Hebrews 1:3a

:00
:15
:30
:45
:60

done

OCT

12

IN other words...

HOLY SPIRIT

The Holy Spirit is the **name** for God's Spirit who lives within Christians. When Jesus left the earth, God gave Christians the Holy Spirit to **guide** them. The Bible reveals the Holy Spirit as having an identity that is one or **equal** with God the Father and God the Son. The Holy Spirit is also given different names within the Bible: Holy Ghost, Helper, Counselor, and Comforter.

The Holy Spirit's **role** is to direct Christians, comfort them, convict them of sin, **help** them understand and obey God's will, and **speak** to God on their behalf.

Today, **pray** that the Holy Spirit would be **evident** in your life.

:00

:10

:20

:30

:40

:50

:60   done

These are the facts concerning the birth of Jesus Christ: His mother, Mary, was engaged to be married to Joseph. But while she was still a virgin she became pregnant by the Holy Spirit. Then Joseph, her fiance, being a man of stern principle, decided to break the engagement but to do it quietly, as he didn't want to publicly disgrace her.

As he lay awake considering this, he fell into a dream, and saw an angel standing beside him. "Joseph, son of David," the angel said, "don't hesitate to take Mary as your wife! For the child within her has been conceived by the Holy Spirit. And she will have a Son, and you shall name him Jesus (meaning 'Savior'), for he will save his people from their sins. This will fulfill God's message through his prophets—

"'Listen! The virgin shall conceive a child! She shall give birth to a Son, and he shall be called "Emmanuel" (meaning "God is with us").'" When Joseph awoke, he did as the angel commanded and brought Mary home to be his wife, but she remained a virgin until her Son was born; and Joseph named him "Jesus."

Matthew 1:18-25

BOY JESUS
IN THE TEMPLE

When Jesus was twelve years old he accompanied his parents to Jerusalem for the annual Passover Festival, which they attended each year. After the celebration was over they started home to Nazareth, but Jesus stayed behind in Jerusalem. His parents didn't miss him the first day, for they assumed he was with friends among the other travelers. But when he didn't show up that evening, they started to look for him among their relatives and friends; and when they couldn't find him, they went back to Jerusalem to search for him there.

Three days later they finally discovered him. He was in the Temple, sitting among the teachers of Law, discussing deep questions with them and amazing everyone with his understanding and answers.

His parents didn't know what to think. "Son!" his mother said to him. "Why have you done this to us? Your father and I have been frantic, searching for you everywhere."

"But why did you need to search?" he asked. "Didn't you realize that I would be here at the Temple, in my Father's House?" But they didn't understand what he meant.

Then he returned to Nazareth with them and was obedient to them; and his mother stored away all these things in her heart. So Jesus grew both tall and wise, and was loved by God and man.

Luke 2:41-52

The Bible is God's **complete** instruction manual to the world. But it's interesting that God gives us very **little** information about Jesus' **teenage** years. For some reason, God doesn't reveal much about Jesus from His birth until His public ministry, which began when He was approximately 30 years old. We **assume** that Jesus grew up like most Jewish boys **except** that He was also **100% God.**

:00
:10
:20
:30
:40
:50
:60

end

311

IN other words...

BAPTISM

Baptism is "an **outward** act that represents an **inward** decision." Baptism **follows** a faith decision and shouts to the world, **"I'm a Christian!"** Baptism without this faith is merely a bath.

In baptism, when the person is **dunked** under water, it is symbolic of the person **dying** to the world and being buried. Then the **rising** up from the water symbolizes a resurrection to a **new** beginning and a new life in Jesus. The old nature of sin is buried in water while the new person (in Jesus) is raised to a **new life**.

If you haven't been baptized, you might want to do it and **show** the world your **commitment** to Jesus.

:00

:10

:20

:30

:40

:50

:60   done

Here begins the wonderful story of Jesus the Messiah, the Son of God. In the book written by the prophet Isaiah, God announced that he would send his Son to earth, and that a special messenger would arrive first to prepare the world for his coming.

"This messenger will live out in the barren wilderness," Isaiah said, "and will proclaim that everyone must straighten out his life to be ready for the Lord's arrival."

This messenger was John the Baptist. He lived in the wilderness and taught that all should be baptized as a public announcement of their decision to turn their backs on sin, so that God could forgive them. People from Jerusalem and from all over Judea traveled out into the Judean wastelands to see and hear John, and when they confessed their sins he baptized them in the Jordan River. His clothes were woven from camel's hair and he wore a leather belt; locusts and wild honey were his food. Here is a sample of his preaching:

"Someone is coming soon who is far greater than I am, so much greater that I am not even worthy to be his slave. I baptize you with water but he will baptize you with God's Holy Spirit!"

Then one day Jesus came from Nazareth in Galilee, and was baptized by John there in the Jordan River. The moment Jesus came up out of the water, he saw the heavens open and the Holy Spirit in the form of a dove descending on him, and a voice from heaven said, "You are my beloved Son; you are my Delight."

Mark 1:1-11

312

JESUS TEMPTED BY THE DEVIL

Then Jesus was led out into the wilderness by the Holy Spirit, to be tempted there by Satan. For forty days and forty nights he ate nothing and became very hungry. Then Satan tempted him to get food by changing stones into loaves of bread.

"It will prove you are the Son of God," he said.

But Jesus told him, "No! For the Scriptures tell us that bread won't feed men's souls: obedience to every word of God is what we need."

Then Satan took him to Jerusalem to the roof of the Temple. "Jump off," he said, "and prove you are the Son of God; for the Scriptures declare, 'God will send his angels to keep you from harm,' . . . they will prevent you from smashing on the rocks below."

Jesus retorted, "It also says not to put the Lord your God to a foolish test!"

Next Satan took him to the peak of a very high mountain and showed him the nations of the world and all their glory. "I'll give it all to you," he said, "if you will only kneel and worship me."

"Get out of here, Satan," Jesus told him. "The Scriptures say, 'Worship only the Lord God. Obey only him.'"

Then Satan went away, and angels came and cared for Jesus.

Matthew 4:1-11

313

Catch THIS

:00

:10

Jesus wasn't **tempted** so God could reward His victory over Satan with two thumbs up and a pat on the back for a job well done. Jesus was tempted for our **OWN** good. Because He went through temptations as a human, He **completely** understands our humanity and temptations.

:20

Jesus used the **same** weapons to fight off temptation that are available to us today. He used the **Scriptures,** the **power** of the Holy Spirit, and **prayer** to defeat Satan. We can use those same tools today... Scripture...the Holy Spirit, and prayer.

:30

:40

Praise God today because He understands everything you are going through. He **cares** about you! That should be enough **good news** to give you **hope** for another week.

:50

:60
done

Just a

thought

If you like to
party,
you can be
assured
that
God is
throwing **one**

that will
never
end!

:00

:10

:20

:30

:40

:50

1:00

FINISH

JESUS' FIRST MIRACLE

Two days later Jesus' mother was a guest at a wedding in the village of Cana in Galilee, and Jesus and his disciples were invited too. The wine supply ran out during the festivities, and Jesus' mother came to him with the problem.

"I can't help you now," he said. "It isn't yet my time for miracles."

But his mother told the servants, "Do whatever he tells you to."

Six stone waterpots were standing there. Jesus told the servants to fill them to the brim with water. When this was done he said, "Dip some out and take it to the master of ceremonies."

When the master of ceremonies tasted the water that was now wine, not knowing where it had come from (though, of course, the servants did), he called the bridegroom over.

"This is wonderful stuff!" he said. "You're different from most. Usually a host uses the best wine first, and afterwards, when everyone is full and doesn't care, then he brings out the less expensive brands. But you have kept the best for the last!"

This miracle at Cana in Galilee was Jesus' first public demonstration of his heaven-sent power. And his disciples believed that he really was the Messiah.

♦ And I suppose that if all the other events in Jesus' life were written, the whole world could hardly contain the books!

John 2:1-5, 6a, 7-11; 21:25

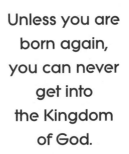

You Must Be Born Again

After dark one night a Jewish religious leader named Nicodemus, a member of the sect of the Pharisees, came for an interview with Jesus. "Sir," he said, "we all know that God has sent you to teach us. Your miracles are proof enough of this."

Jesus replied, "With all the earnestness I possess I tell you this: Unless you are born again, you can never get into the Kingdom of God."

"Born again!" exclaimed Nicodemus. "What do you mean? How can an old man go back into his mother's womb and be born again?"

Jesus replied, "What I am telling you so earnestly is this: Unless one is born of water and the Spirit, he cannot enter the Kingdom of God."

"What do you mean?" Nicodemus asked.

Jesus replied, "You, a respected Jewish teacher, and yet you don't understand these things? But if you don't even believe me when I tell you about such things as these that happen here among men, how can you possibly believe if I tell you what is going on in heaven? For only I, the Messiah, have come to earth and will return to heaven again. And as Moses in the wilderness lifted up the bronze image of a serpent on a pole, even so I must be lifted up upon a pole, so that anyone who believes in me will have eternal life. For God loved the world so much that he gave his only Son so that anyone who believes in him shall not perish but have eternal life."

John 3:1-5, 9-10, 12-16

Unless you are born again, you can never get into the Kingdom of God.

John 3:3

18

o c t

done!

One day as he was preaching on the shore of Lake Gennesaret, great crowds pressed in on him to listen to the Word of God. He noticed two empty boats standing at the water's edge while the fishermen washed their nets. Stepping into one of the boats, Jesus asked Simon, its owner, to push out a little into the water, so that he could sit in the boat and speak to the crowds from there.

When he had finished speaking, he said to Simon, "Now go out where it is deeper and let down your nets and you will catch a lot of fish!"

"Sir," Simon replied, "we worked hard all last night and didn't catch a thing. But if you say so, we'll try again."

And this time their nets were so full that they began to tear! A shout for help brought their partners in the other boat, and soon both boats were filled with fish and on the verge of sinking.

When Simon Peter realized what had happened, he fell to his knees before Jesus and said, "Oh, sir, please leave us—I'm too much of a sinner for you to have around." For he was awestruck by the size of their catch, as were the others with him, and his partners too—James and John, the sons of Zebedee. Jesus replied, "Don't be afraid! From now on you'll be fishing for the souls of men!"

And as soon as they landed, they left everything and went with him.

Luke 5:1-11

Jesus calls His first disciples

If Jesus came to you today and **asked** you to **drop** everything and **leave** everyone to follow Him, how would **you** respond?

Write your answer below.

Give it a try

HEALING ILLNESS;
FORGIVING
SIN

WHAT'S **it** ? mean

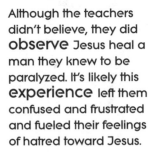

One day while [Jesus] was teaching, some Jewish religious leaders and teachers of the Law were sitting nearby. (It seemed that these men showed up from every village in all Galilee and Judea, as well as from Jerusalem.) And the Lord's healing power was upon him.

Then—look! Some men came carrying a paralyzed man on a sleeping mat. They tried to push through the crowd to Jesus but couldn't reach him. So they went up on the roof above him, took off some tiles and lowered the sick man down into the crowd, still on his sleeping mat, right in front of Jesus.

Seeing their faith, Jesus said to the man, "My friend, your sins are forgiven!"

"Who does this fellow think he is?" the Pharisees and teachers of the Law exclaimed among themselves. "This is blasphemy! Who but God can forgive sins?"

Jesus knew what they were thinking, and he replied, "Why is it blasphemy? I, the Messiah, have the authority on earth to forgive sins. But talk is cheap—anybody could say that. So I'll prove it to you by healing this man." Then, turning to the paralyzed man, he commanded, "Pick up your stretcher and go on home, for you are healed!"

And immediately, as everyone watched, the man jumped to his feet, picked up his mat and went home praising God! Everyone present was gripped with awe and fear. And they praised God, remarking over and over again, "We have seen strange things today."

Luke 5:17-26

Teachers of the Law saw Jesus' act as blasphemous because they believed only God could **forgive** sin. They didn't accept Jesus' claim to be God's Son, so His words and actions were unacceptable to them.

Although the teachers didn't believe, they did **observe** Jesus heal a man they knew to be paralyzed. It's likely this **experience** left them confused and frustrated and fueled their feelings of hatred toward Jesus.

Jesus didn't forgive the leaders because they wouldn't admit they were wrong. Do **you** have any areas of your life today where you **need** forgiveness? Ask God to **forgive** you and cleanse you from anything that is **keeping** you from being **whole**.

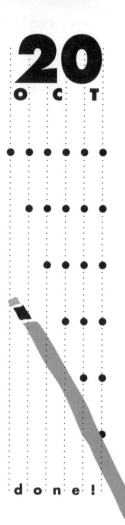

20
O C T

[Jesus] got into a boat and started across the lake with his disciples. Suddenly a terrible storm came up, with waves higher than the boat. But Jesus was asleep.

The disciples went to him and wakened him, shouting, "Lord, save us! We're sinking!"

But Jesus answered, "O you men of little faith! Why are you so frightened?" Then he stood up and rebuked the wind and waves, and the storm subsided and all was calm. The disciples just sat there, awed! "Who is this," they asked themselves, "that even the winds and the sea obey him?"

When they arrived on the other side of the lake, in the country of the Gadarenes, two men with demons in them met him. They lived in a cemetery and were so dangerous that no one could go through that area.

They began screaming at him, "What do you want with us, O Son of God? You have no right to torment us yet."

A herd of pigs was feeding in the distance, so the demons begged, "If you cast us out, send us into that herd of pigs."

"All right," Jesus told them. "Begone."

And they came out of the men and entered the pigs, and the whole herd rushed over a cliff and drowned in the water below.

Matthew 8:23-32

Jesus controls storms and spirits

done!

What are some of the **"storms"** in your life that make you **fearful?**

Give
it a
try

1
2
3

Spend a minute and talk to God about your fears.

318

FAITH & HEALING

The rabbi of the local synagogue came and worshiped [Jesus]. "My little daughter has just died," he said, "but you can bring her back to life again if you will only come and touch her."

As Jesus and the disciples were going to the rabbi's home, a woman who had been sick for twelve years with internal bleeding came up behind him and touched a tassel of his robe, for she thought, "If I only touch him, I will be healed."

Jesus turned around and spoke to her. "Daughter," he said, "all is well! Your faith has healed you." And the woman was well from that moment.

When Jesus arrived at the rabbi's home and saw the noisy crowds and heard the funeral music, he said, "Get them out, for the little girl isn't dead; she is only sleeping!" Then how they all scoffed and sneered at him!

When the crowd was finally outside, Jesus went in where the little girl was lying and took her by the hand, and she jumped up and was all right again!

♦ Is anyone among you suffering? He should keep on praying about it. And those who have reason to be thankful should continually be singing praises to the Lord.

Is anyone sick? He should call for the elders of the church and they should pray over him and pour a little oil upon him, calling on the Lord to heal him. And their prayer, if offered in faith, will heal him, for the Lord will make him well; and if his sickness was caused by some sin, the Lord will forgive him.

Admit your faults to one another and pray for each other so that you may be healed. The earnest prayer of a righteous man has great power and wonderful results.

Matthew 9:18-25; James 5:13-16

:00

:10

:20

:30

:40

:50

:60
done

Catch T·H·I·S

Jesus isn't walking the earth today performing miracles. But that doesn't mean miracles aren't **happening** on a daily basis. God's miraculous healing power hasn't stopped!

Today, healing happens in many **different** ways. One type of healing involves **YOU** if you're a Christian. A verse from today's reading states that healing can come from **sharing** with another person. Here it is again, "Admit your faults to one another and pray for each other so that you may be healed."

There's something **powerful** about confessing your faults or sins to another person. Confession, followed up by **prayer,** is one way in which God **heals.** God wants you to live life to its **fullest,** and unconfessed sin doesn't allow us to live abundantly. If you are feeling anger or hatred toward a person or situation, try **sharing** your pain and **confessing** your faults to another Christian. Pray together and **allow** God to **do the rest.**

319

22 oct

personality plus Satan

Satan was **originally** a big-time angel. His downfall came when he desired to have the **same** power as God. This act of **pride** got him thrown out of heaven.

Today, Satan is intent on **demolishing** God's kingdom and followers. Satan is **effective** in this plot because his methods are discreet. He destroys Christians with temptation, guilt, fear, and doubt. He'd love to see you live a life that doesn't reflect godliness. **Watch out** for his subtle attempts to take your eyes off God. He's not a fairy-tale character, he's for **real!** Don't let him have **any** part of you!

:00

:10

:20

:30

:40

:50

:60

When [Jesus] returned to the house where he was staying, the crowds began to gather again, and soon it was so full of visitors that he couldn't even find time to eat. When his friends heard what was happening they came to try to take him home with them.

"He's out of his mind," they said.

But the Jewish teachers of religion who had arrived from Jerusalem said, "His trouble is that he's possessed by Satan, king of demons. That's why demons obey him."

Jesus summoned these men and asked them (using proverbs they all understood), "How can Satan cast out Satan? A kingdom divided against itself will collapse. A home filled with strife and division destroys itself. And if Satan is fighting against himself, how can he accomplish anything? He would never survive. (Satan must be bound before his demons are cast out), just as a strong man must be tied up before his house can be ransacked and his property robbed.

"I solemnly declare that any sin of man can be forgiven, even blasphemy against me; but blasphemy against the Holy Spirit can never be forgiven. It is an eternal sin."

He told them this because they were saying he did his miracles by Satan's power (instead of acknowledging it was by the Holy Spirit's power).

Mark 3:20-30

the End

JESUS FEEDS

5000

[Jesus] saw a great multitude of people climbing the hill, looking for him.

Turning to Philip he asked, "Philip, where can we buy bread to feed all these people?" (He was testing Philip, for he already knew what he was going to do.)

Philip replied, "It would take a fortune to begin to do it!"

Then Andrew, Simon Peter's brother, spoke up. "There's a youngster here with five barley loaves and a couple of fish! But what good is that with all this mob?"

"Tell everyone to sit down," Jesus ordered. And all of them—the approximate count of the men only was five thousand—sat down on the grassy slopes. Then Jesus took the loaves and gave thanks to God and passed them out to the people. Afterwards he did the same with the fish. And everyone ate until full!

"Now gather the scraps," Jesus told his disciples, "so that nothing is wasted." And twelve baskets were filled with the leftovers!

When the people realized what a great miracle had happened, they exclaimed, "Surely, he is the Prophet we have been expecting!"

John 6:5-14

Just a thought

A little **faith** left in the **hands** of God

can turn into **big** results.

2
3

OCT

:00

:10

:20

:30

:40

:50

1:00

FINISH ☐

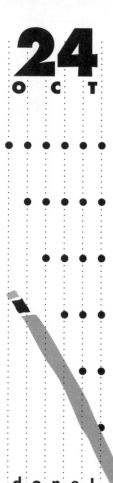

24

O C T

• • • • •

• • • •

• • •

• •

•

d o n e !

When Jesus came to Caesarea Philippi, he asked his disciples, "Who are the people saying I am?"

"Well," they replied, "some say John the Baptist; some, Elijah; some, Jeremiah or one of the other prophets."

Then he asked them, "Who do you think I am?"

Simon Peter answered, "The Christ, the Messiah, the Son of the living God."

"God has blessed you, Simon, son of Jonah," Jesus said, "for my Father in heaven has personally revealed this to you—this is not from any human source. You are Peter, a stone; and upon this rock I will build my church; and all the powers of hell shall not prevail against it. And I will give you the keys of the Kingdom of Heaven; whatever doors you lock on earth shall be locked in heaven; and whatever doors you open on earth shall be open in heaven!"

Then he warned the disciples against telling others that he was the Messiah.

From then on Jesus began to speak plainly to his disciples about going to Jerusalem, and what would happen to him there—that he would suffer at the hands of the Jewish leaders, that he would be killed, and that three days later he would be raised to life again.

Matthew 16:13-21

who is Jesus?

How would you answer Jesus' question?

"Who do you think I am?"

Write a brief description of what you know about Jesus.

Give it a try

322

The Transfiguration

Six days later Jesus took Peter, James and John to the top of a mountain. No one else was there.

Suddenly his face began to shine with glory, and his clothing became dazzling white, far more glorious than any earthly process could ever make it! Then Elijah and Moses appeared and began talking with Jesus! "Teacher, this is wonderful!" Peter exclaimed. "We will make three shelters here, one for each of you…"

He said this just to be talking, for he didn't know what else to say and they were all terribly frightened.

But while he was still speaking these words, a cloud covered them, blotting out the sun, and a voice from the cloud said,

"This is my beloved Son. Listen to him."

Then suddenly they looked around and Moses and Elijah were gone, and only Jesus was with them.

As they descended the mountainside he told them never to mention what they had seen until after he had risen from the dead. So they kept it to themselves, but often talked about it, and wondered what he meant by "rising from the dead."

♦ Christ became a human being and lived here on earth among us and was full of loving forgiveness and truth. And some of us have seen his glory—the glory of the only Son of the heavenly Father!

Mark 9:2-10; John 1:14

ONE MINUTE MEMORY

:00
:15
:30
:45
:60

Christ became a human being and lived here on earth among us and was full of loving forgiveness and truth. And some of us have seen his glory–the glory of the only Son of the heavenly Father!

John 1:14

done

SMALL FAITH
LARGE RESULTS

atch
T · H · I · S

Chances are high you won't have the need or the opportunity to **physically** move a mountain. When Jesus used this illustration, He wasn't referring to the finer points of **landscaping** but to a vital truth having to do with our faith. Jesus wanted His followers to know that **all** things are possible with faith. By using the example of the mustard seed Jesus was emphasizing **littleness**. This means we don't need A **lot** of faith to see God do incredible things. With just a **little** faith, we will be able to move the **mountains** of difficulty facing us.

Faith is **believing** that God is God and He's **TOTALLY** in control. If you believe this to be true, ask God to help you move a mountain in your life and perform the impossible. Remember, it doesn't take a lot of faith... **just a little.**

:00
:10
:20
:30
:40
:50
:60
done

When they arrived at the bottom of the hill, a huge crowd was waiting for them. A man came and knelt before Jesus and said, "Sir, have mercy on my son, for he is mentally deranged and in great trouble, for he often falls into the fire or into the water; so I brought him to your disciples, but they couldn't cure him."

Jesus replied, "Oh, you stubborn, faithless people! How long shall I bear with you? Bring him here to me." Then Jesus rebuked the demon in the boy and it left him, and from that moment the boy was well.

Afterwards the disciples asked Jesus privately, "Why couldn't we cast that demon out?"

"Because of your little faith," Jesus told them. "For if you had faith even as small as a tiny mustard seed you could say to this mountain, 'Move!' and it would go far away. Nothing would be impossible. But this kind of demon won't leave unless you have prayed and gone without food."

♦ [Jesus said,] "In solemn truth I tell you, anyone believing in me shall do the same miracles I have done, and even greater ones, because I am going to be with the Father. You can ask him for anything, using my name, and I will do it, for this will bring praise to the Father because of what I, the Son, will do for you."

Matthew 17:14-21; John 14:12-13

324

ONE MINUTE MEMORY

Once when Jesus had been out praying, one of his disciples came to him as he finished and said, "Lord, teach us a prayer to recite just as John taught one to his disciples."

And this is the prayer he taught them: "Father, may your name be honored for its holiness; send your Kingdom soon. Give us our food day by day. And forgive our sins—for we have forgiven those who sinned against us. And don't allow us to be tempted."

Then, teaching them more about prayer, he used this illustration: "Suppose you went to a friend's house at midnight, wanting to borrow three loaves of bread. You would shout up to him, 'A friend of mine has just arrived for a visit and I've nothing to give him to eat.' He would call down from his bedroom, 'Please don't ask me to get up. The door is locked for the night and we are all in bed. I just can't help you this time.'

"But I'll tell you this—though he won't do it as a friend, if you keep knocking long enough, he will get up and give you everything you want—just because of your persistence. And so it is with prayer—keep on asking and you will keep on getting; keep on looking and you will keep on finding; knock and the door will be opened. Everyone who asks, receives; all who seek, find; and the door is opened to everyone who knocks."

Luke 11:1-10

And this is the prayer he taught them: "Father, may your name be honored for its holiness; send your Kingdom soon. Give us our food day by day. And forgive our sins–for we have forgiven those who sinned against us. And don't allow us to be tempted."

Luke 11:2-4

:00

:15

:30

:45

:60

done X

325

Jesus Welcomes **Little Children**

word

Children

We can **learn** a lot from children. Jesus knew this and referred to them as **examples** that we should **follow** in life.

Look at the following four words that begin with the letters L-I-F-E and try to think of ways you can be more **childlike** (not childish) in **your** faith.

Laughter
Imagination
Faith
Enthusiasm

Ask God to help **you** possess these **childlike** qualities **today!**

Now came an argument among them as to which of them would be greatest (in the coming Kingdom)! But Jesus knew their thoughts, so he stood a little child beside him and said to them, "Anyone who takes care of a little child like this is caring for me! And whoever cares for me is caring for God who sent me. Your care for others is the measure of your greatness."

♦ Once when some mothers were bringing their children to Jesus to bless them, the disciples shooed them away, telling them not to bother him.

But when Jesus saw what was happening he was very much displeased with his disciples and said to them, "Let the children come to me, for the Kingdom of God belongs to such as they. Don't send them away! I tell you as seriously as I know how that anyone who refuses to come to God as a little child will never be allowed into his Kingdom."

Then he took the children into his arms and placed his hands on their heads and he blessed them.

♦ Then he was filled with the joy of the Holy Spirit and said, "I praise you, O Father, Lord of heaven and earth, for hiding these things from the intellectuals and worldly wise and for revealing them to those who are as trusting as little children. Yes, thank you, Father, for that is the way you wanted it. I am the Agent of my Father in everything; and no one really knows the Son except the Father, and no one really knows the Father except the Son and those to whom the Son chooses to reveal him."

Luke 9:46-48; Mark 10:13-16;
Luke 10:21-22

326

JESUS HEALS ON THE SABBATH

WHAT'S **it** mean

One Sabbath as he was teaching in a synagogue, he saw a seriously handicapped woman who had been bent double for eighteen years and was unable to straighten herself.

Calling her over to him Jesus said, "Woman, you are healed of your sickness!" He touched her, and instantly she could stand straight. How she praised and thanked God!

But the local Jewish leader in charge of the synagogue was very angry about it because Jesus had healed her on the Sabbath day. "There are six days of the week to work," he shouted to the crowd. "Those are the days to come for healing, not on the Sabbath!"

But the Lord replied, "You hypocrite! You work on the Sabbath! Don't you untie your cattle from their stalls on the Sabbath and lead them out for water? And is it wrong for me, just because it is the Sabbath day, to free this Jewish woman from the bondage in which Satan has held her for eighteen years?"

This shamed his enemies. And all the people rejoiced at the wonderful things he did.

Luke 13:10-17

The **leader** accusing Jesus of healing on the Sabbath cared more about the **Law** being broken than he did for the woman. Jesus **rebuked** this man by calling him a hypocrite for not seeing beyond the Sabbath rules to the needs of a hurting woman. The religious leader preferred to let the woman suffer or make her return to the synagogue another day instead of breaking the Sabbath rule.

Don't **wait** for good timing to ask for a miracle. Right **now** God is waiting for your words. He's equipped to heal if it's in His plan. It sure **can't hurt** to ask!

Jesus Teaches on Divorce and Celibacy

BIGtime
word

DIVORCE

Divorce is devastating! If your parents are together, that's good news. Most likely you know a friend whose parents are divorced. It isn't easy to live with the pain, loss, guilt, and frustration that go along with being separated from the two people you love the most.

God **hates** divorce and knows the deep pain it brings. If you have been **affected** by divorce, ask God to comfort you. Your pain won't quickly disappear, but be assured that you aren't alone and you don't have to go through it alone. If your parents aren't divorced, pray for the **strength** of their marriage and ask God to provide you an opportunity to **care** for a friend hurt by divorce.

Some Pharisees came to interview [Jesus] and tried to trap him into saying something that would ruin him.

"Do you permit divorce?" they asked.

"Don't you read the Scriptures?" he replied. "In them it is written that at the beginning God created man and woman, and that a man should leave his father and mother, and be forever united to his wife. The two shall become one—no longer two, but one! And no man may divorce what God has joined together."

"Then, why," they asked, "did Moses say a man may divorce his wife by merely writing her a letter of dismissal?"

Jesus replied, "Moses did that in recognition of your hard and evil hearts, but it was not what God had originally intended. And I tell you this, that anyone who divorces his wife, except for fornication, and marries another, commits adultery."

Jesus' disciples then said to him, "If that is how it is, it is better not to marry!"

"Not everyone can accept this statement," Jesus said. "Only those whom God helps. Some are born without the ability to marry, and some are disabled by men, and some refuse to marry for the sake of the Kingdom of Heaven. Let anyone who can, accept my statement."

Matthew 19:3-12

TREASURE IN

HEAVEN

Once a Jewish religious leader asked [Jesus] this question: "Good sir, what shall I do to get to heaven?"

"Do you realize what you are saying when you call me 'good'?" Jesus asked him. "Only God is truly good, and no one else.

"But as to your question, you know what the Ten Commandments say—don't commit adultery, don't murder, don't steal, don't lie, honor your parents, and so on."

The man replied, "I've obeyed every one of these laws since I was a small child."

"There is still one thing you lack," Jesus said. "Sell all you have and give the money to the poor—it will become treasure for you in heaven—and come, follow me."

But when the man heard this he went sadly away, for he was very rich.

Jesus watched him go and then said to his disciples, "How hard it is for the rich to enter the Kingdom of God! It is easier for a camel to go through the eye of a needle than for a rich man to enter the Kingdom of God."

Those who heard him say this exclaimed, "If it is that hard, how can anyone be saved?"

He replied, "God can do what men can't!" And Peter said, "We have left our homes and followed you."

"Yes," Jesus replied, "and everyone who has done as you have, leaving home, wife, brothers, parents, or children for the sake of the Kingdom of God, will be repaid many times over now, as well as receiving eternal life in the world to come."

Luke 18:18-30

Just a thought

Wealth and **happiness** don't always **go** together.

Wealthy people who **don't** know God are spiritually **bankrupt.**

Don't allow **yourself** to love money **more** than you love **God.**

3 1

OCT

:00

:10

:20

:30

:40

:50

1:00

FINISH

NOV

Give me a used
Bible and I will,
I think, be able
to tell you about a
man by the places
that are edged with
the dirt of seeking
fingers.

**John Steinbeck
(1902-1968)**
American Novelist

Jesus Visits a Sinner

As Jesus was passing through Jericho, a man named Zacchaeus, one of the most influential Jews in the Roman tax-collecting business (and, of course, a very rich man), tried to get a look at Jesus, but he was too short to see over the crowds. So he ran ahead and climbed into a sycamore tree beside the road, to watch from there.

When Jesus came by, he looked up at Zacchaeus and called him by name! "Zacchaeus!" he said. "Quick! Come down! For I am going to be a guest in your home today!"

Zacchaeus hurriedly climbed down and took Jesus to his house in great excitement and joy.

But the crowds were displeased. "He has gone to be the guest of a notorious sinner," they grumbled.

Meanwhile, Zacchaeus stood before the Lord and said, "Sir, from now on I will give half my wealth to the poor, and if I find I have overcharged anyone on his taxes, I will penalize myself by giving him back four times as much!"

Jesus told him, "This shows that salvation has come to this home today. This man was one of the lost sons of Abraham, and I, the Messiah, have come to search for and to save such souls as his."

♦ And just as it is destined that men die only once, and after that comes judgment, so also Christ died only once as an offering for the sins of many people; and he will come again, but not to deal again with our sins.

This time he will come bringing salvation to all those who are eagerly and patiently waiting for him.

Luke 19:1-10; Hebrews 9:27-28

333

bIG time word

Influential

Our world has established an **unwritten** standard by which many people measure themselves. This standard usually includes **money, popularity,** possessions, and career positions. People who try to fit into these categories often see themselves as influential and enjoy being noticed for what they have.

The Bible's standard for **influence** is completely different than the world's. Jesus told His disciples that influential people are **servants,** and if they wanted to be influential (or great) they **needed** to serve others.

Try **living** by God's standards and discover ways you can **influence** someone today by **serving.**

NOV 2

IN other words...
DISCIPLE

The **twelve** men Jesus chose to be with Him on a regular basis are called **disciples.** The word "disciple" comes from a root word meaning "to **learn.**" A disciple was one who developed a special relationship with a rabbi and learned from his **teachings.** Today, "disciple" refers to someone learning from another Christian.

Do you know a leader or teacher who is more knowledgeable than you? Could you become that person's **disciple** and learn more about **God's** ways? Such a relationship can be a **great** investment of your time as long as you remember to put your **faith** in **GOD** and not in the other person.

:00
:10
:20
:30
:40
:50
:60 done

Six days before the Passover ceremonies began, Jesus arrived in Bethany where Lazarus was—the man he had brought back to life. A banquet was prepared in Jesus' honor. Martha served, and Lazarus sat at the table with him. Then Mary took a jar of costly perfume made from essence of nard, and anointed Jesus' feet with it and wiped them with her hair. And the house was filled with fragrance.

But Judas Iscariot, one of his disciples—the one who would betray him—said, "That perfume was worth a fortune. It should have been sold and the money given to the poor." Not that he cared for the poor, but he was in charge of the disciples' funds and often dipped into them for his own use!

Jesus replied, "Let her alone. She did it in preparation for my burial. You can always help the poor, but I won't be with you very long."

When the ordinary people of Jerusalem heard of his arrival, they flocked to see him and also to see Lazarus—the man who had come back to life again. Then the chief priests decided to kill Lazarus too, for it was because of him that many of the Jewish leaders had deserted and believed in Jesus as their Messiah.

John 12:1-11

334

As [Jesus and his disciples] came to the towns of Bethphage and Bethany, on the Mount of Olives, he sent two disciples ahead, with instructions to go to the next village, and as they entered they were to look for a donkey tied beside the road. It would be a colt, not yet broken for riding.

"Untie him," Jesus said, "and bring him here. And if anyone asks you what you are doing, just say, 'The Lord needs him.'"

They found the colt as Jesus said, and sure enough, as they were untying it, the owners demanded an explanation.

"What are you doing?" they asked. "Why are you untying our colt?"

And the disciples simply replied, "The Lord needs him!" So they brought the colt to Jesus and threw some of their clothing across its back for Jesus to sit on.

Then the crowds spread out their robes along the road ahead of him, and as they reached the place where the road started down from the Mount of Olives, the whole procession began to shout and sing as they walked along, praising God for all the wonderful miracles Jesus had done.

"God has given us a King!" they exulted. "Long live the King! Let all heaven rejoice! Glory to God in the highest heavens!"

But some of the Pharisees among the crowd said, "Sir, rebuke your followers for saying things like that!"

He replied, "If they keep quiet, the stones along the road will burst into cheers!"

Luke 19:29-40

:00 Jesus entered Jerusalem as the **Messiah** to the world. His arrival had been prophesied for hundreds of years, but

:10 the Jewish people did not recognize Him as their Messiah and Savior. Check out the prophecy in

:20 Psalm 118:22-23, 26: "The stone rejected by the builders has now become the capstone of the arch! This is the Lord's

:30 doing, and it is marvelous to see! Blessed is the one who is coming, the one sent by the Lord. We bless you

:40 from the Temple."

It has also been foretold that Jesus will **return** to earth. This is

:50 called the **Second** Coming. Again, some will reject this truth.

Don't allow yourself to **miss** the signs of

:60 His **return**.

done

335

WHAT'S it mean

THE PARABLE OF THE VINEYARD

Now [Jesus] turned to the people again and told them this story: "A man planted a vineyard and rented it out to some farmers, and went away to a distant land to live for several years. When harvest time came, he sent one of his men to the farm to collect his share of the crops. But the tenants beat him up and sent him back empty-handed. Then he sent another, but the same thing happened; he was beaten up and insulted and sent away without collecting. A third man was sent and the same thing happened. He, too, was wounded and chased away.

"'What shall I do?' the owner asked himself. 'I know! I'll send my cherished son. Surely they will show respect for him.'

"But when the tenants saw his son, they said, 'This is our chance! This fellow will inherit all the land when his father dies. Come on. Let's kill him, and then it will be ours.' So they dragged him out of the vineyard and killed him.

"What do you think the owner will do? I'll tell you—he will come and kill them and rent the vineyard to others."

"But they would never do a thing like that," his listeners protested.

Jesus looked at them and said, "Then what does the Scripture mean where it says, 'The Stone rejected by the builders was made the cornerstone'?" And he added, "Whoever stumbles over that Stone shall be broken; and those on whom it falls will be crushed to dust."

Luke 20:9-18

Jesus **didn't** answer the religious leaders when they questioned Him about where He got His **authority** to drive out merchants from the Temple. Instead, He told them the **parable** found in today's reading.

This parable **illustrates** that some people will refuse to believe Jesus is God's Son. This rejection of the truth will result in their destruction. The message of this parable leaves **no** room for a compromising position with one's faith. Jesus will either **save** you or judge you. There are **no** other options.

Let God know that you have not compromised your faith and that you are **prepared** for His return.

DONE

Then Judas Iscariot, one of the twelve apostles, went to the chief priests and asked, "How much will you pay me to get Jesus into your hands?" And they gave him thirty silver coins. From that time on, Judas watched for an opportunity to betray Jesus to them.

On the first day of the Passover ceremonies, when bread made with yeast was purged from every Jewish home, the disciples came to Jesus and asked, "Where shall we plan to eat the Passover?"

He replied, "Go into the city and see Mr. So-and-So, and tell him, 'Our Master says, my time has come, and I will eat the Passover meal with my disciples at your house.'" So the disciples did as he told them and prepared the supper there.

That evening as he sat eating with the Twelve, he said, "One of you will betray me."

Sorrow chilled their hearts, and each one asked, "Am I the one?"

He replied, "It is the one I served first. For I must die just as was prophesied, but woe to the man by whom I am betrayed. Far better for that one if he had never been born."

Judas, too, had asked him, "Rabbi, am I the one?" And Jesus had told him, "Yes."

Matthew 26:14-25

word

BETRAYAL

Quality relationships are built on **trust.** Betrayal breaks this trust and makes the relationship difficult to repair. **Restoration** isn't impossible, but it's always difficult to forget an act of betrayal.

Humans are **known** to betray other people and even to betray God, but God has **promised** not to betray His people. For thousands of years He has kept His promises, and He's not about to change His ways. This is **good** news! Thank God for this **truth** and think about how you can keep betrayal **out** of your life.

FAITHLESS
FRIENDS

Catch
T · H · I · S

Peter said, "I will **never** desert you no matter what the others do!" Since that day, thousands of Christians have spoken those **same** words at youth retreats or revivals. They say this boldly because they have made a decision to get their act together and follow Jesus. They **promise** they will do whatever it takes to live the Christian life with excitement and **intensity.** But after the retreat is over and the warm fuzzies have worn off, it's usually back to normal Christian living, which translates into very little time, if any, for God. Does this **describe** you?

To maintain a **vibrant** faith takes work. Actually, it's a lot like a marriage. Imagine being married to someone you didn't talk to or spend time with. That marriage would dry up. The same is true in your "marriage" to God; that **relationship** needs time. Go ahead and make **bold** statements like Peter, but be ready to put **time** into your relationship with **God.**

:00

:10

:20

:30

:40

:50

:60
done

"**A**ll of you will desert me," Jesus told them, "for God has declared through the prophets, 'I will kill the Shepherd, and the sheep will scatter.' But after I am raised to life again, I will go to Galilee and meet you there."

Peter said to him, "I will never desert you no matter what the others do!"

"Peter," Jesus said, "before the cock crows a second time tomorrow morning you will deny me three times."

"No!" Peter exploded. "Not even if I have to die with you! I'll never deny you!"

And all the others vowed the same. And now they came to an olive grove called the Garden of Gethsemane, and he instructed his disciples, "Sit here, while I go and pray."

He took Peter, James, and John with him and began to be filled with horror and deepest distress. And he said to them, "My soul is crushed by sorrow to the point of death; stay here and watch with me."

He went on a little further and fell to the ground and prayed that if it were possible the awful hour awaiting him might never come.

"Father, Father," he said, "everything is possible for you. Take away this cup from me. Yet I want your will, not mine."

Then he returned to the three disciples and found them asleep.

"Simon!" he said. "Asleep? Couldn't you watch with me even one hour? Watch with me and pray lest the Tempter overpower you. For though the spirit is willing enough, the body is weak."

Mark 14:27-38

Peter personality plus

But even as [Jesus] said this, a mob approached, led by Judas, one of his twelve disciples. Judas walked over to Jesus and kissed him on the cheek in friendly greeting.

But Jesus said, "Judas, how can you do this—betray the Messiah with a kiss?"

So they seized him and led him to the High Priest's residence, and Peter followed at a distance. The soldiers lit a fire in the courtyard and sat around it for warmth, and Peter joined them there.

A servant girl noticed him in the firelight and began staring at him. Finally she spoke: "This man was with Jesus!"

Peter denied it. "Woman," he said, "I don't even know the man!"

After a while someone else looked at him and said, "You must be one of them!"

"No sir, I am not!" Peter replied.

About an hour later someone else flatly stated, "I know this fellow is one of Jesus' disciples, for both are from Galilee."

But Peter said, "Man, I don't know what you are talking about." And as he said the words, a rooster crowed.

At that moment Jesus turned and looked at Peter. Then Peter remembered what he had said— "Before the rooster crows tomorrow morning, you will deny me three times." And Peter walked out of the courtyard, crying bitterly.

Luke 22:47-48, 54-62

Peter was one of Jesus' **most enthusiastic** and committed **followers.** He was the first disciple and one of the **closest** to Jesus.

Although Peter **denied** Jesus when He was arrested, he later turned around and became very **outspoken** about Jesus' work. In the Book of Acts, we see Peter as an instrumental figure in **starting** the **church** that we are a part of today. Jesus renamed Peter **"the rock."** Although he had his faults, he did become a solid rock and a foundational person in the early church.

You might want to rename yourself **"lucky"** because of all God has **done** for you.

:00

:10

:20

:30

:40

:50

:60

the End

339

:00

:10

:20

:30

:40

:50

1:00

Just a

thought

Jesus could withstand the abuses of others because He had already surrendered to the will of God.

He **knew** God was with Him no matter what people said or **did.**

How about **you?**

JESUS IS SENTENCED TO DEATH

Inside, the chief priests and the whole Jewish Supreme Court were trying to find something against Jesus that would be sufficient to condemn him to death. But their efforts were in vain. Many false witnesses volunteered, but they contradicted each other.

Finally some men stood up to lie about him and said, "We heard him say, 'I will destroy this Temple made with human hands and in three days I will build another, made without human hands!'" But even then they didn't get their stories straight!

Then the High Priest stood up before the Court and asked Jesus, "Do you refuse to answer this charge? What do you have to say for yourself?"

To this Jesus made no reply.

Then the High Priest asked him. "Are you the Messiah, the Son of God?"

Jesus said, "I am, and you will see me sitting at the right hand of God, and returning to earth in the clouds of heaven."

Then the High Priest tore at his clothes and said, "What more do we need? Why wait for witnesses? You have heard his blasphemy. What is your verdict?" And the vote for the death sentence was unanimous.

Then some of them began to spit at him, and they blindfolded him and began to hammer his face with their fists.

"Who hit you that time, you prophet?" they jeered. And even the bailiffs were using their fists on him as they led him away.

Mark 14:55-65

340

JESUS IS CRUCIFIED

WHAT'S it mean

Two others, criminals, were led out to be executed with [Jesus] at a place called "The Skull." There all three were crucified—Jesus on the center cross, and the two criminals on either side.

"Father, forgive these people," Jesus said, "for they don't know what they are doing."

The Jewish leaders laughed and scoffed. "He was so good at helping others," they said, "let's see him save himself if he is really God's Chosen One, the Messiah."

One of the criminals hanging beside him scoffed, "So you're the Messiah, are you? Prove it by saving yourself—and us, too, while you're at it!"

But the other criminal protested. "Don't you even fear God when you are dying? We deserve to die for our evil deeds, but this man hasn't done one thing wrong." Then he said, "Jesus, remember me when you come into your Kingdom."

And Jesus replied, "Today you will be with me in Paradise. This is a solemn promise."

By now it was noon, and darkness fell across the whole land for three hours, until three o'clock. The light from the sun was gone—and suddenly the thick veil hanging in the Temple split apart.

Then Jesus shouted, "Father, I commit my spirit to you," and with those words he died.

When the captain of the Roman military unit handling the executions saw what had happened, he was stricken with awe before God and said, "Surely this man was innocent."

Luke 23:32-34a, 35b, 39-47

Grace is defined as "undeserved **favor.**" God expresses this grace even though we don't deserve it and can do **nothing** to earn it. Jesus expressed grace to one of the criminals hanging on a cross beside His. The crucifixion scene was chaotic. People were yelling at Jesus; He was experiencing unbelievable physical pain, yet He still had **compassion** for the criminal.

Imagine yourself as a criminal charged with sin. Now imagine yourself **receiving** God's love despite your sins. You don't even need to imagine—it's real. Tell someone **today** about God's grace and how much He **loves** you.

:00

:10

:20

:30

:40

:50

1:00

Just a

thought

If you **don't** believe in the **resurrection** of Jesus,

your **faith** is worth **nothing.**

If Jesus didn't **rise** from the grave, He'd still be **dead** and **so** would your **faith.**

(Any questions, see 1 Corinthians 15:17)

THE RESURRECTION

Early Sunday morning, while it was still dark, Mary Magdalene came to the tomb and found that the stone was rolled aside from the entrance.

She ran and found Simon Peter and me and said, "They have taken the Lord's body out of the tomb, and I don't know where they have put him!"

We ran to the tomb to see; I outran Peter and got there first, and stooped and looked in and saw the linen cloth lying there, but I didn't go in. Then Simon Peter arrived and went on inside. He also noticed the cloth lying there, while the swath that had covered Jesus' head was rolled up in a bundle and was lying at the side. Then I went in too, and saw, and believed (that he had risen)— for until then we hadn't realized that the Scriptures said he would come to life again!

That evening the disciples were meeting behind locked doors, in fear of the Jewish leaders, when suddenly Jesus was standing there among them! After greeting them, he showed them his hands and side. And how wonderful was their joy as they saw their Lord!

John 20:1-9, 19-20

342

ALIVE IN **CHRIST**

WHAT'S it mean

D on't let others spoil your faith and joy with their philosophies, their wrong and shallow answers built on men's thoughts and ideas, instead of on what Christ has said. For in Christ there is all of God in a human body; so you have everything when you have Christ, and you are filled with God through your union with Christ. He is the highest Ruler, with authority over every other power.

When you came to Christ, he set you free from your evil desires, not by a bodily operation of circumcision but by a spiritual operation, the baptism of your souls. For in baptism you see how your old, evil nature died with him and was buried with him; and then you came up out of death with him into a new life because you trusted the Word of the mighty God who raised Christ from the dead. You were dead in sins, and your sinful desires were not yet cut away. Then he gave you a share in the very life of Christ, for he forgave all your sins, and blotted out the charges proved against you, the list of his commandments which you had not obeyed. He took this list of sins and destroyed it by nailing it to Christ's cross. In this way God took away Satan's power to accuse you of sin, and God openly displayed to the whole world Christ's triumph at the cross where your sins were all taken away.

Colossians 2:8-15

If you are a **Christian,** you can **rejoice** over the fact that your "old nature" passed away when you gave your life to Jesus. The Bible informs us that the old nature represents your sinful life **before** coming to Jesus. Imagine the word "old" having negative images: **dusty, bad, smelly, rotten, and ragged.**

The new nature represents **light, life, alive, eternal.** These are great words! Jesus' death conquered the old and put it to death. What's that mean to you today? You don't have to live life plagued by the past–that's old–**you're new! Congratulations!**

DONE

NOV 11

NOV

MEMORY

During the forty days after [Jesus'] crucifixion he appeared to the apostles from time to time, actually alive, and proved to them in many ways that it was really he himself they were seeing. And on these occasions he talked to them about the Kingdom of God.

In one of these meetings he told them not to leave Jerusalem until the Holy Spirit came upon them in fulfillment of the Father's promise, a matter he had previously discussed with them.

"John baptized you with water," he reminded them, "but you shall be baptized with the Holy Spirit in just a few days."

And another time when he appeared to them, they asked him, "Lord, are you going to free Israel (from Rome) now and restore us as an independent nation?"

"The Father sets those dates," he replied, "and they are not for you to know. But when the Holy Spirit has come upon you, you will receive power to testify about me with great effect, to the people in Jerusalem, throughout Judea, in Samaria, and to the ends of the earth, about my death and resurrection."

It was not long afterwards that he rose into the sky and disappeared into a cloud, leaving them staring after him. As they were straining their eyes for another glimpse, suddenly two white-robed men were standing there among them, and said, "Men of Galilee, why are you standing here staring at the sky? Jesus has gone away to heaven, and some day, just as he went, he will return!"

Acts 1:3-11

:00

:15

:30

:45

:60

But when the Holy Spirit has come upon you, you will receive power to testify about me with great effect, to the people in Jerusalem, throughout Judea, in Samaria, and to the ends of the earth, about my death and resurrection.

Acts 1:8

Seven weeks had gone by since Jesus' death and resurrection, and the Day of Pentecost had now arrived. As the believers met together that day, suddenly there was a sound like the roaring of a mighty windstorm in the skies above them and it filled the house where they were meeting. Then, what looked like flames or tongues of fire appeared and settled on their heads. And everyone present was filled with the Holy Spirit and began speaking in languages they didn't know, for the Holy Spirit gave them this ability.

Many godly Jews were in Jerusalem that day for the religious celebrations, having arrived from many nations. And when they heard the roaring in the sky above the house, crowds came running to see what it was all about, and were stunned to hear their own languages being spoken by the disciples.

"How can this be?" they exclaimed. "For these men are all from Galilee, and yet we hear them speaking all the native languages of the lands where we were born! Here we are—Parthians, Medes, Elamites, men from Mesopotamia, Judea, Cappadocia, Pontus, Asia Minor, Phrygia, Pamphylia, Egypt, the Cyrene language areas of Libya, visitors from Rome—both Jews and Jewish converts— Cretans, and Arabians. And we all hear these men telling in our own languages about the mighty miracles of God!"

They stood there amazed and perplexed. "What can this mean?" they asked each other.

But others in the crowd were mocking. "They're drunk, that's all!" they said.

IN other words...
SPEAKING IN LANGUAGES

Today, this act of speaking in unlearned languages is called "speaking in tongues" and is listed among the spiritual gifts in 1 Corinthians 12. This particular spiritual gift comes with an instruction: if you speak in tongues in public, the message must be interpreted. The spiritual gift of interpretation allows others to understand the language and be built up or ministered to.

Not all Christians speak in tongues. We can ask God for this gift, but the Bible does not say it's the most important gift. Check them all out and ask God to show you what spiritual gifts He has given you.

:00
:10
:20
:30
:40
:50
done :60

Acts 2:1-13   345

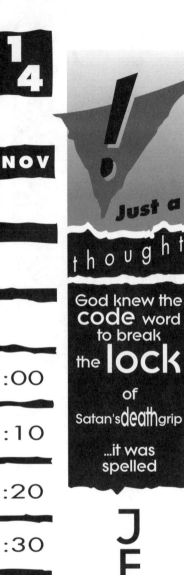

14

NOV

:00

:10

:20

:30

:40

:50

1:00

FINISH

Just a

thought

God knew the **code** word to break the **lock** of Satan's**death**grip ...it was spelled

JESUS

PETER'S FIRST

SERMON

Then Peter stepped forward with the eleven apostles and shouted to the crowd, "Listen, all of you, visitors and residents of Jerusalem alike! Some of you are saying these men are drunk! It isn't true! It's much too early for that! People don't get drunk by 9:00 A.M.! No! What you see this morning was predicted centuries ago by the prophet Joel— 'In the last days,' God said, 'I will pour out my Holy Spirit upon all mankind, and your sons and daughters shall prophesy, and your young men shall see visions, and your old men dream dreams. Yes, the Holy Spirit shall come upon all my servants, men and women alike, and they shall prophesy. Anyone who asks for mercy from the Lord shall have it and shall be saved.'

"O men of Israel, listen! God publicly endorsed Jesus of Nazareth by doing tremendous miracles through him, as you well know. But God, following his prearranged plan, let you use the Roman government to nail him to the cross and murder him. Then God released him from the horrors of death and brought him back to life again, for death could not keep this man within its grip.

"Each one of you must turn from sin, return to God, and be baptized in the name of Jesus Christ for the forgiveness of your sins; then you also shall receive this gift, the Holy Spirit."

Acts 2:14-18, 21-24, 38

PETER HEALS A CRIPPLED **BEGGAR**

WHAT'S **it** mean

Peter and John went to the Temple one afternoon to take part in the three o'clock daily prayer meeting. As they approached the Temple, they saw a man lame from birth carried along the street and laid beside the Temple gate—the one called The Beautiful Gate—as was his custom every day. As Peter and John were passing by, he asked them for some money.

They looked at him intently, and then Peter said, "Look here!"

The lame man looked at them eagerly, expecting a gift.

But Peter said, "We don't have any money for you! But I'll give you something else! I command you in the name of Jesus Christ of Nazareth, walk!"

Then Peter took the lame man by the hand and pulled him to his feet. And as he did, the man's feet and ankle-bones were healed and strengthened so that he came up with a leap, stood there a moment and began walking! Then, walking, leaping, and praising God, he went into the Temple with them.

When the people inside saw him walking and heard him praising God, and realized he was the lame beggar they had seen so often at The Beautiful Gate, they were inexpressibly surprised!

♦ While they were talking to the people, the chief priests, the captain of the Temple police, and some of the Sadducees came over to them, very disturbed that Peter and John were claiming that Jesus had risen from the dead. They arrested them and since it was already evening, jailed them overnight. But many of the people who heard their message believed it, so that the number of believers now reached a new high of about five thousand men!

Peter and John preached the message that Jesus was **alive** and had **risen** from the dead. Jesus' resurrection made it **possible** for them to heal the beggar.

The people that were mad at Peter and John's preaching are the same people that forced the crucifixion of Jesus. They saw the 5,000 new believers respond to the message. They were afraid word of the healing and salvation would **spread** throughout the country.

Events like these made up the **beginning** of the church. The early chapters of Acts record the beginning days of the early church. These events took place almost **2,000** years ago, and yet people are **still** being added to the kingdom day by day...even **today!**

Can you do anything to help the **message** of the **resurrected** Jesus get out today?

Acts 3:1-10; 4:1-4   347

OBEY GOD BEFORE PEOPLE

Catch T·H·I·S

The Council knew that Peter and John had no **formal** educational training, and yet they were **amazed** at their teaching and actions. Years earlier Jesus had also **surprised** the Jewish leaders by His teaching and **actions.** They said, "How can he (Jesus) know so much when he's **never** been to our schools?" Jesus handed down this wisdom to His disciples and they carried on the **Good News.** Ask God to give you godly **wisdom** so you too can amaze others with **God's** Good News.

:00

:10

:20

:30

:40

:50

:60
done

When the Council saw the boldness of Peter and John and could see that they were obviously uneducated non-professionals, they were amazed and realized what being with Jesus had done for them! And the Council could hardly discredit the healing when the man they had healed was standing right there beside them! So they sent them out of the Council chamber and conferred among themselves.

"What shall we do with these men?" they asked each other. "We can't deny that they have done a tremendous miracle, and everybody in Jerusalem knows about it. But perhaps we can stop them from spreading their propaganda. We'll tell them that if they do it again we'll really throw the book at them." So they called them back in, and told them never again to speak about Jesus.

But Peter and John replied, "You decide whether God wants us to obey you instead of him! We cannot stop telling about the wonderful things we saw Jesus do and heard him say."

The Council then threatened them further and finally let them go because they didn't know how to punish them without starting a riot. For everyone was praising God for this wonderful miracle— the healing of a man who had been lame for forty years.

As soon as they were freed, Peter and John found the other disciples and told them what the Council had said.

Acts 4:13-23

348

Stephen martyred for his testimony

God's message was preached in ever-widening circles, and the number of disciples increased vastly in Jerusalem.

Stephen, the man so full of faith and the Holy Spirit's power, did spectacular miracles among the people.

But one day some of the men from the Jewish cult of "The Freedmen" started an argument with him. But none of them was able to stand against Stephen's wisdom and spirit.

So they brought in some men to lie about him, claiming they had heard Stephen curse Moses, and even God.

This accusation roused the crowds to fury against Stephen, and the Jewish leaders arrested him and brought him before the Council.

• But Stephen, full of the Holy Spirit, gazed steadily upward into heaven and saw the glory of God and Jesus standing at God's right hand. And he told them, "Look, I see the heavens opened and Jesus the Messiah standing beside God, at his right hand!"

Then they mobbed him, putting their hands over their ears, and drowning out his voice with their shouts, and dragged him out of the city to stone him. The official witnesses—the executioners—took off their coats and laid them at the feet of a young man named Paul.

And as the murderous stones came hurtling at him, Stephen prayed, "Lord Jesus, receive my spirit." And he fell to his knees, shouting, "Lord, don't charge them with this sin!" and with that, he died.

Acts 6:7a, 8-9a, 10-12; 7:55-60

17

N O V

• • • • •

• • • •

• • •

• •

•

d o n e !

Give it a try

Stephen was **wrongly** accused! Has this ever happened to you? After reading Stephen's response, is there anything you can learn from him in case you're ever wrongly accused of something?

Write out a **strategy** for how **you** would handle it.

PLAN

349

Just a

t h o u g h t

Will **God** have to **k n o c k** you to the **ground** and **blind** you to fulfill **His** plan?

It seems **much** easier

to **give** Him your heart and **save** yourself the **unnecessary** pain.

:00

:10

:20

:30

:40

:50

1:00

FINISH

SAUL
MEETS

And a great wave of persecution of the believers began that day, sweeping over the church in Jerusalem, and everyone except the apostles fled into Judea and Samaria. (But some godly Jews came and with great sorrow buried Stephen.) Paul was like a wild man, going everywhere to devastate the believers, even entering private homes and dragging out men and women alike and jailing them.

But the believers who had fled Jerusalem went everywhere preaching the Good News about Jesus!

♦ But Paul, threatening with every breath and eager to destroy every Christian, went to the High Priest in Jerusalem. He requested a letter addressed to synagogues in Damascus, requiring their cooperation in the persecution of any believers he found there, both men and women, so that he could bring them in chains to Jerusalem.

As he was nearing Damascus on this mission, suddenly a brilliant light from heaven spotted down upon him! He fell to the ground and heard a voice saying to him, "Paul! Paul! Why are you persecuting me?"

"Who is speaking, sir?" Paul asked.

And the voice replied, "I am Jesus, the one you are persecuting! Now get up and go into the city and await my further instructions."

The men with Paul stood speechless with surprise, for they heard the sound of someone's voice but saw no one! As Paul picked himself up off the ground, he found that he was blind. He had to be led into Damascus and was there three days, blind, going without food and water all that time.

Acts 8:1b-4; 9:1-9

350

Paul

personality Plus

Now there was in Damascus a believer named Ananias. The Lord spoke to him in a vision, calling, "Ananias!"

"Yes, Lord!" he replied. And the Lord said, "Go over to Straight Street and find the house of a man named Judas and ask there for Paul of Tarsus. He is praying to me right now, for I have shown him a vision of a man named Ananias coming in and laying his hands on him so that he can see again!"

"But Lord," exclaimed Ananias, "I have heard about the terrible things this man has done to the believers in Jerusalem! And we hear that he has arrest warrants with him from the chief priests, authorizing him to arrest every believer in Damascus!"

But the Lord said, "Go and do what I say. For Paul is my chosen instrument to take my message to the nations and before kings, as well as to the people of Israel."

So Ananias went over and found Paul and laid his hands on him and said, "Brother Paul, the Lord Jesus, who appeared to you on the road, has sent me so that you may be filled with the Holy Spirit and get your sight back."

Instantly (it was as though scales fell from his eyes) Paul could see and was immediately baptized. Then he ate and was strengthened.

He stayed with the believers in Damascus for a few days and went at once to the synagogue to tell everyone there the Good News about Jesus—that he is indeed the Son of God!

Acts 9:10-15, 17-20

The Paul you read about today is **about** to have his life **changed.** He started off with a zealous anti-Jesus crusade and ended his life as one of the **true** heroes of the Christian faith.

After Paul's conversion, he helped **build** up the early **church** by announcing the news about **salvation** through Jesus. Through his many years of traveling and preaching, Paul started several churches. He wrote letters to these churches to instruct them on Christian living. These letters became **books** in the New Testament.

One of Paul's instructions directed his followers to follow him as he followed Jesus. Paul was **worthy** of following because he was **sold out** for Jesus. Read Paul's letters, follow his teaching, and make him one of your **heroes.**

:00

:10

:20

:30

:40

:50

:60

the End

20

nov

personality plus Barnabas

Though Barnabas **never** wrote a book in the Bible, he was known for his **tremendous** encouragement to Paul and John—who, together, wrote much of the New Testament. Barnabas was an **important** figure in the development of the early church because he **empowered** others through his encouragement and **support.** The name Barnabas actually means "son of encouragement." He lived up to his name!

It's tough to encourage others. To be an **encourager** takes confidence in oneself and God's ability to use you. It's much easier to be critical! Criticism doesn't take much time or thought. But encouragement is **life-changing.** You'll be able to see the results if you replace criticism with encouragement. Try to live up to the name "son or daughter of encouragement."

:00

:10

:20

:30

:40

:50

:60

O ne day as [the prophets and teachers of the church at Antioch] were worshiping and fasting the Holy Spirit said, "Dedicate Barnabas and Paul for a special job I have for them." So after more fasting and prayer, the men laid their hands on them—and sent them on their way.

Directed by the Holy Spirit they went to Seleucia and then sailed for Cyprus. There, in the town of Salamis, they went to the Jewish synagogue and preached.

Afterwards they preached from town to town across the entire island until finally they reached Paphos where they met a Jewish sorcerer, a fake prophet named Bar-Jesus. He had attached himself to the governor, Sergius Paulus, a man of considerable insight and understanding. The governor invited Barnabas and Paul to visit him, for he wanted to hear their message from God. But the sorcerer, Elymas (his name in Greek), interfered and urged the governor to pay no attention to what Paul and Barnabas said, trying to keep him from trusting the Lord.

Then Paul, filled with the Holy Spirit, glared angrily at the sorcerer and said, "You son of the devil, full of every sort of trickery and villainy, enemy of all that is good, will you never end your opposition to the Lord? And now God has laid his hand of punishment upon you, and you will be stricken awhile with blindness."

Instantly mist and darkness fell upon him, and he began wandering around begging for someone to take his hand and lead him. When the governor saw what happened, he believed and was astonished at the power of God's message.

Acts 13:2-5a, 6-12

the End

352

Paul and Barnabas
Among the Gentiles

W hile [Paul and Barnabas] were at Lystra, they came upon a man with crippled feet who had been that way from birth, so he had never walked. He was listening as Paul preached, and Paul noticed him and realized he had faith to be healed. So Paul called to him, "Stand up!" and the man leaped to his feet and started walking!

Yet only a few days later, some Jews arrived from Antioch and Iconium and turned the crowds into a murderous mob that stoned Paul and dragged him out of the city, apparently dead. But as the believers stood around him, he got up and went back into the city!

The next day he left with Barnabas for Derbe. After preaching the Good News there and making many disciples, they returned again to Lystra, Iconium and Antioch, where they helped the believers to grow in love for God and each other. They encouraged them to continue in the faith in spite of all the persecution, reminding them that they must enter into the Kingdom of God through many tribulations. Paul and Barnabas also appointed elders in every church and prayed for them with fasting, turning them over to the care of the Lord in whom they trusted.

Finally they returned by ship to Antioch, where their journey had begun and where they had been committed to God for the work now completed.

Upon arrival they called together the believers and reported on their trip, telling how God had opened the door of faith to the Gentiles too.

Acts 14:8-10, 19-23, 26-27

BIG time word

GROW

"Grow" is an important word because **growth** is an important **goal** for us as Christians. Growth is a reflection of what's taking place in our **relationship** with God. If we're growing in this relationship, it will be **evident** in our life and actions.

Are you growing?
Are you moving toward becoming more mature in your faith? What **steps** do you need to take in your **spiritual** life to ensure that you're moving ahead and growing? Growth is like learning to drive...**no one** can do it for you except you.

353

22
N O V

MEMORY

In Everything Give Thanks

Oh, give thanks to the Lord and pray to him… Tell the peoples of the world about his mighty doings. Sing to him; yes, sing his praises and tell of his marvelous works.

♦ Oh, come, let us sing to the Lord! Give a joyous shout in honor of the Rock of our salvation!

Come before him with thankful hearts. Let us sing him psalms of praise. For the Lord is a great God, the great King of all gods. He controls the formation of the depths of the earth and the mightiest mountains; all are his. He made the sea and formed the land; they too are his. Come, kneel before the Lord our Maker, for he is our God. We are his sheep, and he is our Shepherd. Oh, that you would hear him calling you today and come to him!

♦ Always be joyful. Always keep on praying. No matter what happens, always be thankful, for this is God's will for you who belong to Christ Jesus.

1 Chronicles 16:8-9; Psalm 95:1-7; 1 Thessalonians 5:16-18

:00
:15
:30

Always be joyful. Always keep on praying. No matter what happens, always be thankful, for this is God's will for you who belong to Christ Jesus.

1 Thessalonians 5:16-18

:45
:60

done

354

give thanks for God's provision

Say thank you to the Lord for being so good, for always being so loving and kind. Has the Lord redeemed you? Then speak out! Tell others he has saved you from your enemies.

He brought the exiles back from the farthest corners of the earth. They were wandering homeless in the desert, hungry and thirsty and faint. "Lord, help!" they cried, and he did! He led them straight to safety and a place to live. Oh, that these men would praise the Lord for his loving-kindness, and for all of his wonderful deeds! For he satisfies the thirsty soul and fills the hungry soul with good.

Oh, that these men would praise the Lord for his loving-kindness and for all of his wonderful deeds! Let them tell him thank you as their sacrifice and sing about his glorious deeds.

Psalm 107:1-9, 21-22

done!

Give it a try

List **five** things you're **thankful** for today:

1. _____

2. _____

3. _____

4. _____

5. _____

If you did this exercise every day, your attitude and life would change dramatically. It's hard to be depressed when you're continually thankful.

NOV 24

IN other words...

BODY

Imagine a body without a head. Now, imagine Jesus as the head of the body. Imagine **yourself** as one **dot** along with millions of others that make up and fill in the body. The body refers to the **church** body, and Jesus is the **Head** of this body. Christians who make up this body receive their life support from Jesus—who is the Head over **everything.**

Although we have never met, as believers we are part of the same body. We are Jesus' living body and represent Him and His work to the world. To maintain a **healthy** body we must be connected to the Head. Today, check whether that connection is strong so Jesus will be able to use you as part of His **body.**

Shout with joy before the Lord, O earth! Obey him gladly; come before him, singing with joy.

Try to realize what this means—the Lord is God! He made us—we are his people, the sheep of his pasture.

Go through his open gates with great thanksgiving; enter his courts with praise. Give thanks to him and bless his name. For the Lord is always good. He is always loving and kind, and his faithfulness goes on and on to each succeeding generation.

✦ Let the peace of heart that comes from Christ be always present in your hearts and lives, for this is your responsibility and privilege as members of his body. And always be thankful.

Remember what Christ taught, and let his words enrich your lives and make you wise; teach them to each other and sing them out in psalms and hymns and spiritual songs, singing to the Lord with thankful hearts. And whatever you do or say, let it be as a representative of the Lord Jesus, and come with him into the presence of God the Father to give him your thanks.

Psalm 100; Colossians 3:15-17

356

Oh, give thanks to the Lord, for he is good; his loving-kindness continues forever.

Give thanks to the God of gods, for his loving-kindness continues forever. Give thanks to the Lord of lords, for his loving-kindness continues forever.

♦ Whenever we pray for you, we always begin by giving thanks to God the Father of our Lord Jesus Christ, for we have heard how much you trust the Lord, and how much you love his people. And you are looking forward to the joys of heaven, and have been ever since the Gospel first was preached to you. The same Good News that came to you is going out all over the world and changing lives everywhere, just as it changed yours that very first day you heard it and understood about God's great kindness to sinners.

♦ I always thank God when I am praying for you, dear Philemon, because I keep hearing of your love and trust in the Lord Jesus and in his people. And I pray that as you share your faith with others it will grip their lives too, as they see the wealth of good things in you that come from Christ Jesus. I myself have gained much joy and comfort from your love, my brother, because your kindness has so often refreshed the hearts of God's people.

Psalm 136:1-3; Colossians 1:3-6; Philemon 1:4-7

:00 In some of Paul's writings he expresses a **deep,** heartfelt **thankfulness.** The Greek word for "heart" literally means

:10 **"bowel."** You can understand why many biblical translators have changed the word from bowel to

:20 **heart.** In Greek thought (the language of Paul's writings) the bowels were referred to as the **center** of

:30 affection. It wouldn't sound very good if we still used BOWEL instead of HEART. Imagine this, "The

:40 Thanksgiving dinner was **great,** Mom. I mean that compliment from the bottom of my

:50 **bowels!"**

No matter **what** word you choose to use, **express** your thankfulness to God

:60 today for creating hearts, bowels, and **everything** else.

done

357

26 NOV

RECEIVE GOD'S GOOD GIFTS WITH THANKSGIVING

Catch T·H·I·S

The **fitness** craze is everywhere! We have placed a **superficial** importance on looking good and getting in shape. Millions of dollars are spent each year by those in **desperate** search of physical fitness. Unfortunately, billions of pounds of exercise equipment are resting unused in garages. The money to buy the equipment was available but the **discipline** to use it wasn't. Discouragement sets in and people give up. It's tough to get back into shape–especially as you get older.

The Bible instructs us that **spiritual** fitness is a much more important goal. Your physical body will eventually decay and rot away, but your spiritual body will last **forever.** Spiritual fitness requires discipline and hard work. If you're not in spiritual shape, get **started** on a training program that works for you. If you're spiritually fit, keep growing and don't allow your **faith** to get **flabby.**

:00
:10
:20
:30
:40
:50
:60
done

The Holy Spirit tells us clearly that in the last times some in the church will turn away from Christ and become eager followers of teachers with devil-inspired ideas. These teachers will tell lies with straight faces and do it so often that their consciences won't even bother them.

They will say it is wrong to be married and wrong to eat meat, even though God gave these things to well-taught Christians to enjoy and be thankful for. For everything God made is good, and we may eat it gladly if we are thankful for it, and if we ask God to bless it, for it is made good by the Word of God and prayer.

If you explain this to the others you will be doing your duty as a worthy pastor who is fed by faith and by the true teaching you have followed.

Don't waste time arguing over foolish ideas and silly myths and legends. Spend your time and energy in the exercise of keeping spiritually fit. Bodily exercise is all right, but spiritual exercise is much more important and is a tonic for all you do. So exercise yourself spiritually, and practice being a better Christian because that will help you not only now in this life, but in the next life too. This is the truth and everyone should accept it. We work hard and suffer much in order that people will believe it, for our hope is in the living God who died for all, and particularly for those who have accepted his salvation. Teach these things and make sure everyone learns them well.

1 Timothy 4:1-11

358

GIVE THANKS TO GOD **IN HEAVEN**

WHAT'S it mean

Instantly I was in spirit there in heaven and saw—oh, the glory of it!—a throne and someone sitting on it! Great bursts of light flashed forth from him as from a glittering diamond or from a shining ruby, and a rainbow glowing like an emerald encircled his throne. Twenty-four smaller thrones surrounded his, with twenty-four Elders sitting on them; all were clothed in white, with golden crowns upon their heads. Lightning and thunder issued from the throne, and there were voices in the thunder. Directly in front of his throne were seven lighted lamps representing the seven-fold Spirit of God. Spread out before it was a shiny crystal sea. Four Living Beings, dotted front and back with eyes, stood at the throne's four sides. Each of these Living Beings had six wings, and the central sections of their wings were covered with eyes. Day after day and night after night they kept on saying, "Holy, holy, holy, Lord God Almighty—the one who was, and is, and is to come."

And when the Living Beings gave glory and honor and thanks to the one sitting on the throne, who lives forever and ever, the twenty-four Elders fell down before him and worshiped him, the Eternal Living One, and cast their crowns before the throne, singing, "O Lord, you are worthy to receive the glory and the honor and the power, for you have created all things. They were created and called into being by your act of will."

The Book of **Revelation** is John's vision describing what the **end times** will be like. The visions and scenes described in this book have been interpreted many different ways by thousands of scholars. If you struggle to **understand** the Book of Revelation, you're not alone. The big picture is that Jesus is revealed as King and wins the final battle over Satan. That's **definitely** worth reading about.

You'll have **eternity** to praise and thank God for this victory, but why don't you get a head start and **praise Him today.**

Revelation 4:2-6, 8-11

23 NOV

ONE MINUTE MEMORY

Let Everything Praise the Lord!

Hallelujah! Yes, praise the Lord!

Praise him in his Temple and in the heavens he made with mighty power. Praise him for his mighty works. Praise his unequaled greatness. Praise him with the trumpet and with lute and harp. Praise him with the drums and dancing. Praise him with stringed instruments and horns. Praise him with the cymbals, yes, loud clanging cymbals. Let everything alive give praises to the Lord! You praise him!

Hallelujah!

♦ Don't drink too much wine, for many evils lie along that path; be filled instead with the Holy Spirit and controlled by him.

Talk with each other much about the Lord, quoting psalms and hymns and singing sacred songs, making music in your hearts to the Lord. Always give thanks for everything to our God and Father in the name of our Lord Jesus Christ.

Psalm 150; Ephesians 5:18-20

:00
:15
:30

Don't drink too much wine, for many evils lie along that path; be filled instead with the Holy Spirit and controlled by him.

Ephesians 5:18

:45

:60

done

360

In olden times God did not share this plan with his people, but now he has revealed it by the Holy Spirit to his apostles and prophets.

And this is the secret: that the Gentiles will have their full share with the Jews in all the riches inherited by God's sons; both are invited to belong to his Church, and all of God's promises of mighty blessings through Christ apply to them both when they accept the Good News about Christ and what he has done for them. God has given me the wonderful privilege of telling everyone about this plan of his; and he has given me his power and special ability to do it well.

Just think! Though I did nothing to deserve it, and though I am the most useless Christian there is, yet I was the one chosen for this special joy of telling the Gentiles the Glad News of the endless treasures available to them in Christ; and to explain to everyone that God is the Savior of the Gentiles too, just as he who made all things had secretly planned from the very beginning.

And his reason? To show to all the rulers in heaven how perfectly wise he is when all of his family—Jews and Gentiles alike—are seen to be joined together in his Church in just the way he had always planned it through Jesus Christ our Lord.

Now we can come fearlessly right into God's presence, assured of his glad welcome when we come with Christ and trust in him.

Ephesians 3:5-12

:00 Today's reading provides a message that many Christians **need** to hear. Differences should **never** separate us from other Christians. We are **one** in Jesus

:10 whether we are thin, tall, squatty, large, colored, uncolored, transparent, ear-

:20 pierced, or nose-pierced...it doesn't matter. We are **one** in Jesus!

:30 Paul explains this truth in Galatians 3:28-29: "We are no longer Jews or Greeks or slaves or free men or even merely

:40 men or women, but we are all the same—we are Christians; we are one in Christ Jesus. And now that we are Christ's we

:50 are the true descendants of Abraham, and all of God's promises to him belong to us."

:60 **Celebrate** this truth today with a Christian who is **different** than you by telling him or her you're **related.**

d o n e

361

SPIRITUAL GIFTS

Weird or what

:00
:10
:20
:30
:40
:50
:60
end

In the New Testament there are four different **passages** that discuss and describe **spiritual** gifts. It's interesting that none of these passages have the exact same list of gifts. Some believe that the lists weren't intended to be all-inclusive, and others debate that the ones listed are the only spiritual gifts available. Regardless of whether there are nine spiritual gifts or seventeen, we **do** know that God has assigned **each** of us specific gifts to **build** up the Body of Jesus. Read through the spiritual gift passages* and begin to **discover** how God has specially **gifted you.**

* (Also read Romans 12:3-8; 1 Corinthians 12:28-30; Ephesians 4:7-12; 1 Peter 4:10-11.)

And now, brothers, I want to write about the special abilities the Holy Spirit gives to each of you, for I don't want any misunderstanding about them.

Now God gives us many kinds of special abilities, but it is the same Holy Spirit who is the source of them all. There are different kinds of service to God, but it is the same Lord we are serving. There are many ways in which God works in our lives, but it is the same God who does the work in and through all of us who are his. The Holy Spirit displays God's power through each of us as a means of helping the entire church.

To one person the Spirit gives the ability to give wise advice; someone else may be especially good at studying and teaching, and this is his gift from the same Spirit. He gives special faith to another, and to someone else the power to heal the sick. He gives power for doing miracles to some, and to others power to prophesy and preach. He gives someone else the power to know whether evil spirits are speaking through those who claim to be giving God's messages—or whether it is really the Spirit of God who is speaking. Still another person is able to speak in languages he never learned; and others, who do not know the language either, are given power to understand what he is saying. It is the same and only Holy Spirit who gives all these gifts and powers, deciding which each one of us should have.

1 Corinthians 12:1, 4-11

362

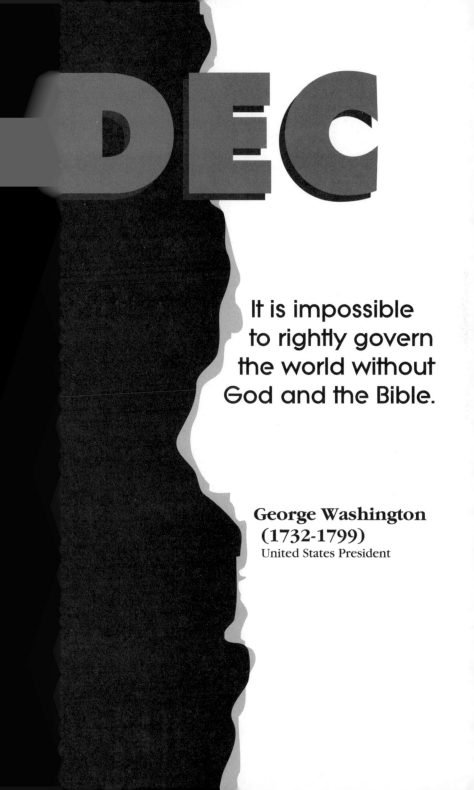

DEC

It is impossible
to rightly govern
the world without
God and the Bible.

**George Washington
(1732-1799)**
United States President

FUTURE HOPE, FUTURE REWARD

CHECK IT OUT

For we know that when this tent we live in now is taken down—when we die and leave these bodies—we will have wonderful new bodies in heaven, homes that will be ours forevermore, made for us by God himself and not by human hands. How weary we grow of our present bodies. That is why we look forward eagerly to the day when we shall have heavenly bodies that we shall put on like new clothes. For we shall not be merely spirits without bodies. These earthly bodies make us groan and sigh, but we wouldn't like to think of dying and having no bodies at all. We want to slip into our new bodies so that these dying bodies will, as it were, be swallowed up by everlasting life. This is what God has prepared for us, and as a guarantee he has given us his Holy Spirit.

Now we look forward with confidence to our heavenly bodies, realizing that every moment we spend in these earthly bodies is time spent away from our eternal home in heaven with Jesus. We know these things are true by believing, not by seeing. And we are not afraid but are quite content to die, for then we will be at home with the Lord. So our aim is to please him always in everything we do, whether we are here in this body or away from this body and with him in heaven. For we must all stand before Christ to be judged and have our lives laid bare—before him. Each of us will receive whatever he deserves for the good or bad things he has done in his earthly body.

2 Corinthians 5:1-10

:00 To a Christian, a future of living with God in **heaven** is good news. We can view death as a move **up** or a **victory.** Paul

:10 expressed this by describing the tension between his desire to live in pain on earth and spread the Gospel

:20 and his **desire** to be with God in heaven. Check out Philippians 1:21:
"For to me, living means opportunities for Christ,

:30 and dying–well, that's better yet!"

There is **hope** for

:40 you! What God has planned for Christians can't be matched by your greatest day on earth. But while you

:50 are on this earth, it's best to live with **celebration** in your heart and a **joyful** eye to your future in

:60 God's presence.

d o n e

365

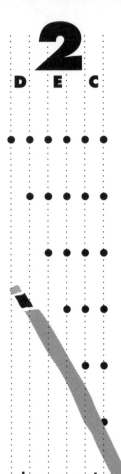

d o n e !

Now all praise to God for his wonderful kindness to us and his favor that he has poured out upon us because we belong to his dearly loved Son. So overflowing is his kindness toward us that he took away all our sins through the blood of his Son, by whom we are saved; and he has showered down upon us the richness of his grace—for how well he understands us and knows what is best for us at all times.

God has told us his secret reason for sending Christ, a plan he decided on in mercy long ago; and this was his purpose: that when the time is ripe he will gather us all together from wherever we are—in heaven or on earth—to be with him in Christ forever. Moreover, because of what Christ has done, we have become gifts to God that he delights in, for as part of God's sovereign plan we were chosen from the beginning to be his, and all things happen just as he decided long ago. God's purpose in this was that we should praise God and give glory to him for doing these mighty things for us, who were the first to trust in Christ.

And because of what Christ did, all you others too, who heard the Good News about how to be saved, and trusted Christ, were marked as belonging to Christ by the Holy Spirit, who long ago had been promised to all of us Christians. His presence within us is God's guarantee that he really will give us all that he promised; and the Spirit's seal upon us means that God has already purchased us and that he guarantees to bring us to himself. This is just one more reason for us to praise our glorious God.

Ephesians 1:4-14

Christians have been **"sealed"** as God's by the Holy Spirit. How does that make you **feel** right now?

sealed for salvation

Give it a try

Humility
and Glory

Is there any such thing as Christians cheering each other up? Do you love me enough to want to help me? Does it mean anything to you that we are brothers in the Lord, sharing the same Spirit? Are your hearts tender and sympathetic at all? Then make me truly happy by loving each other and agreeing wholeheartedly with each other, working together with one heart and mind and purpose.

Don't be selfish; don't live to make a good impression on others. Be humble, thinking of others as better than yourself. Don't just think about your own affairs, but be interested in others, too, and in what they are doing.

Your attitude should be the kind that was shown us by Jesus Christ, who, though he was God, did not demand and cling to his rights as God, but laid aside his mighty power and glory, taking the disguise of a slave and becoming like men. And he humbled himself even further, going so far as actually to die a criminal's death on a cross.

Yet it was because of this that God raised him up to the heights of heaven and gave him a name which is above every other name, that at the name of Jesus every knee shall bow in heaven and on earth and under the earth, and every tongue shall confess that Jesus Christ is Lord, to the glory of God the Father.

Philippians 2:1-11

attitude

Having a **positive** attitude is **vital** in today's world. People are attracted to those with quality attitudes. Christians are typically known for having good attitudes because the Holy Spirit resides in them. The Spirit's indwelling allows Christians to live with **confidence** that God is in control.

When your attitude is positive, people notice that something is different. They can see the security of your peace and **joy**. Is your attitude one that people **notice?** If not, what needs to be done to improve it? If it is noticed, **congratulations!...** you are in a minority of **positive** people.

MINUTE
ONE
MEMORY

Yet if anyone ever had reason to hope that he could save himself, it would be I. If others could be saved by what they are, certainly I could! For I went through the Jewish initiation ceremony when I was eight days old, having been born into a pure-blooded Jewish home that was a branch of the old original Benjamin family. So I was a real Jew if there ever was one! What's more, I was a member of the Pharisees who demand the strictest obedience to every Jewish law and custom.

But all these things that I once thought very worthwhile—now I've thrown them all away so that I can put my trust and hope in Christ alone. Yes, everything else is worthless when compared with the priceless gain of knowing Christ Jesus my Lord. I have put aside all else, counting it worth less than nothing, in order that I can have Christ, and become one with him, no longer counting on being saved by being good enough or by obeying God's laws, but by trusting Christ to save me; for God's way of making us right with himself depends on faith—counting on Christ alone.

No, dear brothers, I am still not all I should be, but I am bringing all my energies to bear on this one thing: Forgetting the past and looking forward to what lies ahead, I strain to reach the end of the race and receive the prize for which God is calling us up to heaven because of what Christ Jesus did for us.

Philippians 3:4-5, 7-9, 13-14

:00

:15

:30

:45

:60

Forgetting the past and looking forward to what lies ahead, I strain to reach the end of the race and receive the prize for which God is calling us up to heaven because of what Christ Jesus did for us.

Philippians 3:13b-14

done

THE SUPREMACY OF CHRIST

Christ is the exact likeness of the unseen God. He existed before God made anything at all, and, in fact, Christ himself is the Creator who made everything in heaven and earth, the things we can see and the things we can't; the spirit world with its kings and kingdoms, its rulers and authorities; all were made by Christ for his own use and glory. He was before all else began and it is his power that holds everything together. He is the Head of the body made up of his people—that is, his Church—which he began; and he is the Leader of all those who arise from the dead, so that he is first in everything; for God wanted all of himself to be in his Son.

It was through what his Son did that God cleared a path for everything to come to him—all things in heaven and on earth—for Christ's death on the cross has made peace with God for all by his blood. This includes you who were once so far away from God. You were his enemies and hated him and were separated from him by your evil thoughts and actions, yet now he has brought you back as his friends. He has done this through the death on the cross of his own human body, and now as a result Christ has brought you into the very presence of God, and you are standing there before him with nothing left against you—nothing left that he could even chide you for; the only condition is that you fully believe the Truth, standing in it steadfast and firm, strong in the Lord, convinced of the Good News that Jesus died for you, and never shifting from trusting him to save you. This is the wonderful news that came to each of you and is now spreading all over the world. And I, Paul, have the joy of telling it to others.

Colossians 1:15-23

369

5 DEC

Just a thought

If people **ask** you what **God is like,** open your Bible and have them check out **Jesus** –He's the **exact** likeness of **God.**

:00
:10
:20
:30
:40
:50
1:00

FINISH

6 DEC

Meeting the Lord
in the Air

word

sorrow

Sorrow is an appropriate **emotion** to express at the death of a loved one. God created you with the ability to **cry** and show compassion. If your sorrow is because of the death of a **Christian,** your tears can eventually become tears of **hope.** You can rest in the truth that death to a Christian is entrance into God's presence and **eternal** home.

As a Christian, you have nothing to fear about your future. If you live by **faith** that your future is sealed, you can live with **assurance.** That's a **great** way to live!

Try it.

And now, dear brothers, I want you to know what happens to a Christian when he dies so that when it happens, you will not be full of sorrow, as those are who have no hope. For since we believe that Jesus died and then came back to life again, we can also believe that when Jesus returns, God will bring back with him all the Christians who have died.

I can tell you this directly from the Lord: that we who are still living when the Lord returns will not rise to meet him ahead of those who are in their graves. For the Lord himself will come down from heaven with a mighty shout and with the soul-stirring cry of the archangel and the great trumpet-call of God. And the believers who are dead will be the first to rise to meet the Lord. Then we who are still alive and remain on the earth will be caught up with them in the clouds to meet the Lord in the air and remain with him forever. So comfort and encourage each other with this news.

♦ When is all this going to happen? I really don't need to say anything about that, dear brothers, for you know perfectly well that no one knows. That day of the Lord will come unexpectedly, like a thief in the night. When people are saying, "All is well; everything is quiet and peaceful"—then, all of a sudden, disaster will fall upon them as suddenly as a woman's birth pains begin when her child is born. And these people will not be able to get away anywhere—there will be no place to hide.

But, dear brothers, you are not in the dark about these things, and you won't be surprised as by a thief when that day of the Lord comes.

1 Thessalonians 4:13-18; 5:1-4

WORK IS GOOD

WHAT'S it mean

Now here is a command, dear brothers, given in the name of our Lord Jesus Christ by his authority: Stay away from any Christian who spends his days in laziness and does not follow the ideal of hard work we set up for you. For you well know that you ought to follow our example: you never saw us loafing; we never accepted food from anyone without buying it; we worked hard day and night for the money we needed to live on, in order that we would not be a burden to any of you. It wasn't that we didn't have the right to ask you to feed us, but we wanted to show you firsthand how you should work for your living. Even while we were still there with you, we gave you this rule: "He who does not work shall not eat."

Yet we hear that some of you are living in laziness, refusing to work, and wasting your time in gossiping. In the name of the Lord Jesus Christ we appeal to such people—we command them—to quiet down, get to work, and earn their own living. And to the rest of you I say, dear brothers, never be tired of doing right.

If anyone refuses to obey what we say in this letter, notice who he is and stay away from him, that he may be ashamed of himself. Don't think of him as an enemy, but speak to him as you would to a brother who needs to be warned.

2 Thessalonians 3:6-15

In today's passage we see an example of **biblical** church discipline. Paul had taught that **Jesus** was going to return. The people in the church believed this and used it as an **excuse** to stop working. Some people even began to sponge food and money from others. They wasted their time by gossiping and getting involved in other people's business. Paul was telling them to get **busy** and begin working.

Work is an important part of your **development.** Some students don't take their jobs **seriously** because the jobs aren't what they want for a career. No matter what kind of job you have, try to do your **best** to honor God with your positive attitude and hard work. Your job will provide you many opportunities to tell co-workers about your **love** for God. Earn their **respect** first by living right and working hard.

DONE

GODLINESS AND CONTENTMENT

Catch T·H·I·S

Do you know someone who loves to **argue?** Some people actually **enjoy** creating and maintaining tension. But arguing just to argue usually results in wasted **chatter.** No real purpose is ever served with **empty** arguments.

Some Christians love to argue about the Bible. They know a lot of **biblical** answers and enjoy to debate non-Christians using their knowledge. Unfortunately, **very few** people enter into a relationship with God during an argument. People are usually **defensive** and less open while arguing...even if what they hear is the truth.

Learn as **much** as you can about the Bible so you can talk rationally, but reserve arguing for another topic. If you replace your arguments with love, you'll find people more **responsive** to the truth. Love works...even if you don't have all the right **Bible** answers. Keep learning, and **replace** arguing with **love.**

:00

:10

:20

:30

:40

:50

:60

done

Some may deny these things, but they are the sound, wholesome teachings of the Lord Jesus Christ and are the foundation for a godly life. Anyone who says anything different is both proud and stupid. He is quibbling over the meaning of Christ's words and stirring up arguments ending in jealousy and anger, which only lead to name-calling, accusations, and evil suspicions. These arguers—their minds warped by sin—don't know how to tell the truth; to them the Good News is just a means of making money. Keep away from them.

Do you want to be truly rich? You already are if you are happy and good. After all, we didn't bring any money with us when we came into the world, and we can't carry away a single penny when we die. So we should be well satisfied without money if we have enough food and clothing.

Tell those who are rich not to be proud and not to trust in their money, which will soon be gone, but their pride and trust should be in the living God who always richly gives us all we need for our enjoyment. Tell them to use their money to do good. They should be rich in good works and should give happily to those in need, always being ready to share with others whatever God has given them. By doing this they will be storing up real treasure for themselves in heaven—it is the only safe investment for eternity! And they will be living a fruitful Christian life down here as well.

1 Timothy 6:3-8, 17-19

372

9 DEC

ONE MINUTE MEMORY

The Profit of the Scriptures

You know what I believe and the way I live and what I want. You know my faith in Christ and how I have suffered. You know my love for you, and my patience. You know how many troubles I have had as a result of my preaching the Good News. You know about all that was done to me while I was visiting in Antioch, Iconium, and Lystra, but the Lord delivered me. Yes, and those who decide to please Christ Jesus by living godly lives will suffer at the hands of those who hate him. In fact, evil men and false teachers will become worse and worse, deceiving many, they themselves having been deceived by Satan.

But you must keep on believing the things you have been taught. You know they are true, for you know that you can trust those of us who have taught you. You know how, when you were a small child, you were taught the holy Scriptures; and it is these that make you wise to accept God's salvation by trusting in Christ Jesus. The whole Bible was given to us by inspiration from God and is useful to teach us what is true and to make us realize what is wrong in our lives; it straightens us out and helps us do what is right. It is God's way of making us well prepared at every point, fully equipped to do good to everyone.

2 Timothy 3:10b-17

The whole Bible was given to us by inspiration from God and is useful to teach us what is true and to make us realize what is wrong in our lives; it straightens us out and helps us do what is right.

2 Timothy 3:16

:00
:15
:30
:45
:60

373

DEC
10

JESUS:
OUR HIGH PRIEST

:00

:10

:20

:30

During Old Testament times, the High **Priest** would present sacrifices to **atone** for people's sins. It's interesting to note that in the New Testament **Jesus** is referred to as our great High Priest. His one sacrifice was **totally** sufficient for **all** of us to be forgiven forever.

:40

:50

As a Christian, you now have **direct** access to God and don't need a High Priest to go before you anymore. Take **advantage** of that direct access and **thank** God for the ultimate sacrifice of **Jesus.**

:60

 end

But Jesus the Son of God is our great High Priest who has gone to heaven itself to help us; therefore let us never stop trusting him. This High Priest of ours understands our weaknesses since he had the same temptations we do, though he never once gave way to them and sinned. So let us come boldly to the very throne of God and stay there to receive his mercy and to find grace to help us in our times of need.

♦ Yet while Christ was here on earth he pleaded with God, praying with tears and agony of soul to the only one who would save him from (premature) death. And God heard his prayers because of his strong desire to obey God at all times.

And even though Jesus was God's Son, he had to learn from experience what it was like to obey when obeying meant suffering. It was after he had proved himself perfect in this experience that Jesus became the Giver of eternal salvation to all those who obey him. For remember that God has chosen him to be a High Priest with the same rank as Melchizedek.

♦ And it was necessary for Jesus to be like us, his brothers, so that he could be our merciful and faithful High Priest before God, a Priest who would be both merciful to us and faithful to God in dealing with the sins of the people. For since he himself has now been through suffering and temptation, he knows what it is like when we suffer and are tempted, and he is wonderfully able to help us.

Hebrews 4:14-16; 5:7-10; 2:17-18

374

heroes of faith: Part 1

What is faith? It is the confident assurance that something we want is going to happen. It is the certainty that what we hope for is waiting for us, even though we cannot see it up ahead. Men of God in days of old were famous for their faith.

By faith—by believing God—we know that the world and the stars—in fact, all things—were made at God's command; and that they were all made from things that can't be seen.

It was by faith that Abel obeyed God and brought an offering that pleased God more than Cain's offering did. God accepted Abel and proved it by accepting his gift; and though Abel is long dead, we can still learn lessons from him about trusting God.

Noah was another who trusted God. When he heard God's warning about the future, Noah believed him even though there was then no sign of a flood, and wasting no time, he built the ark and saved his family. Noah's belief in God was in direct contrast to the sin and disbelief of the rest of the world—which refused to obey—and because of his faith he became one of those whom God has accepted.

Abraham trusted God, and when God told him to leave home and go far away to another land that he promised to give him, Abraham obeyed. Away he went, not even knowing where he was going.

Hebrews 11:1-4, 7-8

DEC 11

done!

Give it a try

Write a **definition** of **faith**:

Share what you wrote with someone who is more knowledgeable than you regarding Christianity. Discuss your definition.

Yesterday you came up with your own definition of faith. Today, look at how Jesus responded to His followers' questions about the amount of faith they needed. Check out Matthew 17:20:

"For if you had faith even as small as a tiny mustard seed you could say to this mountain, 'Move!' and it would go far away. Nothing would be impossible."

Jesus didn't emphasize the **amount** of faith needed, but stressed that **true** faith, even in its smallest form, can do **great** things. Ask God to help you **strengthen** your faith **today**.

:00

:10

:20

:30

:40

:50

:60

Sarah, too, had faith, and because of this she was able to become a mother in spite of her old age, for she realized that God, who gave her his promise, would certainly do what he said. And so a whole nation came from Abraham, who was too old to have even one child—a nation with so many millions of people that, like the stars of the sky and the sand on the ocean shores, there is no way to count them.

While God was testing him, Abraham still trusted in God and his promises, and so he offered up his son Isaac and was ready to slay him on the altar of sacrifice; yes, to slay even Isaac, through whom God had promised to give Abraham a whole nation of descendants!

He believed that if Isaac died God would bring him back to life again; and that is just about what happened, for as far as Abraham was concerned, Isaac was doomed to death, but he came back again alive!

It was by faith that Moses, when he grew up, refused to be treated as the grandson of the king, but chose to share ill-treatment with God's people instead of enjoying the fleeting pleasures of sin. He thought that it was better to suffer for the promised Christ than to own all the treasures of Egypt, for he was looking forward to the great reward that God would give him.

And these men of faith, though they trusted God and won his approval, none of them received all that God had promised them; for God wanted them to wait and share the even better rewards that were prepared for us.

done *Hebrews 11:11-12, 17-19, 24-26, 39-40*

376

WISDOM IN TRIALS

Dear brothers, is your life full of difficulties and temptations? Then be happy, for when the way is rough, your patience has a chance to grow. So let it grow, and don't try to squirm out of your problems. For when your patience is finally in full bloom, then you will be ready for anything, strong in character, full and complete.

If you want to know what God wants you to do, ask him, and he will gladly tell you, for he is always ready to give a bountiful supply of wisdom to all who ask him; he will not resent it. But when you ask him, be sure that you really expect him to tell you, for a doubtful mind will be as unsettled as a wave of the sea that is driven and tossed by the wind; and every decision you then make will be uncertain, as you turn first this way and then that. If you don't ask with faith, don't expect the Lord to give you any solid answer.

Happy is the man who doesn't give in and do wrong when he is tempted, for afterwards he will get as his reward the crown of life that God has promised those who love him. And remember, when someone wants to do wrong it is never God who is tempting him, for God never wants to do wrong and never tempts anyone else to do it. Temptation is the pull of man's own evil thoughts and wishes. These evil thoughts lead to evil actions and afterwards to the death penalty from God.

James 1:2-8, 12-15

377

Catch THIS

:00

:10

:20

:30

:40

:50

:60 done

One of the many **confusions** regarding the Christian faith has to do with God and **temptation.** Many Christians believe God tempts us in order to test our response and measure our faith. Today's passage explains this isn't true. **God doesn't tempt us!** God provides a way for us to escape temptation because He doesn't want us to sin.

When you're tempted, realize it's not God doing the tempting. **Run** from temptation and don't allow the temptation to know where you're going. Better yet, think through potentially tempting situations before they happen. As you think about them, plan your **escape** route so when **temptations** do come along you'll know exactly what to do. With an escape plan, the temptations can become an **opportunity** to run to God for **strength.**

CONTROLLING THE TONGUE

Words can **hurt!** Almost everyone has been hurt by someone's damaging words directed at them. If you haven't, consider yourself lucky but expect it to happen sooner or later.

Jesus said that the words that come from our mouth are a reflection of what's in our heart. Check out Matthew 12:35:

"A good man's speech reveals the rich treasures within him. An evil-hearted man is filled with venom, and his speech reveals it."

Try using **good** words today. Think about the **power** behind the words you use. Your words can either **heal** or hurt. Choose healing words **today.**

:00

:10

:20

:30

:40

:50

:60

If anyone can control his tongue, it proves that he has perfect control over himself in every other way. We can make a large horse turn around and go wherever we want by means of a small bit in his mouth. And a tiny rudder makes a huge ship turn wherever the pilot wants it to go, even though the winds are strong.

So also the tongue is a small thing, but what enormous damage it can do. A great forest can be set on fire by one tiny spark. And the tongue is a flame of fire. It is full of wickedness, and poisons every part of the body. And the tongue is set on fire by hell itself and can turn our whole lives into a blazing flame of destruction and disaster.

Men have trained, or can train, every kind of animal or bird that lives and every kind of reptile and fish, but no human being can tame the tongue. It is always ready to pour out its deadly poison. Sometimes it praises our heavenly Father, and sometimes it breaks out into curses against men who are made like God. And so blessing and cursing come pouring out of the same mouth. Dear brothers, surely this is not right! Does a spring of water bubble out first with fresh water and then with bitter water? Can you pick olives from a fig tree, or figs from a grape vine? No, and you can't draw fresh water from a salty pool.

James 3:2b-12

d o n e

378

THE PROMISE OF
SALVATION

15

DEC

All honor to God, the God and Father of our Lord Jesus Christ; for it is his boundless mercy that has given us the privilege of being born again so that we are now members of God's own family. Now we live in the hope of eternal life because Christ rose again from the dead. And God has reserved for his children the priceless gift of eternal life; it is kept in heaven for you, pure and undefiled, beyond the reach of change and decay. And God, in his mighty power, will make sure that you get there safely to receive it because you are trusting him. It will be yours in that coming last day for all to see. So be truly glad! There is wonderful joy ahead, even though the going is rough for a while down here.

You love him even though you have never seen him; though not seeing him, you trust him; and even now you are happy with the inexpressible joy that comes from heaven itself. And your further reward for trusting him will be the salvation of your souls.

This salvation was something the prophets did not fully understand.

They were finally told that these things would not occur during their lifetime, but long years later, during yours. And now at last this Good News has been plainly announced to all of us. It was preached to us in the power of the same heaven-sent Holy Spirit who spoke to them; and it is all so strange and wonderful that even the angels in heaven would give a great deal to know more about it.

1 Peter 1:3-6, 8-10a,12

Just a thought

When you put your **faith** in **Jesus,** you not only receive a **heavenly** birth but also a **promise** for eternity and God's **strength** to keep you **until** then.

:00

:10

:20

:30

:40

:50

1:00

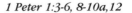

FINISH

379

16 DEC

Living Stones and the Cornerstone

word

Unfortunately, our world has a **lot** of hatred floating around. Hatred displays itself in many different ways. When anger isn't processed or dealt with in a **godly** manner, it usually leads to resentment and then to hatred. This hatred usually shows itself in some form of rebellion or **rage.**

Hatred is the opposite of **peace.** If you choose hatred, you'll slowly destroy yourself and will eventually fall to pieces. But if you refuse hatred, you'll **experience** God's peace. What's your choice?

Peace
or
Pieces?

So get rid of your feelings of hatred. Don't just pretend to be good! Be done with dishonesty and jealousy and talking about others behind their backs. Now that you realize how kind the Lord has been to you, put away all evil, deception, envy, and fraud. Long to grow up into the fullness of your salvation; cry for this as a baby cries for his milk.

Come to Christ, who is the living Foundation of Rock upon which God builds; though men have spurned him, he is very precious to God who has chosen him above all others.

And now you have become living building-stones for God's use in building his house. What's more, you are his holy priests; so come to him—(you who are acceptable to him because of Jesus Christ)—and offer to God those things that please him. As the Scriptures express it, "See, I am sending Christ to be the carefully chosen, precious Cornerstone of my church, and I will never disappoint those who trust in him."

You have been chosen by God himself—you are priests of the King, you are holy and pure, you are God's very own—all this so that you may show to others how God called you out of the darkness into his wonderful light. Once you were less than nothing; now you are God's own. Once you knew very little of God's kindness; now your very lives have been changed by it.

1 Peter 2:1-6, 9b-10

THE MORNING STAR

WHAT'S it mean

We have not been telling you fairy tales when we explained to you the power of our Lord Jesus Christ and his coming again. My own eyes have seen his splendor and his glory: I was there on the holy mountain when he shone out with honor given him by God his Father; I heard that glorious, majestic voice calling down from heaven, saying, "This is my much-loved Son; I am well pleased with him."

So we have seen and proved that what the prophets said came true. You will do well to pay close attention to everything they have written, for, like lights shining into dark corners, their words help us to understand many things that otherwise would be dark and difficult. But when you consider the wonderful truth of the prophets' words, then the light will dawn in your souls and Christ the Morning Star will shine in your hearts. For no prophecy recorded in Scripture was ever thought up by the prophet himself. It was the Holy Spirit within these godly men who gave them true messages from God.

♦ Your words are a flashlight to light the path ahead of me and keep me from stumbling.

♦ I, Jesus, have sent my angel to you to tell the churches all these things. I am both David's Root and his Descendant. I am the bright Morning Star.

2 Peter 1:16-21; Psalm 119:105;
Revelation 22:16

Peter had an **incredible** experience at the Mount of **Transfiguration.** But this experience couldn't replace his love for the Scriptures and his conviction of their truth. Peter instructs Christians to **trust** the **Scriptures** more than experience.

Living by God's Word will provide **light** and guide us in the darkness. Although the Bible is filled with human words, it was **God** who **inspired** the writers with the right words to use. God "spoke" or "breathed" those words into life. They **are** God's words and are as reliable as God himself. When God's words are hidden in your heart, you can't help but be different...
it's guaranteed!

DONE

18 DEC

LOVE ONE ANOTHER

Catch T·H·I·S

The greatest **gift** of all is God's love to us **expressed** through Jesus' death in our place. That's **love!** The Bible is another example of God's love. God has filled the pages with His **timeless** words. Actually, the Bible is God's **personal** love letter to us. From the beginning of time until the end of time, the central theme of the Bible is **love.**

Jesus **expressed** this when He wrapped up all the commandments by using "love" three times. He said to LOVE God with all of our heart, soul, and mind, and to LOVE our neighbors as we LOVE ourselves. This love will not only **change** your life but will also **show** others you are a follower of God. This is especially true if you can love others without any expectations of them. Try loving regardless of how others act or treat you. This type of love isn't easy to express, but if you can do it, you'll find yourself loving just as **God loves you.**

:00

:10

:20

:30

:40

:50

:60

done

My little children, I am telling you this so that you will stay away from sin. But if you sin, there is someone to plead for you before the Father. His name is Jesus Christ, the one who is all that is good and who pleases God completely. He is the one who took God's wrath against our sins upon himself and brought us into fellowship with God; and he is the forgiveness for our sins, and not only ours but all the world's.

And how can we be sure that we belong to him? By looking within ourselves: are we really trying to do what he wants us to?

Someone may say, "I am a Christian; I am on my way to heaven; I belong to Christ." But if he doesn't do what Christ tells him to, he is a liar. But those who do what Christ tells them to will learn to love God more and more. That is the way to know whether or not you are a Christian. Anyone who says he is a Christian should live as Christ did.

Dear brothers, I am not writing out a new rule for you to obey, for it is an old one you have always had, right from the start. You have heard it all before. Yet it is always new, and works for you just as it did for Christ; and as we obey this commandment, to love one another, the darkness in our lives disappears and the new light of life in Christ shines in.

♦ [Jesus said,] "And so I am giving a new commandment to you now—love each other just as much as I love you. Your strong love for each other will prove to the world that you are my disciples."

1 John 2:1-8; John 13:34-35

The Love of the Father

DEC

ONE MINUTE MEMORY

Stop loving this evil world and all that it offers you, for when you love these things you show that you do not really love God; for all these worldly things, these evil desires—the craze for sex, the ambition to buy everything that appeals to you, and the pride that comes from wealth and importance—these are not from God. They are from this evil world itself. And this world is fading away, and these evil, forbidden things will go with it, but whoever keeps doing the will of God will live forever.

♦ See how very much our heavenly Father loves us, for he allows us to be called his children—think of it—and we really are! But since most people don't know God, naturally they don't understand that we are his children.

♦ If you believe that Jesus is the Christ—that he is God's Son and your Savior—then you are a child of God. And all who love the Father love his children too. So you can find out how much you love God's children—your brothers and sisters in the Lord—by how much you love and obey God. Loving God means doing what he tells us to do, and really, that isn't hard at all; for every child of God can obey him, defeating sin and evil pleasure by trusting Christ to help him.

But who could possibly fight and win this battle except by believing that Jesus is truly the Son of God?

1 John 2:15-17; 3:1; 5:1-5

> If you believe that Jesus is the Christ–that he is God's Son and your Savior–then you are a child of God.
>
> 1 John 5:1

:00

:15

:30

:45

:60

done

383

20 dec

personality Plus Antichrist

The word "Antichrist" appears only **five** times in the New Testament, but the theme of an antichrist person is woven **throughout** the Old Testament prophecies. The word "anti" means "in place of" or **"against."** The Bible describes the Antichrist as someone who will try to exalt himself and be worshiped. The Antichrist will be given power by Satan and will try to lead people against God during the end times.

One of God's responsibilities is to take care of history. One of our responsibilities is to remain faithful to God. A strong **faith** in God will replace your fears with the **security** that the Antichrist will have no power over **you**.

:00

:10

:20

:30

:40

:50

:60

the End

Dear children, this world's last hour has come. You have heard about the Antichrist who is coming—the one who is against Christ—and already many such persons have appeared. This makes us all the more certain that the end of the world is near. These "against-Christ" people used to be members of our churches, but they never really belonged with us or else they would have stayed. When they left us it proved that they were not of us at all.

And who is the greatest liar? The one who says that Jesus is not Christ. Such a person is antichrist, for he does not believe in God the Father and in his Son. For a person who doesn't believe in Christ, God's Son, can't have God the Father either. But he who has Christ, God's Son, has God the Father also.

♦ Watch out for the false leaders—and there are many of them around—who don't believe that Jesus Christ came to earth as a human being with a body like ours. Such people are against the truth and against Christ. Beware of being like them and losing the prize that you and I have been working so hard to get. See to it that you win your full reward from the Lord. For if you wander beyond the teaching of Christ, you will leave God behind; while if you are loyal to Christ's teachings, you will have God too. Then you will have both the Father and the Son.

If anyone comes to teach you, and he doesn't believe what Christ taught, don't even invite him into your home. Don't encourage him in any way. If you do, you will be a partner with him in his wickedness.

1 John 2:18-19, 22-23; 2 John 7-11

Stoutly defend the truth that God gave once for all to his people to keep without change through the years. I say this because some godless teachers have wormed their way in among you, saying that after we become Christians we can do just as we like without fear of God's punishment. The fate of such people was written long ago, for they have turned against our only Master and Lord, Jesus Christ.

Dear friends, remember what the apostles of our Lord Jesus Christ told you, that in the last times there would come these scoffers whose whole purpose in life is to enjoy themselves in every evil way imaginable. They stir up arguments; they love the evil things of the world; they do not have the Holy Spirit living in them.

Stay always within the boundaries where God's love can reach and bless you. Wait patiently for the eternal life that our Lord Jesus Christ in his mercy is going to give you. Try to help those who argue against you. Be merciful to those who doubt. Save some by snatching them as from the very flames of hell itself. And as for others, help them to find the Lord by being kind to them, but be careful that you yourselves aren't pulled along into their sins. Hate every trace of their sin while being merciful to them as sinners.

And now—all glory to him who alone is God. He is able to keep you from slipping and falling away, and to bring you, sinless and perfect, into his glorious presence with mighty shouts of everlasting joy. Amen.

Jude 3b-4, 17-19, 21-24a, 25

IN **other** words...

GODLESS TEACHERS

The **problem** addressed in the Book of Jude is still a problem today. There are still godless teachers who are trying to **pervert** or add to the Bible. We need to watch out for these men and women because their teaching can be seductive and subtle. False teachers can creep into the church like worms and lead good people in the **wrong** direction.

One way to identify these teachers is to **observe** how they live their lives. If you are following someone's teachings, you need to ask yourself, "Does this person **practice** what he or she teaches? Does this person hate what is evil?"

Do what it takes to remain in **God's love** and you'll be protected from the ungodly.

:00

:10

:20

:30

:40

:50

done :60

385

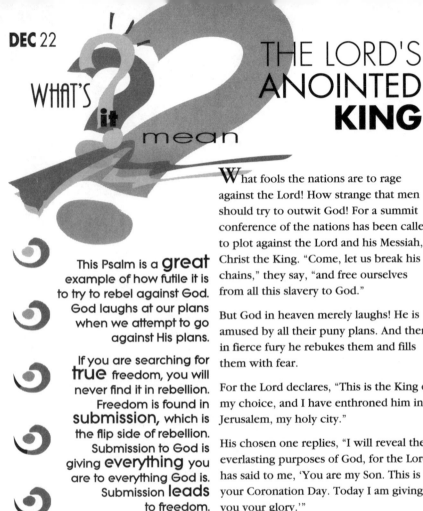

WHAT'S it mean

THE LORD'S ANOINTED KING

This Psalm is a **great** example of how futile it is to try to rebel against God. God laughs at our plans when we attempt to go against His plans.

If you are searching for **true** freedom, you will never find it in rebellion. Freedom is found in **submission,** which is the flip side of rebellion. Submission to God is giving **everything** you are to everything God is. Submission **leads** to freedom.

Don't you think that if God were capable of planning the coming of Jesus that He could also plan **your** life? Trust in His wisdom and be a **part** of His **eternal** plan.

What fools the nations are to rage against the Lord! How strange that men should try to outwit God! For a summit conference of the nations has been called to plot against the Lord and his Messiah, Christ the King. "Come, let us break his chains," they say, "and free ourselves from all this slavery to God."

But God in heaven merely laughs! He is amused by all their puny plans. And then in fierce fury he rebukes them and fills them with fear.

For the Lord declares, "This is the King of my choice, and I have enthroned him in Jerusalem, my holy city."

His chosen one replies, "I will reveal the everlasting purposes of God, for the Lord has said to me, 'You are my Son. This is your Coronation Day. Today I am giving you your glory.'"

"Only ask and I will give you all the nations of the world. Rule them with an iron rod; smash them like clay pots!"

O kings and rulers of the earth, listen while there is time. Serve the Lord with reverent fear; rejoice with trembling. Fall down before his Son and kiss his feet before his anger is roused and you perish. I am warning you—his wrath will soon begin. But oh, the joys of those who put their trust in him!

Psalm 2

DONE

386

DAVID'S SON AND LORD

Jehovah said to my Lord the Messiah, "Rule as my regent—I will subdue your enemies and make them bow low before you."

Jehovah has established your throne in Jerusalem to rule over your enemies.

In that day of your power your people shall come to you willingly, dressed in holy altar robes. And your strength shall be renewed day by day like morning dew. Jehovah has taken oath and will not rescind his vow that you are a priest forever like Melchizedek. God stands beside you to protect you. He will strike down many kings in the day of his anger.

He will punish the nations and fill them with their dead. He will crush many heads. But he himself shall be refreshed from springs along the way.

♦ Under the old arrangement there had to be many priests so that when the older ones died off, the system could still be carried on by others who took their places.

But Jesus lives forever and continues to be a Priest so that no one else is needed. He is able to save completely all who come to God through him. Since he will live forever, he will always be there to remind God that he has paid for their sins with his blood.

He is, therefore, exactly the kind of High Priest we need; for he is holy and blameless, unstained by sin, undefiled by sinners, and to him has been given the place of honor in heaven.

Psalm 110; Hebrews 7:23-26

Just a thought

If you have **Jesus** you have all you need... **forever...**

He has taken care of **everything!**

2 3

DEC

:00

:10

:20

:30

:40

:50

1:00

FINISH ☐

24
D E C

Because Joseph was a member of the royal line, he had to go to Bethlehem in Judea, King David's ancient home—journeying there from the Galilean village of Nazareth. He took with him Mary, his fiancée, who was obviously pregnant by this time.

And while they were there, the time came for her baby to be born; and she gave birth to her first child, a son. She wrapped him in a blanket and laid him in a manger, because there was no room for them in the village inn.

That night some shepherds were in the fields outside the village, guarding their flocks of sheep. Suddenly an angel appeared among them, and the landscape shone bright with the glory of the Lord. They were badly frightened, but the angel reassured them.

"Don't be afraid!" he said. "I bring you the most joyful news ever announced, and it is for everyone! The Savior—yes, the Messiah, the Lord—has been born tonight in Bethlehem! How will you recognize him? You will find a baby wrapped in a blanket, lying in a manger!"

Suddenly, the angel was joined by a vast host of others—the armies of heaven—praising God:

"Glory to God in the highest heaven," they sang, "and peace on earth for all those pleasing him."

Luke 2:4-14

Christ is born

done!

Tomorrow we **celebrate** the **birth** of Jesus. If you could write Jesus a birthday **message,** what would you write?

Give it a try

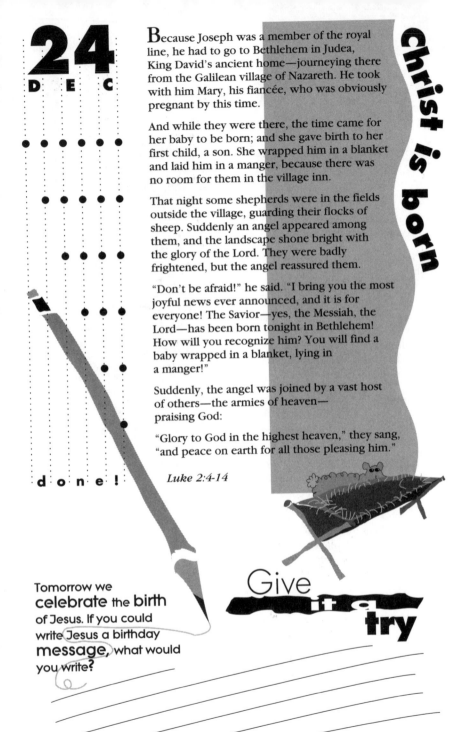

388

Jesus personality plus

Jesus was born in the town of Bethlehem, in Judea, during the reign of King Herod.

At about that time some astrologers from eastern lands arrived in Jerusalem, asking, "Where is the newborn King of the Jews? for we have seen his star in far-off eastern lands and have come to worship him."

King Herod was deeply disturbed by their question, and all Jerusalem was filled with rumors. He called a meeting of the Jewish religious leaders.

"Did the prophets tell us where the Messiah would be born?" he asked.

"Yes, in Bethlehem," they said, "for this is what the prophet Micah wrote:

'O little town of Bethlehem, you are not just an unimportant Judean village, for a Governor shall rise from you to rule my people Israel.'"

Then Herod sent a private message to the astrologers, asking them to come to see him; at this meeting he found out from them the exact time when they first saw the star. Then he told them, "Go to Bethlehem and search for the child. And when you find him, come back and tell me so that I can go and worship him too!"

After this interview the astrologers started out again. And look! The star appeared to them again, standing over Bethlehem. Their joy knew no bounds!

Entering the house where the baby and Mary, his mother, were, they threw themselves down before him, worshiping. Then they opened their presents and gave him gold, frankincense, and myrrh. But when they returned to their own land, they didn't go through Jerusalem to report to Herod, for God had warned them in a dream to go home another way.

Matthew 2:1-12

Jesus is the **key** figure in the New Testament and the **prophesied** Messiah of the Old Testament. Although we know very little about Jesus' life prior to His public ministry, we do know Jesus **is** God's Son, He's the **living** example of the invisible God, He lived a **perfect** life, He was fully human and fully God, He died for our sins, He resurrected three days later, and He promised to return to earth someday. It may not seem like a lot of information, but it's enough to make it possible for **you** to live **forever**.

Today, much of the world **celebrates** the birth of Jesus. But someday every person in the entire world will bow before Jesus and be judged according to his or her faith. **Today** is a special day, but it's not a real holiday unless Jesus is a part of your life. Have a **Merry Christmas!**

:00

:10

:20

:30

:40

:50

:60

the End

DEC
26

NEW HEAVENS
AND A
NEW EARTH

:00

:10 No one knows the **time** of Jesus' return and the establishment of a new heaven. But there are several prophecies concerning the **last**
:20 **days,** some of which include: widespread violence, the rejection of God's Word, the rise of
:30 false prophets and antichrists, abnormal sexual activity, intense demonic activity, extreme materialism, increase of
:40 wars, and political and religious uproar in the Holy Land.

:50 These aren't **all** of the signs but a few to get you thinking. Many of these signs are **already** present in our world. Find **someone** who can help
:60 you better **understand** the end times.

end

"I am creating new heavens and a new earth—so wonderful that no one will even think about the old ones anymore. Be glad; rejoice forever in my creation. Look! I will recreate Jerusalem as a place of happiness, and her people shall be a joy! And I will rejoice in Jerusalem and in my people; and the voice of weeping and crying shall not be heard there any more.

"No longer will babies die when only a few days old; no longer will men be considered old at 100! Only sinners will die that young!

"Their harvests will not be eaten by their enemies; their children will not be born to be cannon fodder. For they are the children of those the Lord has blessed; and their children, too, shall be blessed. I will answer them before they even call to me. While they are still talking to me about their needs, I will go ahead and answer their prayers! The wolf and lamb shall feed together, the lion shall eat straw as the ox does, and poisonous snakes shall strike no more! In those days nothing and no one shall be hurt or destroyed in all my Holy Mountain," says the Lord.

Isaiah 65:17-20, 23-25

Afterward he brought me out again to the passageway through the outer wall leading to the east. And suddenly the glory of the God of Israel appeared from the east. The sound of his coming was like the roar of rushing waters, and the whole landscape lighted up with his glory. It was just as I had seen it in the other visions, first by the Chebar Canal, and then later at Jerusalem when he came to destroy the city. And I fell down before him with my face in the dust. And the glory of the Lord came into the Temple through the eastern passageway.

Then the Spirit took me up and brought me into the inner court; and the glory of the Lord filled the Temple. And I heard the Lord speaking to me from within the Temple (the man who had been measuring was still standing beside me).

And the Lord said to me: "Son of dust, this is the place of my throne and my footstool, where I shall remain, living among the people of Israel forever. They and their kings will not defile my holy name any longer through the adulterous worship of other gods or by worshiping the totem poles erected by their kings. They built their idol temples beside mine, with only a wall between, and worshiped their idols. Because they sullied my holy name by such wickedness, I consumed them in my anger. Now let them put away their idols and the totem poles erected by their kings, and I will live among them forever."

Ezekiel 43:1-9

IN other words...

JERUSALEM

Jerusalem is a **city** that is continually mentioned in both the Old and New Testaments. During biblical times, this popular city was both the **capital** of Israel and its center for **worship**. The Temple, which was the Israelites' symbol for their faith, was built in Jerusalem. After the temple was destroyed, each succeeding temple was rebuilt on the original site. The majority of **Jesus'** ministry took place in Jerusalem as did most of the events surrounding the beginning of the church.

Much of the **prophetic** literature (including today's reading) designates the city of Jerusalem or a Jerusalem-like setting as the place of Jesus' return and rule. If you're ready for His **return**, it won't matter when or where... **so be ready!**

:00 :10 :20 :30 :40 :50 done :60

391

28
dec

personality Plus John

John was one of Jesus' **first** disciples and formed the **"inner group"** with Peter and James. John was **more** than a fisherman who turned author, he was an **intelligent** man who educated himself with Jewish teachings.

He received the nickname **"Son of Thunder"** and is often described as being scrappy and ambitious. He's also known as the disciple whom Jesus **loved.** John's life is really an example of how Jesus could change people. Jesus was able to take a self-centered fisherman and turn him into a man known for his deep love for his Master. **Read** John's Gospel if you want a better **picture** of **Jesus'** life on earth.

It is I, your brother John, a fellow sufferer for the Lord's sake, who am writing this letter to you. I, too, have shared the patience Jesus gives, and we shall share his Kingdom!

I was on the island of Patmos, exiled there for preaching the Word of God and for telling what I knew about Jesus Christ. It was the Lord's Day and I was worshiping, when suddenly I heard a loud voice behind me, a voice that sounded like a trumpet blast, saying, "I am A and Z, the First and Last!" And then I heard him say, "Write down everything you see, and send your letter to the seven churches in Turkey: to the church in Ephesus, the one in Smyrna, and those in Pergamos, Thyatira, Sardis, Philadelphia, and Laodicea."

When I turned to see who was speaking, there behind me were seven candlesticks of gold. And standing among them was one who looked like Jesus, who called himself the Son of Man, wearing a long robe circled with a golden band across his chest. His hair was white as wool or snow, and his eyes penetrated like flames of fire. His feet gleamed like burnished bronze, and his voice thundered like the waves against the shore. He held seven stars in his right hand and a sharp, double-bladed sword in his mouth, and his face shone like the power of the sun in unclouded brilliance.

When I saw him, I fell at his feet as dead; but he laid his right hand on me and said, "Don't be afraid! Though I am the First and Last, the Living One who died, who is now alive forevermore, who has the keys of hell and death—don't be afraid! Write down what you have just seen and what will soon be shown to you."

Revelation 1:9-19

:00

:10

:20

:30

:40

:50

:60

the End

392

THE SAINTS AND THE SERPENT

Then I saw an angel come down from heaven with the key to the bottomless pit and a heavy chain in his hand. He seized the Dragon—that old Serpent, the devil, Satan—and bound him in chains for a thousand years, and threw him into the bottomless pit, which he then shut and locked so that he could not fool the nations any more until the thousand years were finished.

Then I saw thrones, and sitting on them were those who had been given the right to judge. And I saw the souls of those who had been beheaded for their testimony about Jesus, for proclaiming the Word of God, and who had not worshiped the Creature or his statue, nor accepted his mark on their foreheads or their hands. They had come to life again and now they reigned with Christ for a thousand years.

This is the First Resurrection. Blessed and holy are those who share in the First Resurrection. For them the Second Death holds no terrors, for they will be priests of God and of Christ, and shall reign with him a thousand years.

When the thousand years end, Satan will be let out of his prison. He will go out to deceive the nations of the world and gather them together, with Gog and Magog, for battle—a mighty host, numberless as sand along the shore. But fire from God in heaven will flash down on the attacking armies and consume them.

Then the devil who had betrayed them will again be thrown into the Lake of Fire burning with sulphur where the Creature and False Prophet are, and they will be tormented day and night forever and ever.

Revelation 20:1-3b, 4-5a, 6-8, 9b-10

2 9

DEC

Just a thought

The Book of Revelation is no **fairy tale!** Satan is **real** but God **defeats** him.

It's tough to understand and certainly takes **faith** to believe, but God's Word gives you enough **light** to know

a life without **Jesus** means **eternity** in hell...

o u c h !

:00

:10

:20

:30

:40

:50

1:00

FINISH

30 DEC

ONE MINUTE MEMORY

Judgment Day

I saw a great white throne and the one who sat upon it, from whose face the earth and sky fled away, but they found no place to hide. I saw the dead, great and small, standing before God; and The Books were opened, including the Book of Life. And the dead were judged according to the things written in The Books, each according to the deeds he had done. The oceans surrendered the bodies buried in them; and the earth and the underworld gave up the dead in them. Each was judged according to his deeds. And Death and Hell were thrown into the Lake of Fire. This is the Second Death—the Lake of Fire. And if anyone's name was not found recorded in the Book of Life, he was thrown into the Lake of Fire.

♦ Then I saw a new earth (with no oceans!) and a new sky, for the present earth and sky had disappeared. And I, John, saw the Holy City, the new Jerusalem, coming down from God out of heaven. It was a glorious sight, beautiful as a bride at her wedding.

I heard a loud shout from the throne saying, "Look, the home of God is now among men, and he will live with them and they will be his people; yes, God himself will be among them. He will wipe away all tears from their eyes, and there shall be no more death, nor sorrow, nor crying, nor pain. All of that has gone forever."

Revelation 20:11-15; 21:1-4

:00
:15
:30
:45
:60

He will wipe away all tears from their eyes, and there shall be no more death, nor sorrow, nor crying, nor pain. All of that has gone forever.

Revelation 21:4

done

JESUS IS COMING

SOON!

Then the angel said to me, "These words are trustworthy and true: 'I am coming soon!' God, who tells his prophets what the future holds, has sent his angel to tell you this will happen soon. Blessed are those who believe it and all else written in the scroll."

"See, I am coming soon, and my reward is with me, to repay everyone according to the deeds he has done. I am the A and the Z, the Beginning and the End, the First and Last. Blessed forever are all who are washing their robes, to have the right to enter in through the gates of the city and to eat the fruit from the Tree of Life.

"Outside the city are those who have strayed away from God, and the sorcerers and the immoral and murderers and idolaters, and all who love to lie, and do so.

"I, Jesus, have sent my angel to you to tell the churches all these things. I am both David's Root and his Descendant. I am the bright Morning Star. The Spirit and the bride say, 'Come.' Let each one who hears them say the same, 'Come.' Let the thirsty one come—anyone who wants to; let him come and drink the Water of Life without charge."

"He who has said all these things declares: Yes, I am coming soon!"

Amen! Come, Lord Jesus!

The grace of our Lord Jesus Christ be with you all. Amen!

Revelation 22:6-7, 12-17, 20-21

395

3 1

DEC

:00

:10

:20

:30

:40

:50

1:00

FINISH

Just a thought

Begin your year right by **committing** yourself to **Jesus** and remaining faithful the **entire year** (and until His return).

A year **walking** with **Jesus** is a great **year!**

RELATED TEXTS

RELATED TEXTS

January 30
Habakkuk 3:17-19; 1 Thessalonians 5:16-18; Revelation 7:13-17

January 31
Job 19:25-27; Proverbs 11:2-6; Philippians 3:7-11

February 1
Job 4-5; 8; 11; 15; 18; 20; 22; 25; 32-37; Hebrews 12:5-11

February 2
Job 3; 6-7; 9-10; 12-14; 16-17; 19; 21; 23-24; 26-31; Psalm 7; Luke 18:1-8

February 3
Psalm 30; Job 38-41; Habakkuk 1:1-2:1; Romans 9-10

February 4
Psalms 17; 37; Matthew 5:1-6; James 5:11

February 5
Job 34:17-19; Isaiah 57:15-19; 66:2; Luke 6:20; Acts 10:34-35; Ephesians 6:5-9

February 6
Nehemiah 8:1-12; Ecclesiastes 3:1-8; Psalm 119: 49-50; Luke 6:21; 2 Corinthians 1:3-7; 7:8-11

February 7
Psalms 25:12-13; 37:12-40; Matthew 11:25-30; Galatians 5:19-23; 2 Corinthians 10:1-5; 1 Peter 3:8-9

February 8
Psalms 107:1-9; 146; Isaiah 55:1-2; Luke 6:21; Revelation 7:16-17

February 9
Psalm 6; Micah 7:18-19; Zechariah 7:9-10; Luke 6:27-38; 10:25-37; Jude 1:20-23

February 10
2 Chronicles 30:13-20; Proverbs 20:5-11; Mark 7:1-23; Hebrews 3; 12:14-29

February 11
Isaiah 9:6-7; John 1:1-13; Romans 8:9-23; Galatians 3:26-4:7; 1 John 3:1-11

February 12
Job 36:15-17; Isaiah 53; 1 Peter 1:3-9; 4:12-19

February 13
Deuteronomy 7:7-11; 10:14-15; John 3:16-19; Romans 5:8-11; Ephesians 2:4-10

February 14
Deuteronomy 6:1-5; Psalm 136; John 15:9-17; 1 John 3

February 15
Psalm 105:23-25; Acts 7:9-34; 1 Corinthians 7: 21-23; Galatians 3:26-28

February 16
Isaiah 49:13-19; Acts 7:20-22; Hebrews 11:23

February 17
Numbers 32:23; Acts 7:23-29; Hebrews 11:24-27

February 18
Isaiah 6; Acts 7:30-35; Revelation 15:2-4

February 19
Exodus 20:7; John 6:35; 8:12, 58; 10:7, 11; 11:25; 14:6; 15:1; Revelation 1:8

February 20
Exodus 15:1-3; Isaiah 42:5-9; Colossians 3:16-17; Hebrews 13:15

February 21
Isaiah 50:4-11; Acts 4:23-35; Ephesians 5:19-20

February 22
1 Samuel 17:39-51; Isaiah 54:5; Revelation 4:1-8

February 23
Genesis 17:1; 28:3; 35:11; 43:14; 48:3; 49:25; Exodus 6:2-4; Revelation 21:22-27

February 24
Job 28; Psalms 8; 86; 110; Daniel 9:1-19; Philippians 2:5-11

February 25
Genesis 14:18-24; Psalms 7; 9:1-2; 91; Luke 1:26-38

February 26
Genesis 1; 14:18-24; Ecclesiastes 12:9-14; Isaiah 40:27-31; Revelation 4:11

February 27
Deuteronomy 33:27; Psalm 90:1-2; Romans 16:25-27; Hebrews 9:14

February 28
Psalm 16; Isaiah 40:25-31; 54:5; Acts 2:22-39

RELATED TEXTS

February 29
Judges 11:27; Psalms 7; 82; 96; John 5:25-30; Acts 10:34-43; James 4:11-12; Revelation 19:11-16

March 1
Psalms 47; 95:1-7; Isaiah 44:6-8; Jeremiah 10:6-10; Matthew 21:1-5; 1 Timothy 1:17; 6:15

March 2
Joshua 22:22; Psalms 50; 132; Isaiah 49:24-26; Mark 14:60-62

March 3
Isaiah 44:24-28; 54; Luke 24:13-36; Galatians 4:4-5; Titus 2:11-14

March 4
2 Samuel 22:3, 31; Psalms 46; 59:16-17; 71; 91; Isaiah 25:1-5

March 5
Deuteronomy 32; 2 Samuel 22; Psalm 62; Romans 9:30-33; 1 Corinthians 10:1-4; 1 Peter 2:1-8

March 6
Psalm 68:19-20; Micah 7:1-7; Habakkuk 3:16-19; Luke 1:47-55; 2:8-20; John 4:40-42; Acts 5:29-32

March 7
Psalms 23; 80:1-7; Ezekiel 34; Micah 5:2-5; John 10:11-15; 1 Peter 2:21-25; 5:1-4

March 8
Psalms 1; 112; Isaiah 27:2-3; John 15:1-16; Romans 7:1-6

March 9
Deuteronomy 6:4-6; John 14-15; 21:15-17; 1 Corinthians 13; 1 John 4:7-21; 1 Peter 4:7-8

March 10
Psalm 136; Jeremiah 31:3-6; Zephaniah 3:16-17; 1 John 4:7-21

March 11
Nehemiah 8:1-12; Psalms 28:6-9; 30:4-5; Isaiah 61

March 12
1 Chronicles 16:23-33; Nehemiah 8:1-12; Psalm 21:1-7; Isaiah 62:4-7

March 13
Proverbs 12:20; Isaiah 32:17; 57:21; Micah 4:1-5; Luke 2:13-14; Romans 8:1-6

March 14
Ecclesiastes 3:1-8; Romans 15:33; 16:20; 2 Corinthians 13:11; Philippians 4:6-9

March 15
Proverbs 15:18; 16:32; 19:11; 25:15; Ecclesiastes 7:8; Romans 12:9-12

March 16
Isaiah 7:13; 65:17-25; Romans 2:1-4; 3:21-28; 1 Peter 3:18-20; Revelation 21:1-8

March 17
Ruth 1:1-3:10; Proverbs 14:21; 1 Thessalonians 5:15

March 18
Isaiah 53:1-8; Romans 2:1-8; 11:11-24

March 19
Psalm 34:8-14; Proverbs 3:27; 11:27; 1 Peter 2:12-15

March 20
2 Chronicles 6:41; Psalm 84:9-12; Mark 10:17-18; Romans 8:18-28; 3 John 11

March 21
Psalm 101; Proverbs 3:1-4; Matthew 24:45-51; 25:14-30

March 22
Deuteronomy 31:30-32:4; 2 Thessalonians 3:3; 2 Timothy 2:11-13; Revelation 19:11-16

March 23
Isaiah 8:12-15; 1 Timothy 6:3-11; 2 Timothy 2:24-25; 1 Peter 3:1-6

March 24
1 Kings 19:9-12; 2 Corinthians 10:1; Matthew 21:1-12

March 25
Proverbs 1:1-7; 23:23; 1 Thessalonians 5:5-10; 2 Timothy 1:7; Titus 2:11-14; 1 Peter 4:7

March 26
Exodus 34:5-7; Psalm 86:15-17; Joel 2:12-14; Jonah 3-4; 2 Peter 3:8-15

March 27
Genesis 13:12-17; 15:12-16; Haggai 2:4-8; Acts 7:30-36

RELATED TEXTS

March 28
Exodus 1:8-13; 9:13-16; Proverbs 29:1-2; John 10:33-38

March 29
Exodus 8:7, 18-19; Romans 9:14-21; 2 Timothy 3:8-9

March 30
Exodus 7:15-10:29; Deuteronomy 4:32-38; 1 Samuel 4:2-8; Acts 7:30-36

March 31
Exodus 4:22-23; Psalms 105:23-38; 135:8-9; 136:10-12; Romans 9:14-21; Hebrews 11:28

April 1
Numbers 9:1-14; Deuteronomy 16:1-8; 2 Chronicles 30; 1 Corinthians 5:6-8

April 2
Psalm 22; Mark 10:45; Acts 8:26-39; 1 Peter 2:21-25

April 3
Genesis 22:1-19; Hebrews 9:11-28; 1 Peter 1:18-20; Revelation 5-7; 21:9-22:4

April 4
Psalm 16; Matthew 12:38-41; Mark 10:32-34; Luke 24:13-32; Acts 2:14-40

April 5
Psalm 118; Zechariah 9:9; Mark 11:1-11; Luke 19:28-40; John 12:12-16

April 6
Psalm 8; Isaiah 56; Jeremiah 7:9-11; Mark 11:15-18; John 2:13-17

April 7
Psalm 110; Matthew 27:45-54; Mark 1:9-11; Luke 9:28-36; Acts 2

April 8
Jeremiah 31:31-36; Matthew 26:17-30; Mark 14:12-26; Revelation 19:4-9

April 9
Genesis 37; Matthew 26:47-56; Mark 14:43-50; Luke 22:47-54; John 6:35-40; 17:1-12

April 10
Leviticus 24:13-16; Daniel 7:13-14; Mark 14:55-65; Luke 23:63-71

April 11
Psalm 22; Isaiah 53; Matthew 27:33-56; Luke 23:26-48; John 3:13-16; 19:16-37

April 12
Psalm 16:8-11; Mark 16:1-8; Luke 24:1-10; John 20:1-18; 1 Corinthians 15

April 13
Job 19:23-27; 1 Corinthians 15:23-58; Romans 6:1-11; Acts 2:22-36

April 14
Exodus 12-13; John 1:19-36; Hebrews 2:11-18; Revelation 13:8

April 15
Deuteronomy 16:1-8; Psalm 78:41-52; 105:26-38; 2 Thessalonians 1:5-10

April 16
Psalm 37:7; 46:10; Isaiah 59:1; Romans 9:14-24; Hebrews 11:1-2

April 17
Psalms 114; 136:13-15; Deuteronomy 11:1-4; Joshua 24:5-7; Hebrews 11:23-29

April 18
Psalm 136; Ephesians 5:19-20; Revelation 15:2-4

April 19
Genesis 15; Exodus 15:19-18:27; John 6; Acts 7:36-38; 1 Corinthians 10:1-4

April 20
Deuteronomy 4:1-20; Jeremiah 31:31-34; Hebrews 8

April 21
Exodus 18:8-10; Deuteronomy 4:32-39; 5:1-21; 13:1-16; Isaiah 37:15-20; Ephesians 4:4-6

April 22
Deuteronomy 7; Isaiah 44:6-19; Jeremiah 10:1-16; 16:19-21; Matthew 6:19-24; 1 John 5:21

April 23
Exodus 3:13-15; Psalms 20; 86:5-12; Acts 4:5-12

April 24
Genesis 2:1-3; Exodus 16:11-30; Psalm 62:1-5; Mark 2:23-28; Hebrews 4:1-4

April 25
Malachi 4:5-6; Colossians 3:20-21; 2 Timothy 3:1-5; Titus 1:6-9

April 26
Genesis 4:1-16; Numbers 35:9-34; Matthew 15:10-20; John 8:42-44; Romans 1:28-32

April 27
Proverbs 5:1-19; 6:20-35; Romans 1:18-27; Ephesians 4:17-24; Colossians 3:1-7; 1 Thessalonians 4:3-8

April 28
Proverbs 1:10-19; 10:2; Isaiah 10:1-4; Malachi 3:6-12; Titus 2:9-10

April 29
Proverbs 12:17-18; 25:18; Isaiah 29:19-21; Matthew 15:10-20; Mark 14:53-64

April 30
Deuteronomy 31:6; Proverbs 1:10-19; Philippians 4:11-12; 1 Timothy 6:9-11; James 4:1-3; 1 John 2:15-17

May 1
Leviticus 19:18, 33-34; Micah 6:8; Mark 12:28-31; Luke 10:25-37; Acts 4:32-35; Romans 13:8-10; 2 Corinthians 8:13-15

May 2
Deuteronomy 10:17-20; Psalms 68:5; 146:9; 1 Timothy 5:3-16

May 3
Numbers 5:5-8; Matthew 5:23-24; Luke 19:1-10; 1 Corinthians 6:1-11

May 4
Exodus 21:22-25; Deuteronomy 19:16-21; Psalm 103:8-12; Matthew 5:38-42

May 5
Genesis 9:6; Leviticus 24:17-22; Deuteronomy 24:16; Matthew 21:33-44

May 6
Genesis 7:1-4; Matthew 15:1-20; Mark 7:1-23; Acts 10; Romans 14

May 7
Exodus 12; 23:14-17; Leviticus 23; Colossians 2:16-23

May 8
Exodus 20:12; 21:15; Leviticus 20:9; Ephesians 6:1-2

May 9
Psalms 51:1-9; 77:1-8; 103:1-18; Isaiah 66:12-14; Lamentations 3:22-33; Colossians 3:12-14

May 10
1 Samuel 2:1-10; Job 42:12-16; Psalm 127:3-5; Proverbs 17:6; Isaiah 54:1-8; Luke 1

May 11
Exodus 2:1-9; Proverbs 6:20-24; 2 Timothy 1:5; 3:14-17

May 12
Genesis 24; Acts 18:23-26; Romans 16:1-6

May 13
1 Samuel 25:1-42; Proverbs 19:14; Luke 1:26-55; Ephesians 5:21-24; 1 Peter 3:1-6

May 14
Psalm 45; Song of Songs 4; Isaiah 62:1-7; Revelation 19:5-9; 21:1-4

May 15
Exodus 22:16-17; Numbers 27; 30; 36; Deuteronomy 21:10-17; 22:13-30; 25:7-10; Ruth 3-4; 1 Timothy 3:2,12

May 16
Exodus 25-27; 35-40; Mark 15:37,38; Hebrews 9:13-28; 10:19-23

May 17
Leviticus 1-7; 21-22; Numbers 3; Hebrews 7-9; 1 Peter 2:4-10

May 18
Deuteronomy 8:18-9:5; Judges 2:10-23; 2 Corinthians 6:14-7:1; Colossians 4:4-6; 1 Peter 2:1-12

May 19
Deuteronomy 7:9-15; 10:12-13; Micah 6:6-8; John 14:15; Romans 10:5-13; 1 John 5:3

May 20
Genesis 12:1-3; Psalms 1; 84; Luke 6:17-26; 11:27-28; John 20:24-29

May 21
Proverbs 13:9; Mark 9:50; Luke 14:34-35; 1 Peter 4:12-19

May 22
Psalm 119:161-176; Matthew 22:34-40; Romans 3:21-31; 7-8

RELATED TEXTS

May 23
Exodus 20:13; Proverbs 8:12-13; Matthew 5:38-48; Luke 6:22-36

May 24
Deuteronomy 24:1-4; Proverbs 5; Malachi 2:10-16; Matthew 19:3-12; 1 Corinthians 7

May 25
Genesis 12:1-3; Leviticus 24:17-20; Luke 6:27-37; Romans 12:14-18

May 26
Proverbs 11:24-25; Mark 10:17-31; Luke 6:38; 12:32-34; Acts 20:32-35; 2 Corinthians 9:6-15

May 27
Psalm 5; Mark 11:22-26; Luke 11:1-13; 18:1-14; James 5:13-20

May 28
Esther 3-4; Isaiah 58; Jonah 3; Zechariah 7-8; Acts 14:21-23;

May 29
Proverbs 12:25; Mark 13:11; Luke 12:11-34; Philippians 4:6-7

May 30
Romans 14:1-13; John 16:24; 1 Corinthians 5; James 4:1-3; 1 John 3:21-22

May 31
Proverbs 14:11-12; Luke 13:22-30; John 10:1-10; Ephesians 2:13-22

June 1
Deuteronomy 9:7-15; Nehemiah 9:16-19; Psalm 106:19-22; Acts 7:37-41

June 2
Genesis 15:1-5; 22:15-18; 26:2-4; Deuteronomy 9:16-21; Psalm 106:23; Jonah 3; Acts 7:40-42

June 3
Exodus 14; 17:1-7; 32; John 6; Hebrews 2:9-18; James 1:12-15

June 4
Psalms 86:15; 103:8; 145:8; John 3:16-21; 1 John 1:9

June 5
Exodus 33:19; 2 Chronicles 30:7-9; Nehemiah 9:16-19; Psalm 103; Lamentations 3:19-23; Colossians 3:12-14

June 6
Numbers 14:1-35; 1 Kings 8:27-53; Psalm 32:1-5; Daniel 9:1-19; Matthew 6:14-15; 18:21-35

June 7
Numbers 6:24-26; Proverbs 3:33-35; Romans 5:12-21

June 8
Exodus 15:11; Leviticus 22:31-33; Psalm 99; Revelation 4; 15:2-4

June 9
Exodus 33:19; Deuteronomy 4:31; Nehemiah 9:29-31; Micah 7:18-20; Romans 9:11-18

June 10
Genesis 18:14; Exodus 15:1-18; Psalm 29; Mark 4:35-41

June 11
Deuteronomy 4:7; 1 Kings 8:27; John 1:45-49; 14:16-17

June 12
Psalm 94:1-11; Proverbs 5:21; 2 Chronicles 16:9; 1 Corinthians 1:18-25; John 3:19-20

June 13
Isaiah 44:6-8; Malachi 2:10; Matthew 19:16-17; 23:1-10; Mark 12:28-34

June 14
Ezra 9; Psalms 36:5-10; 71; Daniel 9:1-19; Matthew 6:28-33; Acts 3:12-16

June 15
Deuteronomy 32:6; Psalm 2; Isaiah 9:1-7; John 1:12-13; Romans 8; Hebrews 12:1-14

June 16
Exodus 21:15; Leviticus 19:3; Proverbs 10:1; 23:22-25; Ephesians 6:1-3

June 17
Deuteronomy 6:1-9; Proverbs 1:8; 6:20-24; 31:1-9; 2 Timothy 1:2-3

June 18
Deuteronomy 8:5; 1 Samuel 2:12-36; Proverbs 3:11-12; 15:5; Revelation 3:14-20

June 19
Exodus 20:14; Leviticus 20:10; Proverbs 2:16-22; 6:23-35; 7; Ephesians 5:1-3

RELATED TEXTS

June 20
Psalm 45; Song of Songs 1–8; 2 Corinthians 11:2-3; 1 Peter 3:1-6

June 21
Genesis 2:18-25; Hosea 3:1-3; Malachi 2:13-16; Colossians 3:19; Revelation 21:1-4

June 22
Exodus 13:22, 33; 40:34-38; Numbers 14:11-14; 1 Corinthians 10:1-2

June 23
Numbers 11; Psalm 106:1-15; Luke 4:1-13; James 4:1-4

June 24
Deuteronomy 1:19-33; Psalm 106:24-27; Proverbs 29:25; Philippians 2:12-16

June 25
Joshua 5:1-6; John 6:48-51; 1 Corinthians 10:1-6; Hebrews 3:7–4:7

June 26
Psalm 95; Matthew 17:1-5; John 14:15-24; Acts 3:19-23; Hebrews 4

June 27
Psalm 106:16-17; Hebrews 10:26-31; 12:23-29; 2 Peter 1:16–2:22; Jude 1:11

June 28
Exodus 7:19-21; 8:16-17; 17:1-6; Deuteronomy 4:20-22; Acts 5:1-11

June 29
Exodus 16:6-12; Numbers 14:26-37; 2 Kings 18:1-4; Lamentations 3:25-40; 1 Corinthians 10:1-11

June 30
Genesis 12:1-3; Numbers 22-24; Joshua 24:8-10; 2 Peter 2:15-16

July 1
Genesis 12:1-3; 22:15-18; 27:26-29; Deuteronomy 23:3-5; Joshua 13:22; 24:8-10; Revelation 2:12-14

July 2
Deuteronomy 4:1-4; Joshua 22:16-20; Psalm 106:28-31; Hosea 9:10; 1 Corinthians 10:1-8

July 3
Numbers 25; Deuteronomy 21:10-14; Joshua 13:16-22; Judges 6-8; Romans 12:16-21

July 4
Deuteronomy 10:12-16; 11:18-21; Psalms 1; 119; Proverbs 22:6; Mark 12:28-34; Luke 10:25-28; 1 John 5:1-4

July 5
Numbers 21:21-35; Deuteronomy 2:24–3:17; 1 Kings 8:54-57; Hebrews 13:5-6

July 6
Deuteronomy 11:22-25; Psalms 1; 19; 119; 1 Corinthians 16:13-14; Hebrews 3:1-6

July 7
Matthew 1:1-6; Hebrews 11:31; James 2:25

July 8
Numbers 10:1-10; Judges 7:1-22; Matthew 1:1-6

July 9
Deuteronomy 7; 9:1-6; 18:9-14; 20:16-18; Joshua 7-10

July 10
Exodus 24:3-8; Leviticus 26; Romans 6; Hebrews 3-4

July 11
Deuteronomy 4:1-10; 11:18-25; Judges 2:19–3:31; Psalm 78:1-6; Ephesians 2:1-10

July 12
Exodus 15:19-21; Judges 5:1-12; 2 Kings 22:11-20; 2 Chronicles 34:19-28; Luke 2:21-38

July 13
Judges 3:12-30; 5:13-31; 1 Samuel 12:8-11; Hebrews 11:32-34

July 14
Genesis 25:21-24; Numbers 6:1-21; Judges 14-15; Luke 1

July 15
Judges 14-15; Proverbs 5; 6:20–7:27; 31:1-3; 2 Timothy 2:20-23

July 16
Numbers 6:2-21; 30:1-2; Proverbs 11:13; 20:19; Ecclesiastes 5:4-6; Luke 12:47-48

July 17
Psalm 3; Isaiah 1:24; Jeremiah 5:7-9, 29; 9:9; Hebrews 11:32-34

RELATED TEXTS

July 18
2 Samuel 3:14-16; Proverbs 20:6;
Song of Songs 8:6-7; 1 Corinthians 13

July 19
Leviticus 25:25-27, 49-50; Psalm 91;
Jeremiah 32:6-14

July 20
Genesis 38:8-10; Deuteronomy 25:5-10;
Hebrews 13:4

July 21
Genesis 29:31–30:4; 38; Micah 5:2; Matthew 1:1-6

July 22
Deuteronomy 8:2; Proverbs 30:7-9; John 6:25-59;
1 Corinthians 10:16-17; Revelation 2:17

July 23
Psalm 27:1; John 1:1-14; 3:19-22; 12:44-46;
1 John 1:1-7; Revelation 21:2-27

July 24
Psalm 118:17-21; Matthew 7:13-14; 25:1-13;
Luke 13:23-29; John 14

July 25
Psalm 23; Isaiah 40:10-11; Zechariah 11:4-17;
Matthew 25:31-46; Luke 15:3-7;
Hebrews 13:20-21

July 26
Deuteronomy 32:39; John 5:19-26; Romans 5–6;
2 Timothy 1:8-10; 1 John 1:1-3

July 27
Psalm 96; John 1:1-18; 3:13-16; Acts 4:12;
Hebrews 10:19-22

July 28
Psalm 80:8-19; Isaiah 5:1-7; 27:2-6; Luke 6:43-45;
Galatians 5:22-23; Colossians 1:3-12

July 29
Genesis 11:29-30; 25:21; 29:31; Psalm 113:9;
Isaiah 54:1; Luke 1:4-22; 23:28-30;
Hebrews 11:11

July 30
Genesis 8:1; 19:29; 30:22; Exodus 2:24; Luke
1:23-45; Acts 10:25-31; Revelation 16:19; 18:5

July 31
Genesis 4:25-26; Deuteronomy 18:15-19;
Joshua 21:45; Luke 1:13-17

August 1
Deuteronomy 17:14-20; 1 Samuel 8:11-18;
Isaiah 9:6; Jeremiah 10:1-10; 1 Timothy 1:17

August 2
Deuteronomy 17:14-20; 1 Samuel 9:1–10:16;
11–14; John 12:12-15

August 3
Exodus 17:8-16; Deuteronomy 25:17-19;
Micah 6:6-8; Luke 16:10-13

August 4
Psalm 78:70-72; Matthew 5:8; 12:33-35;
Luke 6:43-45; Acts 13:21-23

August 5
Numbers 13:26-33; Deuteronomy 11:22-25;
Psalm 15; Proverbs 14:27; 15:33; 29:25

August 6
Psalms 31:11-18; 97:10; 144; Ephesians 6:10-18;
1 Timothy 4:12

August 7
2 Samuel 21:15-22; Psalm 27; Hebrews 11:32-34

August 8
Proverbs 27:4; Acts 5:12-19; 7:9-10; Romans
13:12-14; 2 Corinthians 11:2; Galatians 5:19-20

August 9
1 Samuel 19–30; Psalms 52; 54; 57; 59;
James 1:13-15

August 10
1 Samuel 28; 30–31; 2 Samuel 1; 16:15–17:23;
Matthew 27:1-5; Acts 16:22-28

August 11
1 Chronicles 17; Psalms 2; 89; Jeremiah 33:14-26;
Romans 1:1-4

August 12
Isaiah 40:10-11; Micah 5:2-5; Hebrews 13:20-21;
1 Peter 2:21-25; Revelation 7:15-17

August 13
Deuteronomy 5:18; Job 31:1; Psalm 119:9-16;
Proverbs 5–6; 1 Corinthians 6:9-11

August 14
Numbers 32:23; 2 Samuel 12:15-25;
Proverbs 26:27; Matthew 1:1-6; Hebrews 13:4

RELATED TEXTS

August 15
2 Samuel 12; Psalm 32; Isaiah 40:28-31; Habakkuk 3:2; Titus 3:3-7

August 16
2 Samuel 7; 1 Kings 1; 1 Chronicles 17; 23-29; Matthew 1:1-6; Luke 12:22-31

August 17
1 Kings 3:16-28; 2 Chronicles 1:1-13; Proverbs 1-4; 8:10-21; James 1:5-8

August 18
1 Kings 10:1-13; Psalm 72; Proverbs 13:10; 16:16; 23:23; Matthew 12:38-42

August 19
2 Chronicles 9:1-12; Proverbs 10:1; 25:1; Song of Songs 1-8; Jonah 3; 1 Corinthians 12:1-11

August 20
Psalm 126; Proverbs 11:18-21; Hosea 10:12-13; Matthew 13:1-17; Mark 4:1-12

August 21
Proverbs 11:30; Matthew 13:18-23; Mark 4:13-25; John 15:1-17; Galatians 6:7-10

August 22
Psalm 45:6; Mark 1:1-15; 4:30-32; Luke 13:18-19

August 23
Psalm 119:169-176; Matthew 18:12-14; Luke 9:22-26; 19:1-10

August 24
2 Chronicles 7:13-14; Proverbs 17:6, 21; Hosea 6:1-3; Acts 3:19-20

August 25
Isaiah 55:6-7; Matthew 18:12-14; Colossians 1:1-14; 1 Peter 2:24-25

August 26
1 Kings 5-9; 2 Chronicles 2-8; Psalm 127; Matthew 12:1-6; John 2:13-21; Ephesians 2:11-22

August 27
Ecclesiastes 1:1-11; Galatians 4:4-5; 6:8-9; 1 Timothy 2:3-6; 1 Peter 5:5-6

August 28
1 Samuel 20:24-42; Psalm 37; Proverbs 17:17; 27:6, 10; 1 Corinthians 4:5; Revelation 20:11-15

August 29
Deuteronomy 7; Ezra 9-10; Nehemiah 13:23-27; 1 Corinthians 7:39; 2 Corinthians 6:14-16

August 30
1 Kings 11:26-40; 2 Chronicles 9:29-10:19; Proverbs 15:1

August 31
Exodus 32; 2 Kings 10:16-31; 23:1-15; 2 Chronicles 11:14-16; Acts 17:15-31; 1 Corinthians 6:9-10

September 1
Deuteronomy 11:16-17; Mark 6:14-15; Luke 1:11-17; 9:7-8; James 5:17-18

September 2
Deuteronomy 12:28-31; 32:36-39; Mark 8:27-29; Luke 9:28-36; James 5:14-18

September 3
Deuteronomy 13; 17:2-5; 18:18-22; 1 Kings 21-22; 2 Kings 9:30-10:28; Philippians 2:5-11

September 4
2 Kings 14:25; Matthew 12:38-41; 16:1-4; Luke 11:29-32

September 5
2 Kings 17:13-15; Psalms 42; 69; Isaiah 44:9-20; Acts 27

September 6
Exodus 32:1-14; Jeremiah 18:1-11; Joel 2:12-14; Luke 11:29-32

September 7
Exodus 34:1-7; Deuteronomy 10:16; Jonah 3; James 4:6-8

September 8
2 Samuel 7; Isaiah 55; Acts 15:1-21; Romans 9-11

September 9
Genesis 19:1-29; Deuteronomy 29:18-23; Zechariah 10:6-12; 2 Peter 3:8-15

September 10
Exodus 3:1-6; 33:15-23; Job 19:25-27; Matthew 5:8; 13:10-17; John 12:37-41; Revelation 4

September 11
Deuteronomy 5:6-10; Judges 10:11-16; Psalms 68:1-3; 97; Jeremiah 26; Acts 1:1-8

RELATED TEXTS

September 12
Deuteronomy 28:14-68; 2 Kings 15:16-20; Acts 7:51-53

September 13
Numbers 21:1-9; Deuteronomy 28:1-14; 2 Chronicles 29-31; Proverbs 25:1; Matthew 1:1-10

September 14
2 Kings 19-20; 2 Chronicles 32; Isaiah 36-39; Acts 12

September 15
Exodus 34:1-7; Jonah; John 3:31-36; Romans 1:18-19; Ephesians 5:5-6

September 16
Psalm 25; 34:1-5; Isaiah 40; Romans 10:9-11

September 17
Psalm 136; Isaiah 6; Luke 1:13-16; 1 Timothy 4:12

September 18
Deuteronomy 28; Joshua 1; Ezekiel 11; 24; 33:1-20; 1 John 5:3-4

September 19
Jeremiah 18:1-11; 19:1-20:2; 38:1-13; Lamentations 3:52-57; Micah 3:9-12; Matthew 16:13-14

September 20
Leviticus 26:1-43; 2 Kings 20:12-18; 25; Isaiah 39; Jeremiah 25; 38; 52; Matthew 1:1-17

September 21
Psalm 137; Ezekiel 19; 24; Matthew 23:33-39

September 22
Genesis 9:5-6; 12:1-3; Romans 1:16-17; Galatians 3:8-14; Hebrews 10:32-39

September 23
Isaiah 13; Joel 3; 2 Peter 3

September 24
Deuteronomy 30:1-10; Psalm 80; Isaiah 40; Ezekiel 36; Acts 17:24-25; 2 Thessalonians 2:7-8

September 25
Genesis 41; Daniel 1-4; Joel 2:28-32; Acts 2:1-21

September 26
Isaiah 47; Daniel 4; Matthew 24:14-22; 1 Corinthians 12

September 27
2 Chronicles 36:22-23; Jeremiah 25:11-12; 29:10-14

September 28
Haggai 2; Zechariah 1-6; 1 Corinthians 3:9-17; 2 Corinthians 6:14-16; Ephesians 2:11-22

September 29
Isaiah 40:1-2; Zechariah 1-6; 1 Corinthians 14:3; 2 Corinthians 1:3-7

September 30
Ezra 3-6; Ezekiel 40-48; Haggai 1-2; John 2:13-21

October 1
Leviticus 26:14-46; Deuteronomy 7:6-15; 28:15-68; Daniel 9:1-19; James 5:13-16

October 2
Nehemiah 2-6; Psalms 27; 51:18-19; 127:1; John 16:33; 1 John 4:4

October 3
Psalm 85; Zechariah 9:9-17; Luke 13:34-35; Ephesians 2:11-22

October 4
Deuteronomy 16:13-15; Ezra 6:19-22; Isaiah 58; Matthew 13:18-23; Acts 17:10-11

October 5
Ezra 4:1-6; Proverbs 31:1-9; Daniel 9:1-2; 1 Corinthians 6:9-10

October 6
Genesis 39; 41; Nehemiah 1:1-11; 1 Peter 3:1-6

October 7
Genesis 12:1-3; Deuteronomy 30:1-7; Esther 4-6; Psalm 44:1-8; Daniel 3; 6; Romans 9-11

October 8
Deuteronomy 23:3-5; Esther 8-10; Joel 3:1-8; Obadiah 15; Revelation 19:11-20:10

October 9
Isaiah 60; Luke 1:1-17; Matthew 3:1-12; 17:10-13

October 10
Genesis 35:14-19; Ruth 4:10-17; 1 Samuel 17:12; Matthew 2:1-6

RELATED TEXTS

October 11
*2 Samuel 7:14; 1 Chronicles 17:13; Psalm 2:7;
Matthew 23:63-64; Mark 14:61-62; Luke 22:67-
70; John 1:32-34*

October 12
Isaiah 7:14; Matthew 2; Luke 1–2; John 4:1-42

October 13
*1 Samuel 2:21, 26; Psalms 26:8; 27:4; 65;
Matthew 2:13-23; John 2:13-17;
2 Corinthians 4:18–5:4*

October 14
*Isaiah 40:3; Malachi 3:1; Matthew 3; Luke 3;
John 1:19-34*

October 15
*Deuteronomy 6:13, 16; 8:3; Psalm 91:11-12;
Mark 1:12-13; Luke 4:1-13*

October 16
*Isaiah 55; Joel 3:16-18; Amos 9:11-15;
John 20:30-31*

October 17
*Numbers 21:1-9; John 1:1-13; 1 Peter 1;
1 John 2:28-29; 3:1-10; 4:7-8; 5*

October 18
*Psalm 51:1-13; Matthew 4:18-22; Mark 1:16-20;
John 1:35-51*

October 19
*Psalm 25:1-11; Micah 7:18; Matthew 9:1-8;
Mark 2:1-12*

October 20
*Deuteronomy 14:8; Isaiah 65:1-4;
Mark 4:35-5:20; Luke 8:22-39*

October 21
*Habakkuk 2:4; Matthew 9:27-30; Mark 5:21-43;
Luke 7:1-10, 36-50; 8:22-25, 40-56; 17:11-19;
18:35-43*

October 22
*Exodus 22:28; Psalm 106:1-37; Matthew 12:22-
37; 13:53-58; Mark 6:1-6; Luke 11:14-23; 12:10*

October 23
*Deuteronomy 8:2-3; Matthew 14:13-21;
Mark 6:32-44; Luke 9:10-17*

October 24
*Isaiah 52:14-15; Mark 8:27-33; Luke 9:18-22;
John 6:67-71*

October 25
*Exodus 40:33-35; Matthew 17:1-9; Luke 9:28-36;
Romans 16:25-27; 1 Timothy 1:17; Jude 24-25*

October 26
*1 Samuel 16:14-23; Mark 9:14-32; Luke 9:37-45;
Romans 4:18-21; 11:1-23; Hebrews 3:16-19*

October 27
*Psalm 89:19-29; Isaiah 9:6-7; Matthew 6:6-13;
7:7-11; Revelation 3:14-22*

October 28
*Psalm 127:3-5; Matthew 18:1-14; 19:13-15;
Mark 9:33-37; Luke 18:15-17*

October 29
*Exodus 20:8-11; Matthew 12:1-14; Mark 2:23–3:6;
Luke 6:1-11; 14:1-6; John 5:1-18*

October 30
*Genesis 1:27; 2:24; Deuteronomy 24:1-4;
Malachi 2:13-16; Mark 10:2-12; Luke 16:18*

October 31
*Exodus 20:12-16; Deuteronomy 5:16-20; Matthew
19:16-30; Mark 10:17-31; 1 Corinthians 13:3*

November 1
Ezekiel 34:7-16; Mark 2:14-17; Luke 7:36-47

November 2
*Psalm 16:9-11; Matthew 26:6-13; Mark 14:3-9;
Luke 7:36-50; John 11*

November 3
*Psalm 118; Matthew 21:1-9; Mark 11:1-10;
John 12:12-19*

November 4
Psalm 118; Matthew 21:33-46; Mark 12:1-12

November 5
*Psalm 41:9; Proverbs 11:13; Mark 14:10-25;
Luke 22:3-23; John 13–17*

November 6
*Zechariah 13:7; Mark 14:26-42; Luke 22:31-46;
John 13:36-38*

November 7
*Psalm 42; Matthew 26:47-56, 69-75;
Mark 14:43-53, 66-72; John 18:2-12, 25-27*

November 8
*Exodus 20:16; Daniel 7:13-14; Matthew 26:59-67;
Mark 14:55-65; Luke 23:63-71; John 18:19-24*

RELATED TEXTS

November 9
Psalm 22; Matthew 27; Mark 15; Luke 23; John 18:28-19:42

November 10
Psalm 16:9-11; Isaiah 53:9-12; Matthew 28; Mark 16; Luke 24; John 20–21

November 11
Isaiah 1:11-14; Acts 2:22-36; Romans 6:1-11; 1 Corinthians 15:12-58

November 12
1 Chronicles 16:8, 23-31; Psalms 67; 72; Isaiah 45:22-23; 49:6; Luke 24:50-53

November 13
Leviticus 23:4-16; Matthew 3:1-12; John 14:15-26; 15:26-27; 16:12-15

November 14
Ezekiel 36:16-28; 39:21-29; Joel 2:28-32; Romans 10:1-13

November 15
Jeremiah 37:15; 38:6; Matthew 15:29-31; 21:1-16; John 5; 14:12-14

November 16
Jeremiah 20:9; Matthew 5:10-12; Acts 5:17-42

November 17
Leviticus 24:10-16; Mark 13:9-13; John 16:1-4; Acts 7:1-54; 8:1-4

November 18
Daniel 8:26-27; Luke 1:18-20; Acts 22:1-21; 26:1-29

November 19
Genesis 20; Numbers 12; 1 Corinthians 15:1-11; Galatians 1:11-24

November 20
Numbers 27:22-23; Deuteronomy 34:9; Matthew 19:13-15; Luke 4:40; Acts 6:1-6; 8:5-25; 1 Timothy 4:11-14

November 21
Exodus 17:1-4; Numbers 14:1-10; 1 Samuel 30:6; John 8:31-59; Acts 7:52-60; 14:1-7; Romans 1:1-17; Ephesians 2:11-22

November 22
Nehemiah 12:27-43; Psalms 77; 135:1-7; 148; Luke 22:14-19

November 23
2 Chronicles 20:14-26; Psalms 104; 118; 145; Matthew 6:25-34

November 24
2 Chronicles 6:41; Psalms 65; 84; 96; Ephesians 5:18-20; 3 John 11

November 25
1 Chronicles 16:34-36; 2 Chronicles 5–7; Psalms 118:1-4; 136:4-26; 2 Corinthians 9:10-15

November 26
1 Chronicles 16:4-14; Romans 8:18-28; 14; 1 Corinthians 10

November 27
Exodus 24:1-11; Isaiah 6; Psalms 103:20-22; 148; Mark 10:17-18

November 28
Exodus 15:1-21; 1 Chronicles 15–16; Colossians 3:16-17

November 29
Isaiah 49:1-6; Acts 15; Galatians 3:25-29; Ephesians 2:11-22

November 30
Exodus 31:1-6; 35:30–36:2; Romans 12:1-8; 1 Corinthians 13–14; Ephesians 4:1-16; Hebrews 2:1-4; 1 Peter 4:7-11

December 1
Ecclesiastes 12; John 11:20-27; Romans 14:1-13; Philippians 1:20-26; 1 Corinthians 15:35-54

December 2
Psalm 113; Romans 8:29-39; Ephesians 2:4-10; Revelation 3:5; 13:8; 17:8; 20:15

December 3
Isaiah 45:22-25; John 13:1-15; Romans 14:11-12; 1 Corinthians 15:20-28; Philippians 2:19-21; 1 Peter 5:5-6

December 4
Psalm 18:30-33; Matthew 5:43-48; Mark 8:34-37; Acts 22:1-21; Colossians 1:24; Hebrews 12:1-3

December 5
Genesis 1:26; John 1:1-18; Romans 5:9-11; 2 Corinthians 5:17-21; Colossians 2:9-10; Hebrews 1:1-3

RELATED TEXTS

December 6
Daniel 12:1-3; Matthew 24; 2 Peter 3; Revelation 3:1-6

December 7
Genesis 1:26-30; 2:15; 1 Corinthians 9; 2 Corinthians 12:12-18; 1 Thessalonians 2:1-12

December 8
Psalm 112:4; Proverbs 11:24-26; 14:31; 19:17; 22:9; 28:8; Luke 12:13-34; 16:1-15; Philippians 4:10-14

December 9
Isaiah 40:6-8; Matthew 5:10-12; Acts 14; 2 Corinthians 4; 12:1-10; 1 Peter 1:23–2:3

December 10
Genesis 14:18-20; Psalm 110; Matthew 4:1-11

December 11
Genesis 1; 4:1-16; 5:23-24; 6-8; 12; Jude 14-15

December 12
Genesis 21–22; Exodus 2-3; Hebrews 10:36-39

December 13
Job 1-42; Matthew 6:9-13; 21:18-22; 1 Corinthians 10:12-13

December 14
Psalm 12; Proverbs 6:16-19; 10:18-21, 31-32; 12:17-19, 22

December 15
Isaiah 52:13-53:12; Zechariah 13:7-9; Hebrews 1–2; James 1

December 16
Psalms 34; 118:22-29; Isaiah 28:16-17; Matthew 16:13-19; Luke 20:9-19; Hebrews 5:11-14

December 17
Jeremiah 26; Amos 3:1-8; Isaiah 61; Mark 9:2-9; Luke 1:1-4

December 18
1 Kings 8:46-51; Psalm 119:9-11; John 14:15; Hebrews 2:17-18; 4:14-16; 7-9; 1 John 3:11-24

December 19
Deuteronomy 30:11-16; John 15:17-25; 1 John 4:7-21

December 20
Proverbs 13:5; Isaiah 44:24-25; Jeremiah 14:14-15; 2 Timothy 3; 2 Peter 2-3

December 21
Amos 4:11; Zechariah 3; Acts 20:28-31; 2 Peter 3; 1 Timothy 4:1-6

December 22
2 Samuel 7; 1 Chronicles 17; Mark 1:1-11; Revelation 2:18-29

December 23
Genesis 14:18-20; Matthew 22:41-46; Hebrews 5:1-10; 7

December 24
2 Samuel 7:8-17; Psalm 89:20-37; Isaiah 9:6-7; Matthew 1:18-25; Luke 1-2

December 25
Exodus 30:22-33; Micah 5:2-5; Mark 15:16-24; Luke 1-2; John 12:1-7; Hebrews 13:15-21

December 26
Genesis 3:1-14; Isaiah 66:22-24; 2 Peter 3:1-14; Revelation 21:1-5

December 27
Ezekiel 1; 3; 8-11; Zechariah 14; Revelation 21:1-4

December 28
Psalm 149; Daniel 7; 2 Timothy 3; Hebrews 4:12-13; Revelation 2-11; 19:11-21

December 29
Genesis 3:1-15; Ezekiel 38-39; 1 Corinthians 6:1-3; Revelation 12-13; 17-19

December 30
Isaiah 65:17-25; 66:22-24; Daniel 12:1-3; John 1:14-18; 2 Peter 3:1-14

December 31
Psalms 1; 37; Matthew 16:24-27; Luke 12:35-40; 1 Thessalonians 4:13-5:11; Revelation 1:1-3

TOPICAL INDEX

A

Aaron 94, 95, 115, 138, 149, 167, 190, 191, 193, 194
Abel 16, 375
Abraham 20-24, 27, 28, 52, 53, 119, 375, 376
abstinence 358
Adam 10, 12-16, 113
adoption 181
adultery 127, 137, 156, 185, 245, 328
Agag 199, 235, 305
aging 60
Ahab 267, 268
Amos 274
Ananias 351
Andrew 321
angel of the Lord 52
angels 47, 48, 112, 212, 255, 280, 313, 344, 379, 388
anger 76, 92, 126, 167, 168, 171, 174, 180, 275, 281
anger of God 167, 168, 171, 174, 180, 275, 281
animals 6, 7
anointing 334
answers to prayer 228
anti-semitism 305
antichrist 384
ascension 344
asking 162
atonement 102, 104, 148, 374, 382
attributes of God 76, 78, 80, 82, 84, 88, 90, 92, 170-180

B

Baal 200, 209, 267-269, 275
Balaam 196, 199, 201
Balak 196
baptism 103, 169, 181, 312, 343, 344, 346
Barak 210, 211
Barnabas 352, 353
barrenness 146, 212, 227, 229
Bathsheba 245-247
beatitudes 39-46, 152
Belshazzar 291, 292
betrayal 109, 213, 214, 337, 339
Bildad 35, 38
birth of Jesus 310, 388
birthright 25
blasphemy 123, 320, 349
blessing 6, 9, 20, 25, 35, 39-46, 134, 151-153, 196, 199, 366, 377, 390
blood of Jesus 44, 73, 108, 114, 148, 172, 366, 369
Boaz 217-219
bread of life 220
burning bush 52

C

Cain 16, 126
Caleb 190, 191
capital punishment 137
celibacy 328
childhood of Jesus 311, 389
children 45, 75, 125, 141, 152, 157, 212, 326, 383
children of God 45, 75, 152, 157, 383
chosen people 39, 75, 83, 119, 120, 150, 249, 344, 366, 380
church 48, 187, 319, 322, 350, 352, 353, 361, 368, 369, 381, 392, 395
clean 138
comfort 40, 141, 152, 171, 244, 295, 367
compassion 76, 84, 88, 141, 146, 170-173, 272, 275, 287
confession 172, 299, 312
contentment 130, 372
courage 203-205, 284
covenant 17, 27, 43, 51, 73, 88, 108, 120, 148, 149, 170, 203, 240, 243, 248, 261, 299, 307
coveting 130
creation 1-3, 10, 11, 354, 369, 375
crucifixion 111, 341
curse 2, 13, 14, 16, 19, 20, 31, 137, 151, 196, 199, 239
cursing 123, 362, 378
Cyrus 293, 296

D

Dagon 215
Daniel 291, 292
darkness 2, 5, 155, 157
David 9, 105-107, 180, 236-249, 258, 261-263, 274, 279, 301, 310, 387, 388
day of the Lord 289
death 15, 60, 76, 104, 223, 244, 322, 324, 333, 334, 336, 338, 341, 343, 367
death of Jesus 76, 104, 223, 244, 322, 324, 333, 334, 336, 338, 341, 343, 367
Deborah 210, 211
defeat 209
deity of Christ 343, 367, 369, 384
Delilah 213, 214
demon-possession 62, 318, 320, 324, 327
demons 47, 163, 358
destiny 212, 304
devil 253, 313, 352, 393
diet 138
discipleship 316
discipline 35, 184
disobedience 167, 168, 194, 195, 200, 209, 235, 261, 267, 270, 278, 380
divorce 156, 328
doubt 377
dreams 26
drinking/drunkenness 303, 360
dry bones 290

TOPICAL INDEX

TOPICAL INDEX

TOPICAL INDEX

M

Magi 389
magic 95
majesty 58
Malachi 307
male and female 10
mankind 8, 10, 11
manna 189, 220

marriage 48, 127, 147, 185, 218, 219, 328, 358
Martha 224, 334
martyrdom 349
Mary Magdalene 112, 342
Mary, mother of Jesus 68, 310, 31., 388
Mary, sister of Lazarus 224, 334
meditation 69, 204
meekness 41
mercy 43, 68, 82, 175, 380, 385
messianic prophecy 11, 63, 80, 90, 102, 105-107, 180, 243, 274, 307, 308, 309, 310, 336, 338, 340, 346, 379, 380, 386, 387, 389
Micah 277, 285
millennium 393
miracles 62, 93-97, 106, 117, 119, 189, 221, 267, 314, 316-319, 321, 327, 347, 348, 352, 353
miracles of Jesus 62, 106, 221, 314, 316-319, 321, 327
Miriam 194
missions 344, 352
money 157
Mordecai 304-306
Moses 15, 50-53, 56, 93-95, 97, 101, 115-117, 120, 138, 167-170, 190, 191, 192-195, 200, 201, 203, 204, 279, 323, 376
mother 68, 140-143, 310, 311, 314, 388
mourning 40
murder 16, 49, 126, 155, 241, 246
music 206
mustard seed 324

N

Nahum 281
names of God 53-63, 67-73, 86, 123, 142, 146, 177, 244, 348, 381, 391, 392, 395
Naomi 216-219
Nathan 246
nations 55, 56, 59, 120, 150, 361, 362
Nebuchadnezzar 286, 291-293
Nehemiah 299, 300, 302
neighbor 133
new birth 315
New Covenant 108
new heavens and earth 82, 390, 394
new Jerusalem 394
Nicodemus 315
Noah 17-19, 375

O

oaths 25, 28, 43, 110, 129, 150, 172, 192, 241
Obadiah 289
obedience 23, 120, 122, 125, 151, 182, 188, 192, 202, 206, 208, 248, 249, 259, 260, 279, 348, 367, 371, 375, 376, 382, 383, 386
offerings 7, 149
omnipotence 176
omnipresence 177
omniscience 178
oppression 49
orphans 134

P

parables of Jesus 252-20., .
parents 125, 137
Passover 101, 108, 114, 139, 337
patience 81, 82, 89
Paul 349-353, 368
peace 41, 45, 79, 80, 89, 259, 301, 308, 335, 356, 388
Pentecost 345
persecution 46, 152, 153, 157, 347-350, 353, 373
perseverance 376, 385
Peter 104, 107, 108, 316, 321, 322, 329, 338, 339, 342, 346-348
Pharisees 9, 140, 154, 160, 255, 315, 317, 328, 335, 368
Philip 225, 321
Phinehas 200
plagues 96
plants 4
polygamy 147
poor 39, 83, 142, 143, 329, 334
power 3, 73, 90
praise 1, 3, 30, 54, 59, 68, 71, 72, 77, 78, 86, 118, 119, 121, 142, 145, 271, 347, 354, 356, 357, 360, 366, 378
prayer 24, 38, 159, 162, 187, 215, 227, 228, 280, 299-301, 325, 338, 352, 353, 355, 374
presence of God 203, 204
priesthood 148, 149, 380
Prodigal son 256, 257
promise 22, 119, 168, 248
prophecy 11, 63, 69, 80, 90, 102, 105-107, 180, 229, 243, 267, 269, 270, 274, 283-285, 294, 296, 307-310, 336, 338, 340, 346, 379, 380, 381, 386, 387, 389, 392
prostitution 147
proverbs 250
punishment 76, 122, 123, 137, 176, 246, 269
purity 44

TOPICAL

INDEX

TOPICAL INDEX

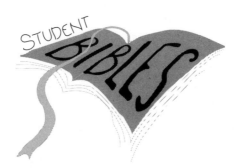

Life Application Bible for Students
Living Bible translation, published by Tyndale

The Student Bible
NIV Bible translation, published by Zondervon

The Youth Bible
New Century Bible translation, published by Word/Group

In Step Student Bible
CEV Bible translation, published by Thomas Nelson